THE
WOODTURNER'S BIBLE

2ND EDITION

WOODTURNER'S BIBLE

2ND EDITION

PERCY W. BLANDFORD

TAB TAB BOOKS Inc.
Blue Ridge Summit, PA 17214

SECOND EDITION
FIRST PRINTING

Copyright © 1986 by TAB BOOKS Inc.
Printed in the United States of America

First edition copyright © 1979 by TAB BOOKS Inc.

Library of Congress Cataloging in Publication Data

Blandford, Percy W.
The woodturner's bible.

Includes index.
1. Turning. I. Title.
TT201.B57 1986   684'.083   85-27715
ISBN 0-8306-0954-7
ISBN 0-8306-1954-2 (pbk.)
Cover photograph courtesy of Shopsmith, Inc.

Contents

Introduction

Wood turning differs from other woodworking craftsmanship because it requires a machine; yet the craftsman still has full control over what he is doing, in the same way that he does when using hand tools on the bench. If there is anything with a family resemblance, it is the potter's wheel, where clay is worked in a similar manner to turning wood. It is the scope for artistic expression that provides much of the appeal in wood turning.

A turner is an artist-craftsman producing objects that may have practical functions; yet he can express himself in the overall design and in the detail work. It is possible for a craftsman to put his individual mark on what he makes in such a way that is not open to any other woodworker, except a carver.

The owner of a lathe can soon master its use in the production of simple pieces; yet it is possible to go on to more advanced work as skill increases. All of this can be done with the basic equipment and with additions made by the turner. Wood turning need not be expensive. A great many items can be made from wood that has been discarded from other woodworking activities.

This shows that the owner of a lathe is possessed with the means of making many things that will give him the satisfaction of seeing a project through from start to finish. It is also a means of making money if the owner is so inclined. Many products are saleable and gladly bought, while antique restorers often want parts made for repairs.

I have found wood turning to be a very satisfying occupation, both professionally and as a hobby. This book is based on experience over a very long time. In it I hope there is all of the instruction that most woodturners will need. I also hope that there are enough suggestions for items to make to give the woodturner ideas in order to keep him, or her, occupied and to also stimulate his/her own original designs.

I have appreciated the help and encouragement of the Woodcraft Supply Corporation, 313 Montvale Avenue, Woburn, MA 01801.

I would also like to acknowledge the help in the provision of pictures of their products by Rockwell International, Power Tool Division, Pittsburgh, PA

15208, and ToolKraft, 700 Plainfield Street, Chicopee, MA 01013.

All of the other photographs are by me or my wife as are the line drawings. The lathe used for most of the action photographs is a Myford ML8.

SECTION I
USING THE LATHE

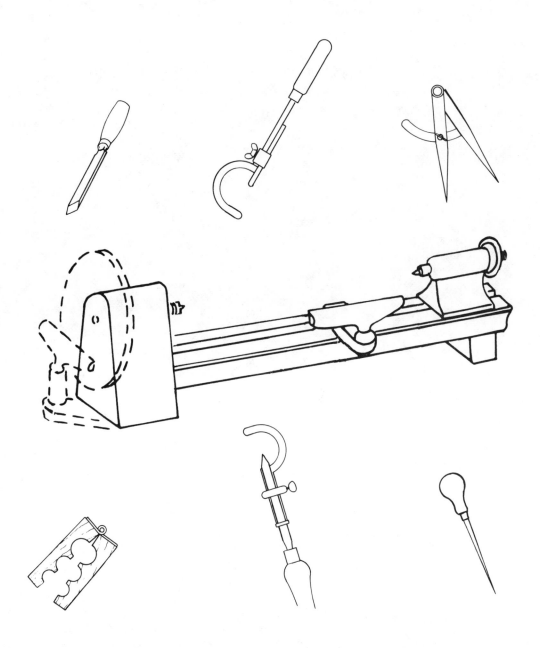

Chapter 1

Turning Origins

The idea of making round things from solid materials by using a tool on them while they rotate goes back into antiquity. Wood is not a sufficiently durable material for turned wood examples to have survived from the earliest days, but it is from early examples of surviving stone turnings that the same techniques must have been applied to wood.

There are Greek and Persian columns and other round objects in stone still standing that were made many thousands of years before the birth of Christ. When our ancestors were living little better than animals, craftsmen of these early civilizations were producing beautiful and complicated turnings.

Another application of the turning technique is seen in the potter's wheel, which is like a vertical lathe. There are surviving early examples of pottery that show they must have been formed on a revolving wheel. The principle used today of *throwing* clay on a potter's wheel and using the hands as tools to shape it while it revolves is much the same as it was in the earliest times. Pottery and blacksmithing are two crafts that a man from

Biblical times would recognize the methods and tools used today.

PRIMITIVE LATHES AND TOOLS

We can only surmise the construction of a primitive lathe, but the work was probably supported between two centers (Fig. 1-1A) and some sort of tool rest arranged in front of it (Fig. 1-1B). Rotation would almost certainly have been by a thong taken around the wood (Fig. 1-1C). Two helpers pulled this backward and forward, so the wood rotated alternately in opposite directions. The turner then used his tool while the wood was turned toward him and withdrew it when direction was reversed.

Early tools were almost certainly pieces of flint or other stone that would take a sharp edge. Then came bronze and eventually iron and steel. Abrasives, in the form of sand on damp cloth or leather, must have been used for some shaping as well as finishing, in order to supplement the cutting of rather crude tools. Surviving examples of

3

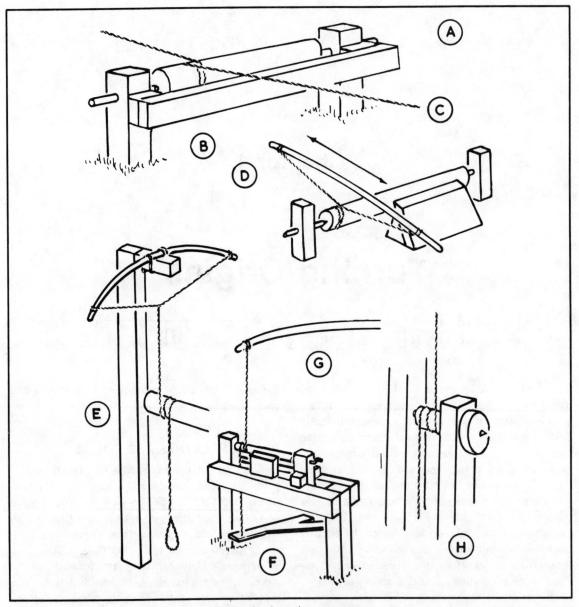

Fig. 1-1. Earl lathes were given a reciprocating motion by a thong or rope.

very old stone turning show that considerable skill and patience must have been exercised to get exceptional results with what were comparatively primitive tools. Most of the examples of workmanship are as good as could be accomplished today.

The method of rotating with a thong is not as obsolete as might be expected. Besides a few primitive peoples who might be expected to still use it, there are variations of the method still used in more civilized countries. Some production work was still being done with a thong drive several years after the end of World War II.

In India, the thong drive is arranged as a bow (Fig. 1-1D). The lathe is close to the floor and the turner sits cross-legged. An assistant may work the bow backward and forward, or the turner works this with one hand while controlling the tool with his other hand and one foot. Much of the decorative turning that comes out of India is still produced in this way.

That method of driving is the same as is used in the Red Indian fire drill used for making fire by friction. It is possible that the fire drill came before the bow-driven lathe. The same idea is used for other applications, such as the turning of a spreader used in the sowing of seeds.

Having a bow to drive a piece of wood being turned means using one of the turner's hands or employing an assistant. The next step is to use foot power, then the turner can have two hands on his tool, while providing power with one foot. A simple way to do this is to fix a large bow above the lathe, then bring the cord down around the work to a loop for the foot (Fig. 1-1E).

A more exact foot control comes from using a treadle with the cord attached to it (Fig. 1-1F). An alternative to the bow is to use a springy branch, either a natural one or a pole suitably supported (Fig. 1-1G). It is this last method that survived until quite recent years. Crude lathes were set up amongst the trees to make legs and rails for Windsor chairs and bowls that were in demand for cash in shops and banks.

Having the driving cord around the work served for what is now often called *spindle* turning, where the work is longer than it is thick and is supported between centers. For a bowl, or other thing of greater diameter than its length, the drive has to be attached to a short spindle supported in bearings with a shaft to drive the wood for the bowl (Fig. 1-1H). This is, in effect, the equivalent of a modern headstock and mandrel nose carrying a faceplate.

All of these lathes suffered from only being usable for 50 percent of their operation. Cuts were made when the wood was turning toward the tool, then there was a pause during the return stroke.

Continuous turning in the cutting direction was the next desirable step. (Fig. 1-2).

POWER DRIVEN LATHES

A lathe could be driven continuously in one direction by a crank handle on the end. Turning is most successfully done at quite a high speed and a direct drive of this sort could not achieve a high enough rate or rotation. Instead, there would be a large diameter wheel away from the lathe and a belt drive. Until the coming of steam and electric power, much turning by wheelwrights and other craftsmen from the Middle Ages onward was done by lathes arranged in this way with two helpers turning the large wheel with crank handles (Fig. 1-3A). A heavy wheel had a flywheel effect to maintain a reasonably constant speed, but no doubt the turner, intent on getting in the best results, would frequently call for more effort from his sweating assistants.

Water power was also used to drive lathes, particularly where the lathe was housed in the same place as saws and other equipment used for converting wood. Water-powered lathes were never very common.

Having one or more men to drive the lathe in addition to the turner had the drawback of employing more than one man for one man's work. The next step was to let the turner use a foot treadle that converted the reciprocating movement to a rotary one. This was done by connecting the treadle to a small crank on a large wheel with a bar called a *pitman* (Fig. 1-3B). If the wheel was light, a steady motion was imparted by having a rocking treadle, so the toe and heel over the axle pressed alternately (Fig. 1-3C). The same idea was used in treadle sewing machines and some improvized lathes have been mounted on old sewing machine stands.

A better and smoother motion is provided by having the large pulley wheel heavy so that it also functions as a flywheel connected to a simple treadle where the operator only has to pump his foot up and down (Fig. 1-3D). The flywheel takes care of the up stroke, where a light wheel needs the toe

Fig. 1-2. A pole lathe is being used for bowl turning. The rope from the pole goes around a mandrel, which is attached to the bowl, and down to a foot-operated treadle.

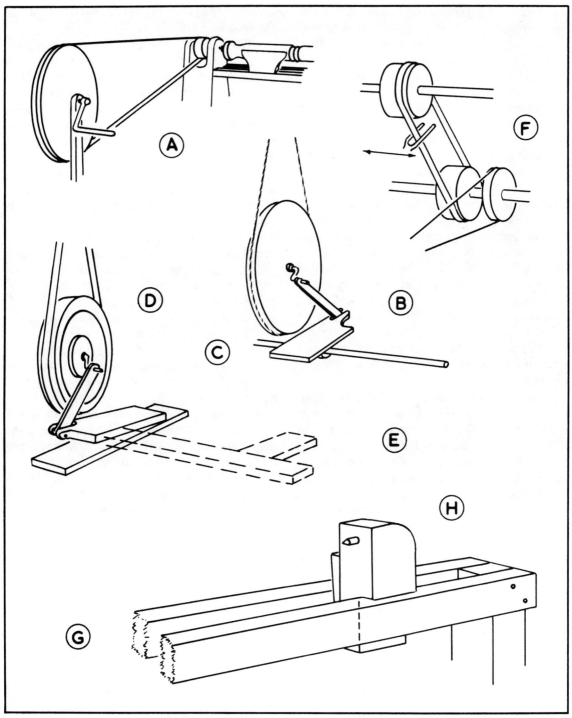

Fig. 1-3. Before the days of electric power, lathes were driven by hand, foot, or through line shafting powered by a steam engine. They were mostly made of wood and construction was quite simple.

and heel action to provide constant rotation. An up and down motion is more suited to a standing position, which is required when using hand tools on a wood lathe. In the later lathes driven by foot, the flywheel was given grooves at different diameters with a matching small wheel to take the drive. In this way, the belt (usually round leather) could be moved to provide different relative speeds—smaller diameters being better turned at high speeds, while the effort required on the foot was reduced if larger diameters were turned at lower speeds.

Nearly all lathes have their power at the left-hand end, so the wheel and treadle are at that end. In a simple lathe treadle, the turner stood on his right leg and treadled with his left. Of course, if the work was long, a point would soon be found where he could not reach with his hands to use the tool as well as treadle with his left leg. An assistant could take over treadling. Later lathes had a long treadle so that the foot could be used at any point along it (Fig. 1-3E). This also had the advantage with heavy work—one or more assistants could add their efforts to treadling without getting in the way of the turner and his tools.

Turning cannot be done from a sitting position, at least not by Western methods, except for very small work. The occasional turner was content to stand and treadle his lathe, but the man who used one continuously arranged a rail that he could lean against. The rail gave him some support without interfering with the leg balance essential to good tool control, and it even provided some reaction to the thrust put on the tool in heavy cuts on hard wood.

The first applications of industrial power used steam, gas, and gasoline engines—none of which were suitable for frequent starting and stopping, and they were mostly not compact enough or suitable for direct connection to an individual machine like a lathe. Consequently, they were of little use where a lathe was the only machine to be driven. It was more usual in a machine shop for the power source to drive shafting that was kept rotating, then the lathe and other machines took their power with fast and loose pulleys and flat belts. A lever moved a fork that slid the flat belt

from a driven pulley to one that was free to idle on the rotating shaft (Fig. 1-3F).

When electric motors were first invented, they were used to drive shafting in the same way. This system of driving through shafting may still be found, but in any new installation it is better and more convenient to have individual electric motors. There need be no shafts and belts exposed, and there is the convenience of easy stop/start as often as required.

Treadle lathes may still be found. Some have been converted to electric power, but a later type of treadle lathe with a heavy flywheel may still make an interesting tool. Much excellent work was done with these machines and interested turners may do so again. For most intending turners, however, a lathe with the electric motor built in directly or via belts from a position under the stand would be the best choice. It is assumed that an electric motorized lathe will be the usual choice and more details are given elsewhere in this book.

Over the very long history of turning, the method of driving has gone through revolutionary changes, but the actual lathe has changed very little in principle. Changes have been mostly improvements and not alterations. A modern lathe is more sophisticatedly engineered, but its parts and their functions are still the same. Drive is provided through a shaft that once had very simple bearings, but now there are ball and roller bearings that reduce play and vibration, which were the enemies of good work in some old lathes with poor bearings. The modern shaft, or *mandrel* may be hollow and have its ends screwed to accept various fittings, but its object is still to rotate the work so a tool can cut it in round patterns.

The other end of long work has always been supported on a tapered point at the same height as the headstock mandrel. In most early lathes the *bed*, which supported the lathe parts, was made of two straight stout pieces of wood (Fig. 1-3G). In the simplest *tailstock*, the center point was through a piece of wood wedged between the sides of the bed (Fig. 1-3H). An improvement used a screw adjustment for the center to take up wear in the wood.

In more recent lathes, the bed is of iron or steel

and is often made in a similar way to the older wooden bed. Precision machining makes for a more accurate bed, but with the tool held in the hands, this is of less importance than in a metal-working lathe, where the action of a mounted tool would be affected by inaccuracies in the bed. Beds of wood turning lathes are also tubular and made with round rods, but only home lathes might have wooden beds.

The tailstock has adjustments in the way it fits to the bed, and there is a more accurate way of screwing the center into the end of the wood. The principle is the same as the primitive lathe. Most turning is done with a plain center, but there are centers with bearings that rotate with the work. This reduces friction and lessens the tendency of the center to wear into the wood and requires periodic tightening as work progresses.

The tool rest may be just a straight fixed bar, but in even the oldest lathes, provision was usually made for it to be moved about on the bed and locked in any position with a wedge or screw so that it could be brought close to the part of the wood being worked on. It might also be given a height adjustment. A modern tool rest is better made, and its adjustments are more precise, but its function is just the same. There is really nothing that can be done to improve the basic concept.

Where work is driven by a cord or strap around it, both ends are supported on simple points. Where the headstock has a shaft to provide drive, there has to be some means of gripping and driving the end of the wood. Quite early in the development of this type of lathe someone thought of using a drive with a long central spike and two or more other spikes or teeth around it to press into the wood. There are variations, but this is still the basic way of driving spindle work.

For bowls and other work of large diameter and short length, there had to be a wheel-like faceplate on the driving shaft. This provided a surface at right angles to the centerline of the shaft to which a flat surface of the wood to be turned could be attached. Early faceplates, or their equivalents, were wood and turned in place on the shaft. They may not have lasted long but were not difficult to replace. More recent faceplates and other holding devices are metal and operate on the same principle.

Most improvements in lathes have taken place in the last couple of centuries since the Industrial Revolution. These are nearly all detail improvements, most of which will be found in modern lathes, so information on them is given elsewhere in this book.

HOMEMADE LATHES

Most would-be woodturners today will buy their first lathe. Actually, it is not difficult to make a simple lathe that will do spindle turning between centers equally as good as that produced on an expensive lathe. Although some quite large lathes have been made, and it is advisable to settle for a small lathe at least for the first project. The main consideration is the headstock assembly, which must have a spindle running smoothly with the absolute minimum of play or vibration. There are bearings and shafts available that could be used. Some of these are intended for mounting polishing heads or grinding wheels. Make sure the chosen assembly will withstand an end thrust. Bicycle wheel hubs have possibilities. The following suggestions are for a small lathe using a bicycle wheel hub as the operative part of the headstock. The center height above the bed is 4 inches and the distance between centers is 18 inches, so the lathe can be used to turn chair and small table legs.

Get a bicycle wheel hub and spindle with as many nuts as possible in order to make and fit parts to it. Particularly useful are longer nuts with tubular extensions, such as are used with some variable gears. Wing nuts for quick-change wheels may have enough metal for making into drive centers.

Use any close-grained stable hardwood for construction. The headstock will determine some other sizes. It can be 1 1/2 inches thick and wide enough to fit between the flanges of the wheel hub. The distance between the two 1-inch square ways that form the bed can then be about 1 inch. Allow enough height to tenon into a strong base (a 1 1/2- x -4 inch section would do). There should be space to reach and turn the wing nuts. The post at the other end matches the headstock (Fig. 1-4A).

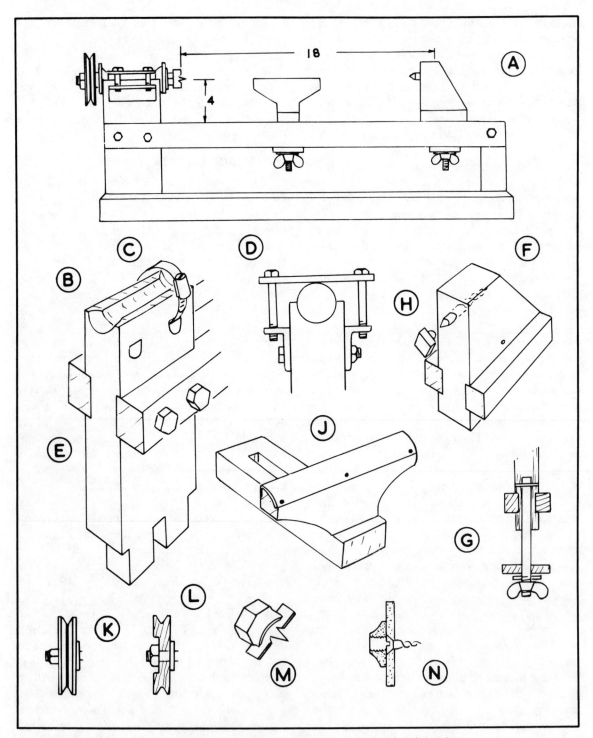

Fig. 1-4. Suggestions for making a lathe using a bicycle wheel hub as the headstock bearing.

Drill through the headstock wood to suit the diameter of the main part of the hub, then cut it across and hollow the ends of the resulting groove to fit over the enlarged ends of the hub (Fig. 1-4B). Secure the hub in place with two worm-drive pipe clips (Fig. 1-4C). Another method, that can be expected to remain tight longer, uses a plate over the hub with screws into tapped holes in angle irons bolted on (Fig. 1-4D).

Notch the ways into the headstock and the end support, preferably with bolts as well as glue (Fig. 1-4E). Mount this assembly on the base piece, which can be drilled for bolting down.

The tailstock is a piece to fit between the ways with slides to travel on them (Fig. 1-4F). Cut the head off a long bolt, so it can go into a hole in the tailstock and project far enough below the ways for a wood pad, washer, and wing nut (Fig. 1-4G). Secure the bolt in the tailstock with a steel pin through a hole—a 3/8-inch bolt with a 1/8-inch pin should be satisfactory. For the center, drive in a large screw, such as a carriage screw about 3/8 inch in diameter. Cut off the head and file the projecting part to a point (Fig. 1-4H) at the same height as the headstock center.

Make the base of the rest about 2- × -3/4 inches with a slot for the square neck of a 3/8-inch carriage bolt. Tenon or screw the rest to it with its top about 1/4 inch below center height. For longer life, fit sheet metal over the edge (Fig. 1-4J). Arrange the bolt with a wood pad, washer, and wing nut, similar to the tailstock.

The drive has to come through a pulley on the end of the spindle. If you cannot find a pulley to exactly suit your needs, use any pulley that can be put on. Then, the first job of the new lathe can be to make a hardwood pulley of the size and type you want. If you have the use of another lathe, a pulley can be turned on that. A suitable thin pulley may leave enough thread projecting for the nut (Fig. 1-4K), but you may have to turn a pulley with a recess for the nut (Fig. 1-4L).

At the other end, a wing nut may be filed to make a drive center, but if you have to use an ordinary nut or a tubular one, file a plate to make a fork center and braze it into a saw cut (Fig. 1-4M). If you take apart another wheel hub, you should find that one cone that holds a ball race can be unscrewed. That might also have a fork center brazed to it, but it may be more use for making a screw center with a sheet metal disc and a wood screw brazed to it (Fig. 1-4N). A larger disc with screw holes in it would make a small faceplate, but it is unwise to expect to turn anything more than a few inches across on a bicycle hub without the support or a tailstock center.

As with lathe parts, turning tools may have had detail improvements but are still basically the same handheld chisels and gouges that have always been used. A wood-turning lathe is a machine tool in the best sense of the term with the emphasis on *tool*, meaning something that a craftsman uses to fashion material. It is the skill of the worker that produces results. A lathe may be larger than most the woodworker's tools, but the woodworker still has to exercise control over it to get the results desired. If skill is lacking, the work suffers. A normal lathe is not a machine that turns out objects automatically once it is set. It is probably the fact that the beauty of turned wood is due to the skill of the craftsman that has contributed to the attraction of the lathe as a working tool throughout history. There are elaborate production lathes that can reproduce identical shapes mechanically, but these do not have the finish of hand turned work. Some of these lathes are ingenious and interesting examples of modern mass-production machinery, but they are outside the scope of this book.

Chapter 2

Choice of Lathe

The most important consideration in selecting a lathe is its capacity. This means what length can be accommodated and how big a circle can be turned. These sizes may not be immediately obvious from the description of a machine. For most general turning, it is advisable to have a lathe that will take more than 30 inches between centers (Fig. 2-1A) as this is needed for table legs. Some lathes are described by their overall lengths and a 4-foot lathe may be needed to accommodate a 30-inch length.

DIAMETER AND HEIGHT

There are two ways of describing the maximum circle that can be turned. Most American lathes are described by their *swing*, which is the largest diameter that will clear the bed (Fig. 2-1B). British and some other lathes are described by the radius or height of centers above the bed (Fig. 2-1C), so a 3-inch British lathe may have the same capacity as a 6-inch American one. In both cases, this is not the size that can be turned for the whole length be-

tween centers as the tool rest base fits over the bed and restricts the size above it (Fig 2-1D). By careful positioning of the tool rest, it is possible to turn a piece of wood with some parts up to the maximum specified size, but the largest parallel cylinder of the full length that can be turned is whatever will pass over the tool rest base. This is not always specified.

In practice, it is rare for a long piece of maximum diameter to be needed, but the maximum clearance is a more important consideration for such things as bowls and floor lamp bases. It is usual for a metalworking lathe (Fig. 2-2) to have a *gap bed*. Metal turning puts a much heavier load on the machine, and the tool is mounted on a slide rest, where its movement is controlled by handled screws. A gap bed allows a greater diameter to be swung on a faceplate, as long as the material is not too thick to go in the gap. Some wood-turning lathes have gap beds (Figs. 2-3 and 2-4), but it is more usual to find the bed continuous and a provision made for turning larger work at the *outboard* or left-

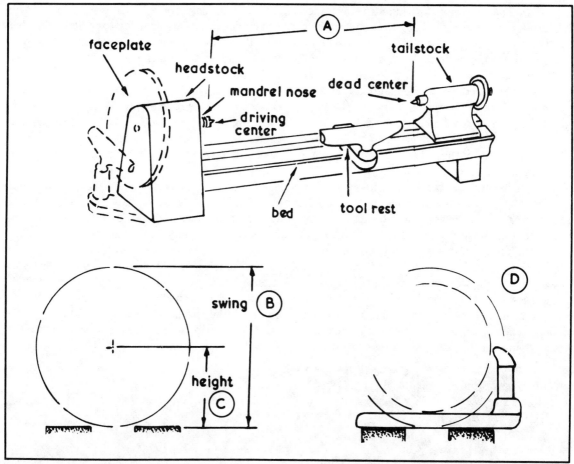

Fig. 2-1. A wood-turning lathe is simple. Its size may be given as the height of centers or the total swing over the bed, but the actual clearance over the tool rest base decides the maximum diameter that can be turned between centers.

hand end of the headstock (Figs. 2-3 and 2-5). If there is a gap, a lathe may be described, for example, as 14 inches/11 inches. This means that the swing over the bed is 11 inches, but the swing over the gap is 14 inches.

The headstock spindle projects both ways and is screwed at the ends if it is intended to take a faceplate at either end. At the right-hand end, there is a normal right-hand thread. The load applied by the tool on the wood then tends to tighten the threaded faceplate or other screwed fitting. If the thread on the left-hand end was also right-handed, the load applied with a tool would tend to unscrew the faceplate, which might fly off. More informa-

tion on faceplates is given in the next chapter.

In some lathes with this arrangement, the tool rest for work at the left-hand end of the spindle fits on a bracket extending from the lathe. Maximum size is then limited by clearance over this bracket. If the lathe is mounted on a bench, clearance over the bench top may be the limiting factor. In some lathes, the tool rest for turning outboard of the headstock may be on a floor stand with no connection to the lathe. This needs to be substantial to hold the tool rest firmly without vibration. It is a method more likely to be found with large heavy production lathes than with those used for lighter occasional work.

A less common way of giving more clearance for turning large diameters is to arrange the whole headstock, with the motor platform, to swivel on the bed, so the faceplate at the normal right hand end of the spindle is brought to the front. The tool rest is moved to a bracket in front of this. The limit of diameter is then governed by clearance over the bench, or if this does not project enough to interfere and the tool rest is on a floor stand, there is no physical limit except the floor. The available motor power will be the governing factor, however.

There is a problem connected with power that restricts the size of work. When a tool is brought to the work and digs in as it starts to cut, the braking effect on a small diameter is not enough to do any more than slightly slow the electric motor. If a similar sort of cut is attempted on a large diameter, with the same motor driving it, the motor might be stalled. Overloading a motor in this way will soon ruin it. Any turner will find there are occasions when he wishes he could turn something larger than the capacity of his lathe, but for most

purposes, a maximum diameter of 12 inches will accommodate average needs. It should be checked with the makers of a new lathe that the motor provided will be powerful enough for the largest sizes to be turned.

As wood is a natural material and the numbers of species of trees commonly used for lumber runs into hundreds, it is difficult to be precise in quoting limits. Even with wood of the same species, there may be enough variation to make the turning of one large piece possible, while another piece of the same sort would cause stalling. Knots and other flaws in a piece of wood may give an interesting effect when a turned object is made from it, but a hard knot may make an otherwise easily turned wood difficult enough to stall the motor.

Although it is impossible and unnecessary to be scientifically correct in arriving at speeds for different sizes of turned work, it is helpful to be able to vary lathe speeds. Choices of speed is largely a matter of experience. Before the days of convenient electric power, a turner might instinctively vary

Fig. 2-2. Shown is a metalworking lathe viewed from above. A rod held in a three-jaw chuck has its end being turned by a tool that is controlled by handles. The handles at the bottom of the picture move the tool in and the other two move it along.

14

Fig. 2-3. This lathe has a gap bed and is mounted on a substantial stand with the motor below the headstock (courtesy of ToolKraft).

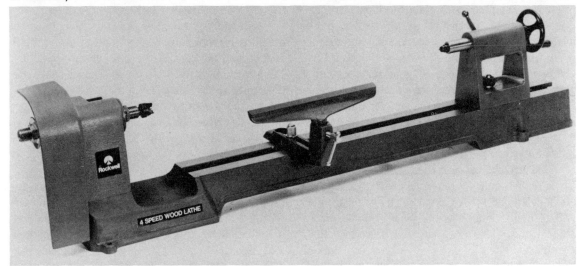

Fig. 2-4. Pictured is a bench-mounted, gap bed lathe with a shielded, four-step pulley. This lathe can turn large wood at the left-hand end (courtesy of Rockwell International).

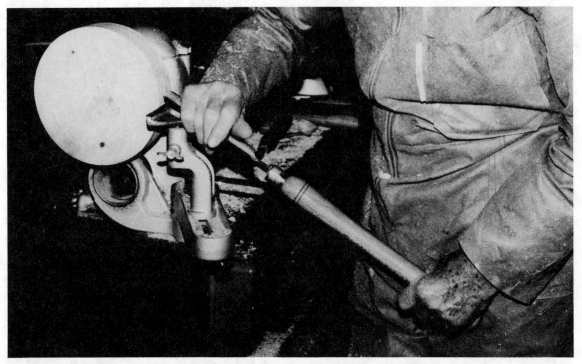

Fig. 2-5. If a lathe is designed to mount wood at the outer end of the headstock, it becomes possible to turn wood larger than could be accommodated over the bed.

speed by treadling faster or slower. Some woods turn better at higher speeds than others, but the important consideration is relative diameter.

It is the surface speed of the work past the cutting edge of the tool that counts. If this was to be maintained the same for all diameters, lathe speeds would have to be infinitely variable. Fortunately this is unnecessary as equally good results can be obtained over a very large range of surface speeds. Surface speeds are relative to diameters, and there is no need to work out the circumference. As an example, the surfaces of work of 1 inch and 6 inch in diameter can be considered.

The circumference is the diameter multiplied by π, which can be regarded as 3.14. So, the distance around a piece of wood 1 inch in diameter is 3.14 inches and around a piece 6 inches, it is 18.84 inches. This is the amount of surface that goes past the tool in one revolution. To maintain the same surface speed on the 6-inch wood as on the 1-inch wood, the revolutions should be cut to

one-sixth. In practice, such a drastic cut in speed is unnecessary, but it is still necessary to be able to vary speeds over a fairly wide range if the best use is to be made of a lathe.

An electric motor has to rotate quickly to be efficient. In wood turning, the lathe speeds required are comparably high, so direct drives are possible. Metal turning is mostly done at a lower speed, so the motor speed is cut down by driving a counter shaft, which then drives the lathe. This arrangement is found in some wood-turning lathes, but it is more usual to drive by a belt directly.

The simplest way to provide variations in lathe speed is to use cone pulleys. There may be two, three, or four steps on the pulleys, which are arranged in reverse manner on the lathe and motor (Fig. 2-6). If the motor is on a pivoting baseplate, it can be moved to slacken the belt, which is then moved to the steps to give the desired speeds. The proportions between pulley sizes are not always as simple as shown, but as an example, assume that

Fig. 2-6. With the cover removed, the four-step cone pulley in the headstock can be seen. The link-type driving belt is on the next to the largest pulley, thus giving the headstock spindle slightly lower rpm than the motor, which has a similar cone pulley the other way around.

the largest pulley is twice the size of the smallest and the other two of the four are spaced between these sizes. If the motor speed is 1725 rpm, approximate lathe speeds are then:

motor pulley		lathe pulley	lathe rpm
2	:	1	3450
1⅔	:	1⅓	2156
1⅓	:	1⅔	1380
1	:	2	862.5

To summarize: any calculated revolutions per minute only apply to the free-running motor, then belt and pulley load will reduce these and cutting wood will reduce them further, even to the extent of stopping the lathe if too heavy a cut is attempted. Heavier cuts can be taken better at low speeds than at high speeds for a given diameter. Normally, small work should run at the highest speed and

most bowls at the slowest speed normally available but much depends on the wood and the heaviness of the cut. Experience will show the best speed for a particular job. If the tool produces dust rather than shavings, the speed is too high. The highest speed that seems acceptable will normally give the best finish. Fortunately, a woodturner does not have to consider speeds in relation to materials and diameters as critically as does a metalturner. Good results are possible on wood within very broad bands of speeds.

An electric motor may be mounted above, behind, or below the lathe. Having it above means a belt coming down to the lathe, which may be dangerous and may get in the way of tool action. This method is rarely found today. Some lathes have an extension to take the motor behind the headstock, and this is convenient. Others, particularly if they are provided with legs or floor stands, have the motor below the lathe. This keeps it out of the way. Wood turning can be very dusty, so whatever method of mounting is used, the motor should be protected from dust as much as is possible.

The older method of driving a lathe with a flat belt is rarely found today. V-belts are used. There are several versions, but the section of the belt grips the sides of the grooves in the pulleys and should not touch the bottoms of the grooves. This gives a positive drive with the minimum risk of slipping.

Control should be by a switch that can be operated by feel and within reach of the turner, whatever his stance. He may have to switch off quickly in an emergency, without looking where he puts his hand. Do not locate a switch so it is necessary to reach across the moving parts of the lathe to operate it. The switch should incorporate an overload device to prevent damage to the motor. There are occasions when it is useful to be able to reverse a lathe. Much depends on the work being done, and some turners never find the need for a reversing switch, but including one in the circuit is comparatively simple.

Many lathes are supplied in a form for mounting on a bench. A floor stand may be an optional extra. Other lathes are only available with legs or stands. A large lathe is best with its own substantial legs or stand, but a smaller lathe is quite satisfactory on a bench.

Considerable rigidity is needed for all but the lightest work. Vibration can only be damped by massive construction of the lathe and its supports. A light lathe will perform better on a substantial wood bench than would a more robust lathe on light legs. Attaching the legs to the floor will help, or if there are shelves, they can be loaded with weights. It is when something asymmetrical is mounted or an unevenly-cut bowl blank starts to rotate that you will know if there is much lack of rigidity. Even with smaller regular spindle turning, lack of rigidity may cause a tool to judder and leave ridges or spiralling marks on the surface. This would not have occurred with a steadier setup.

Working height is not critical to the last inch, and some turners prefer positions higher or lower than standard. A person's own height also affects working position. Having the lathe centers about 36 inches above the shop floor is reasonable, but variations may still be satisfactory. The height of your elbow when standing is another guide to center height.

In many lathes, the bed goes the full length of the lathe and all other parts are mounted on it. The bed is then cast with feet and the usual form has two accurately machined ways to form a base for the other parts (Fig. 2-7A). The bed may be made of one diamond-sectioned rod (Fig. 2-7B) or two parallel bars (Figs. 2-7C and 2-8). The bed of the Myford lathe is a large slotted tube (Fig 2-9).

The headstock is the part where greatest accuracy and mechanical efficiency are required. The bearings in a simple lathe may be plain and without adjustment. These will wear and vibration will develop. In some older lathes, the thrust from turning was taken by a pointed bearing that could be adjusted for wear, and this tightened a tapered bearing at the working end. In better modern lathes, the bearings are ball or roller, sealed to keep lubricant in and dust out, and with fine adjustments.

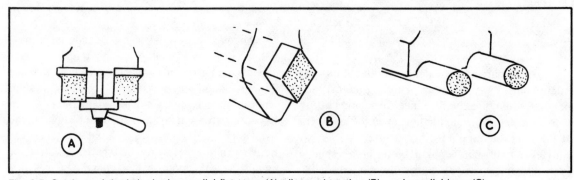

Fig. 2-7. Sections of the lathe beds: parallel flat ways (A), diamond section (B), and parallel bars (C).

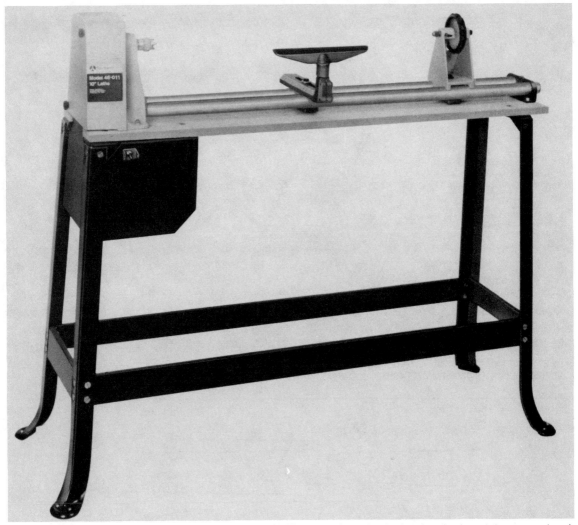

Fig. 2-8. This is a simple lathe with parallel bars as a bed. The motor is under the headstock where it is screened and controlled by a switch (courtesy of Rockwell International).

If much use is to be made of a lathe over a long period, these bearings should be chosen.

It is usual in modern lathes for the headstock mandrel or spindle to be of large enough diameter to be hollow. Besides allowing thin material to be passed through, this allows the ends to be given Morse tapers (Fig. 2-10A). These standard tapers allow centers and small fittings to have their matching tapered shanks pushed in and held by friction, then they can be removed by knocking out with a rod through the hole. There are several sizes

of Morse taper, but those used on most wood-turning lathes are usually Nos. 1 or 2 (No. 2 is the larger).

Some lathes have an indexing arrangement in the headstock. Some turners rarely use it, but it is simple for the makers to provide and is an additional facility worth having. A rotating part (often the large diameter wheel of the cone pulley) has holes around it—the number being such as to divide in several ways, including four, as this is the most needed division. With 48 holes, the possible varia-

19

Fig. 2-9. The Myford ML8 lathe has a slotted tubular bed and an outboard turning position. It may be on a metal stand, but this one has a wooden stand containing drawers for tools and equipment.

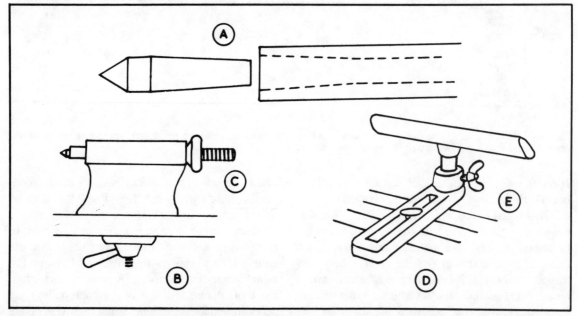

Fig. 2-10. The headstock mandrel and the tailstock are often bored through but given tapered ends to the holes to accept centers. The tailstock can be fixed in several positions on the bed, and its extension is controlled by a hand wheel. The tool rest can be adjusted to bring its edge close to the work in almost any position.

tions are: 4 × 12, 6 × 8, 2 × 24, 3 × 16, and, of course, 48. There is a mating peg or other device in a fixed part of the headstock that can be inserted in any hole in turn as the wood is moved around by hand. This locks the work each time it is inserted, so by using it in the appropriate holes, the work can be stopped and marked equally around the circumference. The tool rest against the work makes a convenient edge to pencil along. This facility is useful for dividing parts to be carved on a turned leg or for locating the positions of holes at right angles for rails into legs. Another use of the device is to secure the spindle so a faceplate or other screwed part can be removed.

There may be other things included in a headstock, but these will be dealt with elsewhere in the book. The headstock should be firmly fixed in relation to the bed.

The tailstock is a much simpler thing. Its object is to support a center at the same height as that at the headstock end. Usually it slides on the bed with guides to keep it straight and a screw through to a nut below (Fig. 2-10B). The nut may have a lever action for quick movement. There is a hollow spindle with a Morse taper for taking centers and other fittings. This is usually given a screw movement operated by a wheel (Fig. 2-10C). Rough adjustment is made by moving the whole tailstock along the bed. When it is secured, fine adjustment is by the wheel. There are several forms of tailstock (at one time called a *sliding headstock*), but any should give firm support to the end of the wood being turned. There must be no vibration present during normal turning.

TOOL RESTS

The tool rest provides something for the handheld tool to bear against at or just below the center height of the wood being turned. It needs to pivot and be moved in and out in relation to the work. Usually the base is slotted to allow in and out movement, and there is a bolt through to a levered nut (Fig. 2-10D) similar to the arrangement under the tailstock. It is convenient to be able to mount tool rests of different lengths, so the T-shaped rest may have a stem to fit a hole in the base, where it can be locked at the required height and angle by a butterfly nut (Fig. 2-10E). For very long tool rests, there may have to be a second base mounted on the bed to take a second stem.

For turning between centers, the tools fit across the tool rest at a slight angle upwards toward the cutting edge (Fig. 2-11A). The angle of crossing the rest will vary according to the height at which it is set. To allow for control as close as possible to the work, the section of the rest should have a curved top to an almost sharp edge (Fig. 2-11B). For turning bowls and similar things with scraping tools, the tool has to slope downwards, preferably with its heel on the top of the tool rest (Fig. 2-11C). So, it would be better to have this flat (Fig. 2-11D). It is unusual for more than one tool rest to be provided with a lathe, and the section used has to be a compromise, so it is not perfect for either type of turning. Some turners grind the top of the tool rest to suit their needs, but ideally there should be several rests of different types.

On most lathes, the tool rest base has a hole to take the stem of the rest, which is held by a screw and can be lifted out. It would not be difficult to have made some alternative tool rests for special purposes. It may be possible to make tool rests of hardwood supported on steel rod to fit in the hole in the base. Angular and curved edge tops are possibilities, particularly for use with scraper tools on bowls and other faceplate work (Fig. 2-11E).

A short rest on a single post can be moved to various positions and angled to bring support to a tool on tapered or intricately-shaped work. This is a help in achieving accuracy, but moving the rest about slows production. In professional turning, rests that are as long as the work are often used. This means that for long flowing curves, the tool can be swept along without moving the tool rest. On parts of the turning, the overhang of the tool on the rest may be greater but with practice it can be controlled satisfactorily. Traditional pole and treadle lathe turners often had quite crude full-length wooden tool rests that could not be adjusted and were not replaced until the edges became badly worn.

Long tool rests with second supports are not

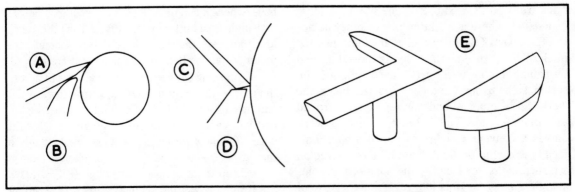

Fig. 2-11. Although the standard tool rest suits many needs, special ones can be bought or made.

available for all lathes. As the tool rest assembly on most lathes uses a base into which a rod on the rest fits, it is not difficult to make a longer rest from wood, using a piece of steel rod (usually about 3/4 inch in diameter) for the main support. Check the height and extension of the existing tool rest and arrange the wood edge to come at about the same position, although its section will have to be thicker (Fig. 2-12A). Allow enough thickness for the rod to go into a hole (Fig. 2-12B), where it can be held with epoxy adhesive. Close-grained hardwood will have the longest life. It should be possible to correct wear on the top by planing many times before the rest has to be replaced.

The wood rest need project no more to the left of the supporting rod than the standard rest does, but the other way make it long enough to extend past the longest wood your lathe will take—preferably overlapping the tailstock in its furthest position (Fig. 2-12C). How that long overhang is supported depends on the lathe. You may be able to make a wood support to mount on the lathe bed. The rest could be held to the tailstock with a clamp and packing (Fig. 2-13). Packings of different thickness would allow for adjustment. You must be able to move the rest up and down a little as well as in and out according to the diameter being turned.

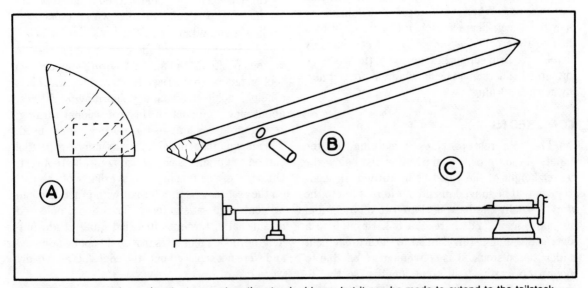

Fig. 2-12. A long wooden tool rest can mount on the standard base, but it can be made to extend to the tailstock.

Fig. 2-13. A long wooden tool rest may clamp to the tailstock with a packing thus allowing long work to be turned without the need to move to a shorter tool rest.

Simplicity is an advantage in a wood-turning lathe. For nearly all turning operations, the turner needs to be able to move his tools to various angles and to many positions without meeting obstructions. Because nearly all lathe tools and their handles are quite long, the arcs through which the turner needs to swing them are of various radii. He does not want to hit a fitting that would prevent the tool from going where he wants to go. There are additions to a lathe that may be worth having on a few occasions, but they should be removable. The headstock rotates the work, truly and without unwanted movement. The tailstock rigidly supports the other end of a long piece. The tool rest gives support where needed and can be moved easily and quickly to a new position. Those are the vital requirements of a lathe for the greater part of its use. It is in the successful performance of these functions that a lathe should be judged.

LATHE MAINTENANCE

A standard wood-turning lathe requires little maintenance. Keeping it clean is something of a problem. Shavings, wood particles, and dust should not be allowed to accumulate, particularly on the bearing surfaces and moving parts. If you don't go to the extent of thoroughly cleaning it, at least make it a practice to brush off all that can be removed after each working session and occasionally stop part way through a job and get rid of all of the unwanted debris.

A narrow brush, such as a paint brush, is useful to supplement the normal hand brush. It gets into the less-accessible places. If the electric motor is within range of the dust cloud, keep that clean by brushing and occasionally vacuum off the dust using the small nozzle of your vacuum cleaner (with power to the motor disconnected). Many electric motors are not as well protected against the entry of dust as we would hope. Air must circulate and dust goes in the same way.

The greatest mechanical load comes on the headstock bearings. If they wear, get distorted, or are damaged in any other way, your work will no longer run true without vibration. There is not much you can do about it except have it repaired, which can be quite costly. Usually, the makers provide plenty of protection for these bearings, but you should keep mandrels and shafts clean in the vicinity of the bearings. You should especially wipe off abrasive grits, which could find their way into bearings and cause damage.

The method of lubrication of the headstock bearings will vary between makes. Check the maker's instructions. Usually, there are oilers. Do not forget them! It is very easy to use the lathe for a long period of time without bothering about lubrication. Inadequate lubrication will cause bearings to get hot, wear more, and revolve less freely. In an extreme case, they could seize. Over-lubrication is better than under-lubrication. If oil leaks and you have to wipe it away, you know there is enough oil in the bearing.

If you have a revolving tailstock center, its bearings will be sealed and not require attention except after extremely long use. Then you should disassemble, and repack them with grease. If you use a plain tailstock center, it has to be lubricated where it supports the revolving wood. Oil on it would be thrown off by centrifugal force. Graphite could be used, but a piece of candle or other hard wax makes a cleaner and better lubricant. Push the point into it each time you mount a piece of wood.

The tailstock and tool rest should move freely along the bed. It is frustrating when they will not move or have to be knocked when you want to make a quick adjustment while turning. Keep the lathe bed clean and smear it with oil occasionally.

Other moving parts on a lathe only require slight and occasional action, but it is worthwhile to clean and lubricate such parts as the tailstock feed screw and the locking parts for the tailstock and tool rest before they get stiff. Accidents occur when they are stiff and difficult to move.

Check the drive from the motor. Many assemblies use V belts, which should bear on the sides of the pulley grooves. If the belt touches the bottom, it has probably stretched and the drive is no longer as positive. There is no need for exceptional tightness of these belts. Have enough tension

to keep the sides of the belt far enough into the pulleys to bear without slipping. Flat and round belts need to be tighter as they depend on the bearing surfaces under them. If there is a countershaft, correct the tension between that and the lathe first, then deal with the belt from the motor.

Electric motors vary in their lubrication requirements. Many have sealed bearings and do not require treatment. If there are oilers, do not over-lubricate as excess oil getting into some electrical parts will stop the motor. It is better to use a little oil often, than to heavily oil the motor at fewer intervals.

You may have a problem with removing such parts as centers, chucks, and faceplates. If the headstock and tailstock mandrels are hollow, a rod can be passed through to knock out centers and other things made to fit the tapered holes. Hold the part being knocked so that it does not fly and damage itself or another part it hits. Wipe out the tapered holes so that the mating surfaces fit closely and accurately. Do this particularly if they have to provide a friction drive as with a fork center. If the mandrels are not hollow, the centers are usually provided with a hole in the side so a rod (tommy bar) can be inserted and jerked round to free the parts.

Parts that screw on, such as faceplates, get a tightening action on them when the lathe is in use. If they make a metal-to-metal joint, the final tightness may be such that they are almost impossible to remove. A fiber or leather washer on the mandrel will do something to prevent this from happening. Even then, it may be difficult to unscrew a faceplate. If the headstock mandrel can be locked with a dividing head or other means, that helps as you try to jerk the faceplate free; otherwise, you can grasp the cone pulley. Remember that if the faceplate is at the outboard end of the headstock, it has a left-hand thread. If holding the faceplate does not give you enough leverage to free it, you can bolt a strip of wood to it (Fig. 2-14A) or make a special tool to engage with holes or slots (Fig. 2-14B).

A very similar problem occurs with small work on a screw center. It helps to include a plywood pad between the work and the metal face (Fig. 2-14C). If you grip the work with a piece of abrasive paper, it will probably unscrew. If it won't, use a punch to give an unscrewing action to the edge of the plywood disc (Fig. 2-14D). That should start the work unscrewing as well.

Included in the listed accessories for some electric drills is a lathe attachment. The drill is mounted in a way that utilizes it as a direct drive headstock. If the original use of the drill is considered, you will see that its designed torque is intended probably for a maximum size wood-burning bit of 1 1/2 inches or less. The loads imposed by wood turning are comparable to those in boring, so a drill/lathe should only be regarded as suitable for small diameter spindle turning. If the limitations are understood, good small work is possible on such a machine, but if anything other than elementary small work is intended, a more substantial lathe is needed.

A good lathe is a comparatively simple thing. It should be rigid enough to damp out vibration. The headstock spindle should revolve without slackness. The tailstock should be easily set and rigidly held. This also applies to the tool rest. The more uncluttered and plain the basic lathe is, the better it is likely to be for its purpose. All the lathe

has to do is rotate a piece of wood. The rest is skilled handwork by the turner, and he needs to be able to move his handheld tools without obstruction. There are just a few essential accessories described in the next chapter, but other attachments and accessories should not be bought until the type of work undertaken shows a real need for them.

SPECIAL LATHES

For most readers of this book, the lathes described in this chapter and throughout the book will serve all of their needs. There are, however, some other lathes that you should be aware of. Much of the professional turning is done on lathes as already described, but in a shop where the needs are for large work as well as the more routine small productions, the lathe will be one made of more substantial casting, with bearings, controls, and accessories in proportion. All of this makes for steadiness when dealing with large and irregular shapes.

There may be provision for turning very large discs. This means that the speed adjustments must allow for quite low revolutions (possibly 50 rpm or less), and the disc will be mounted on the outer end of the headstock spindle with the tool rest on a separate stand on the floor. With this arrangement, a

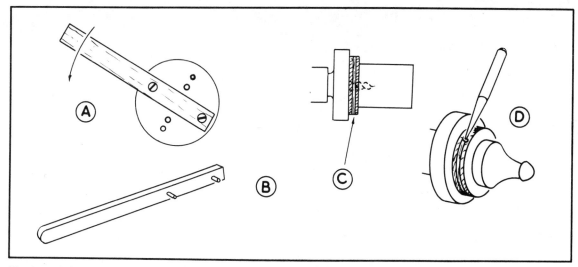

Fig. 2-14. A tight faceplate may have to be levered off. A small object on a screw center can be released with a punch on a packing.

wheel, table top, or other disc can be turned with a radius up to the height of the center above the shop floor.

There are many ingenious lathes for repetitious work, where the wood is fed as needed and cutters turn it to the required profile automatically and quickly. With the extra equipment needed, it is often difficult to recognize the vital turning part comparable with a simple lathe. Other lathes will copy an original. While a sensor follows the profile, a cutter repeats this on the wood being turned. Either of these types of lathe may be used for twist turning, which is otherwise done laboriously by hand. One snag is that the cutters at all stages work on the wood something like the cut of a hand turning roughing gouge pointing straight at the wood. There is not the slicing action finishing cut such as is possible with a skew chisel used by hand. The finish is acceptable, but it is not comparable with good hand work and machine sanding has to compensate for the interior tool finish.

It is possible to turn quite small items on a normal lathe, but for anyone only interested in modelmaking or other regular production of very small items, the comparatively large normal lathe is unnecessary. There are some small lathes available, possibly with only 6 inches between centers and 1 1/2 inch swing. Some of these are precision machines equipped for metal turning as well as hand turning wood and plastics. Quite delicate work to fine tolerances can be made, particularly if special chucks and other equipment are obtained. Small does not necessarily mean cheap. This is the lathe for the specialist. Anyone who only wants to occasionally make small items should choose a normal-size lathe.

Turning tools for a small lathe can be bought, but miniature versions of normal tools can be made easily. Hard steel rod, such as masonry nails, can be ground to shape and mounted in small handles. Very hard close-grained wood is normally chosen for very small items, and the cutters needed are mostly scrapers of various shapes. Any wood with coarse open grain would not be strong enough when turned to small sizes, although it may suit handles and other things made near the capacity of the small lathe. In that case, normal turning tools can be used, although shorter general-purpose gouges and chisels ground to suit will be less clumsy. Carving tools have possibilities for small turning, but they are light-sectioned and must not be expected to do heavy work, even at small sizes.

Chapter 3

Lathe Accessories

The number of pieces of equipment needed in addition to the lathe depends on what work is to be undertaken, but for average needs, there are only a few essential accessories. At the other extreme, if ornamental turning of the type practiced in the nineteenth century and described in detail by John Jacob Holtzapffel in his books of the period is to be tackled, the accessories can almost obscure the lathe on which they are mounted.

There are some accessories that the turner can make himself. The experienced turner will become adept at improvising things to suit the needs of the moment, and some of these will be for a short-lived purpose and then be discarded. Many of these are described in later chapters in connection with particular projects. This chapter is only concerned with the basic accessories that are needed for normal turning and what most turners will acquire early in their activity.

CENTERS

Long work is supported and driven on centers.

These are the points that fit into headstock and tailstock. Such work is often described as *turning between centers* or *spindle turning* to distinguish it from *faceplate turning*. Faceplate turning is done with the wood mounted on the headstock only, usually without calling for support by the tailstock. In most lathes, the centers push into sockets and are held and driven by friction. These are usually Morse tapers and could be No. 1 or No. 2. Adapters are obtainable to fit the smaller No. 1 center into a No. 2 socket (Fig. 3-1), but not the other way around. So, if there is any choice, it is better to have a lathe provided with No. 2 Morse taper sockets, so smaller fittings not originally intended for it can still be used.

Headstock and tailstock mandrels are usually hollow, so a rod can be passed through it to knock out centers. It is also possible to pass thin rods through the headstock mandrel for turning. This is done so that an end can be held by a chuck or parts brought out a little at a time so they can be turned close to the chuck. Doing this avoids the

Fig. 3-1. Several lathe centers: fork or prong, plain, cut and rotating, with an adaptor fitting a No. 1 into a No. 2 Morse taper. The tool at the top is for knocking out centers.

problem of flexing if long thin wood is turned between centers. For drilling long holes (such as lamp standards) there are special tools that can be passed through the tailstock mandrel and/or a matching guide mounted on the tool rest base.

On some lathes, both mandrels are solid and the driving and tailstock centers fit into them or screw on or in them. To release such a center, a rod (tommy bar) is inserted in a hole in the side to provide leverage or there are flats provided for a wrench to be used. The headstock mandrel should be locked or held securely when its center is being unscrewed. A fiber washer arranged between meeting surfaces may be used to prevent screwed centers jamming excessively.

The basic center is a simple point, usually 60 degrees (Figs. 3-1 and 3-2A). This is the angle favored for metal turning and is acceptable for much wood turning. Such a tailstock center does not rotate so the wood rotating at a high speed on it may wear at an amount depending on the hardness of the wood and the amount of lubrication. This means that the tailstock usually has to be tightened soon after work is commenced and often at intervals as work progresses. As the end of the wood is usually scrapped, it does not matter how deeply the center penetrates. In practice, a 60 de-

gree center in the tailstock serves most turners for the majority of their needs. A wider angle, however, would be better for soft woods as it would not tend to penetrate as much and 90 degrees (Fig. 3-2B) or somewhere between that and 60 degrees would be better. Some makers offer centers hard or soft. For wood turning they should be hard.

Another center for tailstock use is a ring or cup type (Fig. 3-1 and 3-2C). A fine spike at the center penetrates the wood, then there is a sharp-edged ring projecting a short distance from a flat base. This center may fit a Morse taper or be made to screw on. In use, the spike locates the wood centrally, then the ring penetrates until the flat base presses on the end of the wood. The cup center is favored for professional production work on a series of similar things turned between centers when the lathe may not be stopped between making parts. In that case, a new piece of wood is forced onto the driving center with a quick thrust from the cup center at the tailstock. After turning, the tailstock is backed away with the right hand and the wood caught off the driving center with the left hand. This is obviously a method not to be recommended for beginners. The use of a cup center can be seen on many production items where its marks show at the end of the wood that is left without trimming off. Whether to use a plain center or a cup center may be a matter of personal choice for general turning between centers. The plain center is better for large work in very hard woods.

There is a metal turning center that is cut away (Fig. 3-2D). For some wood turning this has advantages as it allows a tool to be manipulated at wider angles to the end of the wood.

Letting the wood rotate on a fixed center is not a very good mechanical design, and it is better if the center can rotate with the work. Then the center does not wear into the wood and call for frequent tailstock adjustment. It is important, however, that whatever bearings are used to allow the center to rotate should be free from vibration to quite fine limits. It is possible to obtain ball bearing rotating centers (Figs. 3-1 and 3-2E) that are sufficiently well

engineered to give a good performance for a long time. If much use is to be made of a lathe, one of these centers is worth having. Some of these are arranged to take different center points that are provided.

There are occasions when a plain center is needed at the headstock end as well. Two matching plain centers should be regarded as normal lathe equipment in any case, even if the second is only needed as a reserve if the first becomes damaged.

It is more usual to have a driving center at the headstock end. There have been many patterns made and improvised, but the usual need is for a point to center the wood and some blades or spurs to enter the wood and provide enough grip to transfer the rotation of the headstock spindle to the work. A simple driving center has two projecting

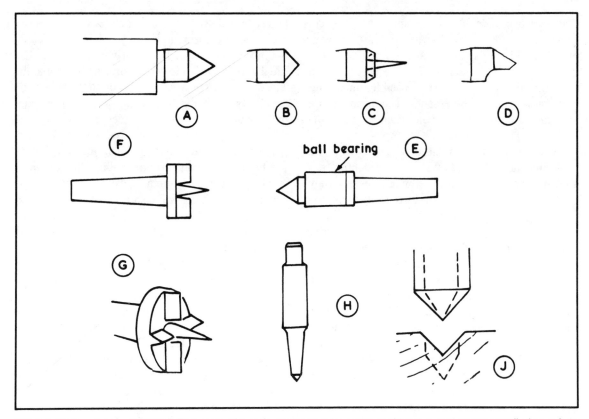

Fig. 3-2. Various types of centers. The angle of a plain center may be acute or obtuse; a cup center usually has a long point. The spur center may be a single pair of blades or two pairs crossing. A ball bearing center in the tailstock is a convenience, because it avoids wear in the end of the wood. It is helpful to use a fairly blunt angled center punch to mark center holes in the end of wood.

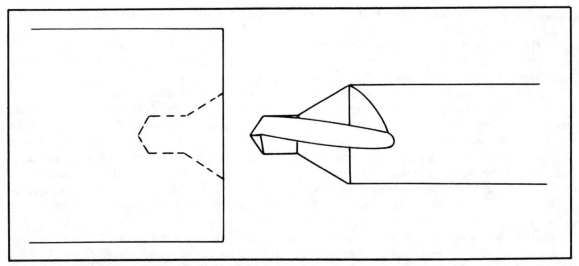

Fig. 3-3. A combination drill will prepare the end of material to be turned to fit on a center.

blades on each side of a central spike that projects further (Figs. 3-1 and 3-2F). A further step has another pair of similar blades at right angles to the first (Fig. 3-2G). Some makers have variations on this and many designs are possible, including removable points. The essential requirement is a central spike projecting further than the parts arranged to provide drive.

It is important that the driving center spike runs absolutely central. With a new center that should be so, but centers suffer in use because they are often hit by a tool during turning. If a point is untrue, it may be possible to bring the tool rest close and use a graver or file to turn its point central. Then, the part behind the point may need more filing when the center is stationary.

The prongs or blades that provide the drive may have regular conical sections as shown in the four-prong driving center (Fig. 3-2G). In others, there may be bevels on one side of each blade, so the sections are like chisel ends with the flat sides towards the direction of rotation. Worn edges should be sharpened at their original angles with a fine file or a small oilstone.

One or more center punches are useful in preparing wood to fit on centers. The common type has a fairly fine point at 60 degrees. For many purposes this is satisfactory. A rather thicker point is

better (Fig. 3-2H) as it will make a wider dent at the same angle to match a center instead of making more of a narrow hole if driven far (Fig. 3-2J). Ideally, the punch and center angles should match. The soft nature of wood in relation to the steel center allows the center to push in and make it thicker or to widen the angle to suit centers. Rotating it against the grinder may not produce the absolute perfection that turning the point would (which cannot be done without first annealing the hardened steel and using a metal turning lathe before rehardening. There will be ample accuracy for the purpose.

Metal turners use a combined center drill and countersink to prepare the end of a rod to take the tailstock center because the center could not press into metal and provide a bearing with just a center punch dot as is possible with wood. Such a combination drill (may be called a Slocumbe drill) would be useful when plastic or very hard wood is to be turned on a wood lathe. The drill, which may be supplied double-ended, has a short straight-fluted small parallel drill and then a countersink at 60 degrees (Fig. 3-3). Drills with several outside diameters are available. The very small ones are intended for fine metal turning, but for general purposes on material for a wood lathe, a drill with a diameter of 5/16 inch or 3/8 inch will do. The small parallel drill part is then about 1/8 inch (Fig. 3-4). Advantages of the small drilled parallel hole are that it relieves the point of the lathe center of wear and it acts as a reservoir for lubricant, such as wax or grease.

If the center of a disc or round rod has to be found and punched, you can use a center square or head but for small circular pieces, such as dowel rods, this is tedious. Another metal turner's tool is more convenient. This is a bell center punch, where a conical part fits over the end of the rod and the punch sliding in the body can be hit to mark the center (Fig. 3-5A). Bell center punches can be obtained to take up to 1-inch, 1 1/2-inch, or 2-inch rod ends.

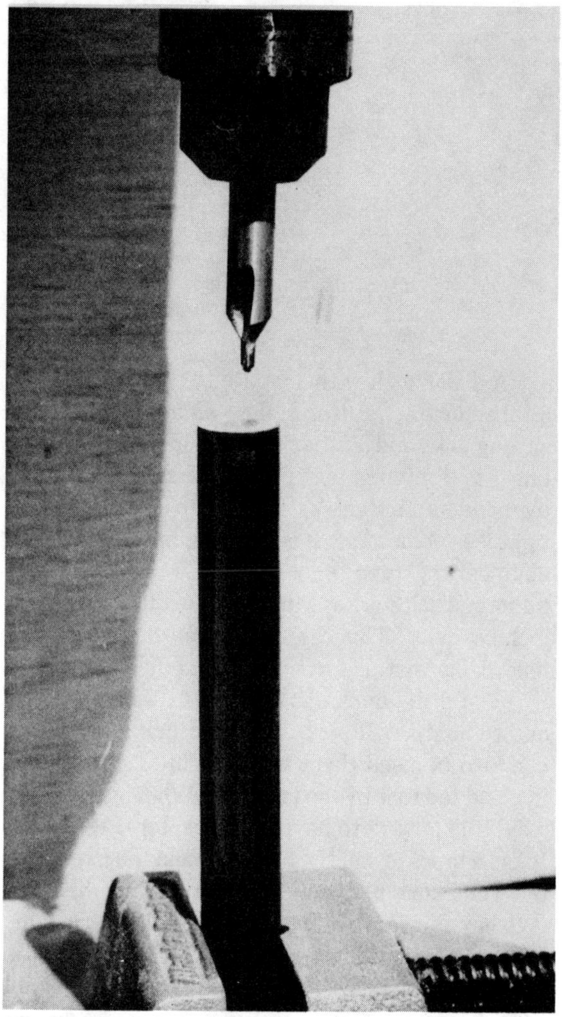

If a bell center punch is unavailable, the engineering alternative is to use hermaphrodite calipers (odd-leg or jenny calipers). Set the tool to an estimated radius, then scribe marks from four or more positions (Fig. 3-5B). The punch position will be at the center of these marks. Without these calipers, it is possible to use dividers in the same way, but you have to be careful to keep the outer leg exactly on the rod edge each time. A marking gauge could be used in the same way with less risk of slipping out of position.

With many woods it is possible to mount a piece between centers with little or no preparation of the ends to take the lathe centers. An experienced turner may put one end on the driving center and bring up the tailstock center to press it on, so there is sufficient grip at both ends to provide a drive

Fig. 3-4. Shown is a combination drill being used to center a plastic rod.

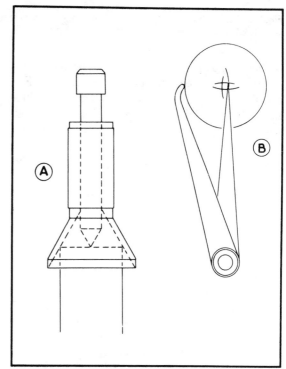

Fig. 3-5. A special punch is used for centering rods (A). Also shown is a method of finding a center with odd-leg calipers (B).

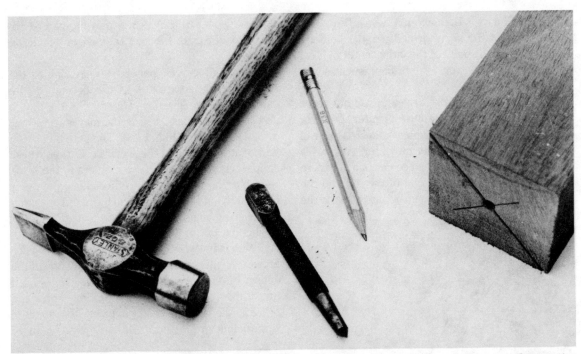

Fig. 3-6. The center of the end of a square piece of wood is found by drawing diagonals. Then, it helps to make a center punch dot and a shallow saw cut for the driving center.

without slipping. For most jobs, the prongs of the driving center need not penetrate very far. For repetition spindle work, this allows quick production with the minimum of operations. A beginner will usually prefer to find the centers of the ends of the wood and make center punch dots. Careful centering is important in any case if part of the wood is to remain square or octagonal; otherwise, any error will show because the round part will not line-up correctly.

It is unwise to drive wood onto the driving center in the lathe with a hammer or mallet because this puts an undue load on the bearings. A spare driving center could be used like a punch with the wood on the bench to make indentations in the driving end of the wood. If it cannot be pushed on, but if the wood is hard, it is better to make a shallow saw cut across the center punch dot to help the prongs enter (Fig. 3-6). Diagonals drawn on the end will find the center of square wood and show the line for the saw cut and a second one if you have a four-prong center.

A drill chuck with a tapered arbor the same as a lathe center is useful. The smallest type with sprung jaws and a capacity of 1/4 inch has its uses, but it is tightened by turning the knurled outside by hand, and there is a limit to the degree of tightness obtainable. It is better to have a precision engineering type chuck that is adjusted and tightened with a key (Fig. 3-7), preferably of 1/2 inch capacity. This can be used in the tailstock to hold drills that are fed into the rotating work.

The drill chuck can be used at the headstock end to hold small pieces of wood being turned. It can also be used there with a drill to make holes in wood fed to it by the tailstock. When used in this way, it is helpful to have a pad center (Fig. 3-8A). It has a taper to suit the tailstock, and the pad keeps the wood at right angles to the drill. A further step is to have a groove across the pad (Fig. 3-8B). This locates round work in relation to the drill and is useful when doing such things as drilling a stool rail to take another (Fig. 3-8C). The grooved pad can be used for similar work to the plain pad as well.

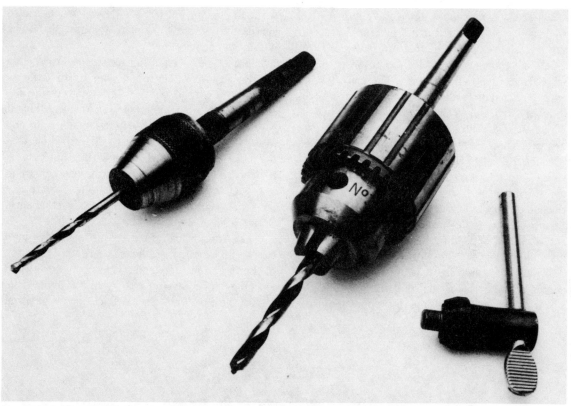

Fig. 3-7. A hand-operated chuck can be used for small drills, but a better grip for any size drill is provided by a key-operated chuck. Both chucks have Morse taper shafts to fit sockets in headstocks and tailstocks.

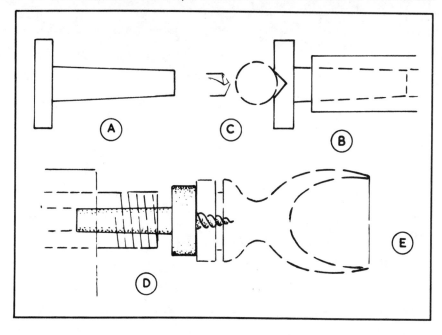

Fig. 3-8. A pad is used when wood has to be supported at the tailstock end for drilling from the headstock. If round work has to be drilled on the side, it is helpful to have a grooved pad. A screw chuck is the best way of holding small items—like eggcups—that have to be turned inside.

A screw center looks like a pad center with a wood screw projecting from it. In its simplest form, the screw is one with the rest of the center (Fig. 3-8D), but this means that if the screw wears, the whole center has to be replaced. There are several variations that use ordinary steel wood screws held in a way that allows the screw to be replaced.

A screw center may be mounted on the headstock spindle to hold small items to be turned without the aid of the tailstock center when that would interfere with turning a hollow. The back center may be used so far, then it is withdrawn for the end turning of a hollow. The screw center may fit into a taper hole in the headstock spindle or screw onto it, depending on the make of lathe. An example of this type of work is an eggcup (Fig. 3-8E). All of the outside can be turned with the back center in place. Then, that is withdrawn and the screw center would continue to support and drive

while the hollow is turned. The screw center also serves like a small faceplate for any disc work within its capacity.

In the type of center in which an ordinary screw is fitted, it is possible to use a length of screw to suit the work, although these fittings all require any screws to be the same gauge thickness. A longer screw provides the best grip, particularly in end grain, but a short screw may be needed when turning a disc or small bowl shape with a thin base. A plywood disk on the center can be used as a pad to reduce the effective length of a screw and to prevent tools coming into contact with the steel parts (Figs. 3-9 and 3-10).

The torque load on the comparatively small screw can be considerable, so there may be a risk of the thread in the wood stripping and the wood loosening. The flat surface of the wood against the face of the center also provides friction for grip and

Fig. 3-9. A screw center or chuck that uses an ordinary wood screw, showing the method of locking it in position.

Fig. 3-10. A screw center with a plywood pad to fit over the screw.

drive, but a few inches in wood diameter is about the limit for most turning on a screw center. Drill a hole only big enough to allow the screw to enter and this will ensure maximum grip. Some screw centers have holes drilled to allow two screws to be driven from the back into the wood, thus allowing the pad to be more of a faceplate and larger diameters to be safely turned.

There are many chucks of various designs, but some are arranged to mount on one make and model of lathe only. The chucks work more positively than a screw center and will drive open-ended work of larger diameter and length without slipping. Most of these work on the collet principle, which is used extensively in engineering. A casing takes three or four jaws that can be adjusted in a very similar way to the jaws of a drill chuck, but with only a limited movement. Therefore, several sets of collets are needed to exchange in the chuck to suit different diameters of wood. A typical set of jaws will hold from quite small up to 1 1/2 inches in diameter. Besides squeezing inwards, jaws can be fitted to tighten outwards. If a hollow is first turned in the base of a bowl or other work, the collets will hold a fairly large piece of wood from inside the hollow.

Other ingenious chucks have been devised, but as spindle noses vary between lathes, it will be necessary to discover what is available for your particular make of lathe. It is possible to improvise chucks for particular purposes, and some of these are described elsewhere in this book. Work too big for these chucks will have to be mounted on a faceplate, while some things are better held with an engineering type of three-jaw chuck. Both of these are described in the next section.

FACEPLATES

If bowls or broad bases are to be turned, the drive and support comes from a faceplate. In most cases, the faceplate does not have to be as large as the work. Only when the work is very thin in relation to its diameter is a larger faceplate desirable and even then a small faceplate can have its effective diameter increased by a wood backing piece between it and the work.

A faceplate screws on to one end of the headstock spindle. It is helpful to have a soft washer for it to press against. This makes removal easier. Besides the screwed part, it is usual for there to be a short length of parallel unscrewed spindle on which the faceplate beds to ensure accuracy. The soft fiber or rubber washer should not take up much of this section (Fig. 3-11A). A faceplate for the inboard end of the mandrel nose will have a right-hand thread. A faceplate intended for the outboard end has a left-hand thread. Screwing in this way ensures the action of a tool on the work has a tightening effect. If the lathe is equipped with a reversing switch, care is needed to watch for any signs of loosening when rotating the other way. Because of the different threads, it is necessary to have separate faceplates for inboard and outboard use—usually a larger one outboard than the one used inboard over the bed of the lathe. There are many sizes to be had. Although a large one may do many of the jobs of a small one, its size can be a nuisance when getting towards the back of something less than the capacity of the faceplate. For inboard use, a diameter of 3 or 5 inches will do, while the outboard faceplate can be about twice these sizes (Fig. 3-11B).

A faceplate may be made of steel or an aluminum alloy. The latter is kinder to a tool that accidentally hits it. Steel is stronger, and there is no risk of wear on the screw threads after long use. In any case, the faceplate should have its accurately machined face and edges backed by sufficient metal for it to resist distortion.

It is usual to fix a pad of scrap wood to a faceplate and mount the work to be turned on that. Most faceplates have a pattern of countersunk screw holes or slots (Fig. 3-12). In practice, it is the screw holes that get most use. The slots have occasional use, but woodworking faceplates seem to be copies of metal working ones; the slots have more applications in bolting on irregular castings and similar things.

CHUCKS

Related to faceplates and their uses are chucks, based on those commonly found on metal turning lathes. There are two types: self-centering, where turning one key operates all jaws; and independent chucks, where the key has to be moved to operate each jaw in turn. It is usual for a self-centering chuck to have three jaws, and an independent chuck, four jaws. Jaw capacity depends on the size of the chuck and the lathe it is to fit. For normal

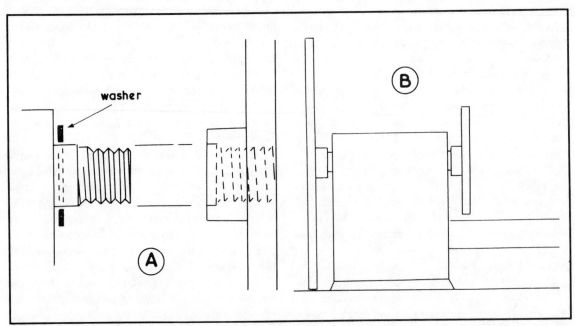

Fig. 3-11. A faceplate screws onto one end of the mandrel, but it is located by a parallel part. The difference in possible sizes is shown by the faceplates at opposite ends of the headstock.

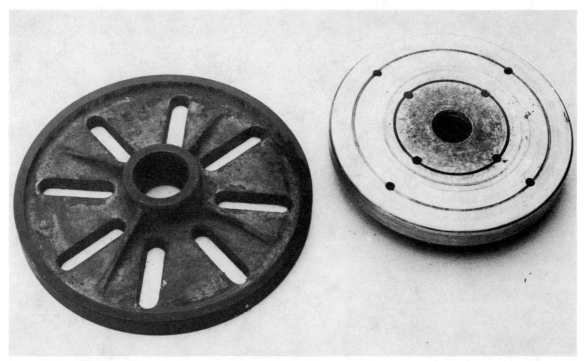

Fig. 3-12. Faceplates are in many sizes, and they may have slots or holes.

lathes, a capacity of 3 or 4 inches is usual. The jaws have steps and may be reversible or another set of jaws can be fitted so the chuck can grip outside solid work or inside hollow work (Fig. 3-13).

These chucks have a backing plate like a faceplate that screws on the mandrel nose. A three-jaw, self-centering chuck automatically locates on round work, but it does not bring square wood very central. An independent four-jaw chuck takes longer to operate, but it is better for square or ir-regular shapes. It is still suitable for round work, so it is the choice for most turners if only one chuck is obtained. Neither of these chucks is essential equipment, but they are convenient for many types of work and are better for some purposes than other fittings or the improvisations and specially-made items otherwise needed.

If there is to be much torque load on a drive, it is better for it to be on the screwed part of the mandrel nose than on the internal taper. In some lathes there are provisions for a screwed draw bolt to pull a Morse taper fitting tightly into its socket

by working from the opposite end. The end of a screw center may have an internal thread to accept this draw bolt.

Any fitting—whether screwed on or pushed in—tends to tighten in use. Some Morse taper fit-tings have flats on them to take a wrench, which can be used to jerk them loose (Fig. 3-14A). This arrangement is needed if the mandrel or tailstock is not hollow right through. If there is a hole through, it is better to use a rod as a knockout bar. This is often any odd piece of wood that will pass through it. It is better to make a rod with a knob end that is slightly longer than the hole it is to pass through. This can be an easy fit in the bore (Fig. 3-14B), which is more effective than an undersize rough piece of wood. The rod may be hardwood or it could be metal, such as brass or aluminum, but softer than the steel it will be touching. To most users, this is a *bumper-outer*, which is a descriptive, not very scientific, name.

Faceplates and large chucks screwed on need the drive locked for removal, then they can usually

Fig. 3-13. A self-centering chuck is a useful tool, because turning the key in one of the slots adjusts all three jaws equally. There are interchangeable jaws for holding work outside or inside.

be held by the rim and unscrewed. If they are too tight a piece of wood can be levered between chuck jaws, or a lever with projections to engage faceplate slots can be used (Fig. 3-14C). Some lathes have a provision for locking the headstock spindle. If the lathe includes a dividing head with a peg to fit into holes in the cone pulley, use that to lock the drive.

Otherwise, it is probably enough to grip the belt

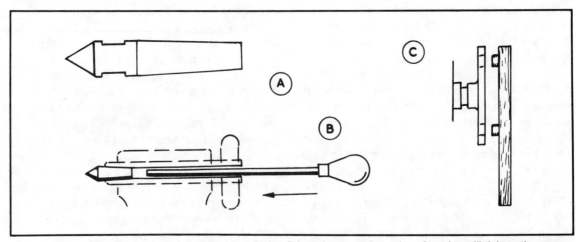

Fig. 3-14. There is a problem of removing centers and other fixings, because the action of turning will tighten the screws. Centers may be loosened by using a wrench on flats, or it may be knocked out of a hollow mandrel. A lever can be used to remove a faceplate.

or pulley with one hand, while levering the faceplate off with the other.

Be careful when removing anything screwed on or pushed in that it cannot drop or fly as it comes off and either damage itself, the lathe, or you. Hold a cloth over a center being bumped out and have wood under the faceplate being unscrewed in case it drops.

Included in the accessories should be an oil can, preferably of the pressure-feed type. The working parts of a lathe revolve at high speeds. Methods of lubrication vary and it is important to follow the advice of the makers. Adequate lubrication at all times is important. If there are drip-feed lubricators or other visible means of lubricating, see that these are full and always functioning; otherwise, follow the lubrication recommendations provided with the lathe. Moving parts should not work dry. Things like the jaws of chucks should be oiled or greased. The screw action of a tailstock needs oiling. Oil and the vital parts of an electric motor do not go well together. Use oil where indicated on a motor, but be careful of letting excess oil go where it should not (see Chapter 2).

When turning, dust is attracted by oil and grease. Most vital bearings are sealed to prevent the entry of dust. Any surface oil that attracts dust should be wiped with a cloth, but do not do this while parts are moving. A loose cloth caught up in a revolving lathe may be almost as dangerous as a dangling tie in the same circumstances.

The accessories described in this chapter are those with general applications that should be of use to any turner whatever his interests. Other more specialized accessories are described in later chapters.

Chapter 4

Lathe Tools

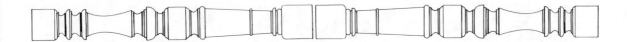

A lathe rotates the wood. What happens to it after that is the concern of the craftsman with handheld tools. He decides how the wood will be shaped, and it is his skill with the tools that settles the quality of the finished object. Consequently, the tools are an important part of the process. Some turners seem to manage with extremely few tools, while others require a very large range. In recent years, there have been many additions to the basic selection that turners have used for centuries. No doubt many of these newer tools have their value, but a beginning turner is best advised to first obtain a few tools of the traditional type before buying a variety of less common ones. A large number of tools bought in the first instance will not guarantee any better results than would be obtained by using a small number of tools and mastering them before deciding that more are needed.

Because wood turning is broadly divided into spindle turning (or turning between centers) and faceplate turning, so are the tools needed. There is some overlap, but tools for spindle turning use something of a slicing action to pare off wood, while those used for faceplate turning cut with more of a scraping action.

The majority of lathe tools are made of simple steel containing the correct proportion of carbon with iron to permit hardening and tempering. This may be described as "high-carbon" or "tool" steel to distinguish it from the low-carbon, "mild" steel (often mistakenly called iron), which cannot be hardened and tempered. Tools of this type are comparatively inexpensive and are all that are needed, unless continuous heavy work or long production runs are expected. Tools made from other grades of steel will keep their edges longer, so pauses for sharpening will be less frequent. The quality of turned work depends on the sharpness of the tools, not on the steel from which they are made.

Tools made from high-speed steel (often described as "H.S.S.") can be obtained. This is high carbon steel with tungsten added. Tungsten increases hardness and is particularly valuable for dealing with woods that contain grit (such as ebony, teak, and cocobola), so edges are retained longer. There is also an increased resistance to the effect of overheating, but that advantage is more apparent when turning metal.

Some turning tools of Japanese manufacture are laminated with hard steel supported by low-carbon steel for strength and toughness. Because the steel of the cutting edge is harder than the normal solid steel tool, it should keep its edge longer. There is a risk of the brittle cutting part splintering, and it is more susceptible to damage by overheating during careless grinding.

GOUGES

Much turning, particularly in the early stages of roughing to shape, is done with gouges. Except for use with very small lathes, these gouges are larger and more substantial than those used for ordinary woodwork. All are sharpened on the outside. There is no use in turning for an *in-cannelled* or inside sharpened gouge. An ordinary gouge is about the same thickness around the curve (Fig. 4-1A). A turning gouge is deeper at the bottom of the curve (Fig. 4-1B) to give stiffness, while one described as long and strong is even deeper (Fig. 4-1C).

Because lathe tools are never hit, there is no need for a shoulder where the tang goes into a wooden handle. This part of the tool is plain (Fig. 4-1D). There is an advantage in length, because it gives leverage, which often helps in directing and controlling a cut. The overall length of tool and handle may be between 16 and 19 inches. The handle usually accounts for more than half of this. Handles are made of close-grained hardwood and are usually fitted with tubular ferrules. Shapes vary, and many turners have their own ideas about tool handles that they make themselves.

Some gouges are available in different sweeps for the same width. The normal curve is part of a circle and makes a good general-purpose tool (Fig. 4-1E). Deep gouges are more of a U-shape and are usually stronger and thicker than the other type (Fig. 4-1F). They are useful for first roughing square or octagonal wood to round. When tilted, the cutting effect is little different from using the flatter normal curve.

Much of the value of long and strong gouges is in the way their bulk and stiffness damp down any tendency to vibration, which would show in the quality of the work. They are rather heavy and could be clumsy for fine work. For more delicate cuts standard size tools are preferable.

There are differences of opinion about how a

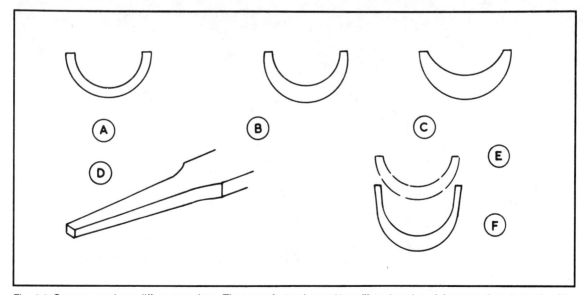

Fig. 4-1. Gouges may have different sections. The tang of a turning tool is unlike a bench tool, because there is no shoulder against the handle.

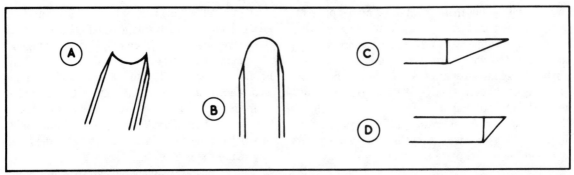

Fig. 4-2. Gouges may be sharpened straight across or rounded on the end. The angle may be acute for some spindle work or made more obtuse for bowl turning.

turning gouge should be shaped on its end. This could be straight across (Figs. 4-2A and 4-3) or it could be spindle-nosed more like a fingernail (Figs. 4-2B and 4-3). The angle of sharpening could be about the same as is used for bench gouge (Fig. 4-2C), or it could be much more obtuse (Fig. 4-2D). Advantages and disadvantages may become apparent when instructions for using the tools are discussed. Not all turners agree on the choice of gouge sharpening, and some get results with one type that other workers say should be done with another. A beginner will probably do best with fingernail ends

in small sizes and straight ends in wide gouges (Fig. 4-3).

A first gouge may be 1/2 inch wide. There will soon be a need for a 1/4-inch gouge, then a wider one (1 inch or 1 1/2 inches) will be useful mainly for reducing rough stock to round. Exact widths of turning gouges are not as important as the widths of bench tools because the shape cut is not so dependent on the width of the tool.

CHISELS

Wood-turning chisels are finishing tools. On

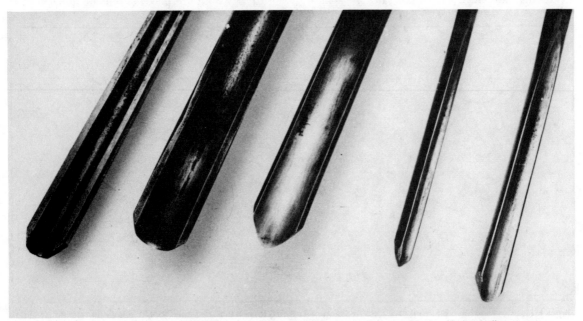

Fig. 4-3. Gouge ends: long and strong, wide-sharpened straight across, and three with rounded spindle noses.

Table 4-1. Sizes of Lathe Tools Commonly Available.

	1/8	1/4	3/8	1/2	5/8	3/4	1	1 1/4	1 1/2	2
Standard gouge		/	/	/		/	/	/		
Long and strong gouge				/		/	/			
L and S deep-flute gouge			/	/		/				
Standard chisel		/		/		/	/			
Long and strong chisel						/	/	/		/
Parting tool	/	/								
Standard scraper				/		/	/			
Long and strong scraper				/	/	/	/			
Beading tool (square section)			/	/						

many parts of a turning they follow gouge work and are used with a slicing action to pare shavings from the rotating wood to leave a surface of comparable quality to planing, although it may be intricately curved. A chisel may be a standard type or long and strong in sizes comparable to gouges and with similar handles. Chisels are sharpened on both sides (Fig. 4-4A). They may be square across the end

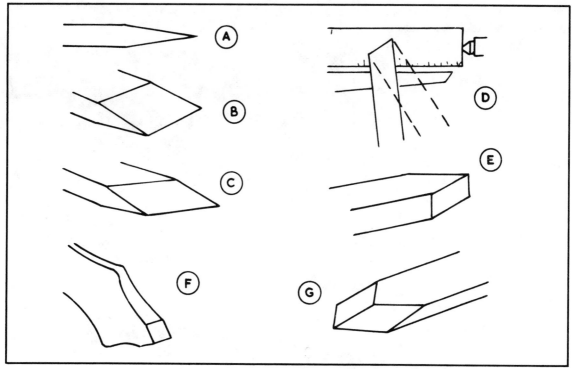

Fig. 4-4. Chisels for turning are sharpened on both sides, usually with the end cut on a skew, and this determines the angle the tool is held in relation to the work. A beading tool is like a thick narrow chisel (E), a parting tool is deeper than it is wide, and it is thinned behind the cutting edge (F), and a diamond-point chisel is not really of much use in turning (G).

(Fig. 4-4B) or skew (Figs. 4-4C and 4-5). For nearly all turning, the difference in effect is in the angle the chisel is held to the work (Fig. 4-4D). Most turners prefer the skew end, which also has uses when the long point is directed at the wood to cut in lines or square ends. The sharpening angle is usually long because the cut has to be a slice comparable to using a bench chisel.

A useful version of a turning chisel is a beading tool, made from steel usually 3/8 inch or 1/2 inch square, beveled on both sides and square across the end (Fig. 4-4E). This is more convenient than an ordinary chisel for forming the beads found in many spindle turnings (see Chapter 6).

Another tool worth having is a parting tool (Figs. 4-4F and 4-6). This has a narrow cutting edge and is thinned immediately behind it. It is thrust straight into the wood and cuts a groove the same width as its edge. As its name implies, it may be used for parting off pieces, but it has many other uses where parts of the work are cut into size before other shaping. Loads on it are not great, and this may be smaller than other tools.

Beading tools are sometimes described as parting tools by suppliers. It is possible to part with one that is 1/4 inch wide, but this takes out a wide groove, and because it is not relieved behind the cutting edge, its sides rub on the end grain as the tool cuts in. Friction is considerable. This, or a relieved parting tool, leaves the cut end grain rough as the fibers are broken when the tool is thrust in, even if it is cutting correctly on the circumference of the reducing waste part. There have been several attempts to make parting tools that cut on their sides as well as the ends. If the tool is grooved on its top surface (Fig. 4-7A), the resulting spiked corners cut something like saw teeth and sever fibers to make better ends on the divided parts.

It is possible to adapt a standard parting tool or a narrow beading tool if you have a narrow grinding wheel or one with a sharp edge. Another version that has been manufactured is grooved along the straight part (Fig. 4-7B) and may be tapered in thickness to reduce binding on the end grain. For light work, there are some carving tools that can be adapted, but they are not robust enough

Fig. 4-5. Chisel ends showing skew and square sharpening.

Fig. 4-6. Special tools: a scraper made from a triangular file, two parting tools, and two gravers for trimming the ends of metal ferrules.

for anything but small work. Rings around the wood are usually cut in with the long point of a skew chisel. A carving V tool (Fig. 4-7C) can be used for these light cuts, but the double chisel formation is difficult to sharpen to get a good point and an even cut. A knife-edge oilstone slip is needed to sharpen inside the angle.

Another tool in some prepared kits of turning

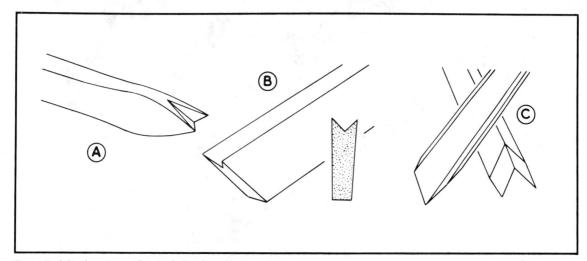

Fig. 4-7. Adaptions to parting tools to give cleaner cuts.

tools is a diamond point chisel. This is usually 3/4 inch wide, flat on one side and beveled to a point on the other side (Fig. 4-4G). It does not appear to have any use. It will not do anything that cannot be done better by other tools. If one is obtained, it can usefully be converted to a scraper by grinding its end.

SCRAPERS

For any faceplate turning except quite small work, the tools should be long and strong. Gouges certainly should be long and strong and their sharpening angle should be fairly obtuse. Scraping tools should be of stout section. Normal spindle turning chisels could be reground to form scrapers for light work. For large bowls, it is necessary to have steel about 1 1/2-×-1/4 inches, or a 3/8 inch section to minimize vibration. Where facilities are

available, it may be possible to grind worn out files to make scrapers (Fig. 4-8).

The sharpening angle of a scraping tool is quite obtuse (Fig. 4-9A). Much work can be done with a tool rounded on one corner and straight for about half the width of the end. For a bowl turned over the bed, the curve should be on the left (Fig. 4-9B). For similar turning outboard of the headstock, it should be the other side (Fig. 4-9C). A scraping tool straight across on the end (Fig. 4-9D) is used on the outside of a bowl and skew one way or the other (Fig. 4-9E) may be more convenient in some places. Other scrapers may have varying degrees of curve (Fig. 4-9F). A scraper may have its shape altered by grinding to suit a particular job (Fig. 4-10).

SHARPENING

As with other branches of woodworking, the

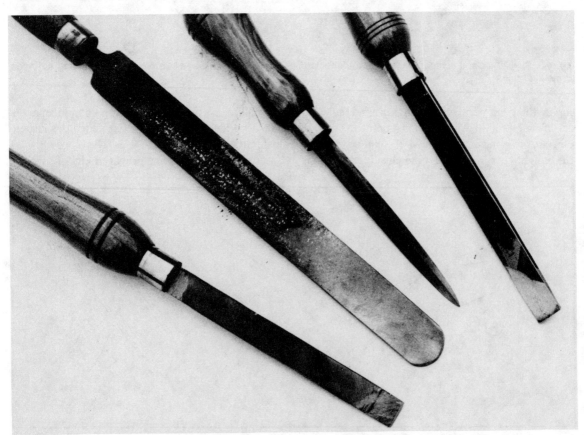

Fig. 4-8. A group of scrapers made from old files.

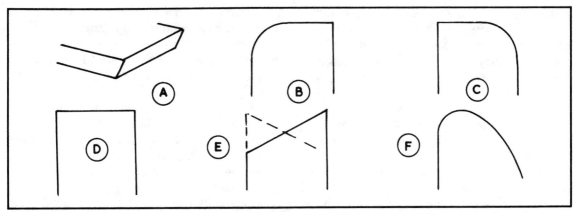

Fig. 4-9. Scraping tools are sharpened at a very obtuse angle. These tools may be given a variety of shapes depending on the type of work they are to be used on, such as the insides and outsides of bowls.

best wood turning is done with sharp tools. Sharpness is a relative term, however, an axe and a razor may both be sharp, yet neither would do the other's job, although each is considered to have a good edge in relation to its purpose. There is something of the same reasoning in sharpening different lathe tools.

An edge is sharp when the two surfaces that form it meet with no thickness of metal between them. Under a microscope no sharpened edge may come up to this state of perfection, but the aim of sharpening is to get as near to this as possible. Ideally, the length of the edge would be a true line, even when viewed under a powerful microscope. Razors and scalpels may come very close to this state of perfection, but for woodworking tools, the quality of an edge does not always have to be to this standard. Sharpening is done with stones made

Fig. 4-10. A straight scraper reversed, one scraper with rounded corners, and two scrapers ground to suit special jobs.

47

with natural or manufactured grits. Quick cutting is done with coarse grit stones. These leave the edge with serrations along it that match the size of grit in the sharpening stone. With some sharpening stones, the serrations left may be large enough to be visible without the use of a lens. Further sharpening consists of wearing away the edge with stones of finer grit. How many successively finer grits are used depends on the purpose the tool. An axe may be satisfactory because it comes from the first coarse grit, but a razor would have its edge worked through many stages of finer abrasives. Each finer grit has to be used sufficiently to remove the saw-like serrations left along the edge by the previous grit.

For finishing tools, the best results on the wood are obtained with an edge approaching the quality of a razor. Tools used for roughing to shape can be effective with a much coarser edge. This means that gouges used for the first general shaping must be sharp—in the sense that the surfaces meet at a finer edge—but serrations left from a fairly coarse grit are acceptable. If the same gouge is to be used for finishing at a later stage, it will have to be worked to a finer edge in readiness for this. Turning chisels, beading tools, and parting tools should always be sharpened to fine edges by working through to fine grit stones.

Scraping tools for faceplate work need the same considerations in sharpening, but the technique is different and a burr raised on the edge is often an advantage. Instructions for achieving this type of edge are given later in this chapter.

SHARPENING EQUIPMENT

Sharpening is broadly divided into *grinding* and *honing*—the later also being referred to as sharpening. In grinding, the grit is in a wheel that revolves, and the tool is held against it. In honing, the abrasive grit is in the form of a stone, usually flat, on which the tool is rubbed. Grinding is normally the coarse stage, but there are honing stones with grits as coarse as those used for grinding, and it is possible to get grinding wheels with very fine grits. There are other ways of sharpening, such as using an endless band coated with grit. Most

turners favor a coarse grit wheel for grinding. Then, the edge is finished on oilstones.

Lathe tools are made of steel, which is iron alloyed with enough carbon to allow hardening and tempering. Overheating in grinding may "draw the temper," meaning soften the steel. Rainbow colors appear at the edge. These are oxides that indicate softening or *annealing*. The oxides can be cleaned off, but by then the damage has been done, even if the evidence has been removed. Only the part where the colors occur is annealed. The tool has to be ground away to pass that part and reach another part still hard enough to hold a good edge.

Probably the best grindstone for woodworking tools is a slow-turning natural sandstone of fairly large diameter that revolves in a trough and has an arrangement where water steadily drips on the stone (Fig. 4-11). It may be turned by hand, treadle, or power. The steady stream of water prevents the tool from overheating and helps the sandstone cut without clogging. Such a stone may be regarded by many as almost obsolete. Its bulk may make it unsuitable for a small shop, but if one is available for grinding turning tools, as well as other woodworking edge tools, it is worth having.

It is more usual to use a high speed stone of manufactured grit (Fig. 4-12A). Something approaching 3000 rpm for a stone about 6 inches in diameter and 1 inch thick is usual. This may be powered directly on the shaft of a suitable electric motor. A high surface speed is necessary. The stone is used dry, and at a low speed it would wear quickly and unevenly as well as not be very effective at removing metal from the tool it is grinding. The friction of sharpening steel on such a high speed dry wheel will quickly draw temper if care is not exercised. There should be a metal or plastic (not glass) container of cold water nearby. The tool should be removed from the stone frequently to dip it in the water to avoid overheating.

Some turners mount a grinding stone on the outboard end of the headstock spindle, so it is easy to move from turning wood to touching up a tool edge on the stone without stopping the lathe or moving from it. There are three reasons why this is not good practice; 1) there is no protection over

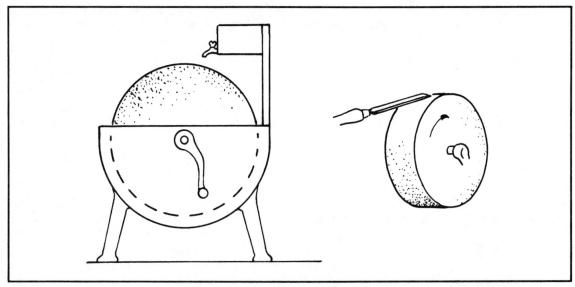

Fig. 4-11. The best grinding tool is an old-fashioned grindstone made of sandstone and lubricated with water.

the stone, and grit flies away from it with possible danger to the user, 2) some of the grit may find its way into the headstock bearings and damage them, and 3) the stone does not rotate fast enough to be effective. With the usual 6 inch in diameter stone intended to be driven at 3000 rpm, the 1000 rpm or less of the lathe will result in the stone wearing away rapidly. This causes excessive grit to fly about and will result in inefficient sharpening.

When a tool is ground on a large diameter sandstone, holding it in your hands is usually satisfactory (Fig. 4-12B) and the resulting ground bevel will be sufficiently near flat for all practical purposes. On a small grinding wheel there is a risk of the

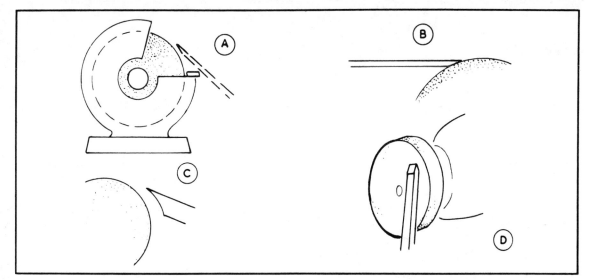

Fig. 4-12. If a tool is ground on a high-speed grinding wheel, it should be moved about to keep a flat bevel and frequently withdrawn and dipped in water to prevent overheating.

49

ground surface being hollow (Fig. 4-12C), although many tools can be ground on the flat side of the stone (Fig. 4-12D). With the need for frequent removal for cooling in water, slight differences in the position held each time on the circumference usually result in a bevel that approximates sufficiently well to flatness. Slight hollowness does not matter and may lessen the effort needed for honing, but an excessive hollow weakens the edge.

Flat sharpening stones come in many sizes, but for lathe tools one stone should be $8 \times 2 \times 1$ inches or larger. There are manufactured stones with one side coarse grit and the other side fine grit. The two sides are usually all that are needed to follow grinding of lathe tools. The stone is best mounted in a wood case and when used with oil, changing sides can be messy; so if much sharpening is contemplated, it is better to have separate coarse and fine stones of this size.

An oilstone should be mounted in a wood box with a lid. It could be made up of separate parts, but one cut from solid wood is usually favored (Figs. 4-13A and 4-14). Slips of wood let in with the ends of the stone are said to take care of tools overrunning the stone (Fig.4-13B) but are not essential. The case may be held in a vise when sharpening, but a strip of leather under each end (Fig. 4-13C) will stop the case sliding on a bench top. Alternatively, there can be nails driven in partly, then cut off, and points filed (Fig. 4-13D) to grip the bench.

Such a new stone can be used with oil or water. The liquid is needed to prevent the stone from clogging, to lubricate the tool being rubbed on the stone, and to prevent the tool from overheating. Oil and water do not mix, so whichever liquid is used at the start must be used throughout. The term *whetting* is sometimes used instead of *honing* and

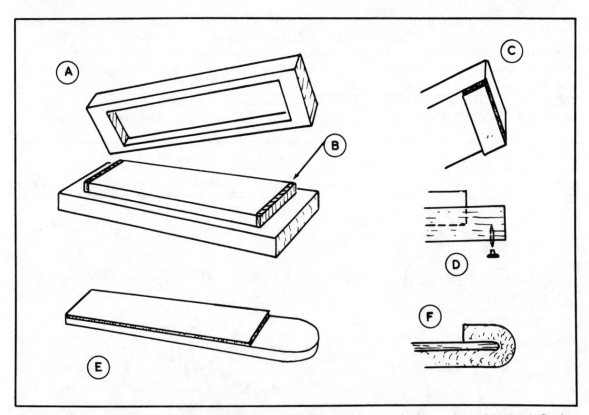

Fig. 4-13. An oilstone is best mounted in a block of wood (A). For stropping a tool edge, a piece of leather is fixed to the wood or wrapped around a thin piece for the inside of a gouge (C).

Fig. 4-14. A useful size of an oilstone, a can of oil with a curved slip stone, and a small stone on a handle for sharpening scrapers.

this probably comes from the use of water, but oil is more satisfactory for shop use. Any thin oil will do. Old-time craftsmen had their preferences for particular and now rare oils, but light machine oil or kerosene will be satisfactory. Motor oil is too thick.

A flat oilstone can be used on tools sharpened on outside curves as well as those sharpened on flat faces. For inside curves there have to be stones with rounded edges. These are usually called *slips* or *slip stones*. Usually a slip is tapered and has two curves (Fig. 4-15). The curves do not have to match the curves of each gouge, but a slip of one radius curve can be used in gouges of this radius and some of bigger radius. It is useless trying to fit a large radius slip in a smaller radius gouge. Some slips have one knife edge. This is for carving tools and is not needed on any lathe tool. Separate slips made of coarse and fine grits comparable to that in the flat stones are really needed, but it is possible to manage with only a medium grit slip.

For most sharpening of turning tools there is no need to progress to any finer grits than are found in the usual oilstones. There are some natural stones that are finer than those of manufactured grit, and one of these may be used as the final stage when the best possible edge is needed. Carvers follow with a strop and this stage could be used on turning tools. A piece of leather is glued to a strip of wood (Fig. 4-13E). It is coated with oil and very fine abrasive powder, which may be bought as strop dressing or a fine engineers' grinding paste can be used. The tool edge is drawn along this and lifted for the return stroke. For the inside of gouges, the leather may be folded back on itself or wrapped around a thin piece of wood (Fig. 4-13F).

GRINDING

There are several ways of grinding chisels, whether skew or square ended. Many come from the makers with rounded bevels on both sides (Fig. 4-16A). This method of grinding can be retained if desired, but flat bevels are just as satisfactory. The flat bevels can go right to the edge (Fig. 4-16B), or there can be a second honing bevel (Fig. 4-16C). All of these types of grinding are used by expert woodturners, so any can be adopted.

Beside wearing the tool away, the grit of the grinding wheel also wears away. There are ways of truing grinding wheels, but if care is taken in spreading the load over the wheel, the surface should keep its shape. A chisel should be moved from side to side on the circumference or over as much as possible of the side of the wheel. When using a tool rest on a dry grinding wheel, the tool can be marked, so it is brought back to the same place after each time it is removed for dipping in water, or a finger grip can be kept in the same position to bear against the tool rest.

A gouge is more likely to cause uneven wear on a grinding wheel. It should be moved across the wheel at the same time as it is rotated through an arc (Fig. 4-17A) to grind all of its outside surface. It is also possible to hold a gouge across the tool rest and roll it on that (Fig. 4-17B) to get an even bevel, but it should still be moved across the stone

Fig. 4-15. The curved edge of a slip stone is used inside a gouge.

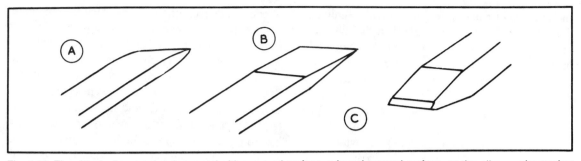

Fig. 4-16. The chisel edge may be sharpened with a curved surface, a broad tapered surface, or the oilstone sharpening surface made slightly more obtuse than the grinding bevel.

to even wear on the surface.

The actual angle to grind is a matter of experience. With the usual thickness of chisels, a bevel a little more than 1/2 inch on each side should be satisfactory. For gouges, used for spindle turning, the bevel may also be about 1/2 inch (Fig. 4-17C), but a more obtuse angle makes a longer-lasting edge (Fig. 4-17D), which is satisfactory for roughing and suitable for faceplate work. It is more important to have fine angle tools when working on softwoods because they cut cleaner with less risk of splitting or tearing the grain. Fine angles are also desirable for finishing hardwoods, but too fine an angle will blunt frequently and much time will be taken with resharpening. A compromise is made with a more obtuse angle for the sake of longer working spells between sharpening sessions.

HONING

Honing normally follows grinding, although it is possible to use a coarse honing stone in place of a grinding wheel if one is not available. There can be many honing periods before grinding is necessary again. Grinding settles the general shape of a cutting edge. Honing successively shortens the bevels until a stage is reached when regrinding becomes necessary to restore the shape and lessen

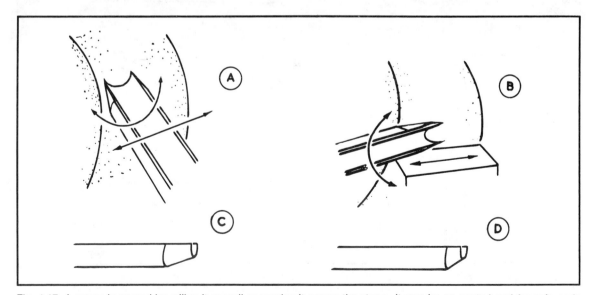

Fig. 4-17. A gouge is ground by rolling it as well as moving it across the stone. It may be an acute bevel for softwoods or some spindle turning, or it may be made more obtuse.

the amount of rubbing on an oilstone. Honing is done at a slightly steeper angle than that used for grinding, whether it blends into the grinding angle or has a distinct angle of its own (Fig. 4-18A). As further honing becomes necessary, the width of the honed area increases (Fig. 4-18B) and honing sessions are prolonged due to the amount to be worn away and regrinding becomes desirable.

To sharpen a turning chisel of any width on a flat oilstone, flow a film of thin oil onto the surface. Put the chisel on the stone with the angle slightly steeper than that needed to keep the grinding bevel on the stone (Fig. 4-18C). This angle has to be maintained as the tool is moved about the oilstone, and this takes practice. One hand grips the tool handle or the upper part of the blade. Use two or more fingers from the other hand to apply pressure near the cutting edge (Fig. 4-19). No turning chisel is as wide as the usual sharpening stone, so to even wear on the surface, the tool should be moved about and the whole surface covered as far as possible. As the tool is moved backwards and forwards, there is a tendency to let it dip as it is pushed forward. This has to be resisted so the angle is kept the same. Stand while sharpening on a stone. It cannot be done satisfactorily while sitting, because it is necessary to sway the body while pivoting shoulder and elbow joints as a linkage controlling the tool.

Use enough pressure to keep the tool in contact—rubbing lightly lets it slide on the film of

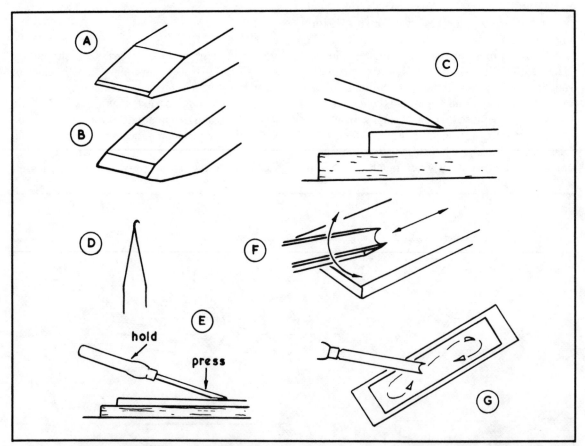

Fig. 4-18. If two bevels are used on a chisel, the sharpening bevel will get long and the whole tool will need regrinding. The handle should be held in one hand and the other hand used to press. Then, move the tool over the whole face of the oilstone. A gouge should also be rolled as well as slid along the surface. When a wire edge can be felt, the two sides have been sharpened. The wire edge can be stropped off or rubbed away by cutting across a scrap piece of wood.

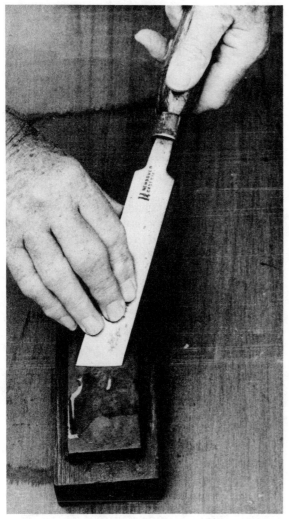

Fig. 4-19. When sharpening a chisel, one hand controls direction and angle while the other hand applies pressure.

meet, there is likely to be a thin sliver of steel that has been sharpened away but is still clinging to the edge. It will be turned over and this *wire edge* can be felt (Fig. 4-18D). It is not usually large enough to be seen. Slice the chisel over the edge of a piece of scrap wood to remove the wire edge. If it is not apparent to the touch, it is a sign that sharpening of both sides should be continued a little more until a wire edge appears. The tool is then as sharp as it can be with that stone.

If a finer edge is needed, change to a stone with a finer grit, but make sure you start again with a clean tool and clean oil. If particles of grit from the coarse stone are allowed to contaminate the finer stone, they will interfere with its action and leave coarse marks in the edge of the tool. The amount of sharpening on the finer stone need only be enough on each side to remove the marks left by the coarser stone. Therefore, sharpening on the fine stone will probably not be as long, although keep in mind that a fine stone is not as fast as cutting. In any case, continue until you can feel a fine wire edge.

If stropping is to follow, the edge should be as good as you can get from the fine stone first, including the removal of the wire edge. Stropping is a slow and fine process. Any wire edge may be too fine to be felt, but slice the edge across scrap wood to remove it before using the tool on the lathe.

Beading and parting tools have cutting edges similar to chisels and are sharpened in the same way. When sharpening a narrow edge, it is very easy to put excessive pressure on one side so the edge is worn away more there than the other side and a distorted cutting edge results. Lift the tool frequently during first rubs on the stone to check if you need to readjust the manner of your finger pressure.

A gouge differs from a turning chisel in having its grinding and honing done on the outside only. This, however, still causes a wire edge inside and slip stones are needed to remove this, although the inside of the gouge remains straight in its length.

A gouge is held on the oilstone in the same way as a chisel with its grinding bevel slightly lifted and the two hands gripping in a similar way (Fig.

oil and if anything happens, it is glazing the surface of the stone so it does not cut as well, rather than sharpening of the tool. Renew oil when necessary. Continue rubbing the chisel on one side until examination after wiping with a cloth shows a good new surface that appears to reach the edge. Turn the chisel over and do the same on the opposite side. Wipe off surplus oil.

Run a finger towards the edge on the opposite side that has just been rubbed on the stone. If the two surfaces have been rubbed away until they

4-18E). The controlling hand, however, has to roll the gouge as it is moved about the surface of the oilstone sufficiently to work on the whole of the cutting edge (Fig. 4-18F). The amount of any gouge in contact with the stone at any time is much less than that of a chisel, so there is more risk of wearing the stone away unevenly. Some turners keep separate stones for gouges and let them become worn hollow. Then, flat stones are only used for turning chisels and other straight-edged woodworking tools.

It is helpful when rubbing a gouge on a flat stone to hold it slightly diagonally to the direction of movement (Fig. 4-20). This makes it easier to roll the tool over its whole cutting edge (Fig. 4-18G). For the best finish, final rubs should have the tool in line with the length of the stone when viewed from above.

Wipe oil off the gouge—inside and out. Then, feel inside for the wire edge by lightly moving a finger along the groove towards the edge. If it is there, use a slip with oil along the inside of the gouge. Hold it in one hand and use it like a file (Fig. 4-15). Do not tilt it, but apply slightly more pressure at the edge than you do along the tool. Move the slip about so as to deal with the whole edge. This may remove the wire edge. To make sure, put the gouge edgewise against a piece of scrap softwood and rotate it so it cuts into the wood. As with chisels, repeat with a finer stone if desired and proceed to stropping if it is a finishing edge you are preparing.

The method of sharpening gouges is the same, whether they have square or fingernail ends. If an end becomes worn different from the shape it is supposed to be or you want to alter the shape of an end, it can be ground by pointing directly at the rotating stone to get the outline needed. Then, the edge is ground fine and finished by honing. The center of a gouge tends to get blunt before the outer parts of the cutting edge. This problem can be reduced by remembering to use the outsides when it is not essential to use the center. Occasionally, it will be necessary to reshape the end.

A scraping tool, whatever the shape of its end, has its angle fairly obtuse. Individual turners have their own ideas about the amount of this angle. It can vary between 15 degrees from a right angle to 45 degrees. Attempting to scrape with a tool sharpened at a long angle, as for a slicing cut, shows an ignorance of the scraping technique and the fine edge would be blunted in a very short time.

A scraping tool does actually cut, and it should remove fine shavings rather than dust. It has to be kept sharp—meaning the two surfaces that form the edge must meet at a line with no thickness and not be rounded or worn away. The top surface of the tool is kept flat and all sharpening is done on the beveled end.

The end may be ground by moving it across a grinding wheel. If the tool is used immediately after grinding it may be found to cut sufficiently well for removal of wood although the surface left may not be good enough for a finished article. For a better edge, honing is done with a stone held in the hand

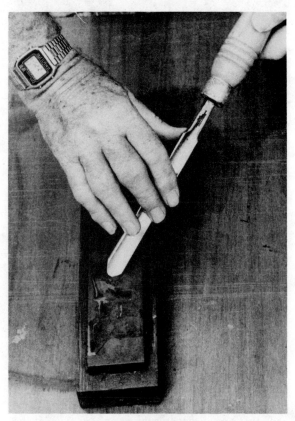

Fig. 4-20. A gouge is held for sharpening like a chisel, it is rolled as it is rubbed along the stone.

Fig. 4-21. The end of a scraper is honed with a stone attached to a piece of wood.

and used like a file (Fig. 4-21). Some workers hold the tool in one hand and hone with the other, but it is easier to be accurate if the tool is held upwards in a vise with padded jaws, then two hands can be used on the stone. Continue honing with a stone coated with oil until the grinding marks are rubbed away. Finally, rub the cutting surface (top) with a circular motion flat on the stone.

This is the way many turners sharpen and use the scraping tools, but there is a further refinement that gives an even sharper edge, which is advantageous when preparing a finished surface. This makes the cutting edge like that of a cabinet scraper by turning over a burr. The tool is sharpened to the honed stage, then a hard steel burnisher or ticketer is rubbed around the edge. The burnisher is a piece of hard steel rod. It could be a round rod in a handle (Fig. 4-22A). Ideally, it should be harder than

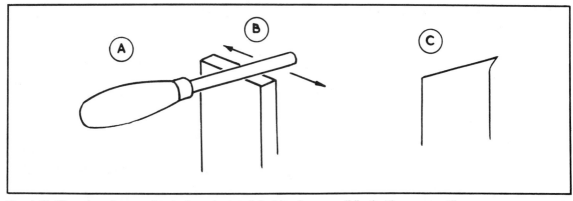

Fig. 4-22. The edge of a scraping tool can be burnished to give a small lip that improves cutting.

the scraper being treated. If it is not, it is possible to use another chisel or gouge as a burnisher. The burnisher is rubbed around the edge with a slight bias towards the cutting edge and the considerable pressure (Fig. 4-22B). The effect is to turn over the edge, something like a wire edge, but in this case it is the actual edge turned over, as shown exaggerated (Fig. 4-22C), although the amount of burr may not be enough to be easily seen. During turning it may be possible to revive the edge by turning over the burr again several times before having to go back to grinding and honing.

Bluntness of a scraping or cutting tool can usually be seen. If the tool is held with its edge near horizontal and the main source of light is on the opposite side to that where you are viewing, the light will be reflected from the blunt edge, which will appear as a white line. It may be necessary to manipulate the tool a little so as to catch the reflected light. A burr cannot be turned on a scraping tool in this state. Both it and any other cutting tool will have to be sharpened on an oilstone or may have to go back to grinding.

As can be seen, grinding wears away both the steel tool and the grit stone. These particles usually fall where they will do no harm, but minute particles of steel or grit getting into bearings of the lathe or its motor could cause damage. Because of this, it is advisable to keep the grinding wheel at a distance from the lathe. Some turners have a grinding wheel mounted on the outboard end of the lathe headstock. This may be convenient, as it is always there ready to touch up a tool without having to go away from the lathe, but there are some snags. Grit may get into the headstock bearings. The wheel may not be revolving at a sufficiently high speed. The top speed of the lathe is probably good enough, but if something is being turned that needs a lower speed and a tool is presented to the wheel at this speed, the wheel may wear quickly and unevenly, so it becomes almost useless. Holding a grinding wheel on a mandrel in a chuck over the lathe bed is even more likely to get grit where it may do damage.

Sharpening on an oilstone should be done cleanly, but oil tends to attract dirt. Wood turning produces much dust as well as shaving. Oilstones should be used far enough away from the lathe to minimize the accumulation of dust. An oilstone is usually maintained sufficiently clean if it is covered after use. If it does become dirty, it can be cleaned off with kerosene or a degreasing fluid. Strops are even more vulnerable to dirt. A strop should be stored out of use by being wrapped or kept in a drawer. Do not allow it to get dry, but keep the leather damp with thin oil.

OTHER TOOLS

A turner improvises gauges and other tools to suit the job in hand, and some of these will be described in relation to jobs in later chapters. There are several other tools needed, which may be bought, and most of these are concerned with measuring.

Rules

Measuring is only a method of making comparisons. Much turning is done by eye and this is where the artistic merit of wood turning comes into its own. Suppose four legs are needed for a table and they all have apparently the same outlines but are of different diameters, the resulting appearance of the piece of furniture will be a failure. A rule is an essential part of a turner's tool kit, but it does not get as much use as might be expected. It is necessary for lengths, but it cannot be used directly across a diameter. The rule may be steel, plastic, or wood. Its markings should start from one end. There should not be an extra piece before measurements start, as on some rules intended for drawing. The markings should be clear and need not be very detailed. With the change to metric measure, it is advisable to have a rule with one edge marked in inches and sixteenths, and the other marked in centimeters and millimeters.

Calipers

Diameters are checked with calipers (Fig. 4-23). The simplest type relies on friction in the joint and is tapped or pulled to the correct size. If a measured size is needed, one leg is put against the end of the

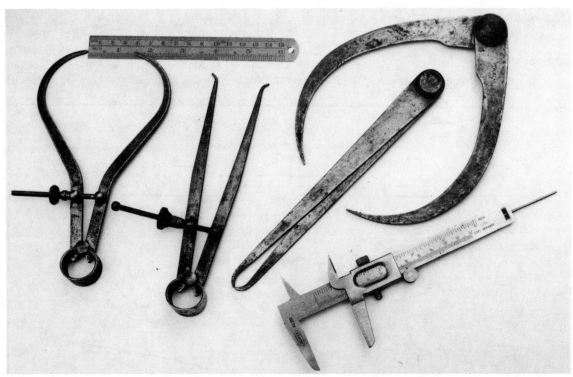

Fig. 4-23. Calipers are made for outside and inside use, and they may have spring bow or friction adjustments. A sliding type suits inside and outside measurement.

rule and the other opened to the correct size. It is possible to overlap the legs of these outside calipers and use them for checking internal diameters, but there are straight-legged inside calipers intended for internal use. Both types are made in many sizes. A large pair of calipers can be used to check small diameters as well as large. Large calipers, however, are rather clumsy to use for small sizes, so it is advisable to have at least one small pair—3 inch and 6 inch will cover most needs for outside curves. Inside turnings are usually smaller so one pair of 4-inch inside calipers should be sufficient. The quoted size is the length of the tool. The diameter that can be spanned is usually a little more than the length.

Metal turners use more sophisticated calipers for the more precise work they do. They are spring bow type with a screw adjustment. These are excellent for wood turning. They are made for inside as well as outside use, but sizes are not usually as

great as those obtainable in plain friction-joint calipers.

Another type of caliper has a sliding piece that can be locked by a butterfly screw (Fig. 4-24A). A development of this is made to be used with a parting tool. The tool is fixed in place with the distance between its cutting edge and the opposite arm set to the diameter to be turned (Fig. 4-24B). In use, the tool is presented to the work and stops automatically at the correct diameter. This is useful for marking depths to which shaped parts have to be worked.

Where the end of a piece of work being turned is accessible, its size can be checked with a hole drilled in a piece of scrap wood. This is helpful when the turning will have to fit such a hole in another part, as it gives a direct comparison of size. Where the turned part cannot be tested in this way, it is useful to have a gauge of some common sizes of your drill bits. Holes are drilled in two meeting edges of strips of wood, which are then hinged so they can be tried over the work (Fig. 4-24C).

Compasses

It is useful to have a substantial pair of compasses or dividers. Light spring bow types are not stout enough. Drawing or scratching a circle on wood puts a load on the arms, which tend to spring or follow the grain. A stout pair of dividers that can be locked to size (Fig. 4-24D) may be about 12

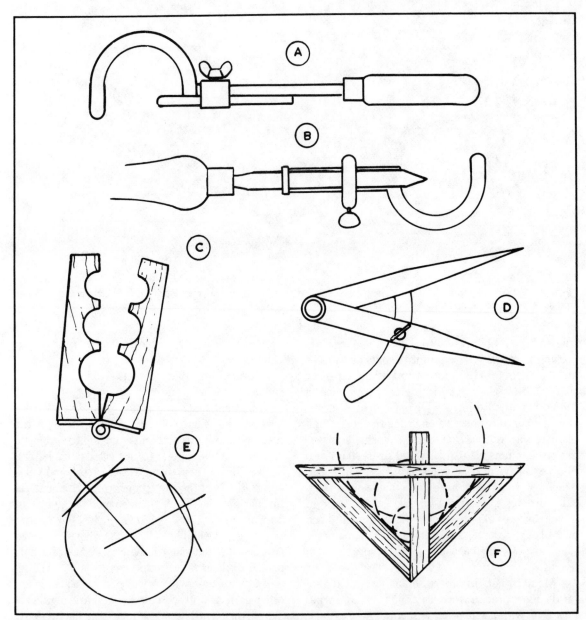

Fig. 4-24. A turner can use a caliper that adjusts in a different way or a similar tool can be attached to a parting tool to cut a definite diameter. A wood gauge is useful for standard curves. Substantial dividers are better than light ones for drawing large circles. A center square can be used in two positions on a circle to find the center by geometric principles.

inches long, then they are useful for marking out most sizes of wood to be turned on the faceplate.

Squares

It is sometimes necessary to find the center of circular work as when the originally centered end has been cut off. The tool for this is a center square. It uses the principle that if two points on a circumference are joined and this line is bisected, the bisecting line at right angles to it will pass through the center. If this is repeated at another position, the two lines will cross at the center (Fig. 4-24E). There are several versions, but for the sizes needed mostly in turned work a tool with a blade bisecting a right angled head is most suitable. One version is obtainable as part of a combination square, which includes a rule on which other parts can be fitted for various purposes (Fig. 4-25). A variation of this that can be made for small work has a blade edge bisecting an angled piece of wood with a crossbar to ensure its rigidity (Fig. 4-24F).

For most spindle turning on a powered lathe, it is satisfactory to mount square sectioned wood between centers and turn the angles off with a gouge. When the turner had to provide the power with his foot, he usually planed off the corners before mounting the wood in the lathe to reduce the labor needed. This is still sometimes advisable. A gouge may catch in the angle of some wood and cause it to split. If it is a large section, there will be quite a lot of wood to be removed when reducing from square to round on the lathe with many readjustments of the tool rest. It may be quicker

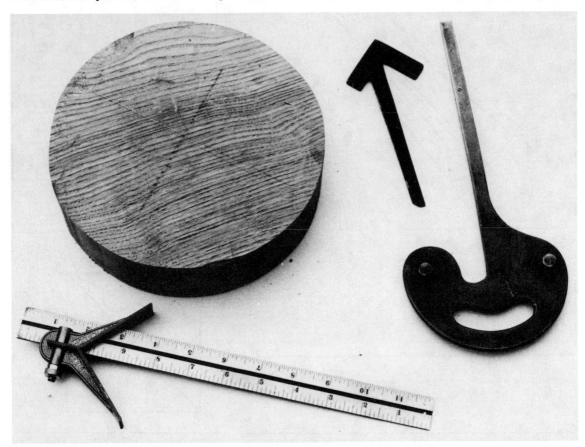

Fig. 4-25. The center of a disc is found by crossing two or more diameter lines found with a center square against the circumference, its blade bisecting angles in the stock or the line between two pegs.

61

to plane off some of the corners first.

When planing corners off, it is useful to have a trough to support the wood. One is made of two pieces, planed to match and fixed together. A stop is formed by a piece of wood let in (Fig. 4-26A). This is conveniently gripped in a vise and should be long enough to support the maximum length the lathe will take. An alternative is a shallower trough

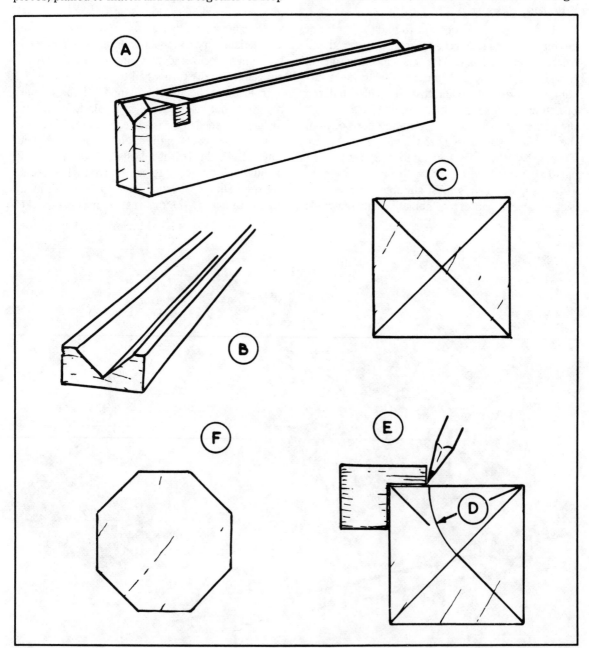

Fig. 4-26. A wood trough is useful for planing off corners in preparation for turning. If an exact octagon is needed, the length of half a diagonal is brought to one side and lines drawn at that distance.

to rest against the stop on a bench top (Fig. 4-26B). There might be two short troughs, which could be used together and moved apart to support longer work.

Precision in planing off the corners is not usually necessary, but cuts are made at about 45 degrees until the newly planned bevels are not quite as wide as what is left on the original square surfaces between them. More accuracy is needed if the finished turning is to have octagonal parts remaining after part of the wood has been turned. The shape then has to be symmetrical and uniform if it is to look right.

To mark square wood for planing to an exact regular octagon, draw diagonals on the end of the wood or on a square drawn elsewhere of the same size (Fig. 4-26C). Measure half a diagonal, or use a compass or dividers to swing up to a surface from a corner (Fig. 4-26D). This could be done both ways from all corners, but one is all that is needed. Notch a piece of scrap wood to this distance (Fig. 4-26E) and use it with a pencil to draw along in each direction on each surface. If the corners are planed off carefully to these lines, all eight surfaces should finish the same widths (Fig. 4-26F).

If it is expected that many square strips will have to be marked for planing octagonal, the need for setting out and making a notched pencil gauge can be avoided by making a simple tool. Decide on what you expect the largest square to be worked on will be. Set out this size to get the positions of the lines that would be drawn along the wood. Mark a strip of wood to take two dowels set into holes with the distance between the inner sides of the dowels the same as the maximum wood to be worked. Suppose the square is 2 1/2 inches—the strip could be 4 inches long, 1/4 × 3/4 inch section and the dowels 1/4 inch in diameter. In line with the dowel centers, mark the positions the drawn lines are to come and cut notches there for the pencil point (Fig. 4-27A).

In use on any size wood, put the tool over the side to be marked and slope it until the dowels bear against the sides, put a pencil in each notch in turn, then draw the tool along (Fig. 4-27B). If you are working on tapered square-section wood, the tool works just as well, providing you keep the dowels tight against the edges as the wood gets narrower or wider.

Depth Gauges

There are occasions when depths have to be checked, like when turning the inside of a bowl, you want to remove enough wood, while not making the bowl so thin as to be weak. There are machinist's depth gauges available (Fig. 4-28), but many of these have a precision greater than is needed in most wood turning, and the base or stock may not be long enough to go across a bowl.

A simple depth gauge can be made with a strip of wood of sufficient length, with a piece of dowel rod through it, held by friction and tapped up and down to adjust its setting (Fig. 4-29A). This is a temporary expedient. A more permanent tool can be given some shaping (Fig. 4-29B). The dowel rod is made to slide easily, and it can be held in any position with a wedge. A piece of 3/8-inch dowel rod, with its end tapered to a rounded point, can be fitted through a stock made from a piece of hardwood 2 × 1 × 12 inches.

Make the wedge from hardwood about 1/4 × 1/2 inch section. Give it a slight taper and arrange a projection at its small end to prevent it falling out of its slot (Fig. 4-29C). Cut the slot for the wedge to the same taper and at a depth that allows the rod to slide freely when the wedge is driven back to the narrow end. Driving the wedge the other way locks it against the rod (Fig. 4-29D).

There are many gauges and templates that can be made to suit the job in hand, particularly when a set of turned parts have to be made to match. Adjustable profile templates are obtainable, and they can be set to any outline and used as a gauge for checking that further turned pieces match the first (Fig. 4-30). Some of these consist of a large number of thin metal pieces that slide over each other within a clamping frame. When they have their ends pressed to the required shape, they can be locked. Unfortunately, the profile templates commonly available will not accommodate more than about a 5 inch length of shaping.

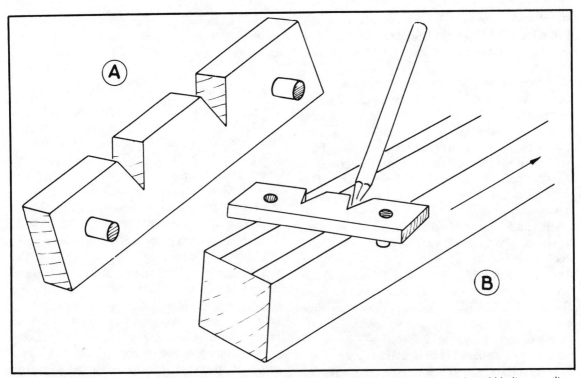

Fig. 4-27. This tool can be used to mark the corner lines of octagons on square pieces of any size within its capacity.

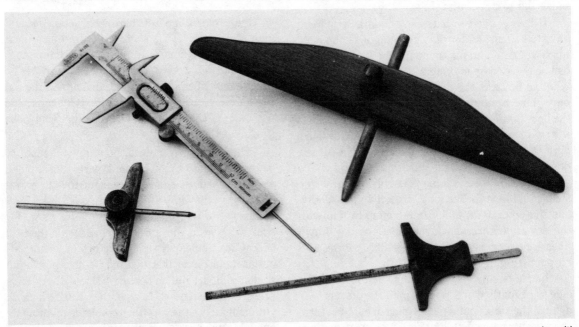

Fig. 4-28. Two machinists' depth gauges and one on the end of sliding calipers, together with a gauge made with a dowel rod through a wooden block.

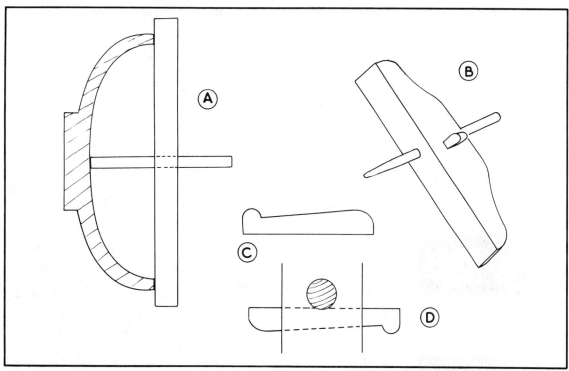

Fig. 4-29. Application of a depth gauge in a bowl, and a method of locking the dowel with a wedge.

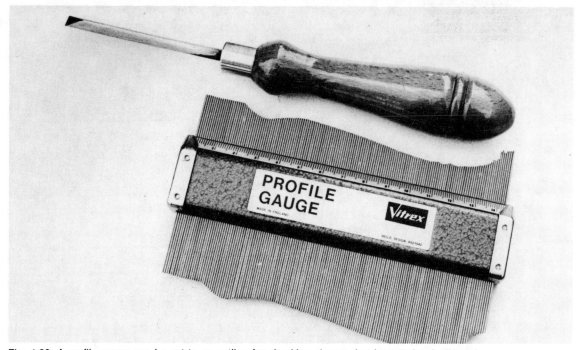

Fig. 4-30. A profile gauge can be set to an outline for checking shapes that have to be duplicated.

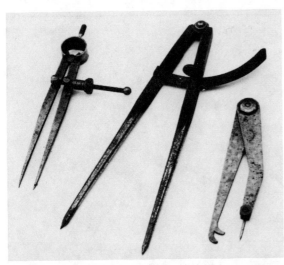

Fig. 4-31. Large stiff dividers are of more use on wood than the lighter machinists' type. Odd-leg calipers are used to scratch lines at a distance from an edge for finding centers of rods.

Dividers

Dividers or compasses are needed, particularly for drawing circles when cutting blanks for bowls. Light machinist's dividers have their uses, but a heavier pair (Fig. 4-31) are more rigid and less liable to be diverted from drawing a circumference by ching in the wood grain. Odd-leg calipers (hermaphrodite or jenny) are a cross between calipers and dividers. They may be used by a turner to scratch a line parallel with an edge or for centering from four or more positions across the end of the rod. The center is then within the marks scratched.

Ideas for making marking and testing devices to suit particular jobs are described with the projects to which they apply elsewhere in this book, and many can be adapted to other work. A prolific turner collects a large number of improvised testing devices made for one job and kept for altering to suit others.

Some turned objects are complete in themselves and need no other work than can be done on the lathe. Others have to be joined to wood that has not been turned, or several turned parts may have to be assembled together. This additional work involves the use of general woodworking tools. Most turners have a kit of other tools and the ability to use them. Most turners have come to wood turning after experience in other branches of woodwork. This book is concerned only with wood turning—instructions in general woodworking, other than those techniques directly connected with turning, would be out of place.

Chapter 5

Safety

A lathe may not have the obvious dangers inherent in such machine tools as circular saws or even the rather similar motion of a drill press, but, like any tool, there are safety rules to be observed. The power source is likely to be a motor of at least 1/2 horsepower. That is stronger than a man, so in any accident that becomes a contest between man and motor, the motor will win. Treat your lathe with respect. Never be casual in your attitude toward it. Concentrate on what you are doing. If you need to refer elsewhere, either stop the lathe or withdraw the tool. Never divide your attention.

Once the work has been reduced to round, there are no projections to bother about whatever the speed of rotation. Before that, be careful of projections, possibly splintery, that may harm you or cause a tool to catch and do damage either to you or to the work. Be careful that the work is secure. If it is between centers, tighten the tailstock occasionally to ensure that wear on the center has not become such that the wood may come away. See that the driving center has a good grip when the wood is first mounted. Similarly, check the security

of screws or other fastenings into faceplate work. Fortunately, if wood becomes loose from the lathe, it tends to drop rather than fly, but do not always assume this.

When work is first mounted, pull it around by hand before switching on the power to make sure it does not foul anything and that it will revolve smoothly and without slackness. The tool rest should be fairly close. Pulling the wood around will show if it has enough clearance. See that machine parts that can be moved are tight before switching on. If the tailstock or tool rest are not properly secured to the bed, they may move to a dangerous position and cause trouble.

The motor should be in a position where it cannot be touched during turning. The belt and pulley on its shaft are out of reach, but at the lathe, there may be a removable cover over the pulley and belt on the headstock. Always have that cover fixed before switching on.

The turner should support himself on his legs, braced a short distance apart. He should not sit and should not lean on the lathe bench. Some turners have a rail to lean back against, but that is a carry-over from treadle days. It does not harm but is of little use.

CLOTHING

Loose clothing should be avoided. In particular, do not wear a tie. There have been cases of turners being strangled by a tie catching in the revolving work or in unprotected pulleys and belts. Short sleeves are satisfactory. If long sleeves are worn, they should be close at the wrist. Long sleeves, un-buttoned and allowed to drop and hang loose are almost as dangerous as a hanging tie. One piece protective clothing is advisable. Apart from safety considerations, turning produces a considerable amount of dust and keeping an overall garment to put on over other clothing is sensible.

Be careful of loose cloths. A pad without stray ends is better for polishing in the lathe. If cloth has to be used, make sure its corners are folded in. The danger is in the possibility of the cloth being caught in a revolving part, rapidly winding up and possibly taking your hand with it. Strips of abrasive cloth may also present a similar risk if carelessly han-dled. Hold both ends and be extra careful near the driving center or a chuck. Draw the tool rest back out of the way, so your hand holding the cloth pad or abrasive cannot become caught against it or knock it.

Wood turning produces dust and sometimes larger pieces of waste, particularly chips and pieces that splinter off during the first roughing to round from square. Fortunately, much of this waste tends to fall or travel along or close to the tool, but sometimes it will rise, and you should be aware of the risk to your eyes. There is also the possibility of breathing very fine dust, often without being aware of it, particularly when sanding. For a short period of turning, there is obviously very little risk of being affected. Even then, it is advisable not to bend closely over the work, and to have your head out of line with the tool and flying chips, and not to breathe through the mouth.

If you have to wear glasses to aid your sight, you may feel they provide all the protection your eyes need from flying wood particles at the lathe or from grit when grinding. Otherwise, a pair of goggles are worthwhile (Fig. 5-1). Many protective goggles can be worn over prescription glasses. Note the risk of a layer of dust building up on goggles or glasses so visibility gradually lessens without you realizing it. Wipe the lenses frequently. Ideally, any eye protection should be safety glass or hard plastic. Remember that plastic goggles can get scratched, so do not just leave them around on the bench when not being worn. The amount of dust and splinters that might reach your eyes depends on the type of wood, and you will soon discover what types are hazardous and justify eye protection.

Fuller eye and face protection can come from a safety shield or visor attached to crown and back straps over your head. The whole carved transparent plastic front of a safety shield can be lowered over your face or lifted horizontally above your head without removing it (Fig. 5-2). This is more of a guard to use when grinding and using the more spiteful power tools, but you may feel it is justified as full face protection when turning some woods.

Preventing dust from getting to your lungs via your mouth and nose is important in prolonged turn-ing, particularly if you do much sanding. Brief ex-posure to dust from sanding turned wood may prove dirty and a nuisance, but otherwise harmless, unless it is one of the woods producing irritant dust. If you expect to be at your lathe for long periods, it is advisable to wear something to allow you to breathe, yet exclude dust from your nose and mouth. You only have to see the amount of dust deposited around you in the shop after such a ses-sion to realize how much could enter your nose and mouth.

The simplest way of protecting your face is to tie a handkerchief or a piece of similar cloth around your lower face in bandit fashion. Better than that is some sort of mask or respirator. There is really no need for the elaborate type of respirator used as protection when paint spraying or using toxic substances, unless one is already available. A simpler type of filter will keep out dust, and that is all you need.

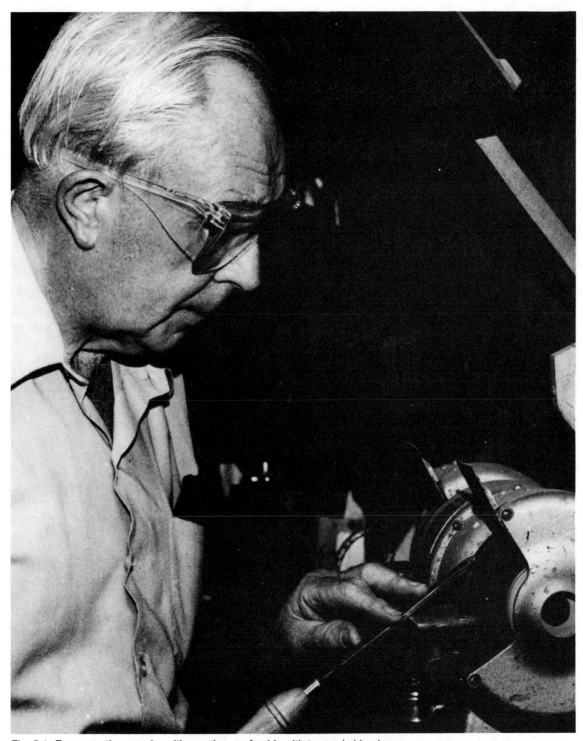

Fig. 5-1. Eye protection may be with goggles, preferably with top and side pieces.

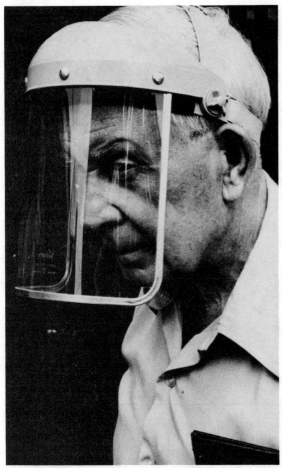

Fig. 5-2. A safety shield or visor protects the face from flying dust and wood particles, but it can be swung out of the way when not needed.

A basic dust mask is cup-shaped over your nose and mouth, with an elastic band to go over your head. The material used holds back dust and eventually it becomes saturated with dust and has to be discarded. Another mask of similar purpose (Fig. 5-3) uses a light metal frame to hold filters, then only the cheap filters have to be discarded. A more advanced respirator is designed as protection against dust, but it looks more like a spray mask with straps to keep it in place. In all cases, you should have a stock of spare filters.

It is unlikely that the work of wood turning will justify the installation of a dust extraction system, even if the lathe is in constant use. If it is one of many woodworking machines and others need dust extraction, the system could be extended to the lathe so as to remove dust and wood particles. In most circumstances, a shop with reasonable ventilation is all that is needed, plus the wearing of appropriate masks when the work justifies them.

Keeping the shop clean and tools that are out of use in their racks or other storage, having wood stocks out of the way of the working area, and making sure that nothing can interfere with your movements or concentration at the lathe, will contribute to safety as well as to tidiness and, therefore, a better standard of workmanship. Risks involved in any sort of work are always less when the place is airy, bright, clean, and free from congestion.

LIGHTING

It is best to have natural light coming from above and in front of the operator. Electric light should approximate to this with light coming from above and slightly ahead of the worker. Do not normally have a lamp as low as the worker's head. For fine work there may be an advantage—both in safety and in the quality of work possible—to have a lamp protected with a deep shade that can be brought low. It is most important that you should be able to see what you are doing. If light is inadequate, stop work and do something about it.

Have somewhere to put down tools where they will not roll off. Form the habit of always putting a tool down with its cutting edge away from you. It is unlikely that many tools will be needed for a series of operations. If there are tools around from a previous stage and they are not needed now, return them to a rack. Many lathe stands have little space for tools to be put down. A wooden bench top under the lathe is better than putting tools across a flat lathe bed or a metal stand.

Keep tools sharp. They are less dangerous than trying to force a blunt tool into the wood. Always hold a tool tightly with both hands. At first, there is a temptation to hold lightly when cutting lightly. Never relax the grip on the handle and normally keep the hand near the end where maximum leverage can be applied if the tool tries to dig in or pull itself out of your hands. The other hand must keep the blade tightly in contact with the tool rest, whether the fingers or thumb are on top. A tool must be firmly held against the tool rest before it makes contact with the wood. Its edge should be lowered onto the wood, so it is rubbing, then moved until it cuts. If you let a tool touch the wood when it is not in contact with the tool rest or only lightly held, it will dig in. Besides spoiling your work, it may kick back or fly and hurt you. If you are using a scraping tool, keep its handle high as the edge approaches the work, then lower to a cutting angle. With an approach lower than it will be held for cutting, it will dig in and jerk as it meets the wood.

When the tool is being manipulated to turn a profile, the leverage may not always come directly down on the tool rest and the hand there has to resist the tool trying to jerk or roll sideways. So far as possible, have the bearing surface of the tool on the tool rest in line with the part of the blade that is cutting. If, for instance, one side of a gouge curve bears on the tool rest while the other side is cutting, there will be a tendency for the tool to roll.

Sometimes such a cut is needed and the roll resisted, but often the stance of the tool can be altered to avoid the attempt to roll.

Calipers are sometimes used on revolving wood. Hold their tops over the far side of the lathe. Besides making it easier to see their ends on the work, this reduces the risk of the calipers being drawn around and jammed against the tool rest.

Do not position the lathe where someone else doing other things may knock or otherwise interfere with the turner. Never let anyone play with the lathe. Do not allow two people to try to use it at the same time. If anyone is under instruction, keep practice and demonstration separate. The instructor may put his hands over the student's hand on one tool, but he should not try to demonstrate with a second tool. The safest place for anyone watching a turner is behind him, although they could be towards the end of the lathe, but would not get as good a view there. Normally, there is not much risk in front of you, but if there is any choice, keep observers behind you.

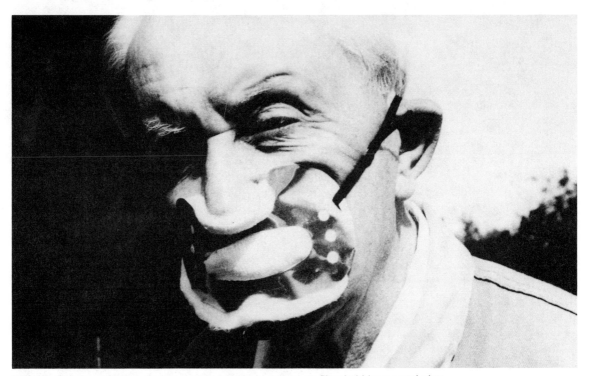

Fig. 5-3. Simple protection against dust is provided by a gauze filter held by a metal plate.

A lathe is not a hazardous machine. There are other woodworking machines with much greater risks in using, but parts are revolving, and the power is more than you can oppose. A lathe and the wood it is turning will not come up and hit you unexpectedly. Usually, if the wood comes away from the machine, it will drop. Do not assume that all will be well, however, as familiarity can lead to carelessness. Always approach the lathe in a positive way, preparing things correctly and doing jobs systematically in the right way. It is the casual approach and being imprudent that can lead to an accident. As with any power tool using sharp cutters, always keep safety in mind.

Chapter 6

Starting Spindle Turning

Turning between centers can mean anything from something the size of a toothpick to a substantial pillar to support a porch. Much depends on the size of the lathe. The same one would not be used for these two extreme sizes. The average lathe is quite adaptable and one with a capacity for table legs or larger can also be used successfully for quite small fine turnings. A small lathe, however, that might be easier to use for tiny delicate work does not require high centers, a large tool rest, or big chucks.

For a practice piece, it is unwise to consider making anything. Merely turn a piece of wood to get the feel of the tools, what they will do, and what they will not do. Almost certainly the wood will be damaged at some stage, so be prepared to scrap it. This is part of the process of learning. When you have discovered how the tools work and learned to control them to get the desired effects on several experimental pieces, you can start to think of making things with every prospect of success. Your first tool handle, candlestick, lamp standard, or other article made between centers will give you as much satisfaction as something much better made at a

later stage in your wood turning experience.

For early experiments use reasonably large pieces of wood. A piece 1 1/2 inches square and 12 inches long gives you scope to try different tool actions. If one part goes wrong, there is more wood to try again further along. If you use smaller pieces of wood, you will have to remove and replace them frequently. Avoid thin wood at this stage. It will bend and spring or vibrate under the tool disconcertingly. It is possible to turn wood that does not start square, but for first experiments, it is better to use a piece that is reasonably near square in section. There is no need to plane a piece that may be 1/8 inch out of square. That be taken care of in the first rough turning.

Although it is possible to turn almost any wood, it is best to avoid softwoods for first experiments. A mistake with a tool may cause such a split that the whole piece of softwood is severed. Early attempts at fine detail in softwoods are likely to cause it to break out if the tool is not sharp or presented correctly to the wood. Open-grained hard woods can also be troublesome in this way. The most forgiving woods to errors in tool handling are the close-grained hardwoods. A piece of wood that is obviously hard, without pronounced grain markings and with little or no obvious pockets in the grain is likely to be easy to work, although exceptionally hardwoods do not respond so well to the slicing action of a chisel. As turning will eventually be done in all kinds of wood, there is no need to be too selective at first. Almost any oddments of square wood will find uses in turning. Short ends of square stock left over from other woodworking should be added to the wood-turning store, and they will make knobs, handles, and other small things.

Find the centers of the ends of the wood, usually with diagonal lines, and make center punch dots. It is also possible to use a marking gauge set to approximately half the thickness from each face, then the dot made in the middle of the resulting small square. It may be possible to push the driven end onto the center tight enough to get a grip. Until you are certain that this can be done satisfactorily it may help to make a shallow cut on one of the diagonals, or both if the driving center has four spurs. If the center in the tailstock is a cup type with a slender point, it may be possible to merely feed the point into the wood without a center punch mark, but even then a shallow punch dot helps to locate the point precisely.

Have the tool rest out of the way. Press the wood onto the driving center. Make sure the screw of the tailstock is far enough back to allow ample movement—about the middle position is usual for starting. Bring the tailstock up to the wood and lock it to the bed. Adjust the tailstock so the center enters the wood. Apply a little lubricant and move the center further into the wood until it obviously holds it without vibration. Bring the tool rest to the work and pull the wood around by hand to see that the angles of the square section will not hit the tool rest (Fig. 6-1A). Often, one corner projects more than the others, unless the wood started perfectly square and precisely centered. Such exactness will be necessary when making a table leg with a square top, or a similar thing where some square part is retained, but if the whole length is to be made round, slight eccentricity of first mounting does not

matter. If you have doubts about the wood being splintery or if the lathe seems underpowered, corners may be planed off the wood to make it octagonal before coming to the lathe, but in most cases this is unnecessary.

An expert turner will bring a square section to round in a very short time, but a beginner should approach his first attempts more cautiously. Experts vary in their choice of gouge for first roughing. Once you understand the effect of the

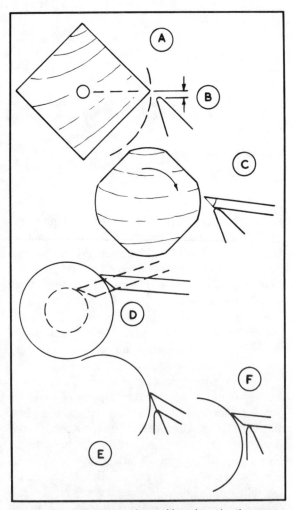

Fig. 6-1. The tool rest must be positioned to miss the square corners, but because these corners are cut away, the rest can be moved in. The tool should be angled so its bevel almost rubs on the cylinder it is producing, then it will cut instead of scrape.

tool, it is possible to get similar results with different gouges. For first experiments, a square-ended gouge about 3/4 inch wide is suitable, although if you only have one with a rounded nose of a different width, the technique is much the same.

At an early stage in your turning you will have to decide on the tool rest height that suits you. This is governed by several factors, which will be explained later in this chapter, but for your first rough turning have it about 1/8 inch below center height (Fig. 6-1B).

Stand with your feet apart and with one leg nearer the lathe than the other. Have one hand on the end of the handle for greatest leverage. A common fault is to slide the hand along until it is almost up to the ferrule. The other hand has to hold the blade on the tool rest. There are two ways of doing this. If the fist goes over the blade and the thumb underneath, maximum pressure can be applied (Fig. 6-2). This allows control of the tendency of the tool to kick and move and is generally preferred for the first reducing of square stock to round. The other way is to only have the thumb on top (Fig. 6-3). The fingers grip below, but there cannot be as much pressure applied this way. An advantage of the second method is that it allows a better view of the end of the tool and the part of the work it is cutting. Both methods are used, and not every turner favors the same method for the same thing. A new turner will soon find himself altering his grip almost instinctively to suit the way he prefers for a particular type of cut. However, for first roughing start with the fist on top.

A woodturner needs to be ambidextrous. You will soon discover which hand you prefer on the handle and which on the blade. For much of the time you can have your hands that way, but there are times when it is more logical to change hands so the tool approaches the work the other way. Trying to get this opposite action without changing hands will result in awkward contortions and difficulty in getting good results. Normally the hand on the handle is braced against the body or the thigh,

Fig. 6-2. For heavy cuts, the fist may be held over the top of a gouge and further steadiness obtained by resting tight against the tool rest.

Fig. 6-3. Where lighter cuts are taken, it is sufficient to have your thumb on top of the tool, so progress is more easily seen.

but there are times when it has to be moved to direct the cutting edge. Certainly, when much leverage can be expected at the cutting edge, as when turning off the square corners, it helps to let the body as well as the hand steady the handle end. The body may touch the lathe stand, but do not lean on it—tool control comes from balance on the legs as well as from arm actions.

The lathe speed is not very critical for experimental spindle turning, but if there are four steps on the lathe cone pulley, have the belt in the groove next to the smallest. If there are three steps, have the belt on the center or smallest steps.

At first experiment with the gouge flat on the tool rest or sloping only a little above horizontal, then feed it into the work (Fig. 6-1C). Maintain this angle, but slide the tool along the tool rest for a short distance. Go back over this part to take off more wood. Stop the lathe and examine the work. What was beginning to look round is now shown to be still square with the corners removed roughly (Fig. 6-4). Remove the rest of the square angles in

the same way down to the same size. Continue turning more off. Keep the work approximately parallel for the whole length.

Both centers will probably wear into the wood. After you have been turning for a short time, try tightening the tailstock screw a little. There may have to be more adjustments later, but in most hardwoods, the first adjustment after starting takes up wear for a long time. If the wood is not much bigger across than the driving center, be careful of hitting that with the tool. It may be advisable to leave that end of the wood oversize as a protection. In most production wood turning, it is usual to have something there to be parted off, just in case. A wide gouge can be worked along by a combination of rolling and sliding. This spreads wear over the whole edge and reduces the frequency of sharpening.

Using the gouge horizontally makes the edge cut as a scraper. This is not the way it is designed and continuing in this way will soon blunt it. It is intended to have more of a cut, which suits the finer

76

angle of the cutting edge, giving an easier action and a smoother finish. Once the wood is round or nearly so, lower the handle so the cutting edge is raised until the bevel almost follows the line of the circumference (Fig. 6-2). Regulate the cut by a combination of feeding into the wood and experimenting with the approach angle. This is the point where you can also experiment with the height of the tool rest. The angle you find best for the gouge is about the same as will be best for most other tools.

It is the relation of the cutting edge to the wood that is important. The tool bevel should be almost rubbing on the circumference of the wood. As the wood is reduced, the angle in relation to the tool rest will be altered (Fig. 6-1D). Have the tool rest reasonably close to the wood at all times, which means moving it in for smaller diameters and angling it so one end can be used in a hollow. If the tool rest is low, the tool has to be held more upright (Fig. 6-1E) to maintain the correct cutting angle. If the tool rest is high, the cutting is done further over the work and the handle has to be held higher

(Fig. 6-1F). The height of the lathe in relation to the height of the worker will affect the favored tool rest height, because this affects the positions of the hands and the best stance to adopt to work comfortably and with the most satisfactory effect. Fortunately, tool rest height is not critical, and it is easy to adapt the way a tool is held to suit the existing height, but each turner will have to find the best arrangement to suit his developing technique. In average conditions, having the tool rest a little below center height suits most workers. It should be set there until you find by experience that you prefer a different height.

With the wood roughed to a reasonably parallel cylinder, try working hollows. The square-ended gouge can be used for wide sweeps. It should be angled towards the lowest point and care is needed to keep the points above the surface at all times to prevent them from digging in (Fig. 6-5A). As the hollow progresses, try tilting the gouge so the leading point goes almost below the surface and the tool is brought round towards the direction it is cutting (Fig. 6-5B). Hold tightly. This gives more of

Fig. 6-4. The hand is lifted to show the wood still has some flat sides, so another cut is needed to make a true circular shape.

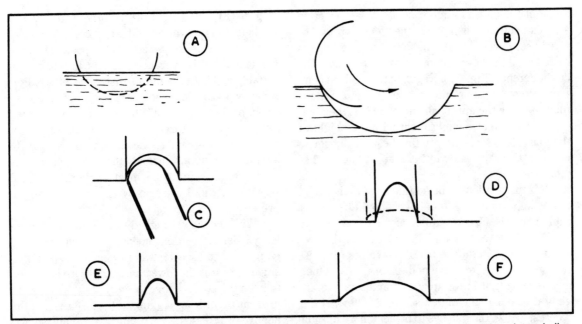

Fig. 6-5. A gouge should always be used so its points are above the surface of the wood. It can be swung into a hollow with a slicing action. A deep elliptical section looks better than a shallow or semicircular one.

a slicing action. After a cut down one side of the hollow, stop the lathe and examine the wood. This side should have a smoother surface than the other side of the slope. The point need not go below the surface, but the cut is made with that side of the cutting edge and is the technique used for getting a smooth finish in a hollow direct from the gouge. Although, as will be seen later, a better effect on a long sweep is made by finishing with a chisel.

Small hollows (*coves*) cannot be made with a square-ended gouge and a rounded fingernail (*spindle-nosed*) shape has to be used. This can be used to slice in a broad sweep in the same way as described for a square-ended gouge. Then one of the sharp sides of the rounded end does the cutting. For a small cove, a suitable gouge is held at the correct angle, but when viewed from above, it is fed squarely in, particularly if the hollow is to be the same size as the gouge end (Fig. 6-6). With a light feed and a sharp tool, the sides of the cutting edge as well as the point will sever wood fibers and leave a surface that needs little sanding.

If the hollow is to be wider than the end of the gouge, the first hollowing should be straight in at

the center, but then it is possible to tilt the gouge slightly to pare down the sides to the required size (Fig. 6-5C). Working in this way with a narrow gouge allows the hollow to be shaped as required. If turned hollows are examined, they will not all be sections of circles (Fig. 6-5D), but may be parts of ellipses. The effectiveness of much turning is in the way it uses shadows. A deep hollow, like the end of an ellipse (Fig. 6-5E) gives more pronounced shadows than a semicircular one or one that is like the side of an ellipse (Fig. 6-5F).

CHISELS

In general bench woodworking, chisels are used for straight cuts and gouges for curved ones. In turning, gouges are mostly roughing tools and chisels are finishing tools on the same surfaces. There are places where a chisel cannot go and a gouge also has to be used for finishing, but in turning between centers, chisels are used after gouges wherever they can be applied.

Handling a chisel calls for more skill than a gouge. If a gouge cuts incorrectly, the result may be a scrape instead of a cut, but the wood is not spoiled, and the surface may be made good by other tool work or by sanding. There is some risk of a gouge digging in and spoiling work, particularly a square-ended one, but the risk of a chisel damaging work when used unskillfully is greater. In general, the wider a chisel, the less the risk of it digging in. For experimental cuts, use a chisel about 3/4 inch wide—certainly not less than 1/2 inch wide.

Some turners prefer a chisel sharpened square across the end, but the majority use a skew end. How much of an angle it is given is a matter of personal preference. The cutting edge has to approach the wood at the same angle, whatever way the chisel is sharpened, so differences are in the angle the tool is held to bring the cutting edge to the same position relative to the wood. A skew chisel sharpened at the angle it comes from the maker should be the first choice. It is unlikely you will ever want anything different, but as your experience grows, you may want to experiment with other end angles.

Use both hands on a chisel in the same way as suggested for a gouge. Cuts are mostly com-

paratively light, so thumb on top gives enough grip and allows you to watch progress (Fig. 6-3). Do not be misled into lightening the grip when only a light cut is needed. The tool must be firmly held at all times. Almost every turned work between centers will require chisel cuts in both directions, so it is important to get used to changing hands as necessary.

Where the wood has been roughed to a cylindrical shape with the gouge, the chisel can be used to remove the roughness and leave a surface that is the wood turning equivalent of planing flat wood. It may not produce a perfect surface the first or second time, but practice will show how this is done and tool control will come.

Have the work rotating and the tool rest fairly close to it. Hold the chisel so its sharpened angle bears on the surface but the cutting edge is clear of it (Fig. 6-7A). The short end of the cutting edge faces in the direction the cut is to be made (Fig. 6-7B). When using a skew chisel for this sort of work, the long point has to be kept clear of the wood at all times. Sometimes the short end may go

Fig. 6-6. A narrow gouge with a rounded end can be fed straight in to make a small hollow cove.

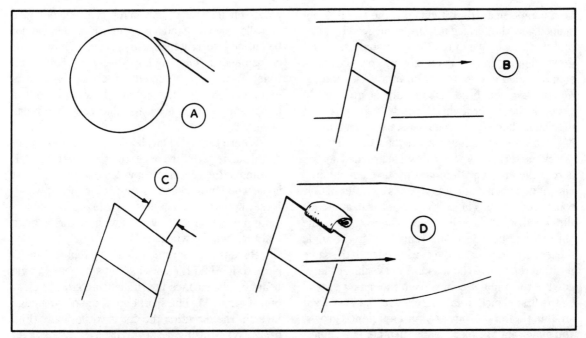

Fig. 6-7. A chisel is used so its bevel is almost flat on the wood, and it is moved along with a slicing action using only the lower part of the cutting edge.

below the surface, but most of the cutting is done with that part of the cutting edge towards the short end (Fig. 6-7C).

Tilt the chisel towards the direction of cut. If necessary, slide it back a little over the tool rest, until the lower part of the cutting edge begins to enter the wood. From this point, use the tool with a slicing action (Fig. 6-7D). Aim to maintain the angle and keep a parallel cut. It helps to have the tool rest exactly parallel with the centerline of the lathe to serve as a guide. If a very light cut is taken, the chisel edge may try to follow inequalities left by the gouge. It is better to make the cut deep enough to just go below the rough surface.

If the chisel is cutting correctly, the wood will come away as shavings that curl off the edge. Of course, further cuts can follow and will almost certainly be necessary to level inequalities. Careful manipulation of the tool and the angle at which its edge is brought to the wood can regulate the thickness of shaving being removed from something delicately thin to quite a coarse piece. However, a chisel is mainly a finishing tool. If much wood has to be removed, it is better to use a gouge to get near to size, so only a light slice has to be taken with a chisel.

When using a chisel or gouge into a hollow, always work from the larger to the smaller diameter (Fig. 6-8). This is with the grain. If you try an experimental cut from smaller to larger, the tool will try to dig in and even if it does not dig, the surface will finish roughly.

When working into a hollow from both directions, the only difficulty is at the bottom. If the two cuts show an unevenness in diameter, so that there is an unequal ridge around the small part, that may be due to play at the tailstock center. Tighten the tailstock and make another light cut. Ideally, the cuts from both directions will meet without a flaw at the bottom of the curve, but grain discrepancies and human error may leave a light ridge or roughness of grain there. The cut down each side of a hollow should finish with a lifting action or scoop upwards at the smallest diameter. Do not start to curve up the other side—that causes roughness. If light scooping cuts do not give a perfect result, unevenness can be corrected when the work is sanded.

It is easier to keep a wide chisel true on a broad expanse. A chisel up to 1 1/2 inches wide is worth having for finishing long parallel cylinders or long graceful sweeps as found on a table leg. The work can be done with a narrower chisel, but it is easier with a wide one. Narrow chisels are needed to go into restricted places. Many turnings have intricate outlines, and the only way to finish a narrow surface where other parts prevent the entry of a wide chisel is to use a narrower one. It is good practice to always use the widest chisel that will go into a restricted place—1/4-inch chisels are needed for these limited uses, but 1/2-inch or 3/4-inch chisels

are most turner's choice for general chisel work.

The bulk of the work with chisels is in finishing flat and curve surfaces with a slicing action. That technique should be mastered thoroughly. The quality of turned wood is most apparent in the surfaces shown in the plainer parts. There should be no flaws in the more intricate parts, but if there are any, they will be less obvious. Unevenness in a long flowing curve or a falter in a part supposedly parallel may be very obvious.

A simple use of a chisel is in cutting rings around turned wood. This is often seen on tool handles, where a series of rings provide a grip (Fig. 6-9). Different patterns of rings allow tools to be identified when their handles are otherwise the

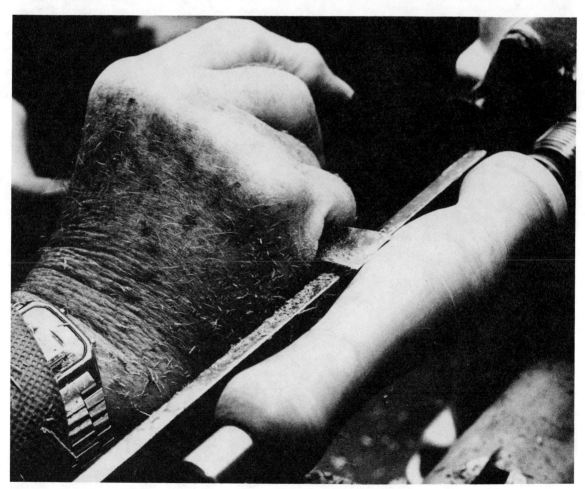

Fig. 6-8. Where the work tapers, cuts are made from the high level to the low level.

Fig. 6-9. Two tool handles with metal tube ferrules and lines cut around them with the long point of the chisel are shown.

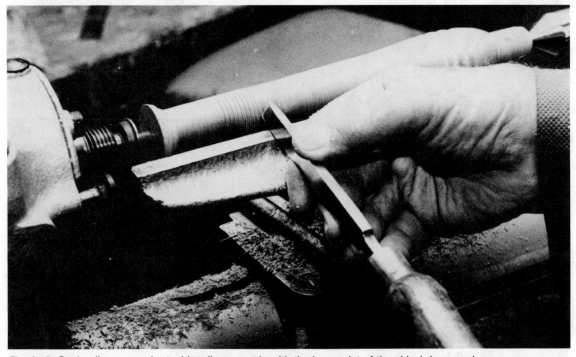

Fig. 6-10. Cutting lines around a tool handle are made with the long point of the chisel downward.

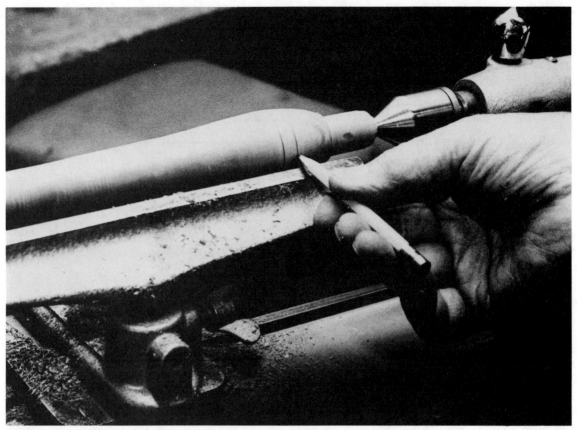

Fig. 6-11. The widths of beads can be marked out by holding a pencil on the tool rest.

same. This is often done with carving tool handles, where the wood carver has large numbers and it helps him to get to know his tools.

The chisel is rested with its long point downward on the tool rest (Fig. 6-10) and fed directly at the revolving wood. It is not usually necessary to press very hard. In any case, it is inadvisable to continue to push hard for long as enough heat could be generated to draw the temper of the point of the tool. If a deep cut is needed, it is better to withdraw the tool and allow it to cool before pressing in again.

It is possible to make a series of lines without any marking and practice soon shows you how to do this evenly. If exact spacing is needed—as when marking around a handle for measuring lines of beads—a pencil can be held against the revolving wood to mark where the cuts are to come (Fig.

6-11). Do this lightly, because the wood will soon wear away the pencil. Any pencil marks that should be removed can be sanded from the revolving wood.

A chisel can also be used point-down to square the end of turned wood. Sometimes both the driven end and the tailstock end of the wood will be parted off and the small pieces that provided support will be scrapped. In many cases, such as with a tool handle, the center mark from the tailstock center is useful for locating the hole to be drilled for the tang of the tool so that the end is not cut off. It is as it came from the saw, however, it may not be smooth and it may not be true.

The chisel is put on the tool rest point downward, like for cutting lines around the wood, but it is angled so the bevel on the side nearer the wood is at about right angles to the centerline of the lathe (Fig. 6-12A). With the tool maintained at this angle, it can be fed in as far as the center and the end of the wood trued with as many slices as are necessary. With a plain center, there is no risk of damaging the tool, because the steel center is not rotating. If a revolving center is used, the cut should finish before the chisel reaches it. Anything left can be cleaned off after the work is removed from the lathe.

The same technique can be used to work a

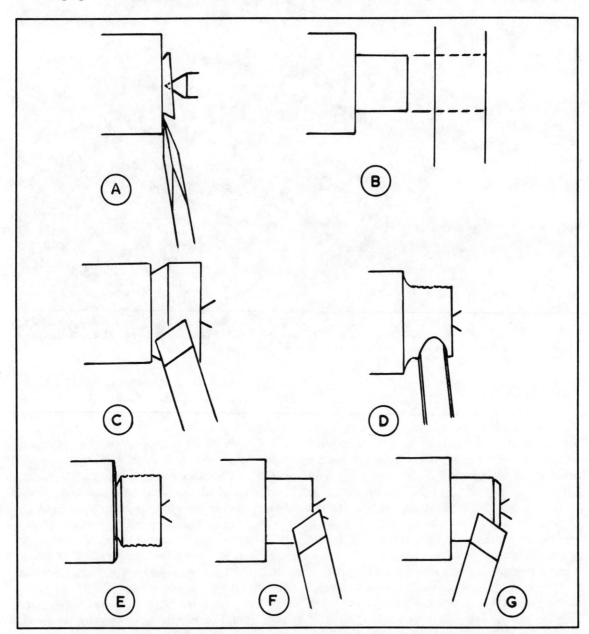

Fig. 6-12. An end of a handle to take a ferrule is first squared with a chisel and reduced with a gouge and a chisel until it will fit the tube. A slight taper on the end helps when driving it on.

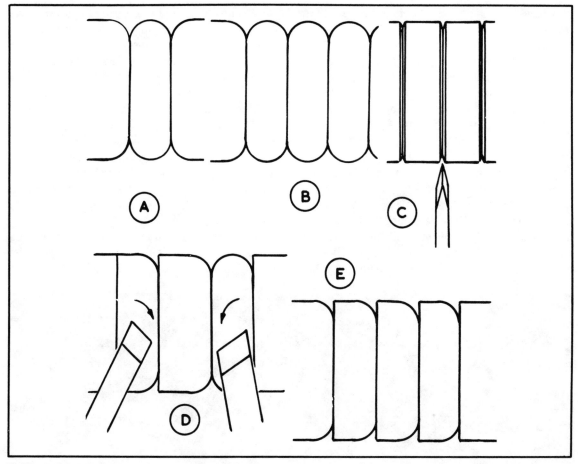

Fig. 6-13. Beads may be single or multiple. They are first cut in with a chisel, then a chisel or beading tool is used to curve down both ways.

shoulder. Many things are turned with a dowel end to fit into something else (Fig. 6-12B). The position of the shoulder is marked with a cut straight in. The reduced side of this can be beveled, using the short end of the chisel (Fig. 6-12C). If there is much wood to be removed, most of the waste can be taken off with a gouge (Fig. 6-12D). The shoulder is deepened. Keep a short distance away from the final line at first (Fig. 6-12E). Use a chisel with the short end leading to turn the dowel to size (Fig. 6-12F), then square down the shoulder on the line, in the same way as described for truing an end. To help the dowel enter its hole, bevel its ends slightly. Use the chisel with the short end leading (Fig. 6-12G).

BEADS

Many pieces of turned work, particularly those following traditional designs, have a large number of *beads*. These are bands of curved section around the work and may be alone or in a series. Even where there is only one, the wood on each side is turned into it like half beads (Fig. 6-13A). With a series, the beads may directly adjoin each other (Fig. 6-13B).

Beads can be turned with a chisel. Using one little more than half the width of a bead allows progress to be observed better than with a wider chisel. The positions of the beads are marked by cutting in lines around the turned wood (Fig. 6-13C). They may not go as deep as the beads the first time, but may have to cut in deeper as work progresses (Fig. 6-14).

The chisel that is to shape the bead is held squarely to the work or angled slightly towards the direction it is to cut with the short end of the cutting edge that way (Fig. 6-13D). One side of the bead is cut from the outside diameter to the bottom of the cut. Even if the short end of the chisel does not enter the wood at the beginning of the cut, it will have to as it gets further around the curve. Hold the tool tightly and roll its cut. Be prepared to resist any tendency for the tool to catch and dig in. An expert will make one side of a bead almost in one quick action. The beginning should do it in several cuts. All cuts one way may be done almost to completion at the same time (Fig. 6-13E), then the tool turned over and all cuts made the other way. Almost certainly there will have to be a return to cutting straight in with the long point and more light cuts to get the desired shape to the beads. First ones may then need sanding, but the aim should be to get correct shapes and a smooth finish from the chisel.

Most beads in the past have been cut in the way just described, but the danger for a beginner is in the short end digging in and making an unintended scoring slice that spoils the work. Much of this risk can be avoided by using a beading tool. This is a chisel sharpened square across the end and made from square steel, usually not more than 3/8 inch across.

The method of making a bead with a beading tool is similar to that with a chisel. A chisel or the beading tool can be used to cut in the lines. The

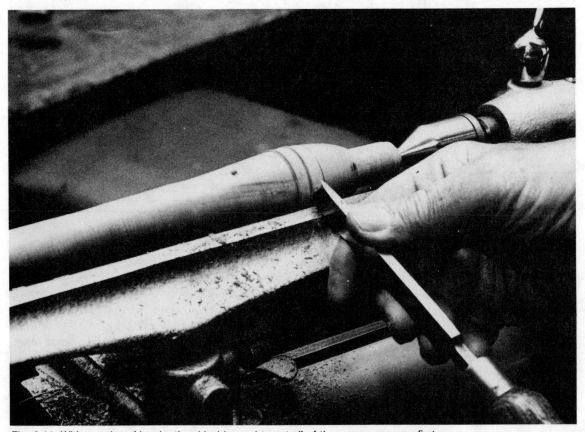

Fig. 6-14. With a series of beads, the chisel is used to cut all of the curves one way first.

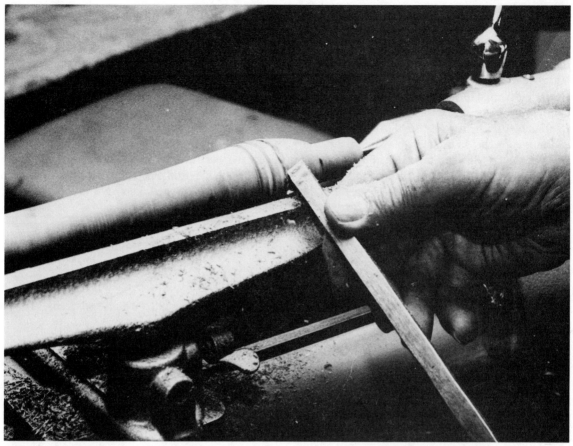

Fig. 6-15. A beading tool can be used both ways, but it is usual to do all of the curves one way first.

tool is then used squarely to the work with the under bevel on the wood. Then it is brought back until the edge is about to cut and rolled on the tool rest in the direction of cut. This is the same as with a chisel, but the leading point starts cutting straight away and the square end minimizes the risk of digging in (Fig. 6-15). The tool does not have to be turned over to cut the other way. As with a chisel, skill brings the ability to make a bead quicker and with fewer cuts, but a beginner will do better with a number of light cuts.

PARTING

Because parting tools are narrow, they are stiffened by being made quite deep and are narrowed further behind the cutting edge to give clearance as they enter the wood. They should be presented squarely to the wood. The cutting edge severs fibers by breaking them, leaving rough edges to the sides of the cut. If the cut edges are to form part of the finished work, allow for squaring cleanly with a chisel later. A parting tool can be taken quite deeply into a piece of wood as the narrowing will give clearance if you keep the cut straight. It is worthwhile making some practice parting cuts in one of your experimental turned pieces of wood to observe the action. Note the effect of the cutting angle in relation to the circumference of the wood as described in the next few paragraphs.

Have the tool rest close to the work. Point the

parting tool directly at the revolving wood. Hold it with two hands in the same way as the other tools. Press straight in. At first, point the tool towards the center of the wood (Fig. 6-16A). After entering a short distance, lower the end of the handle so the cutting edge points more towards the circumference of the circle it is cutting (Fig. 6-16B). Continuing to push in gives the edge less of a scrape and more of a cut, so progress may be easier. The sides of the cut will still be rough. Move the end of the handle as the diameter of the wood gets less in order to keep the cutting angle about the same in relation to the reducing circumference.

Obviously, if the parting tool was pushed in far enough, it would eventually cut to the center and part the wood—hence its name. However, before the center was reached, the wood would start to bend and pinch against the sides of the tool, which would jam and the wood would probably break. In practice, wood is often parted down to the point where the small piece left is beginning to weaken. Then, the work is removed from the lathe and sawn off with the exposed piece planed or sanded true. Careful parting can be taken right to the center if

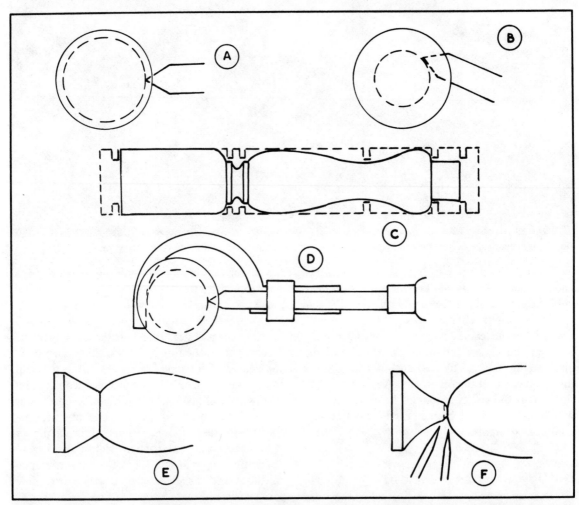

Fig. 6-16. Various parts of a spindle turning can be marked approximately to size by first cutting in with a parting tool, which may be controlled by a special gauge. If one end has to be rounded and cut off, the waste part is turned down towards it and final cuts are made, either with a chisel or parting tool.

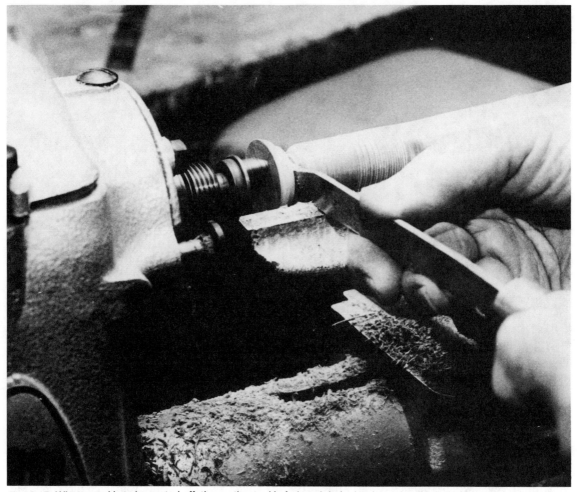

Fig. 6-17. When wood is to be parted off, the parting tool is fed straight in, but it can be tilted upwards to get a better cut.

the work is closely supported as when near the headstock end.

Parting in this way is satisfactory if the rough end grain from the parting tool is acceptable, as it would be if it was to fit inside another part. If the finished end is to be shaped, as it may be if there is a rounded end towards the headstock end, the parting tool can be taken in far enough to leave enough strength (Fig. 6-17), then much of the shaping can be done (Fig. 6-18). This would be a final step. The other turned work should be completed elsewhere on the wood before weakening at that end. Be careful further turning, possibly with a little more use of the parting tool and the pointed end

of a chisel, it should be possible to reduce the curved end almost to nothing. Then, carefully remove the work so sawing and sanding leaves a good finish.

Another use of the parting tool is in marking both positions and depths for other cuts. The rough turned wood has key points marked, then these are cut in with the parting tool (Fig. 6-16C). Depth may be checked with calipers, or a gauge may be attached to the parting tool (Fig. 6-16D) to stop it at the correct depth.

With the wood marked in this way, other shaping can be done. Knowing that if these parting tool cuts are used as guides, the intended sizes will be

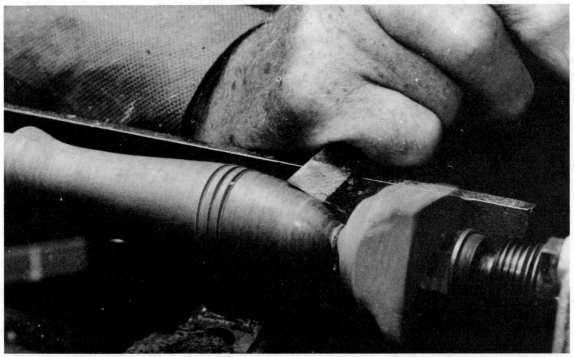

Fig. 6-18. The waste wood at the end can be turned down towards the part that is wanted in order to make it easier to square the final end.

maintained. This is particularly important when making a set of matching parts, such as legs or posts. As the edges left by the parting tool are rough, there should be a small allowance made for cleaning shoulders, where they have to be cut squarely. If edges will be rounded towards the parting tool edges, there is no need for allowance.

Without a parting tool, it is still possible to get to a similar point at an end by using a chisel. At the headstock end the waste part, as well as the shaped part, can be progressively turned down (Fig. 6-16E). Some of the waste can be removed with a gouge, but towards the end the small diameter can be cut away by tapering from each direction (Fig. 6-16F) until a point is reached where the work is taken off the lathe and sawn through.

Chapter 7

Spindle Turning Details

The fundamentals of turning wood between centers have been outlined in the last chapter. It is not always obvious how to set about using these techniques in combination with each other to make particular items, however.

PREPARING THE WOOD

In general, the wood is roughed to a cylindrical shape with a large gouge before going on to other work. If a part has to remain square or another angular shape, those parts that are to be round are roughed to shape, but the gouge work is not brought too close to the square part because there might be a risk of breaking away an angle of the square. If a corner of a square is damaged, it is sometimes possible to hide it by making it an inside angle of a stool leg or other partly hidden place. Obviously, it is better to not do the damage in the first place.

Roughing can be left as a reasonably parallel cylinder and shaping done with other tools, but if the finished item will have a taper or a general cur-

vature in the length, the roughing gouge can be used to take roughing very closely to final measurement. Obviously, you need to watch that roughing does not go undersize or so close to final sizes that there is no surplus left for finishing tools to clean off.

If the wood being turned is longer than the tool rest, it may save time to do most of the work over a part within the length of the tool rest before moving the tool rest, but this will be controlled by the design. If there is a long curve to be turned, getting this right is more important than cutting down on the number of moves made with the tool rest. If the whole length is conveniently divided into sections, each can be treated as one job before moving to another part.

It is sometimes necessary to consider how turning a part will affect stiffness of the wood. If the center of a piece will eventually be thin, it would be unwise to turn that part to size first, because the weak center might bend when tools are used on other parts. If the wood bends and flexes, the surfaces cut elsewhere may have chatter marks, where the tools jumps, or the shapes produced may be uneven.

An expert, particularly if he is turning professionally and his earnings depend on fast production, may produce chair legs of acceptable finish in sets of four in the time a beginner takes to get the first wood roughed to size. From his experience, he instinctively knows the best sequence of work and uses tools in the correct order. He turns key parts to size and uses them as a guide to the diameters to be turned elsewhere. He does a surprising amount by eye and can get shapes matching without using calipers or a rule.

This ability comes with experience and practice. A beginner should set the foundation by tackling jobs after planning how he will do them. With many turning projects, there are several ways of doing them, and individuals have their own preferences. A newcomer has to work out the methods that suit him best. Some turners own and use a large selection of tools. Others seem to get equally good results with only a few tools. Turning is an art as much as a mechanical skill, so a turner may develop his own ways of doing things. The following examples, showing steps in making a few typical things, will indicate how work can be planned to produce good results.

TOOL HANDLES

Many of the first things made on a lathe are likely to be handles for tools of all sorts, such as lathe tools and many general woodworking tools as well as garden and domestic tools. Nearly all tools need a metal tubular ferrule to prevent the wood from splitting when the pointed tang of the tool is driven in. Oddments of metal tube can be collected to make ferrules. Brass or copper polish bright and look good, but aluminum, steel, and anything else that can be found may be used. Diameters may be from 3/8 inch upwards, depending on the tool, but some garden and domestic tools need large handles with ferrules up to 1 inch in diameter. How thick the wall of the tube is does not matter much—for most tool handles, it can be quite thin.

Tube can be cut to length with a fine hacksaw. Do not use a coarse blade. The distance between teeth should be less than the thickness of the tube wall; otherwise, the saw will jump in the metal and not cut evenly. File the sawn ends true. For an average tool, the length of the ferrule should be about the same as its diameter, but this is largely a matter of preference. A thin ferrule may look better slightly longer, while a large diameter ferrule may be shorter. If a metal turning lathe is available, the ferrules can have their ends turned true, but filing will get a reasonable end, and a method of truing in position is described later. Use a round file inside the tube to remove any burrs. There is no need to clean or polish the outside of the ferrule at this stage, because it can be done on the lathe after fixing on the wood.

As an example, steps for making a file handle are given (Fig. 7-1A). Similar handles are used on other tools. Some variations are detailed later. This handle is made from a piece of hardwood 1 1/4 inches square and 7 inches long, using a ferrule 1/2 inch in diameter.

- Mount the wood in the lathe and turn it round for its whole length with a gouge (Fig. 7-1B). Adjust the tailstock to take up wear and prevent vibration. Lubricate a plain tailstock center.
- Set calipers to very slightly more than the internal diameter of the ferrule (Fig. 7-2). Mark about 1/16 inch more than the length of the ferrule from the tailstock end of the wood and use a parting tool to cut in almost to the caliper size (Fig. 7-1C). If a parting tool is unavailable, cut in with the point of the chisel and taper on the waste side towards it as described in the last chapter.
- Use a 1/4-inch gouge to turn the end near to the finished size. Then use a skew chisel to turn the ferrule part to size (Fig. 7-1D). Switch off the motor and hold the wood with one hand to keep it on the driving center and withdraw the tailstock so the ferrule can be tried in position. If the ferrule will not go, turn just the end down smaller. When the size has been ascertained, turn up to the shoulder with the skew chisel (Fig. 7-1E). The point of the chisel will probably have to be used in the angle to finally sever

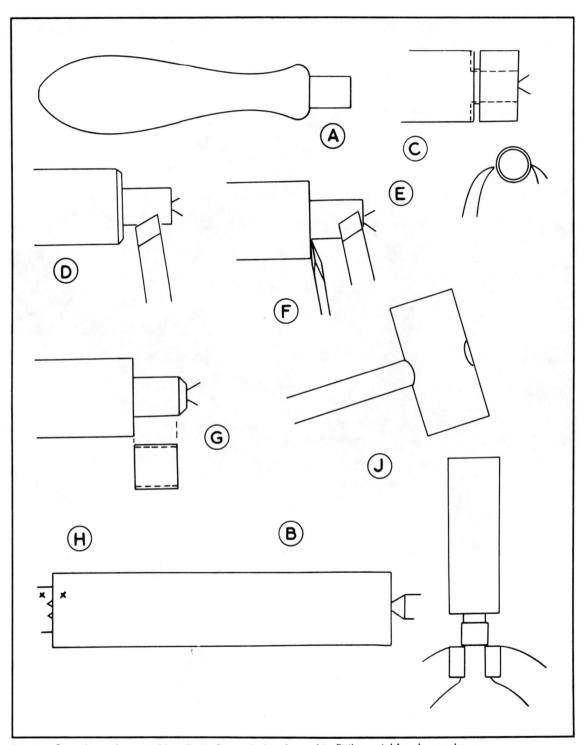

Fig. 7-1. Steps in turning a tool handle by first reducing the end to fit the metal ferrule are shown.

the wood fibers (Fig. 7-1F). Ideally, the wood is given a very slight taper, so the ferrule gets tighter as it is driven on, but in the first instance, the best that can be done will be to turn the wood parallel. Calipers will help, but it is easy to see when wood is parallel or tapered by looking across it. Finally, check that the wood is longer than the ferrule by holding the ferrule

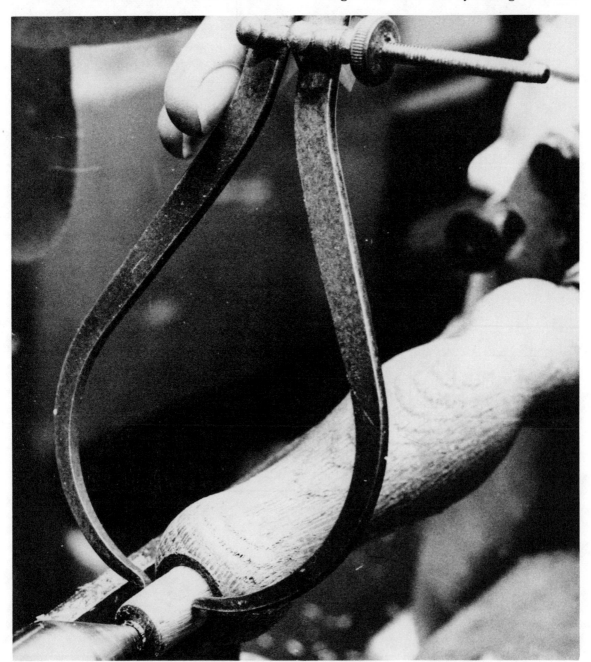

Fig. 7-2. The end for the ferrule on a file handle may be tested with calipers.

against it, then use a chisel to put a slight taper on the extreme end (Fig. 7-1G).

■ Put matching marks on the wood and the driving center (Fig. 7-1H). The wood might still run true if put back in another position, but it is wiser to make sure by using the same location. Remove the work from the lathe. Put the ferrule over the partly opened jaws of a vise and use a mallet to drive the wood into it (Fig. 7-1J).

■ Return the work to the lathe. Lubricate the center again if necessary. If the ferrule runs true, there is no need to do anymore to it. If the end is obviously uneven, it is not difficult to true it with a hand tool while it is revolving in the lathe. The tool can be made from a narrow chisel or from a piece of square hardened and tempered tool steel; 1/4 inch square is large enough. Grind the end diagonally at about 45 degrees (Fig. 7-3A). Put the steel in a handle so it projects 2 or 3 inches. This is called a *graver*. Have the tool rest as close as possible to the ferrule, then hold the graver on it so it can be manipulated until one edge cuts the tube. A file can be used on the rotating tube to bevel or round the end. The metal ferrule can be brightened by using a strip of abrasive cloth against the revolving metal. Keep it moving to reduce local wear on the abrasive. You could follow with polish on a pad, but do not use a cloth with loose ends that might catch in the work.

■ About 1 inch at the driving end will be cut off. Cut in with the parting tool to mark this, but do not go too deeply at this stage—down to about half the diameter is enough (Fig. 7-3B). Use a 1/2-inch gouge to remove wood so you get a pleasing outline. Note there are two high parts—that near the ferrule is not as high as the other end. The hollow should go deep enough to make a comfortable grip and give a pleasing appearance. Remember that the tang of the tool has to go into the wood, and it must not be so thin as to be weakened when a hole is drilled. The shape is best formed by eye, although a drawing may provide guidance.

■ Use a skew chisel to turn the curve towards the ferrule (Fig. 7-3C). Reverse the chisel and turn

over the top of that high part into the hollow (Fig. 7-3D). Turn the other side of the hollow (Fig. 7-3E) from the top of the larger curve. The chisel can be reversed and part of the curve towards the headstock end smoothed, but there will have to be more thinning at the cut-off part before a pleasing curve can be made there.

■ Do all that is necessary to other parts of the handle before reducing further at the headstock end. If there are rings or other decoration to be added, do them now (Fig. 7-4). If the tool work has been good there should be little need for sanding.

■ Sanding revolving wood makes marks across the grain lines. Avoid coarse grits as much as possible as the marks they leave are difficult to remove with finer grits. If sanding seems desirable, use any of the usual woodworking abrasive papers, but keep to fine grits. A folded paper used in the hand and allowed to follow the shape without too much pressure should be satisfactory. Some tuners hold a handful of shavings under the revolving wood, with the tool rest out of the way. Whether this really does anything to the surface is debatable.

■ At the ferrule end, the center will probably enter further than the wood extends from the ferrule. If so, use the long point of a chisel to square the wood level with the ferrule (Fig. 7-3F). If you have left too much wood, square it in level with the ferrule part way, leave enough wood for the center to keep its hold. The surplus will have to be cut off after the hole has been drilled.

■ Withdraw the tailstock and replace the center with a drill chuck. Use a drill of about the same size as the end of the tool tang that is to be fitted. Have the tailstock screw wound back so most of its length is available to feed forward. See that the headstock end of the wood is properly seated in the driving center. Bring the tailstock up until the drill bit is in the hollow left by the center (Fig. 7-5). Lock the tailstock to the lathe bed. The lathe speed can be reduced if you wish, but drilling can usually be done satisfactorily at normal turning speed.

The drill has to be taken in as far as the tang

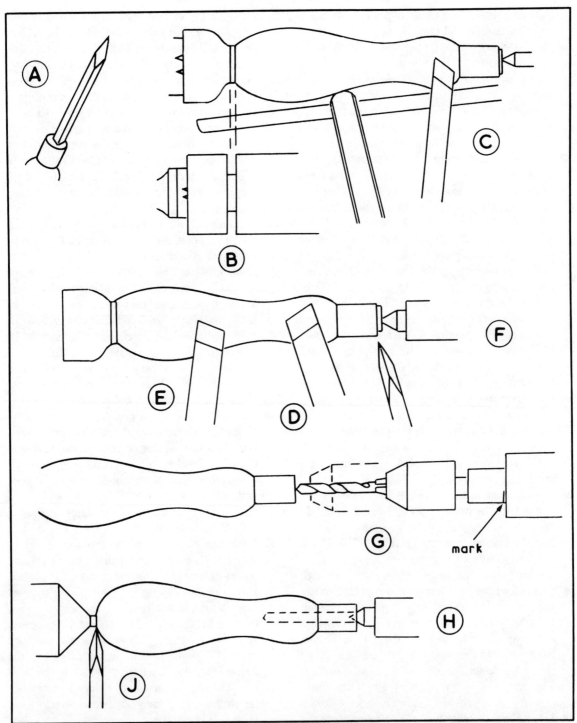

Fig. 7-3. Further steps in making the handle. A graver can be used to clean the end of the metal tube. Chisels and gouges are used towards the thinner parts. A hole for the tool tang is drilled with a drill held in a tailstock chuck.

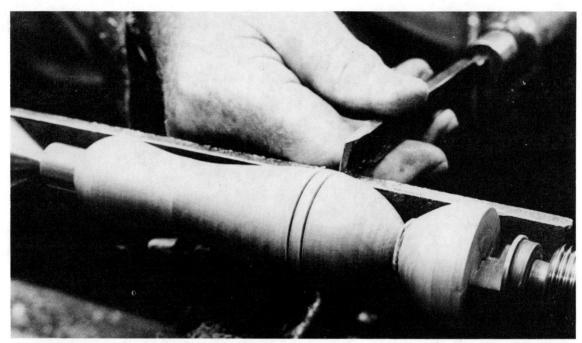

Fig. 7-4. Decorative rings are cut with the long point of a chisel.

is to go. If you do not know how much of the tailstock barrel is projecting and add the depth needed to this, the drill can be fed in until that much of the barrel is exposed and the depth will be right (Fig. 7-3G). Stop the lathe and withdraw the drill. If the tailstock is reversed after drilling without stopping the lathe, it might withdraw the drill cleanly or the drill may grip the wood and pull it off the driving center with the possibility of breaking the drill in the wood. This small hole can be used as a pilot hole for larger drills to go in. They will go in steps to suit a tapered tang, using a hand drill on the bench, or larger drills can be used in the lathe. In both cases, be careful not to take the large drills too far. Hole sizes and arrangements have to be judged so the tang will drive in and grip, yet not be so tight as to risk splitting the wood despite the ferrule, or prevent it entering as far as intended.

For a file tang, metalworking Morse pattern twist drills are suitable. For a large gardening tool, woodworking bits may have to be used. Because they are guided by points at the cen-

ter, it is better to drill the largest hole first, then steps with smaller bits until the full depth is reached. If a small hole is drilled all the way first, there is no wood left to guide the central point of the larger bits.

■ Use a center in the tailstock again (Fig. 7-3H). At the headstock end cut in deeper with the parting tool, but not so far as to feel the wood weakening. Use a chisel with the short end leading to turn down the large part of the curve, but for the last parts use the long point (Fig. 7-3J). By careful work it is usually possible to go down to about 1/8 inch in diameter (Fig. 7-6). Sand the end to match the sanding of the rest of the handle. Remove the handle from the lathe, and saw off the end. Clean off the cut with chisel and abrasive paper.

■ The handle just described is perfectly satisfactory, but it is very like quantity-produced handles. The turner can add his own decoration to the handle that will identify it and aid in sorting tools if many are given similar handles. Simplest is a series of lines cut in (Fig. 7-7A) usually around the large part, but there could

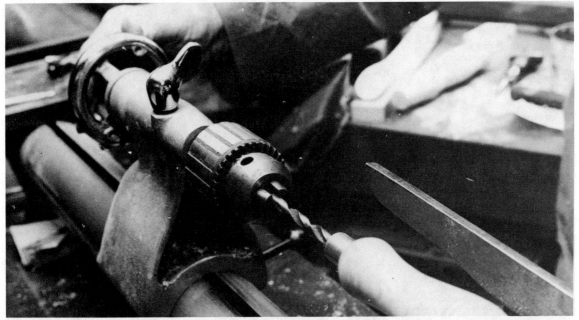
Fig. 7-5. A hole in the handle is made by a drill fed in with the tailstock handle.

Fig. 7-6. The handle end and the waste alongside it can be cut down until very little is left.

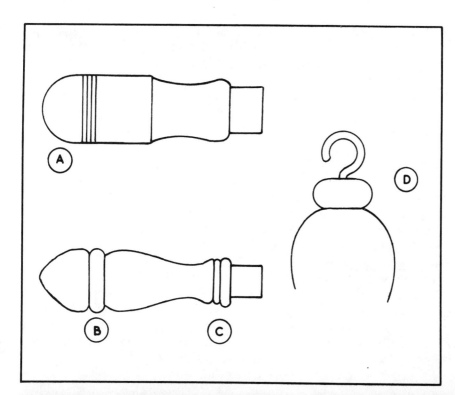

Fig. 7-7. Various tool handle shapes are possible. Beads may be worked or one bead made at the end if the tool is to hang.

Fig. 7-8. A handle for a turning tool is cut from a thick part behind the ferrule with a long sweeping shallow curve.

be others just behind the ferrule. There could be beads, with one or more on the large part (Fig. 7-7B), or a single bead near the ferrule (Fig. 7-7C). There could be a small knoblike bead at the end (Fig. 7-7D), particularly if a hook is to be screwed in for hanging.

Many other handles can be made in very similar ways to the specimen file handle. Turning handles for your tools and domestic equipment can be very satisfying and is a good way to produce worthwhile articles while gaining skill in turning between centers. A tool intended to be pushed will be given a larger knob end, so there is more of a ball to fit in your hand. You will probably want to make new handles for some of your turning tools. Most are made thick near the ferrule and will give you practice in a long sweeping curve (Fig. 7-8). Care is needed to avoid getting slight kinks in the outline. Rings and beads around will break up the outline and disguise slight discrepancies. They also help you to identify individual tools.

Instead of tangs to push into the wood, some tools have sockets into which the wood has to be fitted (Fig. 7-9). Turn the handle with its taper towards the tailstock (Fig. 7-10), so you can turn that first and test it in the socket. Make it oversize at first, then its end can be entered in the socket and you can judge the correctness of the slope and turn to size accordingly. If you accidentally make it too loose, you can turn further into the length of the wood until you get it right before turning the remainder of the handle.

Not all handles need ferrules or sockets. If there is little strain on the tool or implement, its tang can go directly into the wood. An example is a paper knife (Fig. 7-11). Make the wood round and drill a slightly undersize hole for the knife tang. Mount the wood with the tailstock center in the hole and complete the outline (Fig. 7-12).

Many ordinary chisels may now be supplied with plastic handles, but traditionally, they were wood and in three basic patterns. Enthusiastic woodworkers still prefer turned wood handles for their chisels and similar tools because they have a better appearance and feel. The most common type is a *barrel shape* (Fig. 7-13A). This is started like

Fig. 7-9. These garden tools have sockets into which the handles are fitted and held with screws.

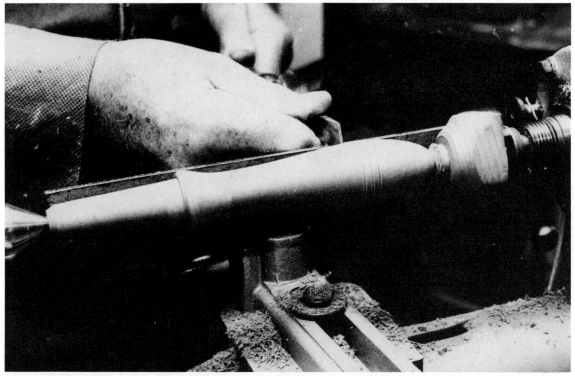

Fig. 7-10. A handle for a socketed tool is best turned with the tapered end towards the tailstock so it can be tested in the socket.

Fig. 7-11. A handle for a paper knife need not have a ferrule.

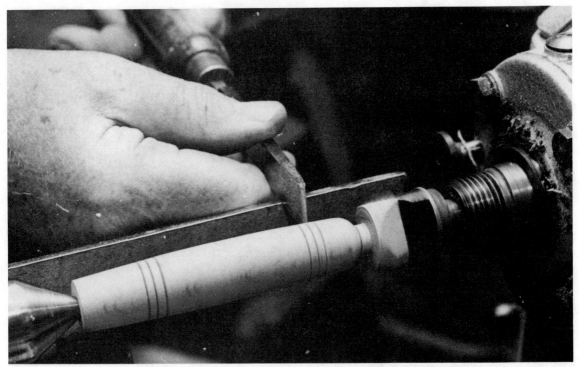

Fig. 7-12. The paper knife handle is turned with the tailstock center supporting in the tang hole.

a file handle, but after the ferrule has been fitted and the other end reduced slightly, the outline is made with a curve that has its thickest part slightly nearer the upper end than the center of the handle. The end may be given a *domed shape* or turned with a slight curve. The domed end is suitable for a hand grip, but the other shape is better if the handle is to be hit with a mallet or hammer.

Another type is similar to a file handle, except the upper part has a parallel section or also known as a *parallel part*, usually with rings cut around it (Fig. 7-13B). Except for the care needed in getting the parallel part true, the turning work is similar to making a file handle.

A wide chisel in one of these handles will resist rolling on the bench, but a narrow one will not. For narrow chisels, particularly those slender paring types, it is helpful to have a handle that will not roll. This can be accomplished by having a part of the handle octagonal (Fig. 7-13C). Except for this, it is similar in outline to the handle with a parallel part. Plane the wood to a regular octagon section

with its centers accurately located as described in Chapter 6. Turn the parts that are to be round, but be careful that the roughing gouge does not ride up onto the part that has to remain octagonal and damage the planed surfaces. The main hollow can blend from the octagon until the point is cutting a full circle (Fig. 7-14). Round the octagon into the top and turn down the waste wood to this size (Fig. 7-13D). Use the parting tool to cut in the end and turn away some of the waste part so you can see what you are doing (Fig. 7-13E). Use the chisel point downward to cut a rounded button on the end of the handle (Fig. 7-15). Go as far as you dare, then remove the work from the lathe and saw off the waste. The small center piece can now be worked smooth.

A row of pegs set into a board is convenient for hanging clothing and many other items. The "Shaker peg" design (Fig. 7-16A) is attractive and it is made much like tool handles. Where tool handles can mostly be individual shapes, pegs have to be made in matching sets, so you have the problem of repeating the design. A single peg can be made to a shape you find pleasing, then use that peg as a pattern for further pegs.

Turn the wood cylindrical to slightly more than will be the finished maximum diameter. Cut in where the shoulder of the dowel will be and where the outer end will come. Use a parting tool (Fig. 7-16B) to do this. Using those cuts as a guide, remove some of the waste wood with a gouge (Fig. 7-16C). Drill a hole the same size that the peg will have to fit into in a small piece of scrap wood. Use

this as a gauge for turning the dowel (Fig. 7-16D). If the tailstock center is small enough, you can hang the gauge on it, so it is easily brought into action. Give the dowel a very slight taper in its length and a steeper taper at its end for easy fitting into the final hole (Fig. 7-16E).

Turning most of the shape is straightforward work with a chisel. Slice along from thicker to thinner (Fig. 7-16F), but the curve inside the enlarged end may be too tight for even a narrow chisel. That can be finished with a gouge turned on edge (Fig.

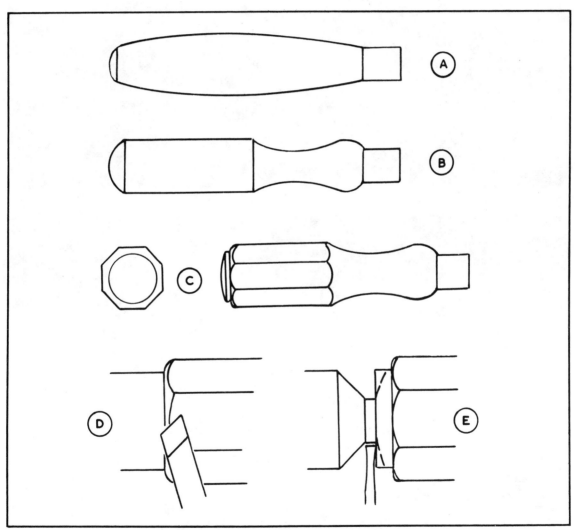

Fig. 7-13. Handles for chisels and similar tools may be barrel shaped, partly parallel, or octagonal to prevent rolling. An octagonal shape is best turned with a round button at one end.

Fig. 7-14. When turning a handle with an octagonal part, care is needed to avoid damage to the unturned part.

Fig. 7-15. The top of an octagonal handle is finished with a knob.

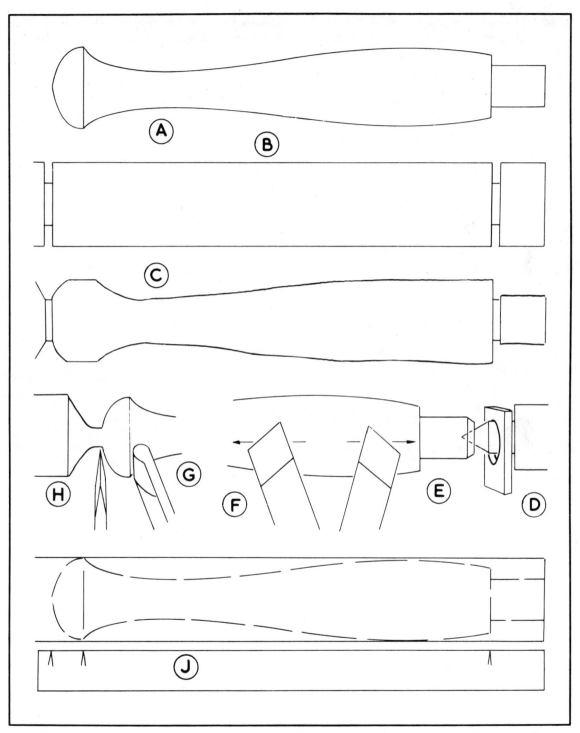

Fig. 7-16. Making a peg board for hanging clothes is much like making tool handles, except that the pegs have to be made in matching sets.

7-16G). Take what will be the end and turn the curve with a chisel, long point downwards (Fig. 7-16H), and cut away the waste part as necessary to give clearance. Do not go very far yet, but leave enough wood for strength while you sand the peg. When you are satisfied with the finish, cut in more at the end. Do not part off completely, because that might leave a rough center where it would show. Go down to about an 1/8 inch in diameter, then remove the wood from the lathe and saw and chisel the remaining wood smooth. Finally, rub it on abrasive paper in the palm of your hand.

While making more pegs to match, have the first peg nearby. Also, set calipers to the largest and smallest diameters and either measure with a rule or, preferably, use the marked edge of a piece of wood as a rod for keeping lengths uniform (Fig. 7-16J).

Chapter 8

Further Spindle Turning

Much of the work involved in turning a piece of wood supported between centers is the application of the basic techniques described in Chapters 6 and 7. With complex turning, the best sequence to adopt is not always obvious, particularly with reproductions of older turnings. Many modern pieces of work that incorporate turning are much plainer than those of maybe 50 years or more ago, and elaborate turning would be out of place. Besides reproduction work, however, there are still such things as table legs and floor lamps that are made with a great many beads, coves, and ornate flourishes within the length that tax the skill of the turner and display his craftsmanship.

Not every turner uses the same method and approach to his work, so it may be that, after a little experience, you will adopt your own method, which may differ from that described here. Turning is a more artistic type of woodwork than most other branches, except carving, and there are always more ways than one to produce artistic results. Most of this chapter is devoted to suggesting sequences of work for particular projects.

If a spindle for a table lamp is being made, it is just one piece that does not have to match anything else. If a preliminary sketch or detailed drawing is made and some part happens to finish a little larger or smaller than originally intended, it does not matter. Much turning of this sort can be done by eye. Overall dimensions may have to be checked. If an end has to be turned as a dowel to fit a hole, that obviously has to be correct, but the decorative part might be worked by eye with little or no reference to a rule or calipers. This technique might also be used if several things have to match. The first piece is turned to what is felt to be a pleasing shape. The matching parts are then turned with measurements taken at key points, but the first part can be kept nearby for reference. How much actual measuring and checking will be needed depends on skill and experience. A beginner would be best advised to use many checks to ensure an exact match, but an experienced worker might make an acceptable series of matching parts with little or no measuring. Commercial production could only be done economically in this way.

STOOL RAILS

The lower rails of a stool or chair require at least two to match and as many as eight if the article is square with double rails. A common form has a bead at the center and a sweep each way to ends that fit holes in the legs (Fig. 8-1A). A simpler version may be without the bead and just a thicker center, possibly decorated with cut lines around. A more elaborate rail might have a longer bulbous center between beads before tapering the ends. Examination of pictures of old furniture will show some very elaborate rails.

In working a rail, it is important that the bead is genuinely central and that the ends make a good fit in the holes in the legs. A strip of scrap wood can be marked as a rod with the length and the intended position of the bead. Check that it is symmetrical by marking on paper or another piece of wood against the marks, then turn it round and see that it matches (Fig. 8-1B).

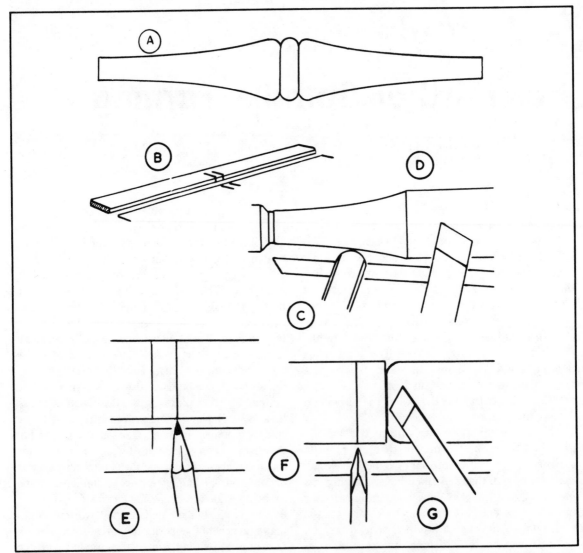

Fig. 8-1. A chair rail must be symmetrical. Tapers are made both with gouge and chisel, then a bead worked at the center.

Fig. 8-2. Beads at the center of a rail break up the profile.

■ Mount the wood between centers. Usually it is advisable to have a little extra at the headstock end to cut off later. Although, if the end diameter is larger than the center at the tailstock end, the wood could be the exact length.

■ Use a roughing gouge to turn the wood round. Bring it to a little more than the final maximum diameter at the center, but some wood can be removed toward the ends (Fig. 8-1C).

■ Check the center area with calipers. For early attempts it may be advisable to turn that part smooth and to size with a skew chisel (Fig. 8-1D). After you have gained a little experience you can go straight into beading, getting the overall diameter correct at the same time as you work the bead.

■ Rest the rod on the tool rest close to the wood. Use a pencil to mark on the revolving wood the positions of the bead and the ends (Fig. 8-1E).

■ Cut in the edges of the bead, either with the long corner of a skew chisel or the end of a beading tool (Fig. 8-1F).

■ Work the bead and curve down the parts on each side of it (Fig. 8-1G and 8-2).

■ Use a parting tool to cut in at the headstock end. Do this also at the tailstock end if anything is to be trimmed off there. Do not go so deep that the wood is weakened, but go a little below what will be the final end diameter.

■ Obtain the diameter the end will have to be from a hole drilled with the actual bit that will be used. It is never wise to assume that any 3/4-inch bit, for instance, is exactly that. It may make a hole slightly over- or undersize. This may happen with some bits that are exactly to size, but they have been sharpened unevenly and cut large, so do not just measure across the bit—a hole from it is the only sure check for caliper setting. A piece of scrap wood drilled with a bit can be used as a gauge at the tailstock end, but calipers will have to be used to check at the headstock end.

■ Reduce the ends to near the final size with a gouge. It will probably be necessary to remove some of the wood that will form the sweep at the same time.

- Bring the ends to size (Fig. 8-3A) with a skew chisel. They should be parallel for the length that will go in the hole, or be given just a very slight taper to ensure tightness. However, a rail in a hole depends for strength on a close contact between as much glued surface as possible and turning the extreme end undersize may make a weaker joint. It is better for the end to be a push fit and the part that will be at the leg surface just a little bigger to make a drive fit. There can be a very slight chamfer on the ends to allow easy entry into a hole.
- Turn the sweeps towards the ends. Bring near to the desired shape with a gouge, then use a skew chisel (Fig. 8-3B). Boldness is needed here. To get a good sweeping taper, the chisel has to be worked along in a controlled slide on the tool rest. It may be necessary to make a few short cuts to remove waste and get the shape approximately correct, but a final light cut should follow through in one line to get a flowing curve without kinks.
- If you have doubts about your ability to get the two sweeps to match by eye alone, a profile gauge of a card template can be made to one sweep and turned over to check the other (Fig. 8-3C).
- Do whatever sanding is required, then part off the wood or remove it from the lathe and saw off the end. Have the first rail in front of you as you turn further ones, so this will aid rod and calipers in getting a matching set.

STOOL LEGS

Stool and chair legs may have square tops and the place where lower rails are attached may also be left square. A low stool may depend on stiffness in fairly deep rails fixed to the square top and be without lower rails. A simple leg of this type is used as an example to show the sequence of turning (Fig. 8-4).

- Because the top is to remain square, prepare the wood by planing it accurately. Allow a little excess length at the top. In assembling the stool, this is probably left on until after joints are cut and made because it reduces any risk of splitting or breaking out. The excess is not cut off until the top of the assembly is leveled. Carefully locate the driving center and the tailstock center. If either of them are far out of true, it will affect the curved work against the square part, resulting in an uneven appearance there. Some workers leave the square part with a sawn surface until after turning, but there is then a danger that the plane may take off part of the turning. I prefer to plane before turning.
- Make a rod for checking lengthwise key places. Reduce the lower part to round with a gouge. Be careful of breaking out the square corners that have to remain. Use the gouge there from square toward round. Do not tilt it the other way or allow its corners to catch in (Fig. 8-5A).
- Use the long point of a skew chisel to cut in with a curved action to shape the end of the square

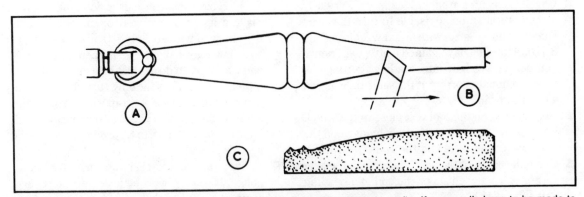

Fig. 8-3. It is important that the ends of a rail should match the holes they are to fit. If many rails have to be made to match, it is convenient to have a template to test them with.

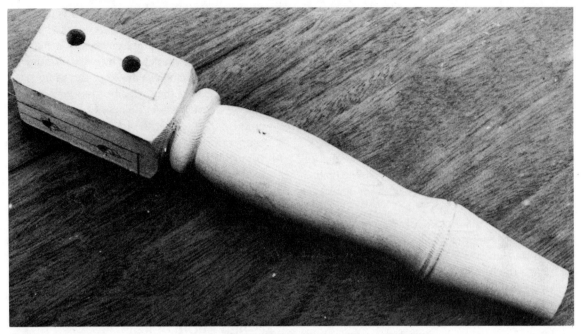

Fig. 8-4. This stool leg with a square top has been drilled for dowels into the top rails.

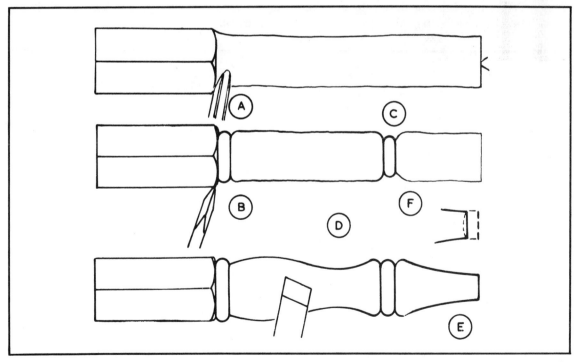

Fig. 8-5. When making a leg, use a gouge away from the square part first, then cut in with a chisel. Turn any beads, and always work the chisel from high to low.

part (Fig. 8-5B). Remove the waste on the round side of the cut.

■ The bead below the square part will be as large a diameter as can conveniently be cut. The other is slightly smaller. Remove some of the waste in the lower area, almost down to size. The wood can be finished smooth with a skew chisel, as suggested for the stool rail, or it can be worked into a bead directly after gouge work.

■ Use the rod and a pencil to mark the bead positions. The foot of the leg will have to be turned true, so allow a little in the length for doing this later.

■ Turn both beads (Fig. 8-5C). Be careful next to the square part that the tool edge does not cut into the square section.

■ Shape the rounded wood adjoining the beads. On each side of the lower bead the curves are similar to those of the bead, but the larger swell takes a more gradual curve towards the top bead. Then, the shape is turned from both higher parts towards the hollow (Fig. 8-5D).

■ Because the large bead and the greater diameter of the swell are almost the same as the distance across the flats of the square part, it is unlikely that calipers will be needed to check them as the series of four legs are made, but it may be wise to back up your checks by eye with calipers to see that the hollows are kept the same size.

■ The part below the lower bead sweeps to the foot with a very slight hollow. Get all four legs uniform diameter at the foot by checking with calipers (Fig. 8-5E).

■ Although making the foot flat should be satisfactory, it will stand better if it is made very slightly hollow. Turn the end true with the long point of a skew chisel or by a cut with a parting tool, then use the chisel to hollow the end very slightly (Fig. 8-5F).

■ When sanding, be careful not to take the sharpness off the square part. A slight accidental rub over the rapidly rotating wood can soon spoil sharp corners.

TAPERED SHOULDERS

There are a few places where accepted techniques cannot be used. One of these is where the large end of a tapered part comes against a shoulder

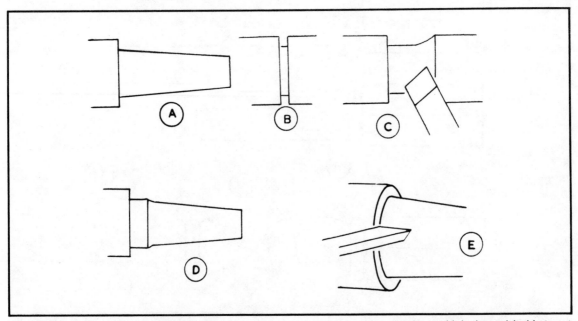

Fig. 8-6. One place where it is difficult to use a chisel from high to low is with an angle, and it is then advisable to cut in with a parting tool and use a scraper for the last part.

Fig. 8-7. These parts of a candlestick are mounted on mandrels through holes for turning between centers.

(Fig. 8-6A). The correct way to turn a taper or any shaped part is from the higher to the lower, from the thicker to the thinner. This is particularly so when using a chisel. A chisel used "downhill" is working with the grain. If an attempt is made to cut up the slope most woods will break out, leaving a rough surface or splinters coming away.

In this example, the shoulder should be cut in, probably with a parting tool at first, then the edge cleaned with a chisel (Fig. 8-6B). The tapered part is roughened to shape with a gouge and the part against the shoulder turned parallel with a skew chisel cutting towards the shoulder (Fig. 8-6C). The greater part of the taper is then turned (Fig. 8-6D). It is possible to get fairly close to the shoulder if cuts are made with the part of the chisel edge near the long point, but care is needed to prevent the point from going below the surface of the taper, or catching in the shoulder. In both cases that would ruin the work.

This leaves a short part of the taper to be removed next to the shoulder, and it will have to be done by scraping. In general, it is bad practice to scrape wood turning between centers, but there is no alternative here. The tool can be a scraper normally used for faceplate turning, or an ordinary woodworking firmer chisel can be used (Fig. 8-6E). Its edge would not last long for much scraping, but it will stand up to this small amount of work.

ARBORS AND MANDRELS

Many holding devices can be improvised, but a simple one for mounting between centers to hold hollow work is called an *arbor* or *mandrel*. It is an oddment of wood turned to a slight taper that will push into a hole in the wood to be turned and drive it by friction. Simple examples are the candleholder and drip ring that will mount on the doweled top of a spindle candlestick (Fig. 8-7). The blanks should be cut approximately to the outline or at least made octagonal; otherwise, the first cuts on the outside may overcome friction and cause the work to slip.

Cut the blank for the ring and drill it. Mount a piece of wood in the lathe. Length is not important, but if the hole is comparatively small, so that the arbor will be slender, keep it no longer than necessary to conveniently hold the work. Otherwise, there may be trouble with vibration. Turn the wood to a taper with the tailstock end slightly less than the size of the hole (Fig. 8-8A). Keep the taper quite gradual.

Mark the end of the wood and the driving center so they will be put together the same way after separating to fit the blank. Take the arbor out of the lathe and push or drive the blank on (Fig. 8-8B). Turning the work (Figs. 8-8 and 8-9) may damage the arbor as tools go over the end onto it, but it should survive for the turning of many drilled blanks, and a stock of arbors to suit different size holes can be kept.

An arbor does not have to go right through the work it supports. It can be used with a hole that is only drilled part way through. If the end of a piece is drilled, possibly for later use with a dowel, an arbor can be turned to push into the hole and pro-

vide something to take the support of the tailstock center (Fig. 8-8C). Or, it can be the driving part at the headstock end, while the work is supported by the tailstock (Fig. 8-8D), depending on which is more convenient for the particular job.

SLENDER WORK

When wood is slim in relation to its length, it is liable to bend under pressure from a tool. Keeping tools sharp and the cuts light will minimize this, but bending causes vibration and this produces uneven cuts and rough surfaces. With extremely slender turnings, the work becomes impossible if nothing is done to stiffen the wood as tools are used on it.

It is sometimes possible to plan the sequence of work, so much of the turning is done while the part that is to be thin and weak is left until later. Keeping it relatively thick until other work is done allows clean cutting without vibration trouble, then

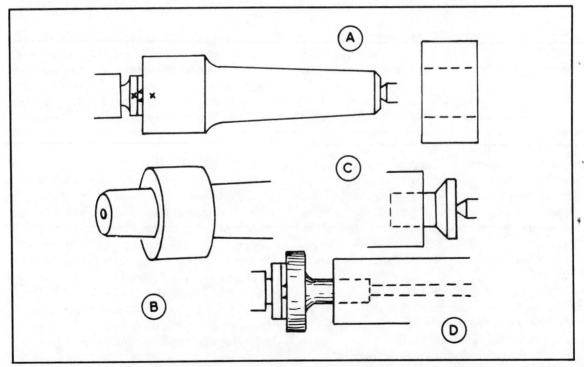

Fig. 8-8. A mandrel can be used for making many small hollow rings. If a drilled end has to be supported, a small plug mandrel can be turned to fit into it.

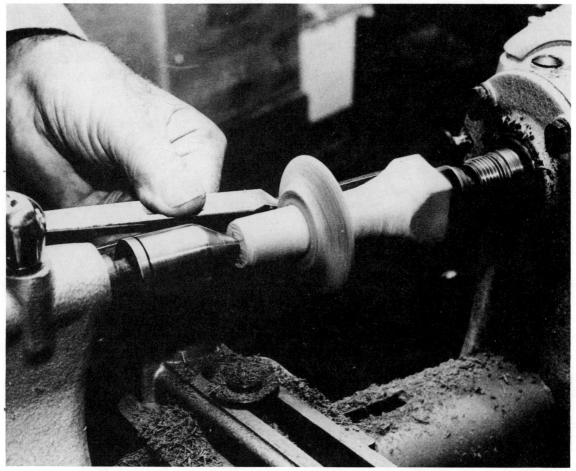

Fig. 8-9. A candlestick drip ring can be turned on both sides while mounted on a mandrel.

only the slender part is left to be dealt with carefully. Much depends on what is being made. If nearly all of the piece being made is slender, this technique cannot be carried far.

For slender items, like drum sticks or conductor's batons, there is no way that you can leave the slender part until all of the other work has been done because the whole thing is slender. The risk of vibrating and possible jumping under cutting loads can be reduced by starting with the wood fairly closely to size. Have a square section only a little too big and plane it octagonal before mounting it in the lathe. You can do some turning near the ends, where the risk of vibration and "juddering" tool marks will be slight, but there is still the

long extent of middle part that will give you trouble. You can probably rough the wood to round with a gouge, without help, but use the tool lightly so vibration marks are kept small. Without support, any attempt to smooth the wood with a chisel will not produce the effect you would get on thicker and stiffer wood. It is likely that you will stop the lathe and see a mass of ridges and hollows diagonally along the wood. The only way to avoid this on wood that is a small diameter in relation to its length is to provide some sort of support.

Some turners steady the wood with their fingers around it and with only their thumb pressing the tool on its tool rest, but care must be taken and it is not really recommended because it could

115

be dangerous. It is better to use some sort of backrest or steady. This presses against the far side of the revolving wood to resist the pushing effect of the tool. The backrest is located so you turn a short length towards it, then it is moved along ready for cutting another short length. If it bears against the wood that has been made round with the gouge but has yet to be turned with a chisel, any marking of the wood by it will be cut off as the chisel does its work.

The simplest backstay is a notched piece of wood. How it is mounted depends on the type of lathe. There may be a way of mounting it on the rear of the tool rest base. Most lathes have a space between the two sides or ways of the lathe bed and the wood can be wedged there (Fig. 8-10A and 8-11). Remove roughness from the surface and edges of the notch to reduce marking the turned wood. A curved notch can be made by drilling a hole and cutting through it (Fig. 8-10B). Choose a size slightly bigger than the diameter of the part of the work to be supported.

The makers of some lathes provide more elaborate steadies. Metal turners need steadies rather more complex than the notched wood and some are quite elaborate. Some have two or three adjustable pieces that bear against the work (Fig. 8-10C). Others have an adjustable notched strip that works like the notched wood, but it is more substantially supported, and with adjustments to get it into the relevant position, the work is more precise. Supports like these may be available for some wood-turning lathes.

A rigid support against the revolving wood causes friction and may wear away the part being turned. In practice, if the backstay is only used briefly on a part not yet finally turned and then moved on, the wear is not enough to matter as it will be cut away. Something that produces less friction by revolving against the work would be better. There are steadies using a pair of rollers pivoted so that they adjust to the work (Fig. 8-10D). If much slender work is to be done, a support of this type could be made from wood.

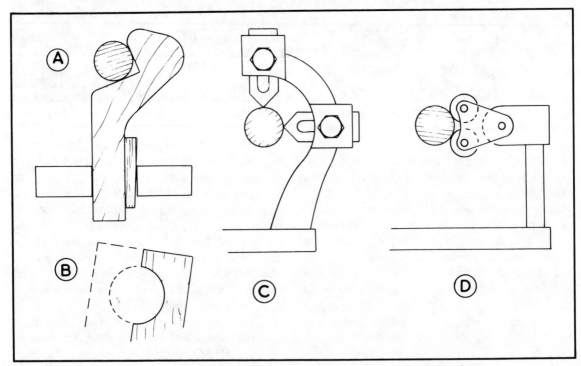

Fig. 8-10. Slender work may be supported with a notched wood steady or a special metal backstay.

Fig. 8-11. A simple notched piece of wood wedged into the lathe bed will support slender turned work.

When the tool rest is brought in close for slender work, there is usually enough of its base projecting to provide a support for a backstay or steady. The example shown (Fig. 8-12) has a support piece tenoned to an upright that is screwed to a metal angle strip. This has a bolt with a butterfly nut and washer underneath to slide in the tool rest slot and provide adjustment.

If the headstock mandrel is hollow and the slender part being turned is thin enough to go through it, a chuck may be used and the wood allowed to project only a short distance. When it is turned, then a little more wood is allowed to project and be turned with the tailstock center brought up for support, until the whole thing has been turned and any slight discrepancies trued by sanding. Even if the slim piece cannot go through the headstock mandrel, there is some advantage in driving the end of the piece with a chuck instead of a fork center because that contributes some stiffness. When sanding slender work, wrap the abrasive paper around the wood and slide it along in your fist,

rather than pull a looped strip from one side and risk bending or breaking the fragile wood.

Care must be taken when turning slender work. It can also be tedious, but some sort of support is needed if the result is to be satisfactory.

BULBOUS TURNINGS

Sometimes a turning has to be made with the center thicker than the ends. If everything is round, this is simple, although wasteful of wood towards the ends, but if it is a bulbous leg with square ends (Fig. 8-13), making it from one piece of wood could be awkward as well as wasteful. The square wood would have to be cut down with a bandsaw or other tool, then the end carefully made square.

With modern strong glues, it is simpler to build up the blank before turning (Fig. 8-14A). It is safer to do the work in two stages. Two pieces are glued on opposite sides, then their edges are planed true, if necessary, before the other two pieces are added. From this point on, turning is done in the usual way. If the bulbous part is large in relation to the lathe,

Fig. 8-12. This backstay is mounted on the end of the tool rest and held with a bolt and butterfly nut, which permits adjustment.

Fig. 8-13. In a bulbous turning, the ends can be reduced to square or the large part can be built up from the end sizes with glued strips.

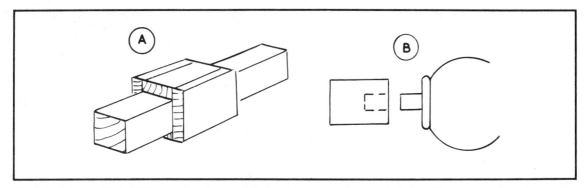

Fig. 8-14. It is possible to build up a piece to make a bulbous leg, or another way is to dowel the large part into short ends.

plane off the corners of the large part before turning to reduce the risk of overloading the motor.

Another way of getting a similar result if the design suits is to make the turned part separate from the square ends and join them together. The central part is made with dowels turned on its ends, then these are glued into holes in the square parts (Fig. 8-14B). Care is needed to see that holes are drilled squarely and the parts are truly in line when the assembly is completed.

SPLIT TURNINGS

Sometimes cabinetwork is decorated with part of a turning glued on. They may be half-turnings (Fig. 8-15A) or something less than that. If half-turnings are wanted, two pieces of wood are joined together for turning and then separated. It is less satisfactory to try to cut down the center of a solid piece of turned wood, as the varied shape of the outline does not offer anything to give even support against a saw guide, and it would be difficult to clean up the sawn surface in any case.

Two pieces of wood are glued together with paper in the joint (Fig. 8-15B). This should hold well enough for turning to be done, but a knife or chisel can be used in the joint to pry the two pieces apart, then the remains of the paper can be scraped or sanded off. To reduce strain on the paper joint, let the driving center go across the joint and not in line with it. At the tailstock end, drill a small hole and countersink it slightly so there is the minimum splitting pressure put into the joint.

It is possible to make quarter-round turnings

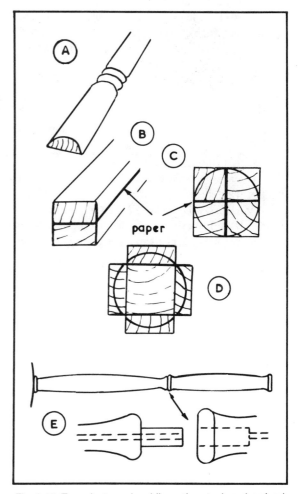

Fig. 8-15. To make turned moldings, the wood can be glued with paper and separated afterwards. If the total length to be made is greater than the capacity of the lathe or auger, parts can be joined together with dowels.

or moldings in a similar way. Four pieces of wood are glued together with paper in the joints (Fig. 8-15C).

Some turned decorations that are fitted to flat surfaces may be quite shallow. They are turned around a square core. The pieces are glued with paper to the four sides, then split off after turning (Fig. 8-15D).

Although some split turnings may be seen on old Jacobean and other furniture with considerable variations in size in the one piece of wood, it is easier to make split turnings when there is not too great a variation between one part and another. There is still scope for much decorative work, but it is not as difficult as something with a large ball shape and slim spindles all in one piece of wood.

LONG WORK

Many things can be made up to the length capacity of the lathe, but in some cases, doing this in one length of wood may not be desirable. If the item being made is slender, vibration may make it difficult or impossible to achieve a good result. If what is wanted is longer than the capacity of the lathe, it is obviously impossible to make the item in one piece. In both cases, it is often possible to build up the length. The slender part may have no

problems if reduced to two pieces approximately half length, while two or more parts can make up almost any reasonable length, whatever the capacity of the lathe.

If you examine a 6-foot tall floor lamp, there will almost certainly be turned beads and other decorations at intervals. If you look closer and examine the grain, you may find differences in grain pattern above and below the decoration. This indicates a joint. Of course, it is possible to make the parts from what was a long length of wood and match the grain at the joint so it cannot be identified, but usually there are some differences. A joint in a plain part would show, but having decorative features around the joint disguises it.

Basically, there is a hole in one part and a dowel turned on the end of the other part. The hole is drilled in the lathe to ensure it being concentric. Beads are turned and the part with the hole in it may be given a slight hollow on the end so the joint comes close on the outside when it is glued (Fig. 8-15E). Making a floor lamp in parts also helps with the problem of drilling a long hole for the wires. This has less risk of wandering when the parts are short, and makes possible total lengths that would be outside the reach of a particular drilling tool in a single length. The method of drilling long holes is described in Chapter 9.

Chapter 9

Open-Ended Spindle Turning and Drilling

There are several things that are turned over the lathe bed that have hollow ends. Examples are eggcups, vases, and cylindrical boxes. They differ from bowls that are turned on a faceplate because they usually have the grain lengthwise, where the majority of faceplate turned items have the grain across. Such open-ended articles can often be turned with support from the tailstock center at certain stages, but the hollow has to be worked when the wood is supported and driven only from the headstock end. There are other things that may not be hollowed, but they have to be turned with something like a ball or point on the end, which are better completed with the tailstock withdrawn. Knobs and finials are examples.

The most common method of mounting the wood is on a screw center or chuck. There are several variations (see Chapter 3). If much of this type of work is to be done, it is advisable to get a screw center that can take an ordinary wood screw because the solid type becomes useless if its built-in screw wears away. Try to have one with the disc backing large enough to have two or three screw holes, then the fitment can be used as a small faceplate or screws driven into a large cylindrical block for extra support and drive. If there is any choice, get a screw center to screw on the mandrel nose. The type that relies on the friction of a Morse taper is satisfactory for turning small work, but it may slip when the tool is cutting something that is 3 inches in diameter. A screw center is a versatile drive for wood, and you may find more uses for it than originally expected.

When wood is to be mounted on a screw chuck, its end should be true as security, and its drive should come from bearing against the plate as well as from the screw thread. This means that it is advisable to mount the wood between centers with what will be the driven end at the tailstock end, then turn it round and square the end (Fig. 9-1A). With this end prepared, turn the wood about and screw it tightly on to the screw chuck. It may be necessary to drill the wood to make the screw enter fully. Obviously, the screw needs to be as tight as possible, so it should screw its own way into the wood with the minimum help from predrilling. Countersink the

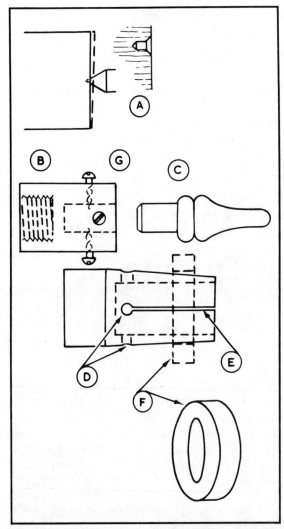

Fig. 9-1. A countersink hole makes a good bearing for a center. Chucks can be improvised from wood for special holding purposes.

bought for some lathes. It is also possible to make a cup chuck with wood. It is unlikely that it can be screwed to go on a mandrel nose, but wood can be mounted on a faceplate or on a screw chuck and turned back to leave a projecting piece that is turned or drilled from the tailstock to make a hole to suit the size of the work. This is useful for such things as decorative knobs or finials that will fix with projecting dowels. The wood can be partly turned between centers, so the dowels are made and some of the decoration in the circumference is done. Then, the dowel end can be pushed into the improvised cup chuck for finishing the end (Fig. 9-1C).

Such a cup chuck depends on accurate turning of the part to be fitted into it because there is no adjustment. This is not difficult, but if there can be a slight variation of size, minor inaccuracies can be taken care of. A split or pinch chuck can be made. This is turned in the same way as the wooden cup chuck on a faceplate. Mark it so it can be replaced in the same position after removing. Mark around the chuck for four, six, or eight holes near the full depth of the hole (Fig. 9-1D). If there is a dividing head on the lathe, accurate spacing is easy; but if the hole positions have to be marked freehand or stepping with dividers, slight discrepancies will not matter. Four holes may be enough for a little chuck, up to about 1/2 inch capacity, but a greater number is better for larger chuck. Turn the outside to a gradual taper, so the edge of the opening is only about 1/8 inch thick. Saw into the holes (Fig. 9-1E).

Make a hole in another piece of wood to push over the chuck so it will squeeze it. Turn the outside smooth while held on an arbor. Pushing this onto the tapered chuck will allow enough adjustment of the bored hole to give a good grip (Fig. 9-1F). If a metal ring or piece of tube can be found in a suitable size, the outside of the chuck can be turned to suit that instead of having to make a wooden ring.

For a simple improvised cup chuck slipping can be prevented by one or more wood screws driven into the work (Fig. 9-1G). This damages the chuck so it would not do if it was intended for prolonged

hole slightly. This prevents the build-up of fibers around the hole, which might interfere with the end bedding tightly against the pad.

Another means of supporting and driving some work is to use a cup chuck. This screw on the mandrel nose and has a hole in it (Fig. 9-1B). The wood is first turned so a waste end will make a push fit in the cup chuck. Drive is then by friction and the waste end is cut off as the last step in turning. Metal cup chucks to screw on the mandrel nose may be use with a great many jobs, but if it is an improvisation for just a few items, it is worthwhile.

Another variation is a coil grip chuck available for some lathes. This is a combination tool that can be used as a screw chuck or a cup chuck, or the back can be used as a small faceplate. The particular value of the coil grip chuck is in the method of positively gripping the end of a piece of wood that has been turned with a shoulder that is then held very tightly when a screwed sleeve is rotated. Any wood to be held for turning in this way has to have its end first turned to suit between centers. The result is considered worthwhile by experienced turners.

One of the best ways of holding work by the end is to use a self-centering chuck (Fig. 3-13). Although these chucks are available to suit the threaded mandrel nose of most lathes, they are not as popular as they might be with expert wood turners. Maybe the feeling is that a self-centering chuck is a piece of metal turning equipment and therefore inappropriate to wood turning. Such a chuck is more expensive than some other types de-scribed, but it positively centers and firmly grips round wood. Because there are three jaws, it does not match four-sided wood, but if the wood is rough-turned round for just the end that will go in the chuck, the jaws grip firmly and concentrically. The waste in the chuck is usually turned off as the last step. The jaws tend to mark the wood they grip. This may not matter if the end is to be a dowel—in fact, the pressed hollows from the jaws could be regarded as ways for air and glue to squeeze out of the final joint. Most self-centering chucks have a second set of jaws for gripping larger work, so it is possible to hold discs up to perhaps 6 inches in diameter, which could be an alternative to a faceplate for some bowls and similar work. Hollow articles can be gripped from inside in a better way than is possible with other holding devices.

EGGCUP

There are a great many hollow articles that can be made on the lathe, but an eggcup (Fig. 9-2) is popular and the steps in making it are similar to those needed for other hollowing. If an eggcup is

Fig. 9-2. The inside of an eggcup may be shaped with a small gouge followed by a scraper.

made according to the following steps, other hollowed work can usually be made with similar technique.

- Allow a little excess length on the piece of wood. Close-grained wood, such as beech or sycamore, are least troublesome for early attempts. Avoid too great a length as the further the overhang, the greater the load on the chuck. If a screw chuck is to be used, 1/4 inch extra length is plenty. If a self-centering cup or coil grip chuck is used, allow enough to enter the chuck and about 1/4 inch outside to what will be the bottom of the eggcup.
- Prepare the end of the wood. In most cases, this involves mounting the wood between centers and turning the end towards the tailstock (Fig. 9-1A).
- Reverse the wood and grip it with the chuck. The tailstock can be brought up to support the wood while the outside is turned cylindrical, but after that it will be kept out of the way. If the outer end is uneven, turn it true.
- It is inadvisable to turn the outside to its final shape, at least in the vicinity of the part that will be hollowed. Making the hollow can put a bursting strain on the wood, so as much wood as possible should be left to resist this until a satisfactory internal shape has been obtained.
- It is possible to turn the hollow entirely with a handheld tool, but it may help to remove some of the waste with a drill in the tailstock chuck. This need not be a large hole, but a 1/2 inch hole is enough to give the tool an entry (Fig. 9-3A).
- Internal work is best done with a scraper. Some workers use a gouge for early removal of waste but there is a risk of digging in and cracking or damaging the wood. The scraper cuts on the near side of the hollow, so its end should be shaped to cut on that side (Fig. 9-3B).
- Have the tool rest across the end of the work and below center height. Tilt the scraper down slightly and adjust its angle of approach to the work so it cuts efficiently. At first some of the hollowing will have to be done from the mouth of the hole inward, but as the shaping pro-

gresses do as much as possible from the bottom of the hole outward, because this works with the grain (Fig. 9-3C) and gives a better cut as well as a smoother finish.
- Eggs vary in size and the hollow will have to be a compromise. Of course, the best template is an actual egg—if you are prepared to risk it. Alternatively, make a paper template, either from an egg outline or from another eggcup, which is known to be satisfactory (Fig. 9-3D).
- On the outside do any turning near the rim first; otherwise, thinning near the chuck may cause vibration problems at the open end. Shape as required with a gouge (Fig. 9-3E). If there is to be much decoration in the thinner neck, the gouge will also be the finishing tool, but for the large sweeps round the bowl, it is better to use a skew chisel. Use a parting tool to make a shallow cut to show where the final base will be. Round the mouth of the cup.
- If the inside was lastly lightly scraped with a sharp scraper from the bottom outward, the finish should be quite good and not require sanding. Sand the rounded mouth of the cup and the outside if necessary. Part off the eggcup to leave the bottom slightly hollow (Fig. 9-4).

An alternative way to deal with the base of the eggcup is to prepare the slightly hollowed end when turned at the tailstock. Use a pad of thin plywood against the screw center when the wood is mounted, then turn the eggcup, and there is no waste wood to part off (Fig. 9-3F). The screw hole remaining in the base will not matter.

BURNING

It is possible to decorate some turned wood articles, particularly open-ended ones such as this eggcup and various jars and pots, by burning. It sounds rather drastic, but is actually charring the wood so dark rings show. Charring is most effective when done on a light-colored hardwood to provide contrast. At least two methods of charring are possible.

If a piece of scrap wood is pressed against the finished rim of an eggcup or similar open item while

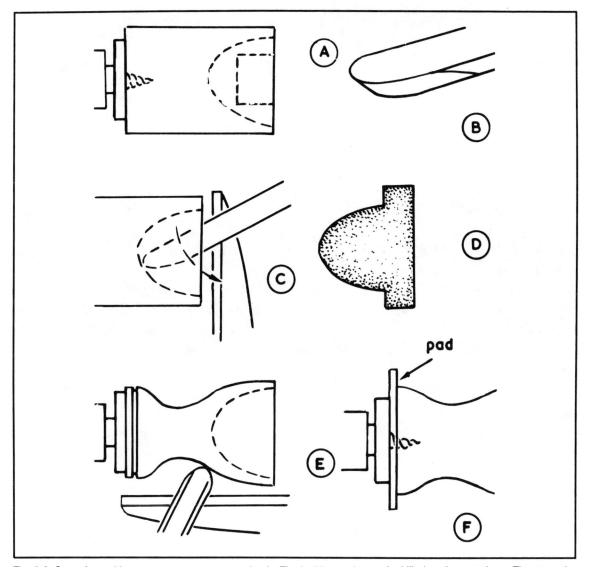

Fig. 9-3. Steps for making an eggcup on a screw chuck. The inside can be partly drilled and scraped out. Then turn the outside in the usual way, either with scrap wood allowed at the end or a pad between the eggcup and the chuck.

it is revolving in the lathe, friction will generate heat so the wood chars and darkens (so will the scrap wood) (Fig. 9-5A). Watch progress and stop in good time.

The other method uses wire to burn in and emphasize cut lines around the wood, such as those on the eggcup (Fig. 9-4). Cut in the lines with the long point of a skew chisel or a V tool. Hold a reasonable length of fine iron wire by its ends so

you stretch and press it down on to a line of the revolving wood (Fig. 9-5B). Friction will make the wire hot and burn into the little groove, darkening it. If the wire is short, you will burn your hands as well. It would be an advantage for stretching and for comfort to wrap the ends of the wire round pieces of dowel or to take it through holes in them (Fig. 9-5C and 9-6).

In both cases, lightly sand the wood near the

Fig. 9-4. The completed eggcup is parted from the waste piece attached to the screw center.

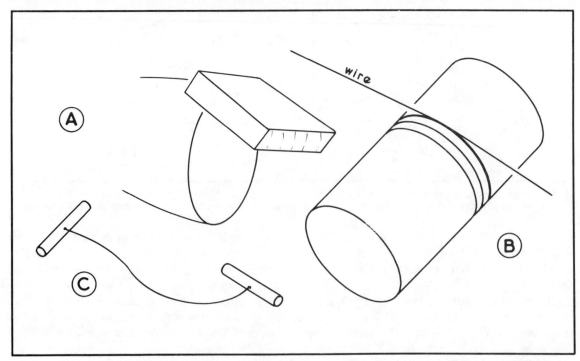

Fig. 9-5. Wood may be charred with the friction of wood pressed on an edge or by a piece of wire pressed into cut lines.

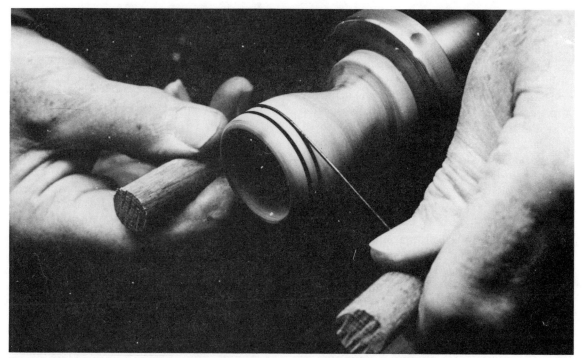

Fig. 9-6. Darkening the cut lines around an eggcup by charring is done with the friction of a piece of wire.

charring to preserve its light color. Varnish or other clear finish will emphasize the contrast.

DRILLING

It may be advisable to differentiate between the meaning of the words *drilling* and *boring*. Most woodworkers use the words for the same thing—making holes with a drill bit. An engineer uses the term *boring* to indicate a method of internal turning with a tool mounted in a slide rest on a lathe, while *drilling* is only making holes with a drill bit. A woodturner follows the woodworking custom of using either name, but it is probably wiser to use only the term *drilling* when that is what is meant.

To conform to metal turning custom, hollowing with a handheld tool might be called *boring*, but use of this word is not yet general practice. It may be more convenient to make a hole, such as would be required in the base of a table lamp, with a tool held in the hand. It is possible to use an ordinary skew chisel to first make a triangular hollow, then turn it in line and go straight in. Occasional cuts

toward the middle will remove waste. It is better to have a scraper tool sharpened with a skew end and relieved on the side. This shape is for turning over the lathe bed. For use on the outboard end of the headstock it would be made the other way. An advantage of boring with a hand tool instead of a drill in a tailstock chuck is that the hole can be adjusted to any size. If the doweled end to fit it is made first, it can be used to check progress as the hole is opened out.

Drilling turned work away from the lathe may be done with any of the usual drill bits, but when holes are drilled in the lathe, this is the equivalent of power drilling, and it is important to use correct bits. Wood bits intended for use in a brace or other hand-powered driver are unsuitable and could behave dangerously.

Where the drill is rotated by the headstock mandrel and the work is stationary, the process is the same as using a drilling machine, but a pad should be mounted in the tailstock (Fig. 9-7A). A piece of scrap wood should be put over it to prevent damage if the bit breaks through. Most drilling is the other way around with the wood, which has usually just been turned to shape, revolving and the drill stationary in a drill chuck in the tailstock.

For small holes that do not have to be given a clean finish, metalworking Morse pattern twist drills can be used up to about 1/2 inch in diameter (Fig. 9-8), which is usually the maximum capacity of a suitable drill chuck. It is possible to obtain these drills on Morse taper shanks so they will go directly into the hollow of the tailstock. It is more usual for them to have parallel shanks to go in an adjustable chuck, however. Standard sizes of these drills have a certain length with each diameter, being longer with the larger diameters. It is possible to get overlong drills, but normally maximum depths are rather limited, although it is often possible to double the depth by working from each end.

There are woodworking bits that look like metalworking bits, but the ends are sharpened to cut clean outlines to the holes (Fig. 9-8). They are excellent bits, but have the same limitations of depth as the metalworking bits.

Another type of power bit looks like a brace twist bit, but the central point is without a screw and the cutters are designed to cut a high speed without seizing or pulling in (Fig. 9-7B). A greater length than normal metalworking bits are available.

Another type of power bit is generally known as a flatbit (Fig. 9-8). This is intended for high speeds when it cuts cleanly. It is not intended to be taken very deeply as it might wander, but for a few inches deep it will make a satisfactory hole. Some bits can be withdrawn while the work is still turning, but it is safer to stop the lathe and remove the bit with the accumulated wood dust.

Sawtooth bits are obtainable in all sizes likely to be needed on shanks that fit drill chucks (Fig. 9-7C and 9-8) because there are cutters all around the circumference, the bits cut cleanly and with little pressure. These bits, like all the others described

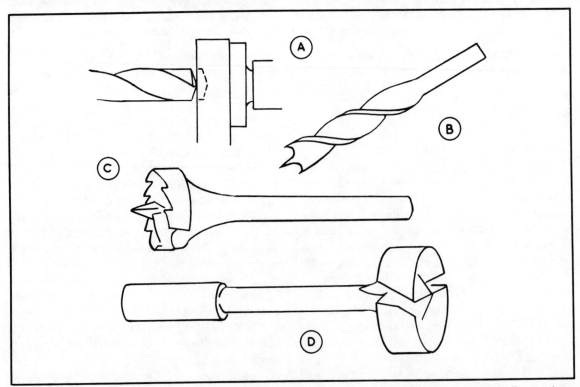

Fig. 9-7. A metalworking drill can be used in small sizes, but one with a spur point is better in larger sizes. For very large holes, a sawtooth drill is useful (C), while a Forstner bit will make a hole without a spur center mark (D).

Fig. 9-8. A drill bit sharpened for wood cuts a cleaner hole than the metal-cutting bit of similar appearance. A flatbit will drill large shallow holes, but the sawtooth bit cuts cleaner at greater depth. The combination bit drills and countersinks to suit lathe centers.

so far, have a central spike that goes ahead of the other cutters and so leaves a hollow at the center of any hole drilled part way through (*blind hole*). This may not matter in most circumstances, but in some cases, it would be better to have the hole finished with an absolutely flat bottom. The only bit that will do this is a Forstner pattern one.

A Forstner bit is guided by its circular rim and not by a central extended point (Fig. 9-7D). It can be used by hand or power, but with power its speed should be kept lower than is usual with other bits. It is not intended for great depths, but for moderate depths it makes the cleanest hole and leaves a flat bottom. It is also one of the most expensive bits.

All of the bits so far described are only suitable for comparatively short drilling. It may be possible, for instance, to make a hole for wires in a floor lamp by drilling from opposite ends up to perhaps 10 inches, but drill lengths make that the limit. The bits are particularly useful for drilling hollows into work held by a screw chuck or other holding arrangement when the whole thing is short in relation to its length. They can be used to make holes

for dowels when one turned part has to fit into another. They will make holes in tool handles that will then assemble to a blade so both handle and tool are truly in line.

The problem of making very long holes, as in wind instruments and tall floor lamps, calls for special bits and ways of controlling them. As wood is a natural material, its characteristics vary, and a bit going into a long length may strike a hard or soft patch that will deflect it from its course if it is not very rigidly guided. This means that a deep drilling bit cannot be made to work successfully by merely lengthening the shank of some of the bits that are very good in shallow holes.

A deep-boring bit needs a considerable parallel length behind the cutting end so this rubs inside the part already drilled and keeps the cutters on course, even when unevenness of grain is met. There are augers available for deep drilling (Fig. 9-9A). Lengths vary, but 24 to 30 inches are usual with diameters between 1/4 and 1/2 inch. Twice this length of hole is possible if the wood can be reversed. The long parallel part of the auger, which is hollowed to take the wood chips, is backed by a solid shank that finishes in a tang to fit into a wooden handle. It may have sufficient grip if it is like a file handle on a small diameter auger, but if more leverage is required, the tang can be pushed into a piece of wood arranged crosswise. When an auger is used, it should not be advanced more than the depth of the parallel part each time, then it is withdrawn and wood chips removed.

Because the auger is probably as long as the lathe bed, it would be impossible to use one in a drill chuck in the tailstock, so deep drilling has to be done with the auger through the tailstock or with the tailstock removed. How this is done depends on the particular lathe. It is advisable to get the equipment intended for use with the lathe you have.

For some lathes there is a guide or auxiliary tailstock that can be mounted in the tool rest socket after the rest has been removed. This is adjustable in height and can be fitted with bushings of various sizes (Fig. 9-9B). To get it correctly lined up with the work, there is a center finder, like an extended center, that fits in the tailstock. It is used to go through the bushing while all adjustments on the

guide and tool rest support are slackened. With the correct position obtained and all screws tightened, the hole through the bushing is true with the centers of the lathe and the wood mounted in it (Fig. 9-9C). Bushings have to be matched to the diameter auger being used. The end of the bushing is shaped like a ring center and a removable pin is provided to accurately center the wood. The center finder point can also be used for this purpose.

The work will already have a dent at its center from where it was supported during turning by the normal tailstock center. If that was a cup center, it is possible there will be a ring that will match the ring of the new bushing. In any case, bring the guide close to the work and engage the bushing with the wood tightly so the ring presses in. Back out and remove the pin or center finder. Re-engage the ring center, but not quite as tightly, and lightly lubricate it.

Push the auger through the hole in the bushing. Start the lathe and feed in the auger with hand pressure. The speed of the lathe and the feed depend on the wood, but it is wise to go slowly in order to reduce the risk of the tool overheating and

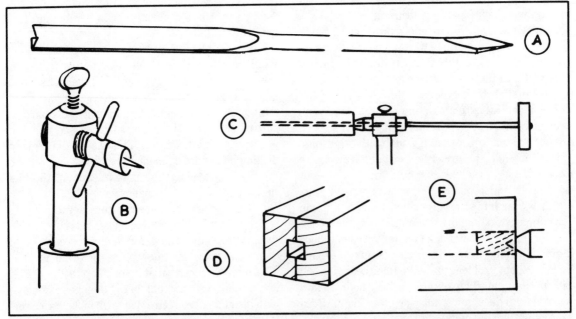

Fig. 9-9. Pictured above is the equipment used for drilling holes in wood. One way of making a long hole without this equipment is to plow grooves in two facing pieces that are glued together.

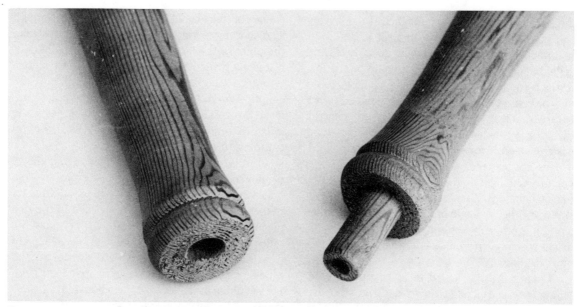

Fig. 9-10. A dowel joint between long drilled parts is disguised by beads on the meeting parts.

its temper being drawn. Feed in the auger until it has penetrated the length of the parallel part behind the cutting edge. Stop the lathe and withdraw the tool. If it is used with the hollow upwards that will help in pulling out the wood chips. With the hole clean, enter the auger again and go in the same amount further before withdrawing and clearing chips again. Either measure along the auger or mark its shank at appropriate intervals so you withdraw at the correct points.

Consider the speed of deep drilling. The cutting end is working where it gets no ventilation and there is often a back-up of waste wood behind the edge. Even if chips are cleared properly, the steel and wood get hot, so much so that the temper could be drawn from the tool or smoke start emerging from the hole as the wood inside chars. To avoid this, have the lathe at its slowest speed—under 1000 rpm is advisable—and withdraw and clear the tool frequently. In an extreme case, with too high a speed and chips building up, the tool could seize in the wood, which may burst, wrecking the job even if the consequences are not more serious.

Drill more than halfway from one end, then reverse the wood and drill the other way. How the reversed wood is driven depends on the design. If it is a floor lamp, there will almost certainly be a dowel to fit into the base. If this starts at the tailstock end, it can be gripped by a chuck when it is reversed. It may be possible to put a temporary plug in the drilled hole and use an ordinary driving center. The end may be pushed into a cup chuck, turned for the purpose on a faceplate. With some deep drilled work, it may be advisable to allow for a waste cylindrical end to be left on for holding, then it is cut off after the hole has been taken right through. There are counterboring bits that have a projecting stem to go into a hole. The extending cutters around it are intended for making an enlarged entrance to the hole. One of these is very much like a normal driving center, except for the central stem, and it could be used to drive a reversed piece of wood with the stem providing accurate centering in the hole.

If the auger is almost as long as the wood being drilled, it is possible to drill almost all the way from one end. Obviously care is needed, particularly if the wood is being driven by the usual pointed and serrated driving center, as the auger and point meeting would damage both parts. Work to careful measurements and take the auger to something like 1 inch of the full depth, then remove the work from the lathe and drill the short distance at the driving end with a brace and bit or an electric drill.

The stage in turning when deep holes are drilled depends on the design. It could be that external turning is completed before drilling, but it may be better to drill through before the detail work is turned. Then, if the hole is not exactly central, the outside can be turned to suit it. Of course, for passing an electric cable through a lamp standard, it does not matter if the hole wanders slightly. If you are making a hole for a metal axle in a roller, for instance, this must be concentric with the outside and is better made first. For much long drilled work, it is probably better to turn the outside cylindrical with a gouge but leave other shaping until after drilling.

If parts will be joined to make up a greater length, one end needs a dowel and the other has to be counterbored to take it (Fig. 9-10). The counterboring should be done after drilling through it. A short temporary plug in the small hole will take the point of the larger drill and can be pulled out if it is not drilled away. For turning after counterboring, a plug can be turned to push into the counterbore to take the center. At the other end, if the through hole diameter is less than that of the tailstock center, it may run directly on it, or you can plug to take a finer center point.

If it is impossible to design a piece that allows drilling right through, the only alternative is to make the wood to be turned in two parts glued together. Grooves or dadoes are worked in the two pieces to make the hole (Fig. 9-9D). To make the glued joint inconspicuous, it may be possible to cut down one piece of wood, make the grooves, and glue the parts together so the grain matches. Temporary plugs in the ends of the wood allow it to be centered for turning (Fig. 9-9E).

Chapter 10

Beginning Faceplate Turning

In spindle turning (turning between centers), the wood is nearly always greater in its length than in its diameter, its grain runs in its length, and it is supported in most cases by a tailstock center as well as a driving center or chuck. The name is still applied when there is support at one end only, but the grain is still lengthwise. If the wood is of greater diameter than length, it is normally driven by mounting it on a faceplate. Usually the grain runs in the direction of a diameter. This type of work may be described as faceplate turning, although it is often called *bowl turning* as bowls are probably the most common things made this way.

At one time, bowl turners and spindle turners tended to be specialists who did not overlap onto each other's work. There is no longer sufficient demand for bowls only or spindle products only, so professional turners have to be adaptable—amateur turners certainly find most satisfaction in tackling all branches of turning. For faceplate turning, there is no need for a long bed, and there are still lathes available that have short or no beds, and these are used in production of faceplate turnings only. Most woodturners have lathes suitable for both types of turning and an outboard mounting for a faceplate gives a normal lathe almost as much scope for bowl and other faceplate turning as a short-bed lathe.

With the grain across the work, it is obvious that any cutting on the circumference will be alternating with and against the grain. Any attempt to slice with a skew chisel would result in digging in where the grain opposed the cut. To a lesser, but still significant, extent attempting to cut on the surface with a slicing tool would be disastrous (Fig. 10-1A). The problem of alternating grain direction in relation to the tool becomes more noticeable as the diameter gets larger. This is why gouges are used for roughing to shape, then finishing is done with scraper tools as described later in this chapter. Chisels, as used for work between centers, have no real use in faceplate turning, except for a few minor roles.

The use of a screw center has already been described and this has some use in holding small diameter work with the grain across. However, this would have to be supplemented with screws

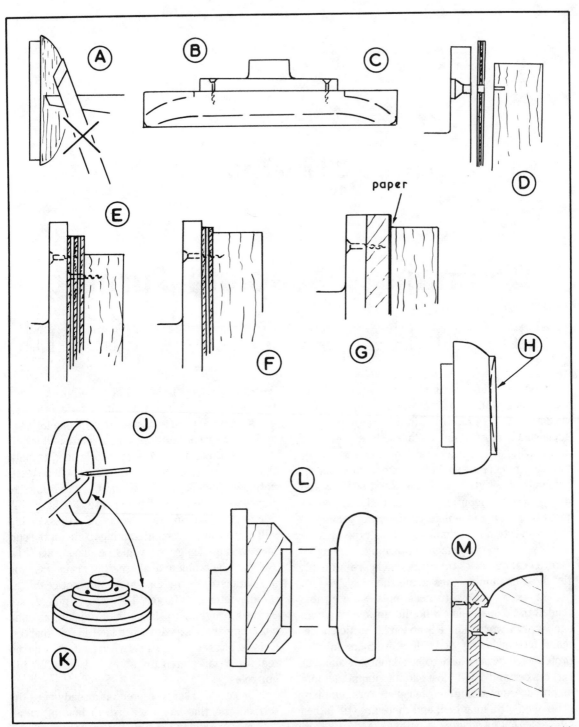

Fig. 10-1. A bowl is turned by mounting on a faceplate, usually by screwing through a pad, although it can be glued with paper in the joint. The pad is then turned down to fit the base of some bowls.

through its pad, so it then functions as a small faceplate. There are some other ways of holding work, but nearly always the basic support is a faceplate.

The work may be mounted directly on the faceplate (Fig. 10-1B). Normally, four screws are used. The layout of holes or slots usually allows for this (Fig. 10-2). There is too much risk of moving if a lesser number of screws are used. This method is satisfactory if the wood is of a larger diameter than the faceplate (Fig. 10-1C) and no work has to be done on the surface in contact with the faceplate.

If all or part of the work goes down to a lesser diameter than the faceplate there is a risk of damaging a tool or the faceplate if the wood is fixed directly. In that case, there may be a wood pad between the work and the faceplate. This could be a plywood disc with the work fixing screws going through it (Fig. 10-1D), or it may be mounted independently and turned true before using more screws to hold the work. In this case, the work may be mounted on the pad only (Fig. 10-1E) or longer screws taken through from the faceplate (Fig. 10-1F).

Screws into a base do not usually matter. The holes that are left can be plugged or hidden under cloth or another base covering. If screw holes must be avoided, it is possible to glue the work to a pad with paper in the joint (Fig. 10-1G). This should hold well enough, but a knife or chisel into the paper will separate the parts when the work is finished and the surplus paper can be scraped or sanded off.

If work has to be done on both sides of the wood, it will be necessary to reverse the wood on the faceplate. This brings problems of concentricity—the second side may not exactly match the first side, so a bowl would have thick and thin parts. For a bowl or other turning of similar form, it is best to turn the outside first.

The block of wood is screwed directly to the faceplate, then the outside turned. It helps if the base that is to come against the faceplate when the wood is reversed is turned very slightly hollow (Fig. 10-1H) so it beds on the metal or pad around its circumference, with no risk of the wobble that could

occur if it was inadvertently rounded the other way. It also helps to hold a pencil against the revolving wood and draw a circle slightly bigger than the faceplate or pad (Fig. 10-1J). When the wood is reversed, this circle helps in getting the bowl mounted accurately (Fig. 10-1K) for work on the other side, which means hollowing in the case of a bowl.

Mounting in this way depends on careful sighting of circle and faceplate rim and slight inaccuracies are almost inevitable, although they may not be enough to matter. Greater precision can be obtained by turning the pad to match the reversed wood. How this is done depends on the particular project, but if a bowl has a parallel part at the base, it is possible. The outside of the bowl is turned on the faceplate, then removed. A pad is mounted on the faceplate and a hollow turned in it to match the

Fig. 10-2. A circle drawn on the sawn disc helps center the faceplate, which should be screwed tightly.

base of the bowl (Fig. 10-1L). This needs careful work until the bowl block can be driven in with a mallet, so the friction drive is good enough to stand up to the work of turning the inside. If even greater security is required, screws can be taken through (Fig. 10-1M). Paper and glue can be used, but the pad may have to be broken away to separate the parts.

If screws are used, they need to be long enough to hold well, but not so long that they will come through when the wood is hollowed. Holes for the screws should not be drilled out any more than is necessary. The more a screw has to force its way into the wood, the tighter its grip should be. In some woods, it is possible to start a screw by tapping with a hammer, then it will cut its way in. In other woods, a small hole may have to be drilled first. A stout gauge screw that matches the faceplate hole as closely as possible is better than an undersize one that may permit movement during turning.

For bowls and other hollow turning, you can do much by observation, but it is useful to have a depth gauge, which is described in Chapter 4 (Fig. 4-29). Without this gauge, however, you can still measure using a straight piece of wood across the rim (Fig. 10-3A). A dowel rod through a hole in a strip (Fig. 10-3B) may be better, particularly if there are several hollows to compare. Slipping can be prevented with a screw (Fig. 10-3C).

A problem with turning wood with the grain across is the tendency to warp and shrink if the wood had not been properly seasoned. This sometimes happens even with apparently well-seasoned wood when a bowl with thin walls is turned from what was quite a thick piece of solid wood. The wood is then affected by moisture in the atmosphere. In production work, bowls are often rough turned and left to dry out and settle into shape. The roughed bowl is left considerably thicker than it will eventually be. This may warp or twist and will almost certainly shrink across the grain so its outline is slightly elliptical. When the turner judges that movement has ceased (maybe several months), he mounts the bowl in the lathe again and turns it true.

If a bowl is to be made from a block of wood believed to have been properly seasoned and it is to have a reasonable thickness, it can be made completely as one process. If there is any doubt or it is to be turned to a thin section, it is worthwhile to put it aside for a few days after the first rough turning to check if it is likely to go out of shape.

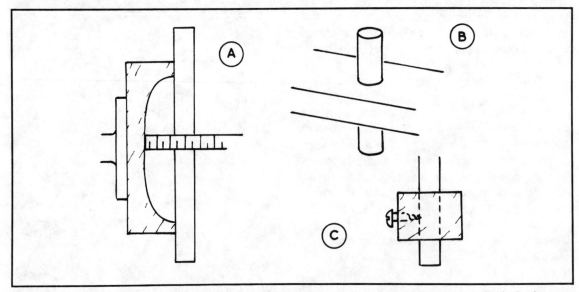

Fig. 10-3. The depth of a hollow in a bowl can be checked by measuring from a crossbar or using a simple depth gauge with a dowel through it.

Then it can be mounted in the lathe again and final cuts made to take out any unevenness. With faceplate turnings that have a general overall greater thickness, there is no need to allow a pause for possible warping or distortion. Unless the wood is unseasoned or only partly seasoned, there should be no risk of things like bases for pedestals, round table tops, and other items that do not taper anywhere to a very thin section going out of shape to any appreciable extent after being made on a lathe.

At one time bowl making as a craft was practiced amongst the trees where the wood was obtained, using primitive lathes operated by treadle. Bowls were turned from newly-felled wood that was completely unseasoned and full of sap. Wood in this state is more easily cleft or split, which had one advantage, but a good finish cannot be obtained and a bowl might warp considerably as it dried out. Many of these bowls were used for coins in shops and banks. Coins could be scooped out of a bowl easily and if it was not truly round, it did not matter.

A technique that has almost disappeared with this craft is the way to make more than one bowl from a block of wood. When one bowl is made from a piece of wood a considerable amount of the original wood is taken away as shavings from the inside of the bowl. This may not matter to the amateur making one good bowl, but to the old-time turner such a waste had to be avoided if possible. He did this by using curved scraper tools (Fig. 10-4A). By having tools of different curves, it was possible to turn the outside of the smallest bowl after working its inside in the usual way, then get a chisel inside and split the bowl away (Fig. 10-4B). The inside of the next bowl was cleaned up and its outside turned with the next curved tool, which was split off, leaving the outside bowl to be finished. Three bowls from one block were common (Fig. 10-4C). The two inner bowls needed some hand planing, scraping, or sanding to get them to a reasonable finish. The inside could be good and this treatment produced bowls acceptable for their purpose with the minimum wastage.

The method is unlikely to be satisfactory with dry seasoned wood, but using sap-laden wood almost straight from the tree gave an almost 100 percent success rate at splitting one bowl from the inside of another.

TOOL HANDLING

If the fibers in a piece of wood are thought of as a number of separate straws, it will be seen that

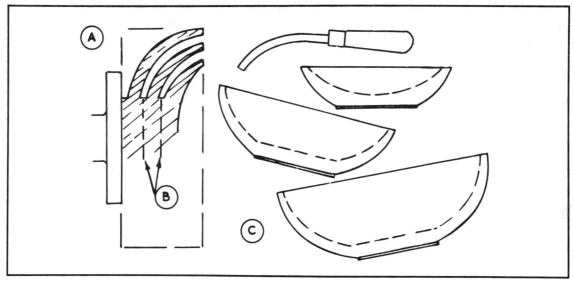

Fig. 10-4. Old-time bowl turners cut several bowls inside each other.

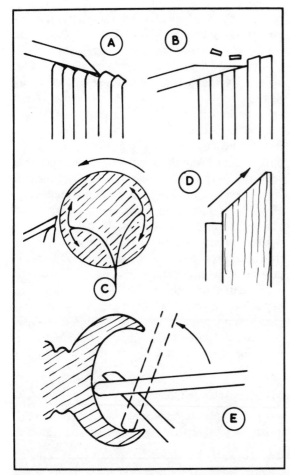

Fig. 10-5. A cut against the grain bends fibers, while a cut with the grain leaves a smooth surface. When turning cross-grained wood, part of it will have to be against the grain, but careful tool manipulation will reduce the trouble.

When a tool is cutting on a parallel circumference, there is nothing that can be done to reduce the tendency of half of the end grain from being against the cut and, therefore, liable to tear up (Fig. 10-5C). If the outline is tapered in cross-section, as it would be in a bowl, working from the smaller to the larger diameter brings a slight advantage of working with half of the end grain (Fig. 10-5D). How much benefit there is in this depends on the amount of taper. It may not be much, but there should be a slightly better surface left from the tool if final cuts are made from the smaller to the larger diameter.

Inside a bowl, some authorities favor cuts from the center outward, while others prefer to work from the rim inward. In fact, most of the hollowing will be done with a combination of the two techniques, but in the final tool work, it can be argued that a better tool finish should result from using a tool that swings around the curve from the center outward (Fig. 10-5E). In practice, there may be little in it, but if the work is stopped and some of the grain seems to be torn up slightly inside the bowl, there is a better chance of eradicating this by using a sharp tool at the correct angle from the bowl center outward than by working from the outside inward. It is largely a case of appreciating the grain structure of wood and developing a "feel" for the material you are turning.

The tools for most faceplate turning, other than small diameter work, ought to be the type most makers describe as "long and strong." There can be considerable leverage on the tool when making a cut on a large diameter, so it is advisable for good work, safety, and ease of handling to have tools that do not flex and that are of sufficient length to allow the leverage due to cutting to be resisted by a hand far enough from the *fulcrum* (the tool rest) to not put undue strain on the operator. For much of the work with a gouge, one hand is over the tool rest with fingers on top so the fist provides a secure hold at that point. The other hand is near the end of the handle, then this hand and the end of the handle can be pressed against the body to provide extra support. What part of the body depends on the angle of the tool, but it is usually the upper part

a cut diagonal to the end grain will tend to turn the straws back instead of cut them (Fig. 10-5A), while a cut the other way does not have as much bending tendency and the cut should be cleaner (Fig. 10-5B). This was seen in spindle turning where cuts from the thicker to the thinner parts of the wood cut more cleanly than any attempt to cut from a hollow outward. In faceplate turning with the grain of the wood across, this tendency to bend back fibers that oppose the tool is more marked. The effect cannot be completely avoided, but a knowledge of the behavior of grain under a tool may help in getting the best result possible in particular circumstances.

of the thigh. The whole body is then in control (Fig. 10-6). As the tool moves around to follow a cut, the operator moves bodily with it and may walk several small steps when dealing with a large turning mounted on the outboard end of the headstock.

So far as possible the tool rest should be quite close to the actual part being cut (Fig. 10-7). This reduces the leverage and is particularly important when taking heavy cuts. Because the tool rest has a straight edge and the work is usually curved, there has to be a compromise. On most lathes, tool rest adjustment can be almost instantaneous, so necessary changes can be made more frequently than some beginners may realize. It is fairly easy to regulate the position of the tool rest when working on an outside surface. When working in a hollow, it may occasionally be necessary to have a tool rest clear of the rim with a large tool overhang. It is possible on many jobs to let the tool rest go inside the hollow, either completely or by getting one end in with the edge askew.

CUTTING AND SCRAPING ANGLES

A cutting tool, such as a gouge or a parting tool, should not be used as a scraper in faceplate turning. It may approach the wood in a scraping attitude, then it is brought up to a cutting angle when the bevel is almost rubbing on the wood (Fig. 10-8A). This is similar to spindle turning. For faceplate turning, a gouge is better for a more obtuse cutting angle (Fig. 10-8B). For roughing work it is found acceptable by many turners to have an edge direct from grinding and not bother to hone the edge with an oilstone. The surface left is not as good as with a honed edge, but at this stage, it

Fig. 10-6. Tools should be held very firmly when turning anything of a large diameter, as in this bowl, where the leverage on the tool has to be resisted by one hand against the tool rest and the other braced against the body.

Fig. 10-7. On the outside of a bowl, the tool should be angled so its bevel is almost flat on the circumference and both hands used to resist leverage and prevent vibration.

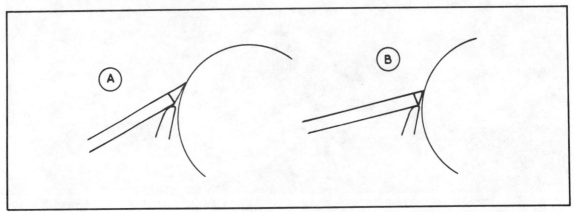

Fig. 10-8. The angle of a gouge against a large bowl should be adjusted according to the amount of bevel on it.

is the removal of waste wood that is more important than getting a quality finish on a surface that has yet to be cut away more. Turning large diameters of some woods soon takes the edge off a tool, so frequent regrinding is necessary and avoiding honing at this stage minimizes delay. For finished surfaces, possibly with the same gouge, the edge should be finished properly on an oilstone and the edge cleaned with a curved slip inside.

When turning the outside of a large diameter piece of wood, the best angle is easily seen with the bevel almost rubbing on the wood. Slight movement of the hands will bring the cutting edge to the optimum position so observation of the shavings or chips coming away tells when the tool is making the best cut. It is not quite so obvious when working inside a large hollow. The cutting angle is less easily seen. The gouge must point upward and not be kept near a horizontal scrape, but the amount of upward slope is best found by feel and observation of the waste wood coming away. Adjust the tool angle until the shavings coming away show a definite cut. When working at the outboard end of the headstock, it is possible to manipulate the tool in any direction without restriction whatever part of a hollow is being cut. With work on a faceplate over the bed, it is sometimes necessary to depart from what may seem the best angle so the tool handle will clear the lathe bed, but even then it is often possible to adjust the tool position and still get a good cut. If a gouge has a rounded end, the side of the cutting edge may be brought to approach the wood with a good cutting angle, while the handle comes clear of the bed, although a similar cutting angle with the center of the edge would have required the handle of the tool to come in an impossible position through the bed.

Scraping is a different technique that follows work with gouges. The tool approaches the wood at a different angle and its purpose is light finishing cuts. Scrapers should not be used for removing large quantities of wood—that is the work of gouges. For large work, scrapers benefit from being "long and strong." There is not always the need for great leverage, but rigidity is important. Any vibration in the tool is transferred as "chatter"

marks on the wood being turned. A scraper must be sharp, and it helps to turn a burr on it as described in the instructions on sharpening. For the best work any tendency to become dull means resharpening. Continuing to scrape with a tool that has developed a rounded edge will only result in a poor surface. Something may be done to it with abrasive paper, but it will not finish with the quality that comes from a sharp tool held at the correct angle.

A scraper may be held with just the thumb on top over the tool rest. The other hand is at the end of the handle and may be braced against the body. The scraping action will set up vibration, even if it is a "long and strong" tool, so bracing against the body does something to counteract this. The best angle for cutting has to be found by experiment and is slightly downward (Fig. 10-9) towards the surface being cut. When a sharp scraper is cutting properly, the waste comes away recognizable as fine shavings (Fig. 10-10). If the angle is wrong or the tool is blunt, the waste comes away as dust. Anyone with experience in using a cabinet scraper on flat wood will see that the need for feeling the correct angle to get true shavings is important.

If a lathe can be reversed, it is possible to do something to remove the effect of stubborn grain, which tears up whatever is done to it the normal way, by lightly scraping when the work is revolving the opposite way. If the tool rest can be mounted at the opposite side, work can be done in the normal way there, or a scraper can be turned upside down on the tool rest in its ordinary position and tilted up so it presents the correct cutting angle (Fig. 10-11A). When a lathe is reversed, the load on the threaded center of the faceplate has an unscrewing effect. Consequently, any tool work should be kept light. Heavy cutting or a sudden digging in could cause the faceplate to unscrew off the spindle nose. A leather or fiber washer behind the faceplate will resist accidental unscrewing. Some workers favor a scraper held in the hand without benefit of a tool rest. The scraper then must be light, and there is little risk of unscrewing a faceplate that has been tightened by work while turning the normal way. The tool can be the usual

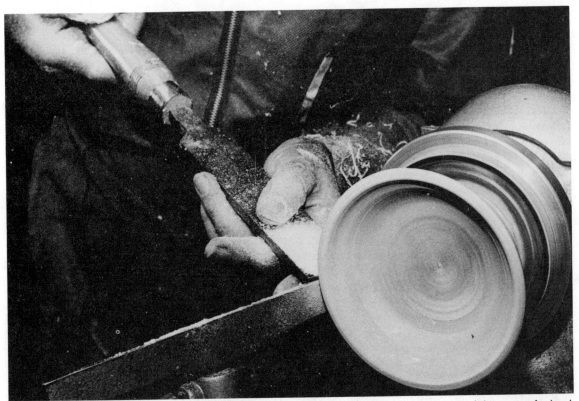

Fig. 10-9. A scraper cuts best when it is pointing slightly downward, then it can be swung around the curve of a bowl to get a smooth finish.

Fig. 10-10. When a scraper is sharp and held at the correct angle, the waste wood comes away as fine shavings.

handled scraper, although this could be a little un-wieldy. It is possible to make or buy a scraper bar, which is just a short length of steel without a handle.

When starting a gouge for an internal cut, there is a risk that it will move sideways and score the surface. It is easier to get a parting tool to make a groove and this will act as a guide for the entry of a gouge (Fig. 10-11B). It should be tilted upward to present a cutting angle and not just act as a scraper. In some constructions, there may be other uses for a parting tool. It can cut in to the required depth as a guide to further shaping and it may be the best tool for cutting an angular recess, although this could be finished if not fully shaped by the cor-ner of a scraping tool.

There is little use for chisels and beading tools in faceplate turning. Because of the risk of digging in opposing grain, a chisel cannot be used with a slicing action on the outside of cross-grained wood and a beading tool would also tend to break out the grain as it was curved over to form the bead. It is better to work a bead with a scraping tool. For a deep bead the end of the tool would be ground to a diamond point so it could get in far enough. For a more shallow bead, it would be possible to do the work with the corner of a square-ended scraper.

The point of a skew chisel may be used to score lines around faceplate turning. It is used with the long end downward in the same way as putting lines around spindle turning. With the comparatively high peripheral speed, pushing the point of a chisel in hard will quickly generate enough heat to burn the wood and take the temper from the steel chisel, so this sort of cutting should be done gently. The point may also be of value in getting into the cor-ner of an angular recess. A parting tool or the square corner of a scraper may fashion the recess, but getting a really sharp internal angle can only be done with a pointed tool. If it is a recess for glass or a lid to fit, a precise angle may be required.

LATHE SPEEDS

Fortunately, lathe speeds are not critical to good faceplate turning, except in a general way, and wide variations can be tolerated. It is important to slow the lathe if faceplate work of much size is to follow spindle turning. For anything more than about 6 inches across, it is better to err towards slow speed than high speed. This means that with most lathes, with three or four steps on the pulley, a middle or high speed may be used for most spin-dle turning, but it is advisable to move to the slowest speed for faceplate turning.

This is particularly important if the work be-ing undertaken is large in relation to the lathe. If it is a fairly light lathe and something of maximum diameter is to be turned, the risk of vibration is con-siderable and this will be aggravated at high speeds.

The problem is greatest before the wood has been turned truly cylindrical. It is usual to saw the

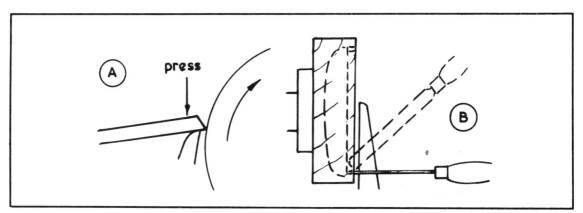

Fig. 10-11. If a lathe can be reversed it is possible to clean off raggedness of cross-grain by using it the other way briefly. For hollowing it is helpful to start the cut with a parting tool.

wood to a reasonably circular shape before mounting in the lathe. This is best done on a bandsaw. By careful cutting, the sawn shape can be very close to a true circle. Even then, it can be mounted slightly out of concentricity so it runs a little out of true, but until its circumference has been cut cylindrical with a gouge, the load on even a substantial lathe can be enough to produce bad, and even dangerous, vibration. If much of this is done there can be wear on the bearings, enough to affect the precision with which the lathe may be expected to perform. This means that, even if a higher speed may be preferred for later turning, the lowest speed possible should be chosen for the first turning of sawn wood.

With large faceplate turning, the surface speed of the wood past the tool is considerably more near the rim than near the center. It is not the usual practice to speed up the lathe for work near the center, but it will be found that cuts have to be much lighter near the rim than towards the center. Vibration, if it persists, is likely to be more towards the rim than near the center. Some slight damping of this can be obtained by first turning the central area only enough to make it round, but leaving the removal of bulk there until later—assuming the center is to be reduced as it would be in a bowl—then work is done to the outer part, either completely or almost to completion, before attention is given again to the center area. A large disc revolving behaves like a flywheel, and leaving a large boss near the center is a help towards smooth running.

Consideration of lathe speed is important to any finishing work. Modern abrasive paper has the grit bonded with a heat and waterproof glue, but pressing a sheet against the outside of a large fast turning piece of wood may cause the paper to tear and disintegrate as well as burn or cut your hand. Use a slow speed for sanding and use only light pressure when working towards the rim. Greater pressure may compensate for the lower surface speed towards the center, but treat the outer part with caution. Good tool work should require little sanding, but it is usual to follow even the best tool turning with light sanding. However, do not tackle large faceplate work with the same degree of pressure on abrasive paper that can be used on spindle turning.

Chapter 11

Faceplate Turning Advanced

Although a great many other things are turned on a faceplate, many of them are parts of other constructions and not so easily defined collectively, so bowl turning, besides being a very satisfactory operation, is also used as a description of faceplate work as a whole. Bowls certainly form the largest part of the output of turners who prefer faceplate turning to spindle turning.

CHOOSING THE WOOD

Most bowls are made from single solid pieces of wood. With the aid of modern glues it is possible to laminate and build up blocks for turning. More about these versions will be given later in Chapter 12, but anyone starting on bowl turning should use solid wood for early attempts. Wood of suitable size for bowls should be selected and kept, possibly when wood is being prepared for other things. A square off the end of a board may not be big enough for most other things, yet it shows possibilities as a bowl to the discerning eye. This also applies to wood that has too twisted a grain

or some flaw that does not affect its strength. It may have been cut out of a board to free another straight-grained part for cabinetwork. Grain that is too wild in its convolutions to suit normal woodwork can often be turned into a bowl with a most interesting grain pattern. Special bowl blanks, as available from some suppliers, may be very welcome. It is possible, however, to find suitable pieces amongst ordinary lumber stocks, and quite often what is needed for a bowl would be regarded as no more than firewood by another type of woodworker.

Obviously, a piece of wood selected for a bowl should be sound. There should be no obvious flaws. The extreme end of a board sometimes develops cracks along the grain. They may not be obvious on a sawn surface, but planing will reveal them. Even then it may be advisable to cut off a few inches from the end of a board that shows signs of weathering or seasoning by the discoloration of the end grain so any minute cracks are removed. Flaws that cause a bowl to crack during turning only mean wasted effort.

Knots or other flaws should be examined. If there is no weakness, it is possible that the flaw will provide an interesting appearance in the finished bowl. A dark rim around a knot usually means it is loosening and would probably break out during turning. Flaws that have open parts (*shakes*) mean the wood should be discarded as these may extend or even deeper parts may already be wider cavities that will appear as wood is turned away.

BOWL TURNING

The simplest bowl to make is one with a base of a diameter greater than that of the faceplate that is to carry it. Such a bowl can be made in one mounting—inside and outside can be worked without removing the wood until the work is finished so avoiding any risk of lack of concentricity. To make such a bowl, use a compass to draw a circle slightly bigger than the bowl on a surface that has been planed flat (test with a straightedge in several directions). With the same center, draw a circle just that much bigger than the faceplate to be seen outside it when the faceplate is screwed on. Cut carefully around the outer circle. Put the faceplate on the wood, using the guide circle to locate it. Drill for screws and drive them tightly (Fig. 10-2). As with tightening car studs, give final tightening with opposite pairs. The penetration of the screws should not be more than you judge sufficient. In the usual hardwood blank for a fruit bowl, 1/2 inch into the wood is more than enough—3/8 inch may be plenty if the bowl is to be turned deeply. Know what the penetration is for later safety checks.

Make sure the spindle nose is clean, both around the threads and on the parallel part. Also wipe inside the mating portion of the faceplate. On many lathes it is a good idea to have a fiber or leather washer on the spindle nose for the faceplate to tighten against. Check that the assembly is hand tight; the action of turning will bring the joint tighter. Locate the tool rest across the outside. Pull the work around by hand to make sure it cannot foul the tool rest. If the tool rest is just below center height that is probably satisfactory but much depends on the relative heights of the lathe and the operator. A worker who is short in relation to the lathe may prefer the tool rest lower than would a taller worker. The size of the work also has an effect. What is important is a comfortable working angle for the gouge used for roughing. Most people find it best to have the end of the handle at the height of the upper part of their thigh. A satisfactory position will soon be found by experiment. If you need to hold the tool handle end too high to get a satisfactory cut, the tool rest should be lowered.

Use a gouge sharpened straight across to get the outside cylindrical. This may be 1/2 or 3/4 inch wide and ground to a fairly obtuse angle, although one with a more acute angle used for spindle turning can be used. Have the gouge angled upward (Fig. 10-7) and take off the high spots first. The gouge may slide from side to side on the tool rest or progress can be by rolling, so different parts of the cutting edge share the work. This gets rid of any eccentricity in the sawn disc so vibration is damped and the disc runs smoothly.

Usually in a one-off bowl, there is no exact size to work to and the outside diameter can be any size. If a pair of bowls are being made, the disc may have to be turned to a definite size. It can be checked with calipers, but it is easier to measure across the flat face. Much bowl turning is done by eye, but a beginner will find it helpful to have a half-drawing showing the probable outside and inside shape (Fig. 11-1A). If the final shape worked by eye is not exactly the same as the drawing it will not matter, providing it has a pleasing appearance. If matching bowls are made, it will be advisable to use templates.

Start roughing the outside to shape by taking off an angle of waste wood on the faceplate side of the block (Fig. 11-1B). Some turners prefer to advance the tool from the outside toward the center. It is easier to watch progress this way. Because it is only a roughing cut and much more wood has yet to be removed, the state of the surface does not matter much. Obviously, it is important to avoid breaking out the wood so splintering pieces crack as far in as the faceplate and the area that is to remain flat. To reduce this risk, cuts may be from near the faceplate outward, using a tool rest mounted diagonally (Fig. 11-1C).

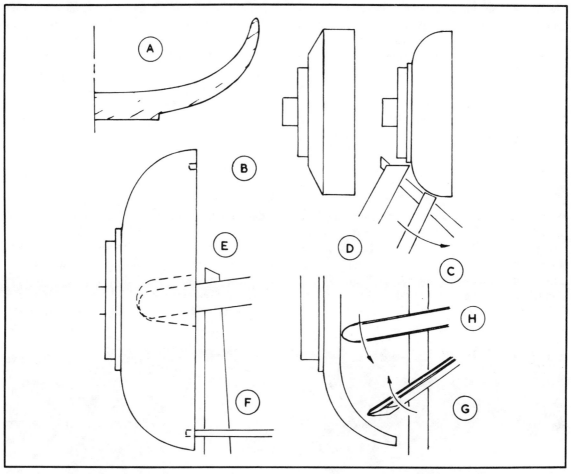

Fig. 11-1. After shaping the outside of a bowl, the inside may be hollowed from the center outward or worked from a parting tool groove inward with a gouge.

Use the gouge to further turn the outside to approximate shape. Cut inward with a parting tool if there is enough clearance at the headstock to allow this to mark the limit of shaping (Fig. 11-1D). If this cannot be done, mark in the same place with the corner of a scraper tool. The gouge can be used both inward and outward around the curve, but later cuts are likely to produce a better surface if cuts are only made from the smaller to the larger diameter.

All of this can be done with a 3/4-inch gouge, which will remove the bulk of the waste most efficiently. When the shape is near to what is required, it is easier to get a smoother finish with a 1/2-inch gouge still working outward from the smaller diameter. Some turners prefer to follow this with a 1/4-inch gouge, but it is sharpness of the tool and the way it is handled that are more important to the quality of finish than the width across the tool.

It would be possible to go ahead and complete the outside at this stage, but shaping of the inside can be started and all scraping done at the same time later.

There are several techniques for removing the waste and shaping the inside of a bowl. One may be no better than another, so it is advisable to experiment and settle for the method or combination of methods that suit you. Cuts can be started near

147

the rim and the hollow worked progressively from there. With a very large bowl, it is advisable to leave a boss near the center as an attempt to limit vibration while turning the larger diameter. Only remove this when the inside near the rim is near size. In a more moderate size bowl, cuts can start near the middle and hollowing be worked outward. In any case, there is a considerable quantity of wood to be removed. Any method of roughing is acceptable, providing the tool is not allowed to go where it should not, either scoring over the rim or hollowing too deeply.

A gouge can be used near the center of the disc to work a hollow almost as if it was a shell bit drilling (Fig. 11-1E). This can be opened further and a start has been made at hollowing. Toward the rim, there is a risk that a gouge in inexperienced hands may be thrown outward and spoil the rim. A parting tool can be used on the waste side of the final width of rim to make a shallow groove, which can be used as a guide for the gouge (Fig. 11-1F).

It is a matter of personal choice whether hollowing is done with a gouge sharpened straight across or with a rounded nose. With a rounded nose, there is less risk of digging in. With an end sharpened straight across, the trailing edge (the one away from the direction of movement of the tool) must not be allowed to go below the surface because this will dig in and the tool will score across the wood or break it out. It is better if neither corner becomes buried. Some turners roll the gouge on the tool rest, or it can swing in arcs.

As the bowl begins to hollow, cuts are better slicing down the inside of the area near the rim with the gouge on its side (Fig. 11-1G). It can then progressively sweep toward the center. If it is preferred to make the cuts from the center outward, a similar sweep action can be made that way (Fig. 11-1H). If it is a shape that goes in quickly from the rim and may even have a turned in lip, the outer part should be turned from the rim around the immediate curve (Fig. 11-2), but the flatter area can

Fig. 11-2. When using a gouge inside a bowl, tilt it so that there is no risk of it digging in. Work in from the rim to avoid wood breaking out.

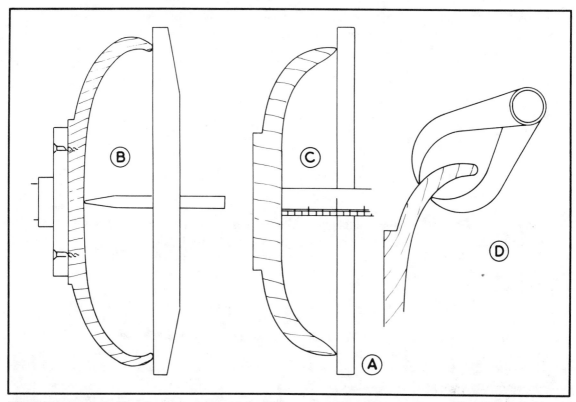

Fig. 11-3. Besides checking the depth of a bowl, use calipers to test thickness. A delicate appearance can be obtained by thinning towards the rim.

be turned from the center out to meet these cuts.

Besides watching the curve to get a pleasing shape, frequently check the depth of hollowing and the thickness of the remaining wood. Allow for the finishing cuts that will follow and reduce the wood even more. Know how much the screws through the faceplate are penetrating the wood. Their points mark the absolute limit of depth, but you may not want to go that far. If weight is wanted, the bottom can be left fairly thick. The most attractive and useful bowl is made by hollowing as much as reasonably possible, bearing in mind strength and the risk of later warping or cracking of thin-section wood. Much depends on the wood. With a close-grained hardwood, you can make the bowl to finish much thinner than if the wood is open-grained. Bowls are not usually turned in softwood, but if they are, possibly to match pine furniture, the thickness left should be about twice as much as in close-grained hardwood.

In any wood, too thin a rim may break or crumble. An appearance of thinness can be obtained by tapering and rounding towards the rim (Fig. 11-3A) leaving the wood further down much thicker. With experience, you can judge the progress of bowl hollowing by eye, but checking depth and thickness may surprise you. A depth gauge will tell you how far you have cut and what thickness is left at the base (Fig. 11-3B). Without a depth gauge, you can put a strip of wood across and use a rule (Fig. 11-3C). The gauge can be used away from the center. To check wall thickness, use calipers (Fig. 11-3D). The curve inside does not have to be related to that outside, but both have to be fair curves that look right, with the wood getting thinner towards the rim in most cases, rather than attempting to keep a uniform thickness from the base to near the rim. Without checks it is possible to get the wood thinner lower down than it is towards the rim. In an extreme case, you might cut right through if you had not been making checks.

Gouges are used inside and outside to remove unwanted wood, but as you get near the intended shape, try to produce as good a gouge finish as possible. If the gouge tears out ragged hollows in the against-grain parts of the circumference, there will have to be a lot of scraper work that may take the wood thinner than intended to remove blemishes. You may want to change from a broad gouge to a narrower one towards a tighter curve near the rim. Whatever you use, have the cutting edges very sharp and make the final cuts lightly.

Ideally, the curve of the bowl inside goes progressively from a tight curve near the rim to nearly flat at the center (Fig. 11-4A). This shape is more difficult to get than may be expected. Errors in shaping the cross-section may not be made apparent until a gloss finish shows them up. Shaping to a slightly conical center can happen, but this is usually very obvious (Fig. 11-4B) and can be corrected. A more subtle flaw is making the deeper part further out than the center (Fig. 11-4C). This may be only slight and not obvious until polishing or varnishing. Holding something with a straight edge across the inside helps to see what the shape actually is (Fig. 11-4D). A card template of the intended hollow may be a better guide (Fig. 11-4E).

One way to avoid troublesome discrepancies in the final appearance is to let the central area be flat (Fig. 11-4F). This is acceptable if there is doubt about obtaining the first cross-section. Although a reasonable flatness should be attempted with gouges, final and definite flattening can be obtained later with a straight-edged scraper.

The outside is worked with a straight-edged, long and strong scraper. Mark the edge of the base with a clean cut, lightly trimming it with the long point of a skew chisel or the square corner of a scraper. Use the scraper at an angle that brings away true shavings and not just dust, and sweep it around the curve (Fig. 11-5). In this way high spots should be leveled and a smooth flowing curved profile be produced. The smoothest finish should be obtained by working from near the faceplate to the rim.

Inside the hollow, a scraper with a rounded end can be used for the part inside the rim. What the curve of the scraper end is does not matter, so long as it is less than the curve it is to cut (Fig. 11-6A). For the center area, it is easier to use a scraper with a flatter curve. If the tool rest is well inside the bowl, the scraper can be worked from the center outward. Adjust the height of the tool rest so when the scraper is sloped down at an angle that produces a proper cut. Its edge is at the same height as the center of the bowl. The tool can then be taken from

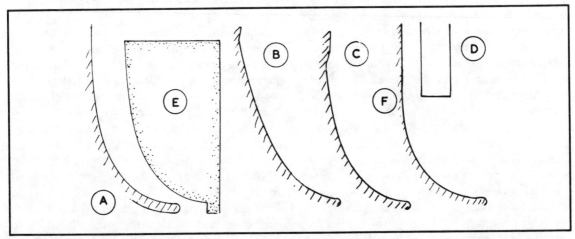

Fig. 11-4. If an exact shape is needed inside, a template can be used. It is important to check that there is a fair curve across the inside of a bowl, because imperfections will show up after polishing.

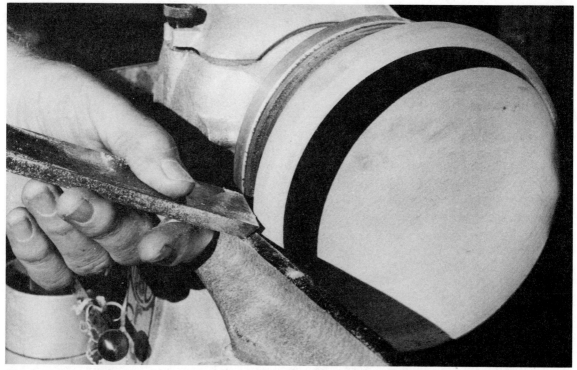

Fig. 11-5. Bring a scraper at a high angle to the outside of a bowl, then lower the handle as it starts cutting until the waste comes away cleanly. Follow the shape around to get an even curve. Watching the far side of the bowl shows where there may be high spots in the section.

the center outward without difficulty. When working in this way, it is possible to see fairly accurately if the bottom is following the intended curve that

is nearly flat at the center and blends progressively into tighter curves toward the curves coming down from inside the rim (Fig. 11-7).

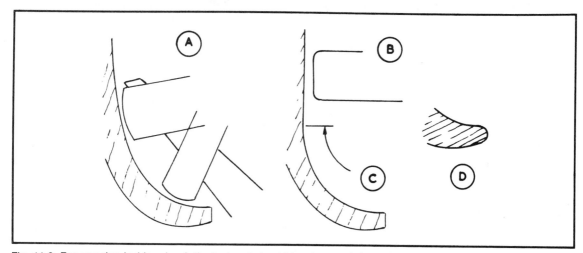

Fig. 11-6. For scraping inside a bowl, the tool rest should be close and the scraper swung from side to side.

Fig. 11-7. Use a board scraper with a moderate curve to get a good shape across the center inside a bowl.

It is also possible to make the inside bottom flat with a slightly curved scraper drawn outward at right angles to the lathe bed, possibly using the carefully set tool rest as a guide, but it is better to have a scraper with a straight end. It may be straight across only, or it can be straight with a slight rounding at the corners (Fig. 11-6B). It may help to mark where the intended limit of flatness is to be with a pencil circle. Flatten the center area first, then bring the curve down to it. Be careful to blend in (Fig. 11-6C) without dipping deeper just before meeting.

Up to this point, it is usually best to leave the rim flat. The safest way to round it is to use a scraper only. The edge may be semicircular in section at its edge, but may widen like part of an ellipse a short distance down (Fig. 11-6D) to give strength.

If the lathe rotation can be reversed, any roughness may be removed by lightly scraping while the bowl revolves the other way. Otherwise, the best finish that can be obtained with sharp scrapers the normal way will have to be accepted.

This is followed by sanding. Aim at a good tool finish, then only light sanding with fine abrasive paper will be necessary. Coarse abrasive scratches around a bowl will show through a finish, so avoid coarse abrasive by aiming at a tool finish, then those scratches from fine abrasive will be so slight they won't show. If you have to use a coarse abrasive for any reason, follow with progressively finer abrasives, using each sufficiently to remove the scratches left by the previous grade.

Be satisfied that everything that has to be done on the lathe has been done before removing the bowl from the faceplate. It is almost impossible to mount anything perfectly a second time. There may be a little roughness around the edge of the base. That can be put right with hand sanding. The screw holes will almost certainly have pulled up the grain around their edges. Even if the bottom is to be covered with cloth glued on, it is advisable to plug the holes. The plugs can be pointed slivers of wood dipped in glue and driven in. Leave trimming the ends level until the glue has set; then saw or chisel off the waste wood and level the bottom by rubbing it on a piece of abrasive paper put on a flat surface.

If the base of a bowl is smaller than the diameter of the faceplate, there are at least two ways of dealing with it. If the bottom is to be flat, like the bowl just described, a plywood disc may be included in the assembly to provide a pad between the work and the metal faceplate (Fig. 11-8A). When turning is done toward the base, the pad will almost certainly be cut into, but it will protect the tool from the faceplate. Except for this, the method of turning is the same as has just been described.

In another method the outside and inside are turned as separate operations, as described in Chapter 10.

Prepare the disc as for the first bowl. There is no need to plane the base, but the top, which will be first toward the faceplate, must be made flat, and there should be a guide circle for positioning the faceplate. Because the screws will be going into a considerable depth of scrap wood, they can be longer than otherwise chosen if greater strength is felt necessary.

Mount the disc in the lathe and turn first to a cylindrical form followed by shaping of the outside. As the whole base is exposed, it may be turned right across. It can be merely flat (Fig. 11-8B), slightly hollow to give a more definitely rigid stand (Fig. 11-8C), or there can be a rim turned with a hollow inside (Fig. 11-8D). The hollow can be quite shallow, but it leaves the rim to provide a steady base.

The shaping of the curve toward the bowl rim is the same as for the earlier bowl. It is advisable to do the work completely at this stage, including scraping and some sanding, although final sanding may be done when the bowl is the other way.

The bowl can be removed from the faceplate and reversed so it is fixed with screws into the base, but there is then difficulty in getting it exactly centered. It is better to turn a pad with a recess to take the bowl base. If the rim of the bowl base is shallow, make the pad quite thin so screws can pass through it into the bowl. If the rim is 1/4 inch or more deep, which will provide a friction drive, use a thicker pad. The pad may only be scrap wood, but it should be a wood at least as hard as that used for the bowl; otherwise, there is a risk of it breaking out under the driving pressure.

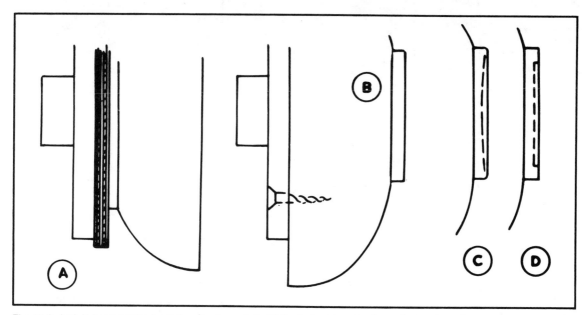

Fig. 11-8. A plain base can be turned against a pad, but if the bottom is to be shaped, the block of wood must be mounted in reverse before it is hollowed.

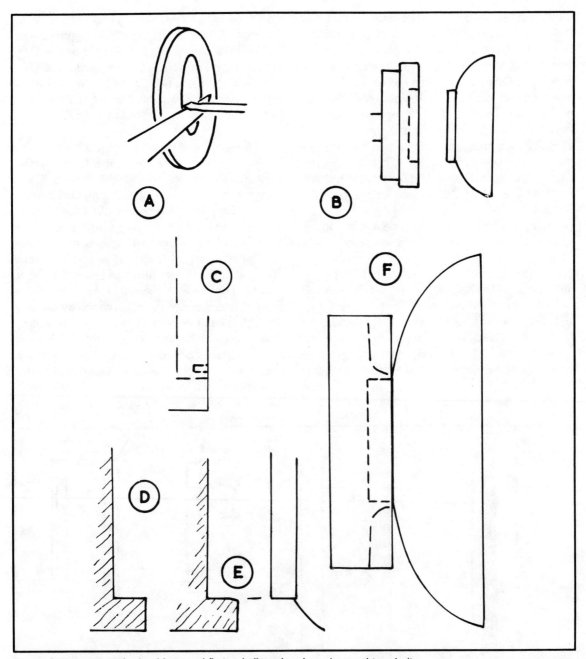

Fig. 11-9. If the base of a bowl is turned first, a hollowed pad can be used to grip it.

For a shallow pad, mount the wood with screws outside the bowl base area if possible, otherwise, use short screws where faceplate holes permit in the part that will be hollowed. Turn the face of the pad true. Use a pencil to draw a circle of the same size as the bowl base. Cut in on the waste side of this with a parting tool (Fig. 11-9A) and remove the waste wood inside this with a gouge. Let the depth be slightly more than the depth of the base, so it goes in far enough to bear on the bowl itself when fully home.

Use the square corner of a scraper to turn out the recess until the bowl just fits in (Fig. 11-9B). Unscrew the faceplate from the mandrel nose, but do not remove the pad from it. Put this assembly on the bowl, then drill and screw into the bottom of the bowl to secure it. From this point, turning the inside is the same as the earlier bowl.

For a bowl with a base rim deep enough to take a friction drive, use a thicker piece of wood for the pad. Turn its surface true. Turn most of its outer edge circular to reduce vibration. Pencil on a circle to match the bowl base, then start hollowing (Fig. 11-9C). Again go a little deeper than the base. Use the square edge of a scraper to bring the recess out to size, but this time check with the actual bowl frequently (Fig. 11-9D). When the size is judged to be almost there, chamfer the edge of the recess slightly with the scrape (Fig. 11-9E). Keep this chamfer very slight as it is only intended to act as a countersink to permit the base to enter, and too much of it would limit the gripping area. The joint needs to be tight enough to require driving or squeezing together. Giving the bowl base a very slight taper may help, but this should be minimal. Similarly, the recess may have a very slight taper. Take the faceplate and pad off the lathe and either

drive the bowl in with a mallet or a piece of scrap wood under a hammer, or squeeze it in with a vise or with clamps. Make sure it goes in evenly so the pad is bearing equally all around against the curve of the bowl next to the base. From this point on, hollowing the inside of the bowl is the same as before.

If the recess is inadvertently cut too large, it may be possible to still use it by turning it out a little more so a strip of paper can be wrapped around the base. If this is still doubtful, the paper could be glued on both sides, then glue and paper particles scraped and sanded off when the work is finished.

When a friction drive is used, the joint will probably be so tight that there is no way of prying the pad and bowl apart without causing damage. The pad will have to be sacrificed to release the bowl undamaged. After all work has been done on the bowl, the outside of the pad is turned down until only a small amount is left in way of the recess (Fig. 11-9F). Obviously, care is needed to avoid any fixing screws. Turning down the pad will weaken its grip, and the bowl will usually come away before turning has been carried right down to the recess size. If screws prevent turning down the pad, the faceplate can be removed and the pad sawn across to weaken it so it can be sprung or broken away from the bowl base.

Chapter 12

Laminated Turning

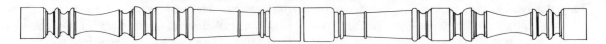

Although most turning is done with solid wood, it is also possible to build up several pieces together and turn the result. Such laminating may be done for strength or for appearance. It may also be the only way of making a part from pieces of wood that are too small.

Usually the parts are simply glued together because any screws or other metal fastenings would interfere with turning and be hazardous for the tools. It may be possible to include glued dowels between parts for extra strength, but with modern glues simple glued joints can be expected to have adequate strength without any extra reinforcing arrangements.

Any of the usual woodworking constructional glues can be used, but for greatest strength, particularly for anything that may get damp, it is advisable to use a waterproof boat building glue. Many of these glues are in two parts to be mixed just before use or applied to meeting surfaces, so a chemical reaction sets the glue when the two parts meet. These glues may be regarded as absolutely waterproof for all practical purposes. Joints should

be close-fitting and the wood clean and dry. If the glue maker's instructions are followed, the joint should be strong as well as waterproof.

Meeting surfaces should be hand-planed flat. Machine planing may case harden the wood surface so it does not absorb glue. It may help to coarsely sand the surface or drag a saw blade across it in several directions to expose more fibers. Clamping should be enough to hold the parts in close contact while the glue sets, but not excessively tight as that might starve the joint by squeezing out too much glue.

As wood is a natural material its characteristics vary, but all wood will absorb and give up moisture. When this happens it may warp. Usually a solid block of properly seasoned wood will hold its shape, but if the thing being made has to be as stable as possible, laminating may be the answer. Decorative work does not have to be dimensionally stable, but if the turning is part of a machine or is a pattern for casting metal, it must keep its shape and dimensions.

If wood is to be used in a construction where

it is very important that it keeps its shape, as in a fairly slender rod forming part of a scientific instrument, it will be better laminated than made from a single solid piece. Before turning, a piece could be cut down the center and one half reversed and glued on the other (Fig. 12-1A). Alternatively, there could be three or more pieces glued to make up the thickness (Fig. 12-2). In this way, internal stresses in each part should be balanced by those in others after turning. The whole thing should remain straight, despite changes in the moisture content.

If a bowl is to be turned of wood to match other things, but it is a type with a reputation for warping in thin sections, the blank for the bowl can be built up by gluing several pieces together with their grains at right angles (Fig. 12-1B). It may be possible to save some working time by cutting the centers out of upper pieces (Fig. 12-1C). This type of laminating can be clamped while the glue sets by using C-clamps, putting in a vise, or standing on the bench with weights on top.

A piece of wood with a twisted grain or some other decorative feature may be turned for the sake of its appearance, but the characteristics that make it look attractive also make it weak constructionally. A piece of straight-grained matching wood may be laminated to it to form the strength part to stiffen the decorative piece and make any joints to other parts.

It is more often that woods of contrasting color are laminated for the sake of appearance. Ideally, the woods should be of comparable hardness and characteristics, but this is not always possible. It would be unwise to mix softwoods and hardwoods, but hardwoods of rather different density and contrasting colors can be used. Avoid oily woods or those with an excess of resin because these may interfere with gluing success.

For spindle turning, there may be four or more strips glued together (Fig. 12-1D). When turning is done, the varying amounts of each color will give a pleasing appearance, but the joints will show straight along the article (Fig. 12-1E).

A different appearance is obtained if wood of one color is glued around a core of another color (Fig. 12-1F). The proportions of the parts should

be arranged to suit what is to be turned, so the effect of turning parts to various sizes breaks through from one color to the other and the outer color is left as a pattern on the thicker parts (Fig. 12-1G). Yet another spindle turning arrangement that gives a varied effect is having several pieces arranged diagonal to the final lengthwise form (Fig. 12-1H). The effect varies according to the chosen angle.

Items turned on the screw center or a small faceplate can be laminated in different color woods. Amusing eggcups can be made from small pieces that would otherwise be wasted. However, laminating is particularly useful for round boxes. Instead of turning from a solid block with the grain lengthwise, the base is a solid disc, then the body is built up with rings of wood glued so they are of alternating colors and directions of grain (Fig. 12-3A). A lid can be made with two pieces in the same way. A knob may be a separate piece of color in contrast to the top of the lid (Fig. 12-3B).

LAMINATING BOWLS

Bowls are good decorative laminating projects. It is possible to use a great variety of methods of cutting and assembling parts to make a bowl blank. It is usual to arrange the parts so the result is symmetrical, but using varying size pieces arranged in no particular order may produce an interesting result. However, there is a certain amount of chance about this, and it is better to keep the design uniform with symmetrical pieces.

Attractive bowls can be made from blanks built up from strips arranged side by side. It is usual to have strips all of the same section but in contrasting colors (Fig. 12-3C). The bowl looks best if the total number of strips is an odd number, then the outer strips are the same at each side and the center of the circle is at the center of a strip and not in a joint. Glue sufficient strips and cut the circle on a bandsaw. Turn the bowl in the same way as for solid block. There may be a boss at the base for attaching to a faceplate, and a final section of any type desired, but a curled-in edge shows the two colors to advantage (Fig. 12-3D).

Many laminated bowls are made up with wedge-shaped pieces in contrasting colors. These

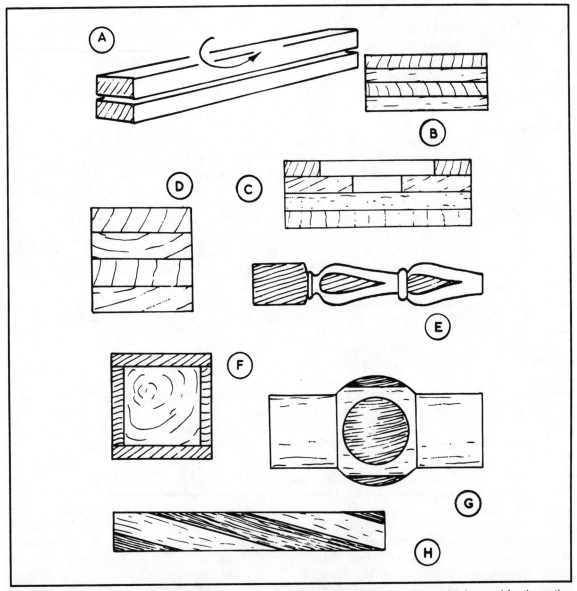

Fig. 12-1. Laminating can be used to provide strength or built up to a suitable size. It can also be used for decoration by gluing woods of different colors together.

need to fit closely and be securely glued. It is not impossible to cut the pieces by hand, but the work is easier if a table or other power saw is available with an angle setting guide. The best blade is hollow ground without teeth set.

The number of segments determines the angle of cut. With 360 degrees in the complete circle a

total of eight segments means one-eighth of 360 as the angle at the center, which is 45 degrees (Fig. 12-4A). The assembly may be for something like a lamp base, a table top, or a bowl. Besides cutting the sides of the segments, the outline should be sawn to a curve to make up into a circle. This is necessary so the parts can be glued together. The

Fig. 12-2. Strips can be laminated to make a square section when it is important that the completed turned part should be stable and resist warping.

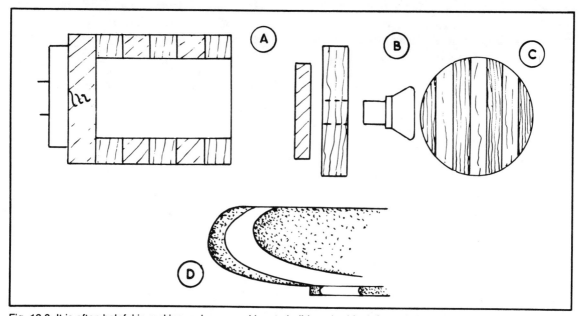

Fig. 12-3. It is often helpful in making a deep round box to build up the blank from circles glued together. A lid can also be made to match and an interesting bowl is formed by gluing strips of different colored woods across each other before turning.

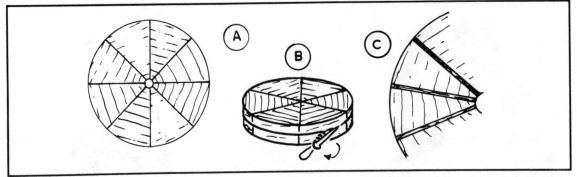

Fig. 12-4. If segments are glued together, the grain can be across so the wood is easier to turn. This will also produce an interesting pattern.

only way triangular segments can be pulled together is by squeezing around the circumference, and the outline needs to be sawn reasonably round for this.

There is a choice of grain direction. If each wedge-shaped piece has the grain across, this will be in the direction of turning and there will be no problem of the tool meeting end grain. If the grain radiates from the center, all turning is across the grain and not against it. The grain may even be through the wood, so it will be parallel with the lathe centerline when mounted for turning.

With wedge-shaped pieces taken to the center, it is possible to clamp with a Spanish windlass. Take a piece of rope around the glued blocks, knot the ends together so the rope circle is loose, then put a piece of wood in the rope and twist it up (Fig. 12-4B). If the assembly is fairly deep, there can be two or more Spanish windlasses applied. There are more sophisticated ways of clamping circular things, but this works quite well on this type of assembly.

Segments going to the center are appropriate for such items as bases for table lamps, but even then there can be a hole at the center for the base of the stem or for passing an electric wire through. If it is necessary to have the disc solid to the center, fitting the fine angles there needs to be carefully done, so if taking each segment to a point can be avoided, that is advisable. A variation on simple segments is to separate them with thin strips of contrasting color. This has the effect of making

a hole at the center (Fig. 12-4C).

For a bowl, there could be segments of the full depth, so the glued up block is treated in the same way as a solid piece. This is a waste of wood, however, and it is better to have a base of solid plywood or segmented wood, then build up a rim of sufficient thickness to allow for turning but with no appreciable amount of wood projecting into the center of the bowl. A difficulty then is in getting the parts assembled symmetrically.

Segments of this type can be marked out geometrically. It is advisable to make a drawing of at least part of a circle with sufficient thickness to allow for turning later (Fig. 12-5A). Lines taken to the center can divide the circle into whatever number of segments will suit the design. The best way of cutting the segments is with their grain running around the circumference of the bowl. If each piece is long, quite a lot of wood is cut to waste, so a fairly large number of segments is better for economy of wood, although the more pieces there are, the more joints there are to cut accurately.

The rim can be made up with just one circle of thick segments. This may be advisable for a first shallow tray or bowl of this type, but building up the blank with segments laid like bricks in a wall will produce the most interesting designs.

The angle at the ends of segments can be found from the full-size drawing, but it is also easy to calculate. The three angles in a triangle total 180 degrees. If the angle at the center is deducted from 180 and the result divided by 2, that is the angle

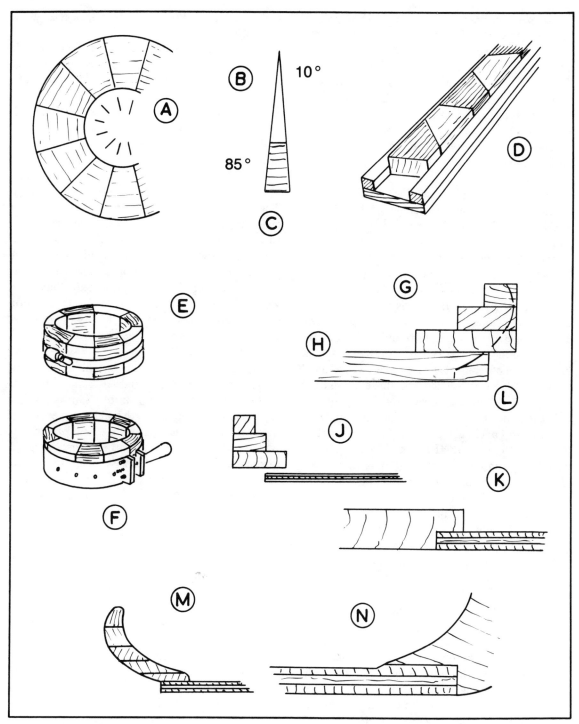

Fig. 12-5. If many pieces of wood are to be glued together to make a bowl or other round object, they have to be securely clamped and accurately matched.

at a corner. For instance, if there are 18 segments making up a circle, the center angle is 1/18 of 180, or 10 degrees (Fig. 12-5B). Taking 10 from 180 and dividing by 2 gives a corner angle of 85 degrees (Fig. 12-5C). If a table saw or another type saw with an adjustable fence or guide is available, that is the angle to which it should be set.

With a large number of small segments to make up a circle, it is difficult to keep the assembly true during gluing. It is helpful to have a circle of the right size drawn on a piece of paper laid on a flat surface. The parts are assembled on that. If the strips for the segments are planed in a long length to the right size, particularly thickness, they will go together with level surfaces. This is important to get flat mating surfaces with the next layer or the bottom. It is difficult to plane the surface of the built-up ring afterwards with any chance of securing a perfect flatness. If there is any doubt about matching thicknesses, the cut segments can be planed together in a simple trough (Fig. 12-5D). Make sure the end pieces agree in thickness and keep that set of segments for one layer. There could be trouble if they get mixed with those for another layer, even if they are apparently the same.

It is difficult to keep joints close enough without some sort of circular clamp. A Spanish windlass can be used (Fig. 12-4B), but something more positive aids in positioning as well as tightening. Hose clips can be used. A large one may be sufficient for a small assembly, but for a larger circle the worm-drive type can be opened and linked so several will make up a sufficient size (Fig. 12-5E). This method of clamping gives a very precise degree of pressure. Check that the outline still conforms fairly closely to the circle drawn on paper as the clips are tightened.

A better arrangement is a band of flexible steel. The "Flexi-Clamp" has a 3-inch wide steel band 5 feet long in the standard form (Fig. 12-5F). Bands of other lengths are obtainable, but the standard band will hold work up to 19 inches in diameter. The screw clamping arrangement can be attached at various points so the clamp can be adjusted to any size circle. An advantage of broad spring steel is that it naturally wants to form a circle and there

is not such a need to check and adjust the outline of an assembly.

There are band clamps available, which could also be used. These work in a similar way, but the band is canvas or webbing, usually of a synthetic fiber material. Considerable pressure can be put on, but the band conforms to whatever shape the assembled segments take up and does not, in itself, maintain a circle. A band clamp can be taken around square and other shapes, but for laminated bowls the steel "Flexi-Clamp" is more convenient.

A set of segments should be tried together dry. They should be pulled together with whatever clamping arrangement is available, then the assembly held to a light to examine each joint. If any light shows through, the meeting edges will have to be adjusted by careful planing. Joints must be good, or there is a risk that a space filled with glue will have little strength and the action of turning will cause the bowl to break up with a danger from flying pieces as well as the loss of the work you have put into it.

Rings of segments should be built up and glued as one stage. The glue should set. Some of the synthetic resins set to an apparently hard state in a fairly short time, but strength builds up over several days. If any work has to be done on a ring, due to uneven assembly or some other cause, it is advisable to wait this time before working on it. With several rings prepared, try an assembly of the rings without the base. For many bowls, the bottom layer may be wider (Fig. 12-5G). It is usual to keep the circumference the same for the sake of lining up the assembly and simplicity in cutting segments, but it is possible to set in the lower layer if that suits the ultimate shape.

Glue the rings together, staggering the segments to give a uniform pattern. Some pressure is needed to hold the parts in contact. There may be scrap wood discs above and below to allow several C-clamps to be put around the assembly. The discs may have holes through their centers for a nut and bolt to put on the pressure. If the assembly is not too large, it may be put in a vise.

If the base is to be part of the shaping of the bowl, it should be solid wood in the form of a disc glued on after the glue joining the rings has set (Fig. 12-5H). It may be satisfactory to use a piece of plywood. It is glued on and its edge turned true as a base (Fig. 12-5J). If it is set will under the curve of the bowl, the ply edge appearance will not be obvious.

An alternative for a better treatment of plywood for a base is to turn the plywood disc true, then turn a recess for it in the bottom of the built-up ring (Fig. 12-5K). This hides the plywood edge completely.

If solid wood is used at the bottom of a bowl, it will be of sufficient thickness for the inside to be turned into it (Fig. 12-5L). If plywood is used, the bowl shape may have to be turned so the plywood is not cut into (Fig. 12-5M). This presupposes perfection in the thickness of the plywood and its mounting. If possible, choose plywood made from thick veneers, then the plywood can be turned into very slightly to produce a new surface inside the bowl, usually with a little step down at the joint (Fig. 12-5N).

CENTERING

Accurate centering in the lathe is important for spindle and faceplate turning. Suppose a spindle turning is made up of a square center and pieces of contrasting color glued around it (Fig. 12-6A). If the square part is not mounted centrally on the lathe and the outside turned to a bulbous shape, the amount of the outer pieces of wood left will be different sizes. The oval outlines on the bulbous parts will not match (Fig. 12-6B). It may be worthwhile

having some excess length on the square piece that has been tested for right angled corners and equal dimensions of the section. Find the centers of the ends, and center punch dots there. Mount the square in the lathe and turn the ends with a parting tool just far enough in for the circles to come below the square outline (Fig. 12-6C). This will show if centering is accurate. If it is not, a little of the spare wood at the end can be cut off and another center marked and tried. This can be done before the other pieces are glued on the outside.

For a bowl or other segmented assembly on the faceplate, centering has to be the same as for mounting a solid block, but with extra care to get the perimeter as near true as possible. Slight unevenness of a built-up rim may not be as apparent as the laminations of a spindle turning that are out of true, but it is obviously best to get the assembly as accurately mounted as possible.

The paper drawing used in getting segments assembled accurately can have a circle of the size of the faceplate drawn on it, then this can be transferred to the wood. If there is a center of the whole assembly marked on the base, use this for the point of a compass to draw a circle. If the bowl is to be mounted on a pad on the faceplate, turn this on the faceplate first so its outline is a circle. If this is smaller than the base of the bowl, draw a circle to match it on the bowl. If the bowl is to be smaller, draw a circle on the pad as a guide for mounting the bowl.

Try pulling a mounted laminated bowl around by hand with the tool rest nearby. If points around the rim vary very much in their distance from the

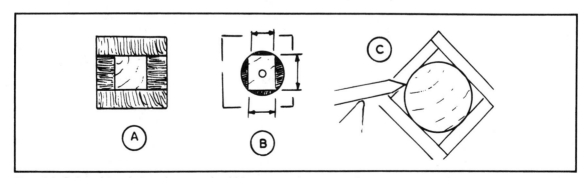

Fig. 12-6. Strips of wood around a core should be accurately centered for turning.

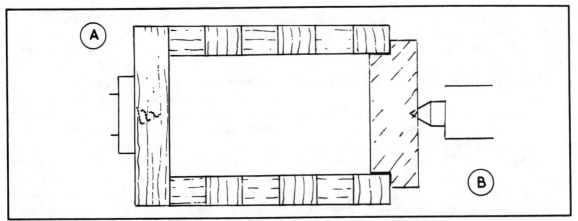

Fig. 12-7. In making a deep laminated box, it is helpful to make a plug for the open end so that it can be supported by the tailstock.

tool rest, it is advisable to try mounting again with screws in different positions to bring the assembly nearer true.

Despite the strength of modern glues, a built-up assembly being turned presents safety problems, particularly in the early stages when the rough shape is being brought to a true circular form. It is helpful to have the first sawing as accurate as possible. It is unwise to leave lumps projecting to be turned off as might be acceptable with a solid block.

A fairly low speed is advisable for faceplate work with laminations—600 rpm will do, but usually the lowest speed of the lathe is acceptable. With laminated spindle turning, speed is not so critical and most turning can be done at the same speeds as would be used for solid wood of the same size or very slightly less.

Although gouges are used for roughing a bowl made of solid wood to size, it is safer not to use them on laminations. A gouge removes wood quicker than a scraper, but its tendency to dig in is greater and cutting heavily puts a considerable strain on the glued joints.

Turn a laminated faceplate project to shape completely with a scraper. Keep initial cuts light, but once the tool is cutting a full circle, shavings as thick as the scraper will produce and can be taken off without undue risk of shattering the bowl. It is important when scraping at any time to keep

the tool sharp, but this is even more so with laminated work.

It is not advisable to turn down a laminated bowl to too thin a section. A bowl made from a solid block can often be made safely down to quite a thin section, tapering off to only a slight radius section at the rim. This looks very attractive. In laminated construction, it is better to settle for a rather thicker section throughout and a large radius section at the rim. it is inadvisable to go to less than about 3/8 inch thick at any point. The possible lack of delicate appearance at the edge is compensated for by the different colors of the laminations, which show up better on a thicker rim.

If laminations are used to build up a cylindrical container, which is supported on and driven by a screw center or a self-centering chuck (Fig.12-7A), the outer laminations may be some way from the support. This also applies to a solid block turned in the same way, but the laminations have their glued joints that may be slightly suspect. It is advisable to arrange some sort of support from the tailstock, at least during the early stage of turning when the work is being brought to a circular shape. This might be something like a lid, turned to fit in and pressed against the work (Fig. 12-7B).

As with turning a laminated bowl, this sort of thing is safer turned with a scraper only. A gouge might be practicable in skilled hands, but even then there is a risk of digging in or breaking out grain adjacent to a joint so the assembly disintegrates.

There should be little risk in turning laminated parts, unless the work has been rushed and the glued joints are not as accurate as they should have been. If fracture occurs and a part of the bowl flies outward, it will normally be thrown by centrifugal force in the direction of a diameter, so it is advisable not to stand in line with that direction. Some sort of eye shield made of shatterproof material may be worn.

Joints that are not fitting properly ought to be avoided under all circumstances because most glues are not gap-filling. If used in bulk to fill a space between surfaces, the set glue will probably craze, so it has a pattern of tiny cracks in it, and the strength of the joint is then minimal. Although it should never happen in good craftsmanship, if a point is reached where a large series of joints are good and one just will not close properly, it is possible to mix

sawdust with the glue that goes in it to make a joint that should be trustworthy. The glue then bonds to the sawdust as well as to the surfaces and crazing should not occur. This is a technique borrowed from boat building, where the compound shapes involved often result in some joints not being as accurate as they should be.

Some glues will soften with heat. Quite a lot of heat may be generated by the action of turning, more so with blunt tools than with sharp ones. If waterproof boat building glues are used, the majority of these are also immune to the effect of heat, so there is no risk of tool friction causing joints to weaken. These glues are also very hard. As with turning plywood in which the glues are of a similar type, tools will quickly blunt from the effect of the hard glue that is being turned with the wood. Be prepared to sharpen tools frequently when working on laminations.

Chapter 13

Fitted Parts

Although many useful things can be made from single pieces of wood, there are many that have to be built up from more than one piece, either as a permanent assembly or as take-down parts, such as a lid and box. This adds to the interest of turning and is usually straightforward, although care and ingenuity may have to be used on some projects.

If one part meets another at an angle, the fitting may have to be done away from the lathe, so accuracy may depend on the skill of the craftsman or the use of jigs or other machines. If the parts have to be concentric, all of the work should be done on the lathe, then there should be no risk of final assemblies finishing out of true.

A common assembly has a dowel turned on one part to fit into a hole in another part (Fig. 13-1A). If both parts are turned, as they would be when fitting a stem and base to a lamp standard or candlestick, the hole in the base should be drilled from the tailstock, preferably with a dent made by the back center to ensure accurate positioning. This can be used to test the size the dowel is turned, although

it may be better to use the same drill to make a hole in a scrap piece of wood and use that as a gauge.

The end of the dowel should be given a slight bevel to help enter it in the hole. Usually, the dowel is turned parallel. If there is any taper, let it be very slight towards the end.

If the dowel is to go right through and will show in the finished work, make it slightly too long and plane it flush after fitting (Fig. 13-1B). In some constructions, as when fitting ladder rungs, there may be a wedge driven into a saw cut. This should come across the grain of the part with the hole (Figs. 13-1C and 13-2). At one time these joints were made dry in outdoor woodwork, but this was because the glues available were not waterproof. It is better now to glue both the dowel and the wedge. Let the glue set after the wedge is driven, then cut off the projecting wood and plane the end level.

Sometimes a dowel has to go into a *blind* hole. The action of driving the dowel is like a piston into a cylinder, so it is advisable to cut a groove in the dowel to let surplus air and glue escape (Fig. 13-1D); otherwise, there might be a risk of bursting

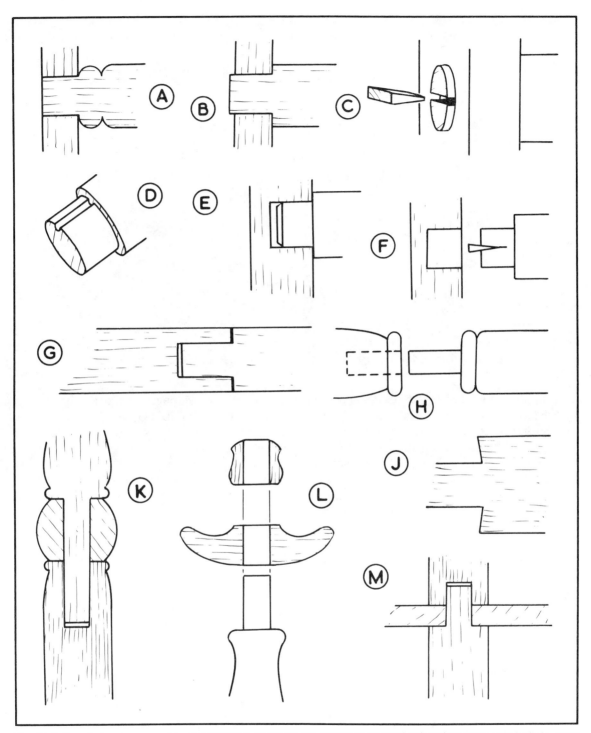

Fig. 13-1. Doweled ends are used in many turning constructions. They can be used to lengthen parts or to include other parts like drip rings of a candlestick.

Fig. 13-2. Dowels can be tightened with wedges driven across the direction of grain of the outer wood, then the ends can be trimmed flat after the glue has set.

a light construction. In this sort of assembly, it is best to have a shoulder to limit the penetration of the dowel, then leave a little extra at the bottom of the hole (Fig. 13-1E). If it is a stool or similar assembly with several rails doweled into holes, the shouldering prevents one part from going deeper than another and ensures a symmetrical assembly. The fact that the dowel does not meet the bottom of the hole will have little effect on strength as glue only has a poor hold on end grain in any case. The strength in the glued joint is around the circumference.

It is possible to wedge a dowel in a blind hole and this can be very strong if sizes are carefully judged. A wedge of suitable size and taper is jammed into a sawcut, then the glued joint driven tight (Fig. 13-1F), so the wedge hitting the bottom of the hole spreads the cut and tightens the dowel.

Dowels can be used to make up spindle work longer than the capacity of the lathe. If a long standard has to be drilled through and the means of drilling will not pass through the total length, parts can be joined. There is a risk in very long drilling

of the drill wandering, despite the equipment available to control it. This is minimized if only comparatively short parts have to be drilled and joined to each other later.

In the simplest assembly, a dowel on one part fits into a hole in the other part (Fig. 13-1G). How far it goes in depends on the size of the whole job. A short assembly may have a short dowel, but anything long and comparatively slender benefits in stiffness and straightness with a long joint. For instance, two parts about 2 feet long and 2 inches in greatest diameter might have a dowel of up to 1 inch in diameter penetrating about 3 inches.

Although it should be possible to join two parallel cylinders in this way and have only a hairline of a joint showing, it is much easier to disguise a joint if there are turned features adjoining it. Usually the joint comes in the hollow between two beads or other rounded parts (Fig. 13-1H). It helps in getting a close joint if one of the pieces is slightly undercut (Fig. 13-1J).

With this sort of joint, the best results come from letting the first assembly be the last; in other words, avoid repeated trial assemblies. The dowel may be tested in a similar hole in a piece of scrap wood. Make sure the hole in the job is clear and there is no roughness at the base of the dowel, then have confidence in your workmanship and push or hit the parts together.

Another use for this type of joint comes when an intermediate piece has to be incorporated. It may be just a piece of a different colored wood, made like a napkin ring, and included for effect (Fig. 13-1K). Another similar assembly is the drip ring for a candlestick. There is a dowel of the same diameter as the candle and this passes through the drip ring and the actual candle holder goes on top (Fig. 13-1L).

The same idea is used if a turned tray has to be fitted part way down a column. The joint is made in the same way as for joining two parts end to end, but sufficient space is left to take the tray (Fig. 13-1M). A variation on this comes when turned legs are to appear to pass through an intermediate shelf. One part—it does not matter if it is a top or bottom section—is long enough to take in the shelf and go far enough into the other part.

LIDS

Many turned lids are really only variations of the doweled joint with one part having a projection to fit into a recess in the other (Fig. 13-3A).

There are several ways of making a turned box with a lid, depending on its design and size, but small pots can have their lids turned from the same piece of wood. A piece of wood long enough to make both parts with something to spare should be turned cylindrical between centers and the tailstock end turned true to fit on a screw center. Mount the wood on the screw center and turn the other end true. Bring up the tailstock and let the back center provide some support. Turn the outside true—it may be slightly eccentric due to remounting.

Cut in where the top of the pot is to come. This may be done with a parting tool, but the roughness this leaves may have to be cleaned off with a chisel. What is left will make the lid. The lid can be made the right way round or it can be reversed.

If the lid is to be made the right way round, take

the parting tool in some way, but not far enough to weaken the wood. Turn down the plug part of the lid to the size that will suit your intended hollowed pot (Fig. 13-3B). The outside part can now be turned in the pattern you want the lid. It can be comparatively shallow and have a knob with a dowel added (Fig. 13-3C). It could be made deeper and the knob turned in the same wood (Fig. 13-3D). When the lid shape is satisfactory, complete parting off.

If the lid is made in the reverse way, the plug part is turned on the exposed end (Fig. 13-3E). If the underside of the lid is to be hollowed, the tailstock is withdrawn and this work done. No other shaping is done on the lid at this stage, and it can be parted off.

The inside of the pot has to be hollowed in stages. A large drill bit can be used to remove some of the waste. Have the lathe on a low speed and feed the bit in just fast enough to keep it cutting. Too high a speed or too fierce a feed may burst the wood or cause it to slip on the screw center. Have the tool rest across the end of the wood and below center height. Use a scraper with a skew end and sloping down slightly. Work from the drilled hole outwards. When the hollowing is approaching the correct size, use the plug of the lid to test progress. Get the entrance to the hole to size first. Follow in to make the hole parallel and the bottom flat (Fig. 13-3F). The recess for the lid need not be the same as the inner diameter of the rest of the pot. It can be stepped (Fig. 13-3G), although a parallel inside surface is satisfactory.

If the lid was made reversed, it should be a push fit in the pot. Push it in and bring up the back center to give preliminary support. This will provide a friction drive, which should be adequate providing excessively heavy cuts are avoided. Turn the outside to size as far as possible with the back center supporting (Fig. 13-3H), then withdraw the center and finally work the lid to shape at its center (Fig. 13-3J).

The outside of the pot can be decorated with beads or lines cut in with a chisel. The lid does not have to follow on the outline of the pot but can be given a rounded edge, which may be set back like a bead or allowed to overlap (Fig. 13-3K).

The final work is parting off the pot from the screwed center. This should be done far enough away to clear the end of the screw. Care is needed not to cut into the screw and damage both tool and screw. The pot will stand better if the bottom is turned slightly hollow so it rests on its rim.

Lids can be made for glass or other containers.

A finished lid may be the same as one turned for a wooden pot with its knob turned integrally or fitted with a dowel. If the knob is part of the lid, the wood can be mounted, with a little waste thickness, on a screw center, then the top and knob turned on the outward side. The part to fit into the container is shaped with caliper checks before the lid is parted from the waste wood.

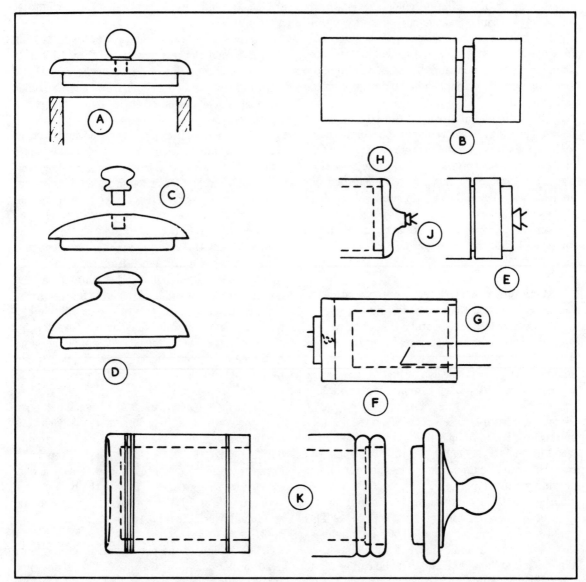

Fig. 13-3. A box and lid can be made from the same piece of wood and may have separate knobs or have the knobs turned as part of the main construction.

Fig. 13-4. A lid on the screw center is tested for fit before turning over to complete the other side.

If there is to be a separate knob, it is easier to turn the lid with the recessed part outwards at first, because the hole for the screw center will be enlarged later for the knob dowel (Fig. 13-4). This allows you to test fit the lid in the container. When that is satisfactory, the wood may be reversed on the screw center for you to turn its top.

Another type of lid is needed to fit a bowl of the fruit or powder bowl type. It is possible to fit a lid later to a bowl that was made without considering a lid. It is likely to have a rounded edge and the lid can have a lip to fit over this (Fig. 13-5A). If the bowl is being made at the same time as the lid, it is better to have a flat edge to the bowl (Fig. 13-5B). An alternative is to cut a recess in the edge of the bowl so the lid drops in (Fig. 13-5C).

The lid may be almost flat, and little more than a disc with a knob. This may suit some purposes, but the sweeping shape of a bowl is best matched with a lid that carries on the same theme. The making of such a lid is, in many ways, similar to bowl turning and forms an interesting project.

It is helpful to turn a wood pad on the faceplate and mount the block for the lid on that (Fig. 13-5D). The bowl should be finished first. Turn the outside of the block to a circle slightly larger than it is in-

tended to finish. True the flat surface.

The exposed part of the mounted wood will be the underside of the lid. Turn the lip to fit the bowl (Fig. 13-5E). The parting tool can cut in, but the square corner of a scraper is needed if it is to have an angular section, and the point of a small gouge on its side may make a rounded shape (Fig. 13-5F). Test for size with calipers and the actual bowl. If the lid is to have its other side turned while mounted on the bowl, it will have to be a push fit, but otherwise it should be an easy drop-in fit.

Hollow the inside of the lid in the same way as a bowl. Use the tool rest across the work and gouges and rounded scrapers. Although the shape may look best if the hollowing is taken close to the lip (Fig. 13-5G), this weakens the wood and there is a risk of breaking out during turning or possible damage later on. It is better to leave a flat (Fig. 13-5H) or nearly flat area for strength. When the inside shape is satisfactory, sand it to a final finish, because it cannot be worked on again on the lathe. If a rubbing polish is to be used on the inside, this might also be done now.

A start can be made at shaping the outside of the lid, but this cannot be taken very far because of the screws and the pad. However, removing

171

some waste at this stage may reduce the load on the mounting used when the lid is reversed.

If the bowl cannot be mounted to drive the lid (Fig. 13-6A) or it is a loose-fitting lid in any case, it is better to use the pad that was used for mounting the lid for turning its underside and adapt it by turning a hollow to match the lid lip (Fig. 13-6B). This can be done with a parting tool. The roughness this leaves around the hole will help grip the lid. Make the hollow deep, so when the lid is pressed in or tapped in with the fist or a mallet it bears around its edges on the surface and not by the bottom of the hollow.

The tailstock can be brought up to give addi-

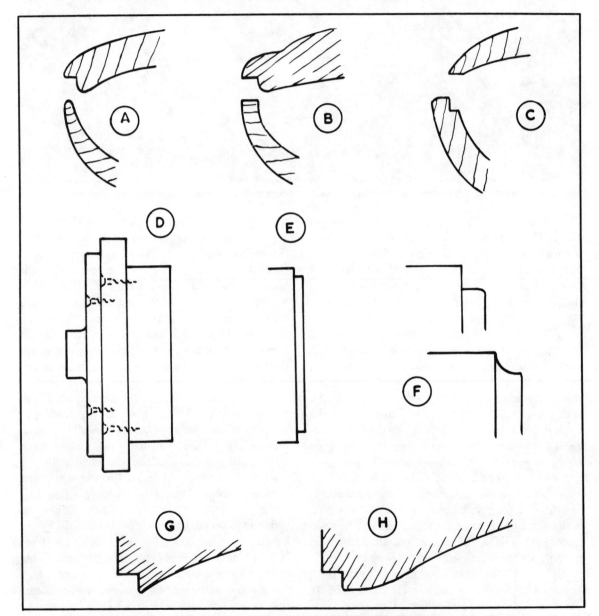

Fig. 13-5. Lids can be made to suit bowls, and they can be arranged in several ways around the rim.

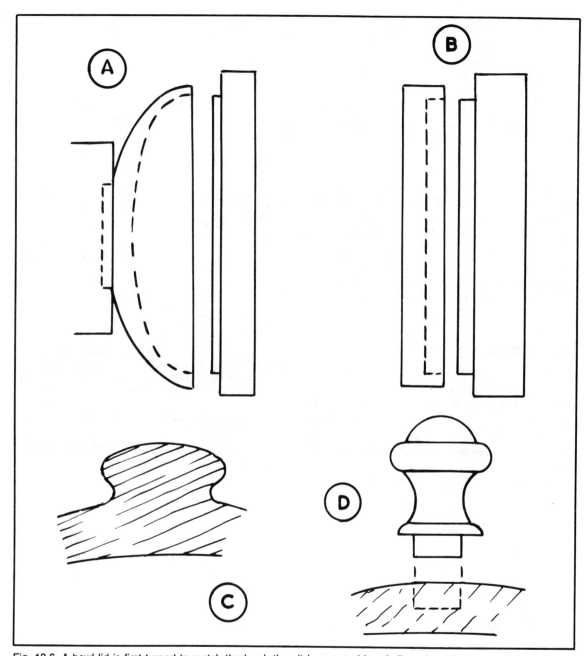

Fig. 13-6. A bowl lid is first turned to match the bowl, then it is mounted in a hollowed pad for turning the outside.

tional support. Turn the outside with gouges and scrapers. It is possible to turn a knob in the same wood (Fig. 13-6C), but this should not be too small nor with intricate detail as the wood is cross-grained, and there is a risk of pieces breaking out.

Such a knob should be fairly large and with a bold outline. This would suit a fairly large bowl and lid, where a good grip is needed. For a small bowl of more delicate appearance, it is better to make a knob separately and fix it with a dowel.

For an integral knob allow a small waste piece at the center so the tailstock can provide support for as long as possible. Do all of the rest of the turning except for this, including sanding, then withdraw the tailstock and turn off the waste piece.

If there is to be a separate knob, the dent made by the center will serve to locate the drill for the knob dowel, so there is no need to plan to allow waste there for turning off. Turn right down to the center, then use a drill in a tailstock chuck to make a hole. Do not go right through. There is little load to be taken so quite a shallow dowel will do, and this will avoid risking the point of the drill breaking through to the inside (Fig. 13-6D). A knob in a wood of contrasting appearance looks good, unless there is a need to keep to a uniform appearance for the sake of matching other furniture. The construction of knobs is described in Chapter 14.

LEGS AND RAILS

If a stool, chair, or table is made with turned legs and rails, there is a problem of assembly. It is unwise to tackle an assembly other than a right angled one at first. Complications arise when something like a Windsor chair is made with its splayed turned legs and the need to drill holes for rails at the correct angles.

A doweled end to a rail gets much more glue surface and, therefore, more strength if the leg is a square section (Fig. 13-7A) than if it is round (Fig. 13-7B). This is particularly so if there are two rails meeting in the leg at the same level. Even if they are carefully mitered, there is not much strength unless the circular section is made much larger across than the equivalent square section leg. For lower rails, it is usually possible to bring them in at different levels and so get greater penetration and strength.

Having square parts to the rails where dowel holes have to be drilled also helps ensure accurate drilling as using a drill press will automatically get the holes at right angles to the surface. Without a drill press, the drill can be mounted in a chuck at

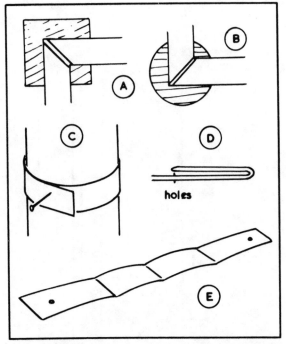

Fig. 13-7. Doweled joints in square parts have more glue area. The spacing around a round leg can be found by folding a piece of paper after marking around it with a pin.

the lathe headstock and the wood held against a pad in the tailstock.

If holes have to be drilled at right angles to each other in a round leg, spacing can be arranged with a strip of paper. Wrap the paper around so its ends overlap. Stick a pin through the overlap (Fig. 13-7C). Open out the paper. The distance between the holes made by the pin will be the circumference of the wood. This could be divided into four by measuring, but it is simpler to fold the paper so the holes meet, then fold again so the first fold comes over the holes (Fig. 13-7D). When opened out, there should be a crease at each quarter-circumference (Fig. 13-7E). Wrap the strip back around the wood. Position it with the pin through the holes if you wish. Make marks at two quarter-circumference positions, and these are the points at which you drill holes at right angles to each other. If the holes are to be staggered, project along from one point to the new position.

Chapter 14

Small Items

There are many small things that can be turned, mainly for use with pieces of cabinetwork. A wood-turner is able to find uses for pieces of wood too small to be of much use to any other woodworker, and it is worthwhile accumulating a stock of off-cuts that other workers throw away. Quite often, a small piece of wood with confused grain, which would be difficult to work by ordinary tools, can turn to make an attractive lathe project. The difficult grain formation that caused someone else to discard the wood is just what makes the turned item appealing.

For most work, there is no need to have special tools. If a piece of wood being turned is only a few inches long, there is no need for the larger and heavier tools. A 1/4-inch gouge with a long curved point will do most roughing to shape and some finishing, while chisel work can be done with only part of a chisel blade, so a 1/4-inch chisel should take care of most things. If there is very fine intricate work to be turned, it may be necessary to make small scraping tools. Although it may be possible to put a temporary cutting edge on the end

of a screwdriver or an awl, then regrind it for its original use afterwards.

Wood for small items should be hard and close-grained if possible. The more open-grained and softer woods are more difficult to turn with fine detail. There is too much risk of delicate parts breaking out as they are being turned. However, if something is being turned that has to match the wood to which it is being fixed, the work may have to be done in less suitable wood and extra care is needed. This means keeping tools very sharp, taking light cuts, and getting the lathe speed right. Small items can usually take the highest speed of which the lathe is capable, but it may be advisable to slow the machine if you are doubtful about the wood.

KNOBS

A frequent need is for handles and knobs for drawers and doors. There are many metal and plastic alternatives to be bought, but there is more satisfaction in using a knob you have made yourself,

175

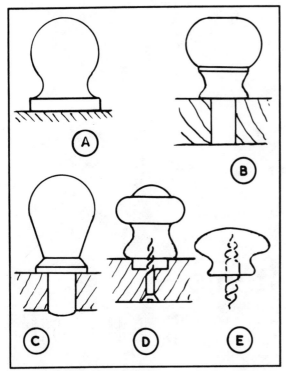

Fig. 14-1. A knob may be glued to the surface or made with a dowel. It can also be screwed.

14-1D) serves to accurately position the knob, although the screw takes the load. Another screwed pattern utilizes a double-ended screw that is driven into a hole turned centrally in the knob (Fig. 14-1E), then the knob is turned to drive the other end into its final location. If it is every likely that the knob will have to be removed, one of the screw fixings is advisable; otherwise, it is better to rely on glue alone or with a screw.

A knob or handle may be turned with a flowing curve without any steps (Fig. 14-2A). This probably gives just as good a grip as any other pattern, but most turners try to break up the plainness. The part that is grasped may be spherical or elliptical, joining a conical base with an abrupt change of

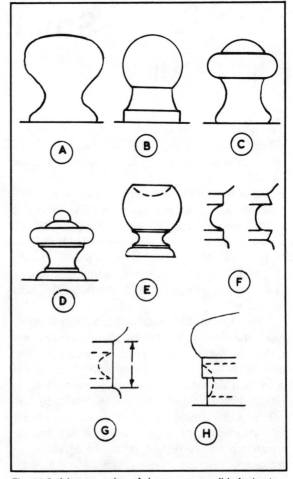

Fig. 14-2. A large number of shapes are possible for knobs.

particularly if the piece of furniture is of a reproduction type where the original could not have taken advantage of factory-made items.

A knob may be turned just to the shape that is visible (Fig. 14-1A). It then has to rely on glue only or a screw driven through from the back. It is better to turn the knob with a dowel to fit a hole that either goes through the wood or stops in a blind hole. A dowel through the wood gives a greater glue area (Fig. 14-1B), but having the end exposed inside may not be appropriate. If some antique furniture is examined, dowel ends may be seen rounded inside (Fig. 14-1C) to give a better appearance. A blind hole does not mar the inside, but if a normal bit with a long point is used, take care that it does not penetrate the inside surfaces.

If there is a reasonable length of dowel in a hole, there should be enough glue area to provide ample strength. Sometimes, as when a heavily-loaded drawer has to be pulled, it may be felt safer to use a screw. Even then, a very short dowel (Fig.

shape (Fig. 14-2B). The large part may have a bead around it (Fig. 14-2C) with or without a central pip (Fig. 14-2D).

Steps between concave and convex outlines are always considered better design than letting one curve blend directly into each other, so the first example can be adapted to show small, but distinct, steps at the changes of outline (Fig. 14-2E). Usually the surfaces of the steps should be kept parallel with the axis of the knob, although they may be angled in sometimes for effect (Fig. 14-2F). Angling the other way spoils the appearance. If both sides of a hollow have steps the same diameter, it is best to turn straight across and work the hollow afterwards (Fig. 14-2G). This is impossible if the steps are of different diameters (Fig. 14-2H), but even then the steps can be turned wider than their final size at first, then the hollow worked to give a clean cut-off at the edges of the steps.

Although a knob could be turned with the dowel toward the tailstock, this leaves the other end of the knob to be parted off with a possibility that

the center would be broken or marked. Because this is the part of the knob most obvious when it is in use, it is better to turn in a way that will allow better attention to it while the work is still in the lathe.

One way to turn a single knob is to have a piece of wood long enough to allow a waste end and to mount this between centers so it can be turned to the maximum diameter and a dowel turned (Fig. 14-3A). Some of the outline can be turned, but at what will be the front of the knob, part off with enough to spare so there is no risk of roughness at the final position (Fig. 14-3B).

If a self-centering or other chuck is available, the work can be held by its dowel for the knob to be finished. If the drill chuck has a capacity of a 1/2 inch, that can be used in the headstock to hold knobs up to this size. If a suitable chuck is unavailable, a block of wood can be mounted on a screw center with its grain lengthwise. Turn its outline true and square the end, then use a drill mounted in a tailstock chuck to make a hole to suit the dowel. Let the hole be slightly deeper than the

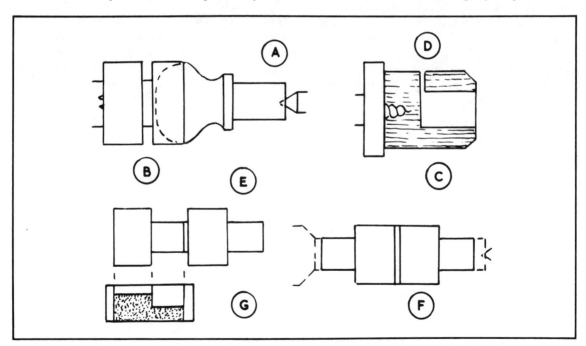

Fig. 14-3. A single knob can be turned between centers. If several knobs are needed, they can be made in one length. If a pad is used to support the dowel end of a knob for finishing, it is helpful to drill a small hole into its side so trapped air can escape.

177

length of the knob dowel. Keep the amount of overhang to a minimum by letting the wood only be long enough to allow the hole to be drilled without the drill touching the screw (Fig. 14-3C).

The knob dowel should be a push fit in the hole so it is friction driven. The dowel may be turned with a very slight taper, and it will help to chamfer its end. So that air in the hole can be released when the knob is mounted, drill a small hole into the bottom of the main hole (Fig.14-3D). It is best if the dowel goes in far enough for the underside of the knob to bear against the block of wood. It is more likely to run true than if part of the dowel is projecting.

With the knob mounted in this way, the exposed part can be turned right to the center and a good finish obtained.

It is more common for there to be at least a pair of knobs needed. This means that more care is needed to ensure the second knob matching the first. The wood can be prepared to suit two or more knobs. How many can be made in a strip depends on rigidity. If too many are included, the wood may flex too much during turning. Short thick knobs obviously permit more grouping than long thin ones.

For multiple turning, the strip is turned to the maximum diameter and lengths marked. Dowels may all be the same way (Fig. 14-3E), but by reversing one, thinning and flexing near the center of the strip can be reduced (Fig. 14-3F). If a rod is made for lengthwise divisions of one knob, it can be moved to check individual turning (Fig. 14-3G). Calipers will be needed to check comparable reduced parts, although turning a parallel cylinder should ensure that outside diameters will be the same.

More knob designs are discussed in Chapter 29.

TOES

For many furniture items, there have to be toes or feet to support the carcasses off the floor. If the piece of furniture has to be moved, there may be casters, but even when these are used, there may have to be a block-type toe to serve as a secure base and attachment for the caster fitting—either deep enough to be drilled for its spindle or wide enough to take the fixing screws through its plate. Without casters, the toes come directly against the floor. They should be rounded so as not to mark carpeting or other floor covering, or they may be broad if there is a considerable load to be taken and support is more important than protection of floors.

Similar, but more delicate, toes may be fitted to boxes and other lighter items that have to stand on a table. It is steadier to support anything with a fairly broad base on three or four points than it is to let the whole base make contact. Slight unevenness in the base or the surface on which it rests can cause wobbling. Three feet will stand firm on any surface, but as most items are rectangular, it is more usual to have four, and this is the next best arrangement.

The simplest toes are little more than buttons that glue in place (Fig. 14-4A). The lower surface should be rounded and smooth. The upper surface must be flat to make a good glued joint. The best way to make these toes is to use a piece of wood long enough for a set and to turn them one at a time from its end. The wood is turned to the intended outside diameter and is held in a chuck or with a drilled pad on a screw center. The curved end is shaped, then that toe is parted off (Fig. 14-4B) and the next toe can be made. See that the parting tool goes straight in to leave a flat surface.

These toes and deeper ones are best made with dowels in a similar way to that described for knobs. If the toes are to be at floor level and under an overhanging carcase, there is no need for elaborate turning. Something like the button-shaped toes can be deepened and given dowels (Fig. 14-4C). They may be spherical, but turning a true sphere is difficult if it is to look right, so it is better to deliberately let the outline be a little off (Fig. 14-4D).

Where the toe is more obvious, it can be turned with steps between concave and convex outlines. It will usually look better if the greater diameter is higher than a smaller diameter (Fig. 14-4E), although it might provide a broader support area for a heavy load with the lower part larger. If a caster is to be fitted, the size will be governed by its needs—either deep enough for boring to take its

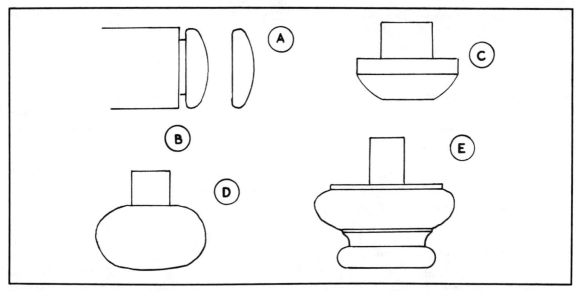

Fig. 14-4. Feet are made in a very similar way to knobs.

spindle or broad enough to accommodate its screwed fixing plate.

TERMINALS

Small turned items can form terminals or finials as decorative items on the ends of posts and other parts of furniture. They make a neat and decorative finish to what might otherwise be a plain and abrupt part. A larger version can be used at the end of a ridge roof, surmounting the gable end. Except for being quite large, its design and construction are similar to furniture terminals.

Terminals always have dowels to locate them. The extremity usually has a smaller diameter than the base, although it often finishes in a knob. A finial standing up on the end of something like a mirror support is very much a design feature and eye-catching, so it should be well-made and a pair should be an exact match.

Simple terminal ornaments (Fig. 14-5A) do not project far, but they have broad bases and taper to shaped ends. As with the better handles and knobs, there are steps between differences in curves to emphasize them and catch the light. Rather more am-

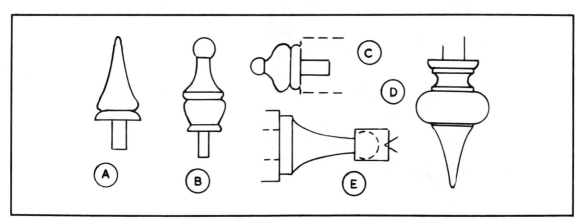

Fig. 14-5. Terminals are used to give a decorative end and are not expected to be pulled or stood on.

bitious terminals may be generally bulbous near the base and taper off toward the ends (Fig. 14-5B). Not all terminals stand upward, but they may be on horizontal rails, and the projection is generally kept short, rather more like drawer knobs (Fig. 14-5C), or they may hang down, when a more pronounced taper is applicable (Fig. 14-5D).

A terminal that does not run off too slender can be turned in the same way as a door knob, but if there is a slender part, it is better to use support from the tail center as long as possible. A finial with a slender tapered neck finishing in a knob can be turned almost to completion with the tail center in position (Fig. 14-5E). If the work up to that stage has been between centers, the terminal can have its dowel pushed into a hole in a block mounted on a screw center for the final delicate work on the end. This allows you to sand and finish right to the center of the end to give a good appearance to this prominent part (Fig. 14-6).

SPINDLES

There are many cabinetmaking constructions where there are a number of small turned pillars or spindles. They may support a rail above a desk top, hold a shaped top around a book rack, and in many Victorian pieces and older furniture, there are rows of spindles between parts. Usually they are not very large—being only a few inches long and often no more than 1 inch in greatest diameter. However, they are often quite close together and this means that great care is needed to ensure they match. Sometimes the end ones of a row are a different pattern, and this may serve to obscure slight discrepancies between inner spindles. Making a set of spindles is a good test of a woodturner's ability to do repetitive work accurately.

Spindles may have tapers towards their ends and be made similar to chair and table rails (Fig. 14-7A). While this allows the amount of penetration into holes to vary there ought to be shouldered

Fig. 14-6. A dowel on a small terminal has been pressed into a hole in a block mounted on a screw center for final shaping of its end.

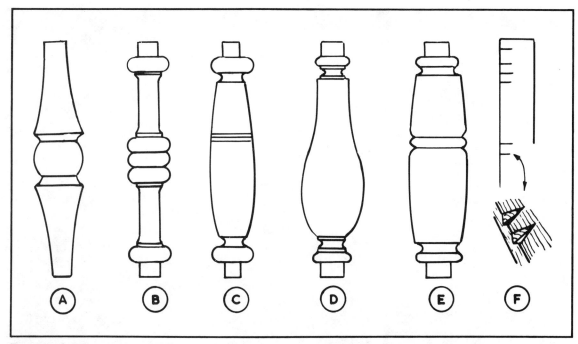

Fig. 14-7. Spindles can be used in many situations, but because they are usually in a series, it is important that they all should match.

rails at the ends to keep the parts parallel. Usually all rails are shouldered. The pattern chosen is usually symmetrical, whether the spindles are to be in the usual upright position or horizontal (Fig. 14-7B). This means they could be turned end for end when mounting. If symmetry is perfect, this does not matter, but it is probably better to arrange the design so there is at least one feature to indicate top or bottom (Fig. 14-7C). This means you only have to watch that spindles match each other one way as you make them, and do not have to check that they will look the same if reversed.

In some cases, it is better to use a pattern that could not be reversed. There are many Greek ornaments and vases, as well as other items that can provide ideas for spindle shapes. Usually the greater diameter is towards the bottom (Fig. 14-7D), or there is decoration off-center (Fig. 14-7E). Remember that a row of spindles will be looked at as a group, and it is not necessarily the individual shape that provides a design feature.

Spindles are straightforward turnings between centers. It is helpful to have several pairs of calipers

so different parts can be compared between successive spindles without the frequent readjustment of one pair of calipers, which could lead to discrepancies. It is also important to have a good rod marked out and work carefully to it. It may help to ensure uniformity to file or chisel notches to take the pencil point at each position (Fig. 14-7F).

Besides using a rod and calipers, it is helpful to have the first spindle behind the lathe and as close to the work as you can reasonably get it. With this in front of you, it is possible to judge progress by eye and see what may need a little more off or a slight adjustment to the sweep of a curve. If all of the spindles of a row are shouldered, the curve of an end bead will disguise any slightly open joint. It is helpful to have one large pair of calipers set to the length between shoulders, or use a notched piece of wood as a lengthwise gauge (Fig. 14-8). Even if the dowels are not turned to their full depth at first, the shoulders are turned to match the gauge before the other features are turned to match the rod and calipers.

More spindle designs are shown in Chapter 23.

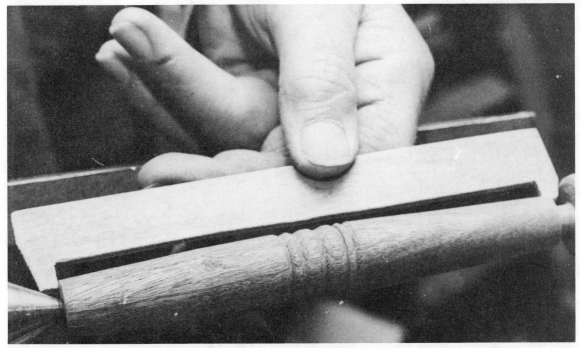

Fig. 14-8. A notched strip will serve as a length gauge when several pieces have to be made to match.

CHESSMEN

If you examine chess sets, you will see that designs of the individual men vary considerably, but basically the majority of sets are primarily turned parts. Some may be elaborately carved and some turning may be quite intricate. Some of the more complicated parts are made of ivory, which can be turned in a similar way to metal, and finer detail than is possible in wood can be cut.

It is possible to use two different colored woods. Ebony is the obvious choice for the black parts, but is not the easiest wood to turn and not so easy to obtain. It is usually better to make the whole set of a close-grained, light-colored hardwood and stain half of the pieces. The smaller the pieces, the more important it is to use hardwood with tight grain and no risk of parts breaking away. For general use and a first attempt, it is advisable to make a set with a king about 4 inches high.

The set shown (Fig. 14-9) is from a fairly simple pattern that avoids much of the multiple beads and hollows found in some sets, particularly those

based on Victorian and earlier sets. Modern preferences in chess sets and other things are for less ornate designs. The pieces are almost completely turned. The ornamenting that has to be done away from the lathe is simply sawing or filing. The cross and horse's head can be carved and given small dowels to fit into holes. The horse may be elaborately carved if you are sufficiently skilled and artistic, or it can be a simplified stylized outline. Notice that the overall greatest diameter should be about the same for all pieces, but they vary in height. If there are differences in diameter, keep all of the same pieces the same size and if any pieces are thicker, it is better that they should be the taller ones.

As with the other small parts described in this chapter, it is the exposed tops of chessmen that are most obvious to the eye, so it is advisable to turn the ends while they project unsupported. The pieces could be given dowels for plugging into a hole, then the dowel cut off later. Another way is to use a screw center. The hole left from the screw can be plugged or filled with stopping later. If the bottom is covered with self-adhesive cloth, the hole will be hidden in any case.

Wood of a length sufficient for several men can be turned between centers. It is probably advisable to start with pawns. Square the end with a chisel into the center. If it is not flat, it is better to be slightly hollow than to finish rounded. This will be the bottom of the first pawn. Start shaping it. The bottom bead and some of the bulbous body can be made to the finished stage, but further parts of it may be reduced with the gouge, and some waste

material left for finishing on the screw center (Fig. 14-10A).

Use a drill that suits the screw center to make a hole. Work with a tailstock chuck. Part or saw off the first pawn. Bring the tailstock up so the back center supports the cut end and make the next pawn up to the same stage. Make all of the pawns up to this stage before moving onto the next stage. Do the same later with the full numbers of other men.

Mount each pawn in turn on the screw center and turn its end to shape (Fig. 14-10B). There is

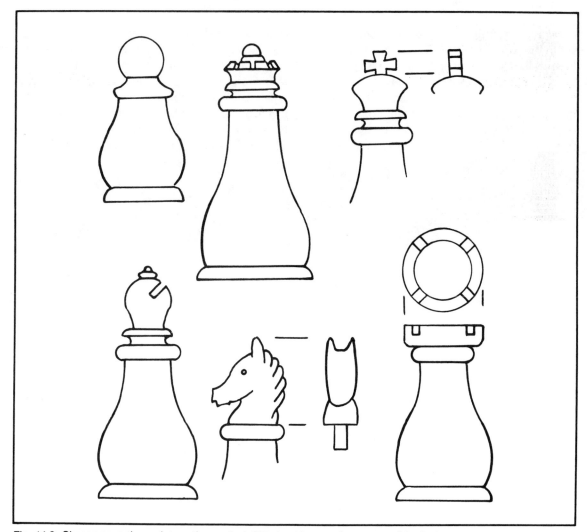

Fig. 14-9. Chessmen make an interesting project. This is only one of many possible designs.

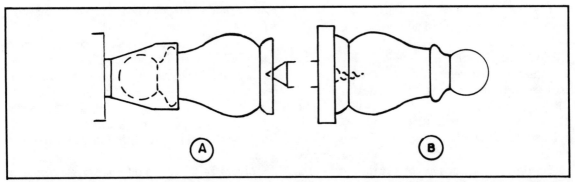

Fig. 14-10. Chessmen can be turned with the base toward the tailstock for the major part of turning. Then, reverse them on a screw chuck for finishing.

no need for a pad against the faceplate because that part of the pawn has already been turned and a tool does not have to be taken close to the metalpad.

With any part that is to have a top piece doweled in the tail, the center can be brought up for support. This will also mark the center for the dowel hole. It is still better to start by making the base to the right and reverse the piece onto a screw center for final turning.

Chessmen may be sanded and cleaned up in the same way as other turned work, but it is not usual to give the wood a high gloss. The best sanding finish that can be obtained in the lathe should be given. Then, it may be sufficient with most woods to use wax on a cloth against the revolving wood. The final patina comes with age and use.

Chapter 15

Balls and Rings

Turning a true sphere is a difficult task. If the ball is to be of an accuracy that will permit it to roll without deviating off its path, perfection has to be absolute. Fortunately, such accuracy is not always a requirement and a ball turned to wider tolerances may be acceptable. A ball that is intended to be thrown in a game can be some way from spherical and be just as acceptable. If the ball is to have a hole through it and be strung on cord in the manner of beads, it may even be better if it is more elliptical than spherical.

SIMPLE BALLS

If a ball does not have to be exceptionally accurate, it is possible to turn it between centers with ordinary tools. A piece of wood long enough to allow some waste at each end is turned to a cylinder of the size the ball is to be. Each side of the ball is then roughed out with a gouge (Fig. 15-1A). These cuts should be kept well on the waste side of what will be the eventual shape, so the first outline produced will tend to be elliptical with the longer axis lengthwise.

Measure a length equal to a diameter and cut in with the long point of a chisel slightly on the waste sides of the lines (Fig. 15-1B). Turn away a little more with the gouge toward these marks. Work by eye, but keep clear of the final outline you visualize. One of the stubs will be used to mount the ball later. This is most conveniently the one toward the tailstock. Turn this to size. In most cases, it will push into a hole drilled in a pad mounted on a screw center or faceplate (Fig. 15-1C). If the lathe has tapered holes for mounting centers, the stub could be turned to a suitable shape to push into the hole in the mandrel nose, instead of using a pad.

Make a template of the intended outline of the ball. It should be wide enough to cover about one-third of the circumference. This could be cut from a card, but it may be better made from thin metal, such as a piece of discarded can, cut with snips (Fig. 15-1D).

Make light cuts with a chisel, working from the greatest diameter over the curves toward the ends. Check with the template. So long as the curve

185

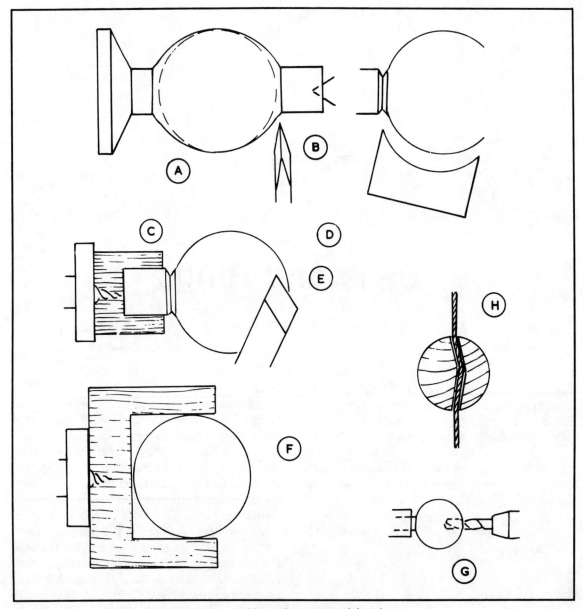

Fig. 15-1. A true ball shape is difficult to turn, and it needs some special work.

turned is flatter than that of the template—its points touch instead of its center—you have not gone too far. Continue in this way until the curve of all of the ball that can be reached matches the template.

At the headstock end of the ball, the diameter of the waste part can be reduced so the shape of the ball can be taken further, but do not go so far

as to weaken the wood. Do not part off as this may cause fractured fibers that may go below the final surface of the ball. Remove the ball from the lathe and saw off the waste piece at the headstock end. Mount the ball by the stub on the other end and turn the exposed part to size (Fig. 15-1E).

How the remaining piece is dealt with depends

186

on the quality of ball required. If the finish is not very important, the stub can be sawn off and the end finished by hand with a chisel and abrasive paper. If the end is to be finished in the lathe, the ball can be mounted in a wood chuck. This is a piece of wood turned with a hollow having a slight taper into which the ball can be pressed and driven by friction (Fig. 15-1F).

If more than one ball has to be made, two or three may be turned from one cylindrical piece of wood. The stubs for the inner balls cannot be turned very small or the whole thing will flex. However, it is possible to rough turn a series of balls then deal with the end one and cut it off so the next can be turned.

If balls are to be drilled, the problem of dealing with the cut-off end grain parts is reduced. A ball can be turned to the point where it is mounted by one stub, then a drill in a tailstock chuck used to make the hole. If the drill is about the size of the remaining wood, it will serve to part off the ball as well (Fig. 15-1G).

An amusing variation on this is to drill holes from opposite sides by hand so they are slightly on the skew (Fig. 15-1H). If the ball is threaded on a cord, which is held upright without much tension, the ball will slid down and the cord reversed for it to slide back, but if the operator tells the ball to stop, it mystifies the audience by doing this. In fact, the operator pulls the cord tight and it then jams in the crooked hole.

Small balls with holes through them can be used as beads. Larger wooden balls are used as separators on fishing gear and are known as *parrels* in some sailing rigs.

ACCURATE BALLS

For a more accurately made ball, it is necessary to be able to move it around so turning is done in directions other than the first cuts. This necessitates making some holding devices. It is advisable to grind a scraper tool to the intended shape of the ball.

A cup chuck has to be made (Fig. 15-2A). This should be close-grained hardwood, and its greatest diameter should be about one-third of the diameter

the ball is to be. It can be turned to push in the tapered socket of the headstock mandrel, or it can be mounted on a screw center. The vital part is that which presses against the ball. Its hollow should be deep enough for the rim, and not the bottom, to take the thrust from the ball and the outer part turned away so an almost sharp edge is exposed to the ball.

There has to be a pad at the tailstock end. This is a smaller diameter than the cup chuck, but it is given a hollow to bear on the ball in the same way (Fig. 15-2B). If possible, have a rotating ball bearing center in the tailstock. Turn the pad to come some way up the slope of the center, or even go right over it to the parallel part if it is comparatively small. If a plain center has to be used, the pad should be a good fit on the point, but as it has to revolve with the ball, use grease inside the pad.

If a special scraper is ground to the curve of the ball, let it come to points at the side. The width of the scraper and the width of the cup center should be the same (Fig. 15-2C).

Turn a cylinder between centers the same diameter as the ball. Rough out the shape without going too far. Do this the same way as for the first ball. Turn the center portion to the exact curve, either with a chisel and a template for comparison or by using the prepared scraper. Use a pencil to mark a line around the center of this recess (Fig. 15-2D). Check with calipers and a template. Turn away more of the waste at each side of this first cut, but be careful to keep oversize. Checking with calipers at an angle will show what progress is being made (Fig. 15-2E). Turn down until only small nibs are left at each side of the ball. Remove the wood from the lathe and saw these off so as not to tear the fibers.

It is the penciled circle that now provides a check on the shape when the ball is turned, so the ball is put between the cup chuck and pad with the penciled circle lengthwise (Fig. 15-2F). If the wood is now turned just down to the pencil line without going below it, the result should be a sphere of a fine degree of accuracy.

Keep a good thrust on the tailstock so the cup center drives the ball without slipping. Turn the outside to shape. Watch the pencil line as cutting

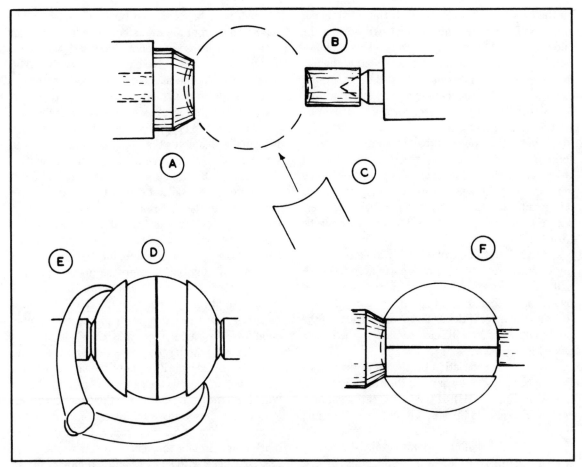

Fig. 15-2. One way of turning a ball is to work it in two directions.

progresses. The line can be seen revolving, but it may be advisable to stop the lathe occasionally and check where it is necessary to remove a little more. When tool work is finished, the pencil line should still be intact, but barely.

When the shape from the tools is satisfactory, the ball may be sanded. Pressure can be released and the ball moved to several other positions so sanding comes in many directions and the final outline is smooth all over and without tool marks showing.

RINGS

Another turning problem comes when parts have to be turned with large holes through them,

as with large rings or circular picture frames. Small, thick pieces can be mounted on a mandrel, but larger, slender-sectioned items need a different technique.

It may be possible to turn a ring with its center solid and cut this away as the last action. A pad may be mounted on a faceplate, then the wood to be turned screwed to it. If the central hole is large, the fixing screws can be driven from the front, if that is more convenient than the usual way (Fig. 15-3A).

Outside shaping is done first. Do this in the same way as working a bowl using gouges and scrapers. Some of the inside is turned away with a parting tool (Fig. 15-3B), then the inside worked to the required size with a scraper. Cuts may be taken almost through to the other side. All of the finishing work can be done before the ring is parted off by cutting through it (Fig. 15-3C).

This method leaves a rough edge inside the ring where the cut goes through. With careful work it is easily cleaned off by hand away from the lathe. This method does not permit any turning on the face of the ring toward the pad on the faceplate, so it is unsuitable for anything that needs turning on both sides, as is necessary with a round picture frame. An exception is when the part being turned is much larger than the pad on which it is mounted. Then, turning can be done on the other side and the final parting cut made from that side in order to give a clean edge.

A picture frame needs a rabbet in the back, and it is usual to turn the front surface in some form of molding, which may be just a few lines cut around or a more elaborate section based on a traditional shape. Such a frame can be started in the

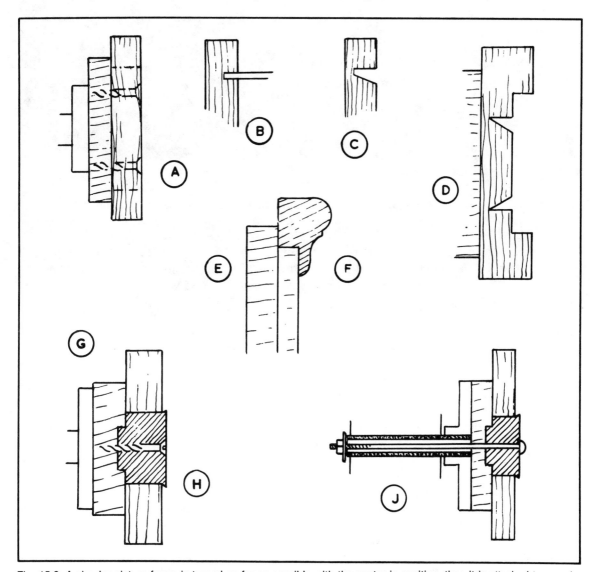

Fig. 15-3. A circular picture frame is turned as far as possible with the center in position, then it is attached to a pad.

Fig. 15-4. A small circular picture frame has its rabbet pressed onto a shaped pad while the outside molding is turned.

same way as the ring just described, but the rabbet is turned in the back before the ring is cut through (Fig. 15-3D).

The pad on the faceplate is turned down to fit into the rabbet and provide a friction drive (Fig. 15-3E). This allows the inner part to be turned clean and the front worked in any way desired (Fig. 15-3F). If the pad is kept smaller than the outside diameter of the frame, the edge can also be turned to complement the face molding (Fig. 15-4).

Another way of mounting a ring after the central hollow has been cut out is to use a matching plug. This is turned parallel, except for a slight enlarging toward the outside. If the work is to be mounted on a pad, it helps in getting the work to run truly if a part of the plug fits into a hollow turned in the pad (Fig. 15-3G). The plug is secured by a wood screw driven through its center into the pad (Fig. 15-3H), but with a hollow mandrel, there can be a bolt taken right through it (Fig. 15-3J).

A wooden ring of circular section is an interesting project. It requires a slightly different technique from a simple rectangular or picture frame ring if it is to be both round in outline and

in section. Use a piece of wood as large as the ring is to be and slightly thicker. Cut it to a circular outline and mount it on a faceplate or screw center of smaller diameter than the inside of the finished ring is to be. Do not use a pad between it and the faceplate (Fig. 15-5A).

Turn the rim to the finished outside diameter. Turn both sides so the remaining thickness is that of the finished ring (Fig. 15-5B). Turn the outside to a semicircular section. Check this with a template. One can be made by drilling a hole of the correct size in a piece of thin plywood, then cut it in half (Fig. 15-5C).

Pencil a line around to indicate what will be the inside of the ring. Cut in on the waste side of this with a parting tool, then use a skew-ended scraper to remove more of the waste, and shape the inside of the ring. Check with the template, and it will be possible to get the section correct for about three-quarters of its circumference (Fig. 15-5D). This much can be cleaned up and sanded before parting off. Part off by cutting mostly from the front, but also cut in lightly from the back. Check the depths of cut from both sides and make the final breakthrough lightly and preferably at a low speed. Be ready to catch the ring. If the section is small in relation to the overall diameter, try not to let the ring fly from the lathe as this may crack the short-grained parts.

For the remaining quarter of the section, prepare a pad that will grip the ring from the outside. This should have a hollow that allows more than half the thickness of the ring to penetrate and be gripped by friction (Fig. 15-5E). Turn the final quarter section of the ring by light scraping cuts pressing outward and backward into the pad.

With the present day greater use of plywood, it is possible to turn rings in this material. However, care is needed to keep scrapers sharp and presented at the correct angles; otherwise, there

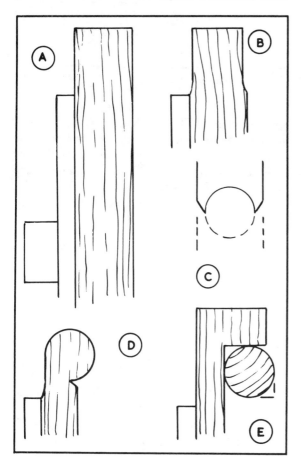

Fig. 15-5. A ring can be three-quarters turned with the center retained, then it is parted off and held in a hollowed pad.

is a risk of surface veneers breaking out. Plywood rings of simple section can be made (Fig. 15-6A) in the same way as described for solid wood. If edges are slightly rounded, these are stronger for use in games than solid wood.

It is possible to laminate pieces of wood to make rings. Joining blocks edgewise may not be satisfactory, but an interesting pattern can be built up with layers put together like bricks (Fig. 15-6B). This is stronger than solid wood and may be done for the sake of strength in something constructional, but if the woods are in contrasting colors, there will be an attractive appearance as well as strength. With a rabbet turned in the ring, the assembly can make a picture frame or have a base set in to make a tray (Fig. 15-6C).

A ring can be turned to make an edge to strengthen and improve the edge of a pot turned with the grain lengthwise. A tongue turned on the pot fits into a groove in the ring (Fig. 15-6D), which may be solid or laminated wood.

Although, by the nature of the process, only complete rings are turned, there are cabinetmaking constructions where only part of a ring may be needed. This happens when moldings have to be carried around curves. Then sections of turned rings are used to butt against straight moldings, either to follow a design around directly (Fig. 15-6E) or reversed to give a special effect (Fig. 15-6F). Care is needed in cutting the miters and in getting the section of the molded ring to match the straight molding. Although something is lost in sawcuts, it is usually possible to get two semicircles from a complete ring with only negligible loss due to a fine saw.

Although any wood may have to be turned into rings to match other parts, if there is any choice, avoid softwoods and hardwoods with open grains, particularly for any design that is a light section in relation to its overall diameter.

PLYWOOD TRAYS

In general, turners prefer to avoid working with plywood. If suitable pieces are chosen, however, it is possible to turn plywood cleanly and produce an interesting result with the many thin laminations

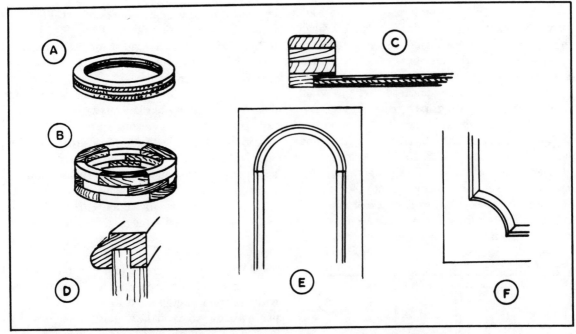

Fig. 15-6. Molding can be turned, either solid or laminated, and cut to shape afterwards.

showing through a clear finish, or the work may be painted to hide the ply edges. Very open-grained woods used in some plywood, such as Douglas fir, are difficult, although not impossible, to turn without some of the grain breaking out. Plywood made from hardwood veneers is better. Rims for the plates and trays just described could be made with several layers of plywood glued together to make up a suitable thickness. If you will be showing the plywood edges of the rim, you may as well omit the recess for the bottom and show the edges of that as well.

This method can also be used to make round trays of considerable size. The only limitation would be the capacity of the lathe, but an example is a stand of moderate size for a coffee or tea pot (Fig. 15-7A) with an outside diameter of about 10 inches. This has 1/4-inch plywood for the base and two pieces of 1/2-inch plywood sawn into rings and glued to make up the blank for turning (Fig. 15-7B). The rim is painted, and the base has Formica inside.

You could mount directly on a faceplate with four bolts through it (Fig. 15-7C). In that case, draw a circle of the size of the faceplate on the plywood

base, then position the faceplate on the wood and drill through it. The bolt holes may be enlarged later to take dowels from feet or they could be plugged. If cloth is glued under the base and a disc of Formica is fitted inside, the holes will be hidden in any case. If you want to avoid having holes through it, mount the blank on a disc of wood, either with screws (Fig. 15-7D) or glue and paper (Fig. 15-7E), so the joint can be levered apart later. Screw the mounting block to the faceplate.

Sharp tools are essential for clean cutting of plywood edges. Cut to shape as far as possible with gouges. Use fairly light cuts to avoid digging in or tearing end grain. Follow with a scraper. Have a burr turned on its edge and again use lightly. There may be a problem of surplus glue inside where the rim joins the base. It is difficult to turn this away without cutting into the base. It is probably best to deliberately cut in slightly, but obviously not through the surface ply (Fig. 15-7F).

With most plywoods and sharp tools used correctly, the finish should be good. You will have to follow with abrasive paper, and you may have to do some hand sanding after removing the job from

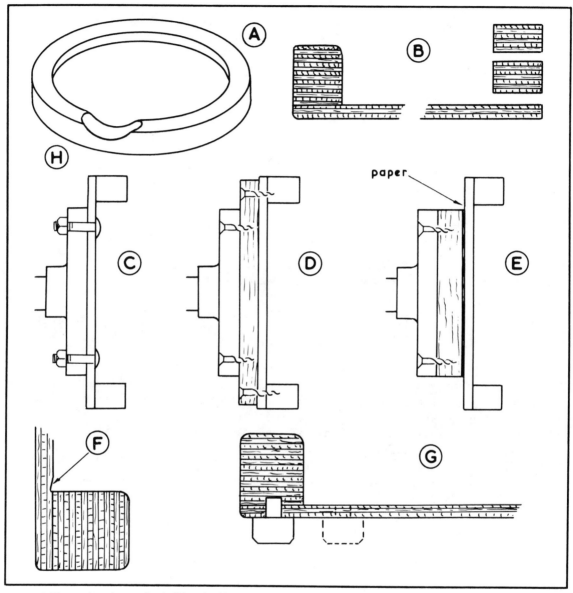

Fig. 15-7. Plywood can be used to build up the blank for turning a tray with a choice of methods of mounting on a faceplate.

the lathe if there are some stubborn end grain fibers.

If you want to fit feet, they can have dowels into holes (Fig. 15-7G), either at the faceplate bolt positions or further out for stability. Many jugs and pots have handles coming close to their bases. You can allow for them by hollowing the rim. There is a secondary benefit from this. If you want to cut

the insides of the pieces of plywood for the rim, as well as the outsides, with a bandsaw, you can cut through to the inside, then arrange the hollow where the cuts have come. If the hollowing does not need to go through to the base, the saw cut through in the lower ring can come elsewhere, where it will be hidden, and the hollow made at the cut in the top ring.

Chapter 16

Twist Turning

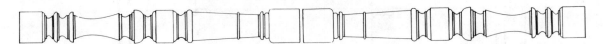

Turned spindles with grooves spiraling around them make attractive variations on straightforward turning for such things as candlesticks, table legs, and bed posts. The work is sometimes described as Jacobean, but its scope is much wider than just that period. For commercial production, there are elaborate combination lathes that work the spiral shape automatically, but these are limited to basic patterns and the hand worker can cut patterns that are impossible for the machine. Working a spiral pattern by hand is a combination of turning and carving that calls for patience rather than a high degree of skill. It can be time consuming, so it is not something for economic commercial production but is more the type of work for a craftsman to do for his own satisfaction.

In effect, a twist turning is a screw thread made around a cylindrical piece of wood. It may be single, double, or with an even larger number of threads. A single thread is probably best for a first attempt to grasp the technique, but a double thread looks best for most things. A further step is to separate the *bines*, so the threads go around with a space be-

tween them. This is usually done with a double thread and is probably visually most effective, but as a test of skill, a larger number of threads can be separated.

There are two screw-cutting terms that should be understood. The *pitch* of a thread is the distance from the top of one ridge to the next, measured lengthwise along the cylinder. The *lead* is the distance a screw would travel into a nut in one revolution. With a single thread or spiral, pitch and lead are the same. In a double spiral or *two-start thread*, the lead is twice the pitch. With any other number of multistart threads, the lead is the same number times the pitch as the number of spirals. This information is necessary when laying out the spirals.

It is possible to arrange pitch at any distance you choose, but it is necessary to consider appearance and the nature of the wood. Grain is weak if its lines are cut across closely. If a deep thread is cut with as tight a twist as seen in metal screws, the tops of the ridges might break during cutting or in use afterwards. There are tools for cutting

194

threads in wood screws and nuts, but the threads are quite coarse, and it is important to choose a suitable close-grained wood. For twist turning, the pitch is much greater. As a rough guide, the bines should spiral around the cylinder at about 45 degrees (Fig. 16-1A). Variations are possible, but this is a starting angle to work on. Very long angles are not as attractive, but if the item is to take a considerable load, longer angles and grooves that do not go too deeply may be advisable to retain enough strength.

The turned work does not have to be a parallel cylinder, but for early work, it is advisable to make the part that is to have the twist parallel. Any ordinary turning that will come at the ends can be done at the same time as this is turned, or the ends can be left square or octagonal until the twist has been completed. Then, the work can be mounted in the lathe and the final turning done. There is some risk of tools going where they should not and leaving the ends with waste wood on reduces the risk of damage there.

Turn the parallel cylinder. Use a pencil to mark the limits of the twist and put lines around to mark the positions of complete threads. Divide the length into equal parts, but let them be about the same as the diameter or slightly more, rather than less (Fig. 16-1B). Further divide these spaces into four with lighter lines (Fig. 16-1C).

SINGLE TWIST

For a single twist, divide the circumference into four and draw lines lengthwise. If the lathe has a dividing head, that can be used to get accurate spacing. Without that an easy way of dividing is to wrap a strip of paper around and push a pin through it. Open the paper and divide the space between pin holes into four. Put the paper back around the wood and mark it from these spacings. The tool rest can be brought close to the cylinder and used to draw along (Fig. 16-1D).

For our single twist, a pitch is one complete circuit, starting where a lengthwise line crosses the end circle to where it crosses the next *pitch circle*. This means the line of thread crosses the other intermediate circles at the other lengthwise lines. It

is possible to draw around it freehand and get a sufficiently accurate result, but it is better to twist a string around it or use a piece of adhesive tape (Fig. 16-1E) to draw along. Another way is to make a sort of set square with its height equal to the pitch and its base equal to the circumference. If this is cut from thin card (Fig. 16-1F), it can be wrapped around and gives a firmer line to draw along than tape or string.

The first line drawn should indicate the ridge of the spiral. Lines can be drawn around at each of the other positions. Those on each side of the ridge line indicate the width of the first cuts to make the hollow. The line opposite the ridge line will be cut away quite soon, so it may be omitted. Shading with pencil the part that will be hollow will reduce the risk of wrong cuts (Fig. 16-1G).

It is hard work with saw, chisel, and gouge from this point. The wood may be supported in the lathe or it can be removed and held in a vise. Square ends will help to secure it in a vise, but if round wood is to be squeezed, pad it well. Another way of holding round work is to have a trough, either in a vise or on the top of the bench. A strap can pass over the work and foot pressure in a loop (Fig. 16-1H) will hold it. When the wood has to be moved—as it frequently needs to be—releasing the foot pressure is a quicker action than having to operate a vise. The first sawing can be done against a bench hook in a trough or in a vise.

Use a small back saw and go around the waste part making cuts diagonally from alternate sides of the groove to remove small triangular-sectioned chips. Obviously, the cuts should not go deeper than the hollow is intended to be (Fig. 16-1J). If the wood has only a small diameter, a start can be made at removing the waste in the grooves by using a deep carving gouge or a carving V-tool. Keep cuts light at first, then as the hollow deepens, use the tool on the side that cuts with the grain and reverse to cut back on the other side.

Another way of removing the waste is to make a first saw cut around the line that marks the center of the hollow. Then chisel toward it from each side. Use a firmer chisel with its bevel downward.

With the bulk of the waste removed, the next

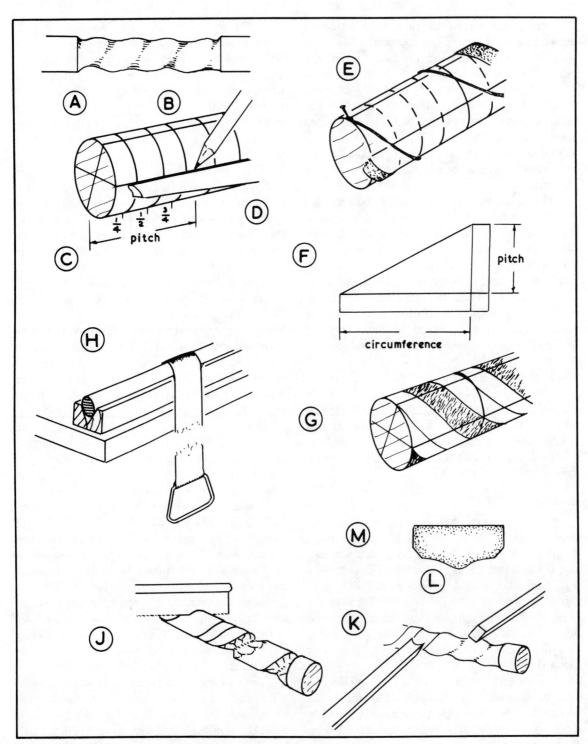

Fig. 16-1. Steps in marking out twist turning for sawing and carving.

step is to clean out the hollow, followed by rounding the top of the ridge. The hollow can be worked with a deep gouge that can keep its corners clear of the wood. It may be possible to use a turning gouge, but a shorter firmer gouge that can be hit with a mallet is easier to use. Work around the groove with cuts with the grain, so the sides of the grooves have to be cut opposite ways. Alternatively use a round file or Surform tool. If this approximates to the final curve, the hollow can be brought to a reasonable shape quite quickly (Fig. 16-1K).

The top of the ridge is rounded by using a chisel in the direction of the grain (Fig. 6-1L). For large work it may be possible to use a small plane. It is not always easy to keep the hollowing even. When one part has been done, a card template made to it can be used to check other parts as they are worked (Fig. 16-1M).

Leave the line around the apex of the twist visible for as long as possible. This helps keep the various steps symmetrical so the twist is even. When hollows and ridges have been brought to a reasonable form by work with tools, change to sanding. Abrasive paper can be wrapped around a piece of dowel rod to work the hollow, but for most of the spiral, a folded piece held in the hand is better. Work through progressively finer abrasives. Pay particular attention to the end grain exposed at the sides of the spiral, which may rise and show roughness under the final finish.

The ends of the spiral will have to blend into the plain turning. It is possible to take the shaped work right up to an abrupt stop against a bead. It usually looks better if the hollow is allowed to reduce towards the surface of the cylinder and the top of the spiral flattens in sections until the shapes disappear into a full circle.

DOUBLE TWIST

Once a single twist is understood, the making of a double or other twist is a simple progression. The basic cylinder is marked out in the same way, except it should be noted that, as the lead of a double twist is twice the pitch, the ridge line goes around to meet its lengthwise line at the second pitch circle (Fig. 16-2A). This has the effect of steepening the angle of twist. Draw two ridge lines at opposite sides (Fig. 16-2B). In the preliminary layout, the pitch circles could be brought closer together to lessen the steepness of the spirals—a spacing equal to about two-thirds of the diameter would be reasonable.

To get the widths of the grooves, the circumference needs to be divided into eight. This can probably be done by estimating points between the four, although for greater precision a dividing head or the pin and paper method can be used. Draw around at these other positions and pencil shade the two opposite parts that will form the hollows (Fig. 16-2C). The method of marking can be any of those suggested for the single twist, but if the set square

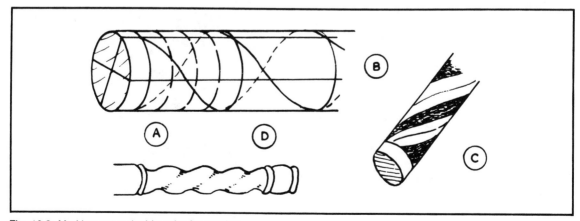

Fig. 16-2. Marking out a double twist for carving.

method is used (Fig. 16-1F), the height will be the lead (twice the pitch).

The work from this stage is similar to that for a single twist, except that two opposite hollows have to be worked. The raised and hollowed parts of a double twist are narrower than those of a single twist of the same overall diameter. Hollows should be worked relatively deeper. In a single twist, a hollow that is rather less than a semicircle in depth will usually be effective, but with a double twist, a rather deeper hollow in relation to its width is needed to get the best effect of light and shade (Fig. 16-2D).

A treble twist has to be marked out with three ridge lines going over three pitch circles and angled accordingly. To give attractive angles, the pitch circles can be brought even closer together than for a double twist. This means that the ridge lines start at one-third circumference spacing and suitable intermediate lines have to be marked, making a total of 12, instead of the eight for double twists. There is no reason why the idea should not be taken further. Increasing the number of bines means reducing their width in relation to the overall diameter with a lessening of the amount of shaping. So, a greater number of twists may be an interesting exercise, but the visual appearance is probably not as good as the simpler double twist.

OPEN TWIST

A further step is to separate the bines to make a hollow or open twist turning (Fig. 16-3 and 16-4A). This is usually arranged as a double twist. It cannot be done with a single twist, but it could be worked with any number greater than two. The only time a larger number might be effective is when the diameter of the pillar or other part is considerable in relation to its length. If the overall diameter is smaller, the effort put into separating the bines is not repaid by the visual effect, as the bines are too close together for the spacing to give a much different effect from a normal closed twist.

If a greater number than two is contemplated, an even number is much easier than an odd number. As will be seen in the description of a double open twist, there are holes right through it, but with an

odd number of bines, the hole on one side is opposite a bine on the other side and waste cannot be removed by drilling through it.

An open double twist is started like a closed double twist. It is marked out with a line around the center of the shaded part indicating the hollow. There are three ways of removing the waste. In the first method, the hollows are cut with saw and other tools, but taken fairly deeply (Fig. 16-4B). Outside shaping need not be done yet.

Next, a series of holes are drilled through the bottoms of the hollows (Fig. 16-4C). The holes are

Fig. 16-3. An open-twist candlestick has the helical center part carved or whittled.

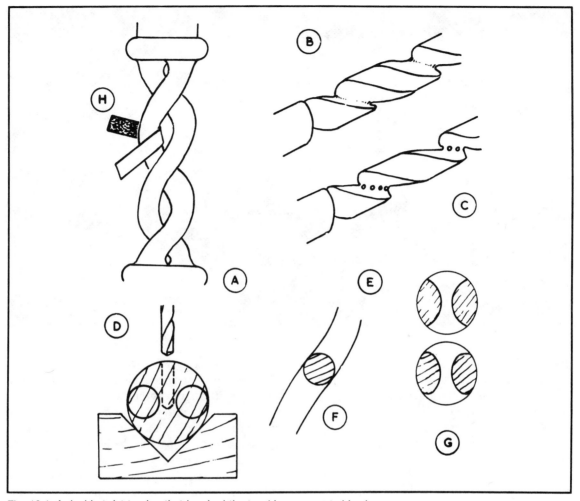

Fig. 16-4. A double twist turning that has had the two bines separated is shown.

fairly close together. A pointed knife or a narrow chisel can be used to break away the waste between the holes and open up the gap.

In the other drilling method, it is advisable to have the wood supported in a trough or V-block on the base of a drill press or a hand electric drill mounted in a stand. This method is not so suitable as the first for freehand drilling. With the wood able to be moved around under the drill, use a bit slightly smaller in diameter than the final spacing is intended to be. Then go around the line marking the center of the hollowing. Holes may be drilled right through, but this might cause splintering and breaking out on the far side, so it is better to drill only

as far as the center of the wood from the lines marking the centers of both hollows (Fig. 16-4D).

A carving expert may prefer to break through without drilling. This is done by using a very deep narrow gouge called a *veiner*. Work progressively deeper around the centers until opposite grooves meet. Even then, some holes drilled through allow the amount of wood yet to be gouged out to be seen, thus a better check is kept on progress than gouging blindly.

The first opening will be quite rough inside, but this can be worked to shape and smoothed with a round file or the point of a knife. Aim to get a smoothly rounded inner surface (Fig. 16-4E). Shape

Fig. 16-5. The open twist can have the bines sanded while the wood is supported by lathe centers.

the outsides to match the insides (Fig. 16-4F). The section of each bine should be circular at right angles to its axis, but at right angles to the pillar it will be elliptical (Fig. 16-4G).

Although you can get some way by filing and whittling, final shaping and smoothing of the inside surfaces will have to be done with narrow strips of abrasive paper or cloth pulled backwards and forwards while being moved along each bine (Fig. 16-4H). If you can remount the turning between centers in the lathe, that is a convenient way of holding the work during this operation (Fig. 16-5). At the ends, each bine has to blend into the full turned parts. They can widen to finish as a bead or other turned decoration.

VARIATIONS

An alternative way of dealing with closed or open twists is to turn the twisted part as a separate piece with dowels at the ends. Further parts of the pillars are turned separately with holes to take the dowels, and assembly is not until all of the work on the twist has been done. This keeps the solid end turnings out of the way of the tools used to make the twists.

Twist turnings need not be parallel. For most purposes, it is better if they are, but there are exceptions when a different outline is needed. If the whole column tapers, it is unwise to retain the same pitch and lead throughout the length. This would have the effect of varying the angle of the twist. It is better to vary the pitch according to the diameter. If the pitch is kept approximately the same as the diameter at that point, the angles will be kept the same. If a different relative pitch is used, let it change proportionately with the pillar diameter.

If the overall shape is not a regular taper, the same rule should be applied, letting the pitch vary proportionately to the diameter in the vicinity. A bulbous outline, with the entwined parts following a tapering outline from the center toward the ends, will make an interesting table lamp or candlestick.

A further development uses open twists, then each bine is treated like the stem of a plant with leaves and flowers added. That is the realm of the carver and is some way from straightforward turning.

Chapter 17

Special Turning

A lathe is designed to make round things—that is the object of the machine tool. However, there are many special techniques that can be used to make it perform other tasks besides the production of straightforward fully rounded articles. There are adaptions to facilitate the rapid production of similar items and gadgets that can be made to widen the scope of a lathe. With some lathes, it is possible to obtain attachments that allow it to form the base of a planer or saw, but these are really using the lathe power source to drive a different machine. Such attachments are not really developments of turning, although they may be performing useful functions, particularly in a shop where space for individual machines is limited. This chapter is concerned with alterations to lathes or the techniques of using them to provide special turning effects.

SQUARED CHUCK

If a great many square pieces of wood of the same section are to be turned, it is convenient to be able to set up the driving end accurately and quickly. This applies to pieces that will be fully rounded and particularly to those that will be left with a square part, such as most table legs. The square part then has to be accurately centered in the lathe or the junction between square and round will show a distorted or eccentric effect.

A wooden driving chuck can be made to mount on a faceplate (Figs. 17-1A and 17-2). To get it accurately centered, the block of wood should be fixed to the faceplate and turned true around the circumference and on the face. A circle—of a size that would just fit in a square to match the wood to be turned—is then marked with a pencil to locate the cut-out. The wood and faceplate should be marked so they can be reassembled in the same position. Then remove the wood and mark and cut out the square (Fig. 17-1B).

The square socket need not go right through the wood and the mounted wood for turning can press against the bottom of that hollow. If the hole goes through the end of the wood, it can press onto a plain center in the mandrel nose (Fig. 17-1C). If

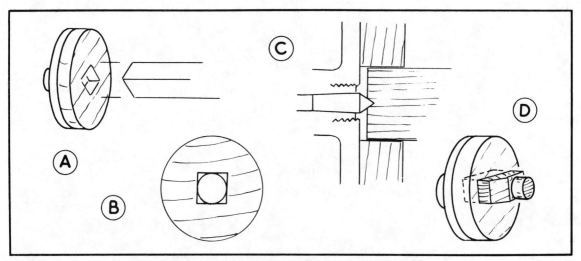

Fig. 17-1. A square pad on a faceplate can be used for driving square legs or a similar pad will hold a blank for a tobacco pipe.

a piece of wood to be turned happens to be slightly undersize, so it could wobble in the square socket, the plain center pressing into it prevents it from moving once turning has commenced, but the square socket still provides drive.

A similar idea is useful if there is to be a part turned off-center on a block of wood. If the main part is fairly large in relation to the turned part and will be revolving off-center, this can set up strains due to the eccentricity of the work. Besides wobble and vibration, there is a risk that the whole thing may fly off normal centers. In any case, the lathe

Fig. 17-2. A pad with a square hole mounted on a faceplate allows quick change when several similar parts have to be turned.

should be run slowly under these circumstances.

A special block can be fashioned to accommodate the unturned part and provide drive, then the tailstock brought up to center the turned part as well as keep the whole thing pressed into the pad on the faceplate (Fig. 17-1D). In an extremely uneven loading, there could be a balance weight added to the faceplate pad.

TOBACCO PIPE

A rather similar holding problem is encountered when making a tobacco pipe. It is possible to turn the outside and inside of the bowl, and turn the outside of the stem and drill it through in the lathe from a sawn blank (Fig. 17-3A), thus leaving a corner to be carved to shape (Fig. 17-3B). To hold the wood securely, a chuck can be made with a block of wood either mounted on a screw center or projecting from a pad on the faceplate (Fig. 17-3C). The grain should be parallel with the centerline of the lathe.

The jaws are notched to seat the pipe blank. For one or two pipes it will be possible to get sufficient compression with a wood screw, but if the chuck is to be used for several pipes, it would be better to pass a bolt through and use a nut on it. Keep the amount of projection of the bolt end to a minimum, so it does not present a hazard nor cause vibration due to the eccentric load. Work on the pipe is obviously done with the blank held successively in two positions. Because the bowl part of the blank is heavier, it may be preferable to turn that first.

WHEELS

Small wheels for toys and other purposes are usually needed in sets of four, and it is important that they match. This means that it is advisable to do as much work as possible on all four at the same time. Depending on size, two methods are possible.

If the wheels are of no great diameter in relation to their thickness, the grain may be across the thickness of the wheel. Four wheels can be made by turning a cylinder between centers (Fig. 17-4A). Turn the cylinder parallel and mark the wheels by cutting in a short way with the parting tool. Round the outsides with a beading tool. Use a drill in a tailstock chuck to make the axle hole right through the block (Fig. 17-4B).

If there are to be rings or other shaping cut on the surface of each wheel, square the end of the first wheel with the tailstock center supporting in the axle hole, do the surface work, then part off that wheel (Fig. 17-5). Bring the center up to the new position and do the same to the next wheel, and so on to complete the set. If the wood can be held in a self-centering chuck, there will be no need to use a center, and there will be less to impede tool handling when doing surface work on the wheels.

For wheels that are rather large in relation to their thickness, it is better to have the grain in the direction of the diameter of the wheel. These wheels can also be made of plywood. Glue four discs together with paper between them. It will help in mounting them on the faceplate if a fifth disc is added to act as a pad for screwing. Turn the wheels to size and drill the axle hole. Do whatever surface

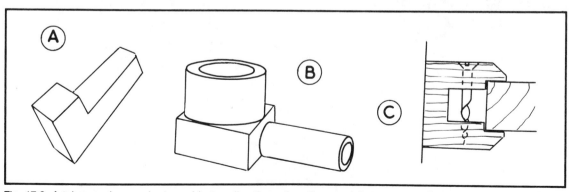

Fig. 17-3. A tobacco pipe can be turned in two directions, then the remaining part carved away.

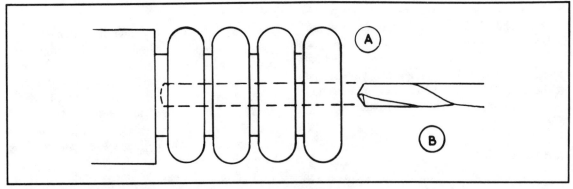

Fig. 17-4. Small wheels are best made in a series and then parted from each other.

work is needed on the first wheel (Fig. 17-6A), then break it off by inserting a knife or chisel in the paper joint (Fig. 17-6B), and make the next wheel.

This method can also be used if the wheel boss is to be thicker than the rim, which is better for giving a broader bearing surface on the axle. Turn the end wheel to shape, including rounding the rim and shaping the boss or hub (Fig. 17-6C). The back will remain flat, but because this is usually toward the body of the toy, it will not matter.

Any other series of small turnings that have to match may be made in a strip in this way. The limit comes when the length of the parts in relation to their diameter is such that a strip would be too slender to turn without wobble.

SPICE DRAWER KNOB

A knob for pulling a drawer can be turned within the thickness of the drawer front. This allows a block of drawers to be arranged without

Fig. 17-5. Several wheels are turned from the same piece of wood with each wheel parted off in turn as its face is finished.

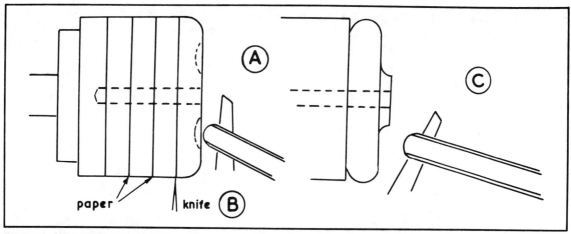

Fig. 17-6. Wheels can be turned by gluing several pieces of wood together with paper between it, then the pieces are split off in turn for finishing.

projections, which is an advantage if a door has to be closed over the drawers or if there are projecting knobs, which are hazardous to anyone passing in a restricted space. This is generally known as a "spice drawer knob" because of its use for that type of drawer in old-time stores and kitchens, although there are many other applications. Because the knob has to be gripped by the fingers and thumb only, this arrangement is best kept for small light drawers that do not require much effort to pull.

The front of the drawer must be reasonably thick—7/8 inch is about the satisfactory minimum. It must also have a diagonal within the limits of the lathe capacity, because it has to rotate on a faceplate (Fig. 17-7). The section turned should be arranged so fingers and thumb can be inserted (Fig. 17-8A). This shape also allows a narrow gouge to be used at the correct angle to undercut behind the knob. Turn straight in with a gouge far enough and at the diameter of the knob (Fig. 17-8B). Remove waste wood at the outside of the recess (Fig. 17-8C), then use a gouge behind the knob (Fig. 17-8D). Follow with a narrow scraper to clean out the recess. Be careful of the extending corners of the front as it revolves; they could become damaged or they could damage you.

ANIMALS

The makers of wooden animals for Noah's Ark

and others who have to produce small figures in quantity may have to do the bulk of their work by hand carving, but they can lessen the labor by making use of the lathe in the preliminary stages. This was a practice used by primitive turners with their pole and treadle lathes. The technique is still used by Swiss and Austrian carvers and turners and could be worthwhile and interesting on a modern lathe.

In the simplest method, a piece of a log is used so its grain is in the direction of its length. This is mounted in the same way as a bowl. This is more suitable for a figure that will finish higher than it is wide (Fig. 17-9A). If the base of the figure can be flat, it is possible to turn the block without having to do work on the side toward the faceplate or pad.

The figures are turned so they radiate from the center (Fig. 17-9B). After turning the log circular and flat on the surface, the wood is turned to match the profiles of the animals, but with a hole through the middle. This allows a tool to get at what will be the backs of the animals as well as the top surfaces and their fronts. With a little ingenuity and the use of templates of the profile, it is possible to bring the shapes quite close to the final outlines.

Parts then have to be separated. The primitive turner split the log with an axe, but today it would be better to use a power saw, making each cut radial (Fig. 17-9C). This gives the animal a tapered thickness, which may not matter as subsequent carving will remedy this. Although, if some modern carved animals are examined, it may be found that front and back pairs of legs are different widths, indicating that they were roughed out in this way.

Primitive Noah's Ark animals were probably made from logs that had not been seasoned, so fine detail was difficult, but the sap in the wood made it cleave easily as the animals were separated with an axe. With seasoned wood, a better outline can be obtained and separating by sawing is easier to do with dry wood than with "green" wood.

In another method, a block is prepared for each animal or other toy, and this is cut as a segment of a circle in a similar way to building up for making bowls with different colored woods (Fig. 17-9D). Similar care with angles is needed as when making a bowl, so joints are a reasonable fit and there is no risk of the assembly coming apart while revolving.

The larger the number of segments and the larger the central hole is in relation to the whole size, the slighter will be the angle of each animal. This method of preparing blanks allows the grain to radiate and be lengthwise. An animal is better made this way (Fig. 17-9E).

Any glue can be used. It is unwise to use a weak one with the hope that joints can be pried

Fig. 17-7. A spice drawer knob is turned within the thickness of the wood while the drawer front is mounted on a faceplate.

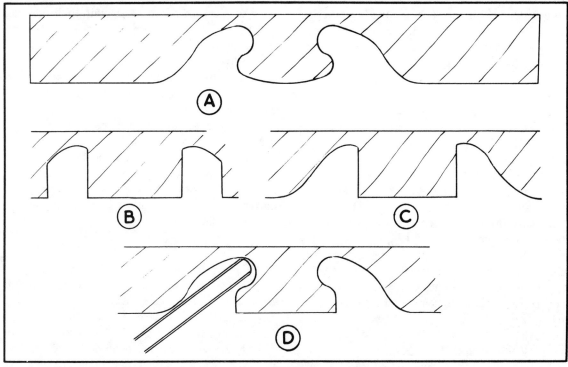

Fig. 17-8. Shown is a section of a spice drawer knob and the steps in shaping it.

apart—they may come apart too early. It is better to use a reliable glue and separate the animals eventually by sawing along the glue lines.

OVAL TURNING

It is possible to turn wood to a fair approximation of an oval (more correctly *elliptical*) section en-

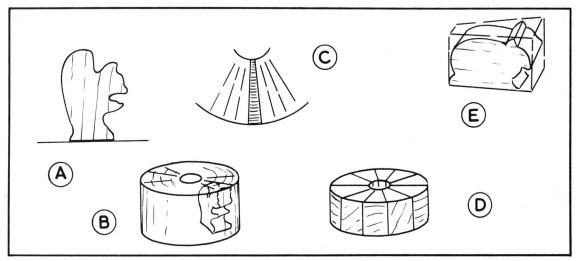

Fig. 17-9. It is possible to turn a number of blanks for animals and other small items as shown. After turning and separating, further work is done by carving.

tirely in a normal lathe. This is done by centering at two positions on each end. The amount of difference between the major and minor axes is determined by the spacing of the two center positions. The amount of shaping need not be much for something like a hammer handle, where its purpose is to guide the hand to hold the hammer in the right direction. However, it is possible to turn an elliptical section that is quite thin in relation to its greater axle.

It is advisable to experiment with a drawing before marking the wood. Work on a square. Find its center, either straight across (Fig. 17-10A) or diagonally. Mark two compass centers a short distance on each side of this (Fig. 17-10B). Draw curves with a compass using these centers (Fig. 17-10C). If your drawings are now visualized as the end of the wood, the lathe centers at each end can go in one of the side positions and the outline turned to the size drawn (Fig. 17-10D). When this is to size, the centers are moved to the other position and the wood turned again (Fig. 17-10E).

This would be the technique for turning a piece parallel in the length. Shaping, such as would be needed for a hammer handle, is done on one side, then care is needed at the second position to avoid taking off more at one point than on the mating part turned at the other side. Stop the lathe frequently and examine the meeting points. When both sides have been turned the same amount, their meeting will be straight along the wood. Any wandering from a straight line indicates uneven turning. In the finished work, there may have to be some sanding along the meeting lines between the two turned sides, but, otherwise, the elliptical shape is all tool work in the lathe.

It is possible to turn a piece of wood that is round in part and elliptical elsewhere, as might occur when a handle with an elliptical section has to have a round dowel end to fit in another part. The elliptical part is turned using the two side centers, and the round part is turned with the lathe centers in the middle positions.

CLUB FOOT

Corner legs of a stool or table may be given club feet, in which the round foot is surmounted by a slender leg that is tapered to meet the foot in an off-center position (Fig. 17-11A) with a nearly straight corner facing the center of the piece of furniture. This is also sometimes called a *cabriole leg*, but some workers prefer to keep that term for a similar leg that is made to shape by sawing and carving. The ordinary club foot is turned with the use of two center positions at the tailstock end. At the headstock end, which is usually square, the driving center remains central.

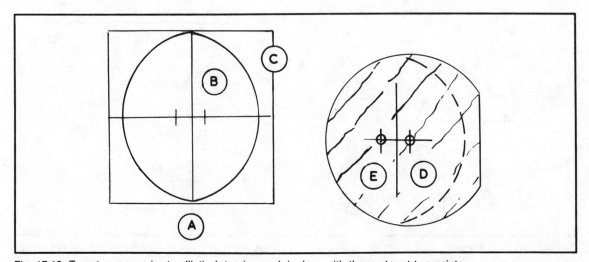

Fig. 17-10. To get an approximate elliptical, turning work is done with the center at two points.

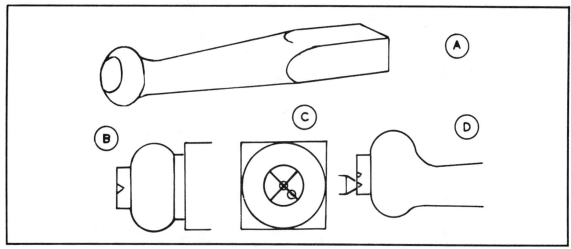

Fig. 17-11. A club foot can be turned by moving the center after making the foot.

At the bottom of the leg, allow a small amount of waste wood. Then, turn the ball (Fig. 17-11B), which may be a simple curve or can be elaborated with beads and other cuts.

Mark a second center diagonally from the first in the direction of one of the corners of the square section (Fig. 17-11C). The distance this is from the first controls the amount of taper of the leg. It needs to be moved sufficiently to give a pleasing shape, but going too far may make the leg too weak for strength. Moving off-center not more than 1/4 inch should be about right for a 1 1/2-inch square leg.

Turn the taper with this off-center position (Fig. 17-11D). If nothing has yet been turned off the square angles toward the foot, do the first gouge work carefully as one corner is quite high and has to be lowered with fairly light cuts to avoid splits. Turning is continued until the smaller part is turning a complete circle. From this point, stop the lathe and inspect progress frequently. It is unwise to judge the finished appearance from the rotating work. Carry the taper as far onto the square as required. The rear corner will blend into the curves.

It is possible to turn the taper with the off-center position first and make the foot with the true center afterwards. A true Queen Anne or cabriole leg is shaped by sawing a square outline, which is then worked to shape by carving techniques. The only actual turning is the foot.

SQUARE TURNING

There are two types of turning that may be described as square turning. One is a modern type in which a pillar or other piece of wood is turned so it is square in section with the corners turned off, so the higher parts of the turning have flats on them (Fig. 17-12A).

One way of producing this type of spindle with flats would be to make it round and plane off the high spots (Fig. 17-12B). This would be wasteful of wood and necessitate starting with a large section that would be cut away. The alternative would be to use wood of the intended square section and carefully center it in the lathe, so when turned, there will be the same amount taken off each corner (Fig. 17-12C). By keeping the wood symmetrical in the lathe, this will produce a pattern on the flat surfaces that is the same on each face (Fig. 17-12D).

Care is needed to avoid breaking out when the tool hits the far side of a cut (Fig. 17-12E). If it is possible to reverse the lathe, this edge can be cleaned when sanding. With the usual one-way lathe, however, there may have to be some hand sanding to smooth those far edges.

The other form of square turning has pillars and other designs with outlines that are usually associated with turning, but on wood that is square throughout (Fig. 17-12F). These shapes are pro-

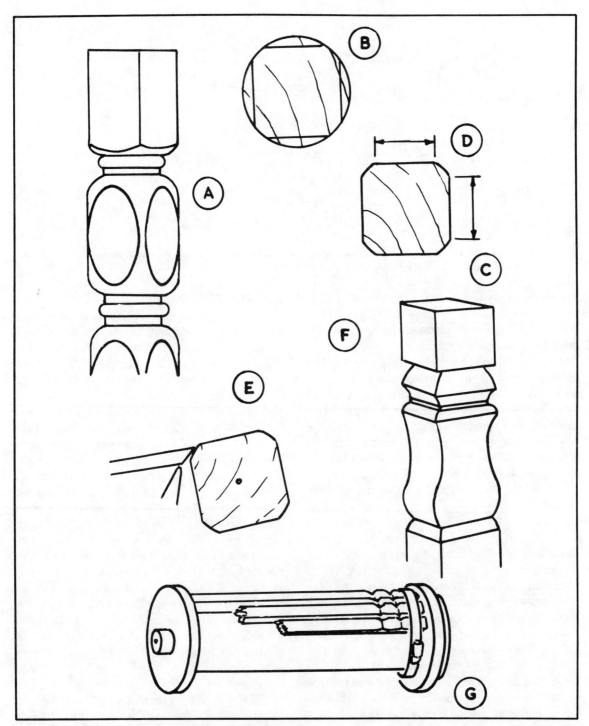

Fig. 17-12. One type of square turning merely takes the corners off squares, while another type is made approximately square by turning a large number of pieces around a drum.

duced commercially by machines that cut the profile on each face as a separate operation. Wood of true square section cannot be made to profiles with a lathe, but there is a way that was used commercially (sometimes called *therming*) that may still have applications for anyone possessing a lathe. The results have slight curves across the surfaces, but the effect is very similar to true square turning.

A cylinder is used, which can be solid wood or be built up. It has an axle with ends to suit the lathe centers. The axle could be wood for an experimental assembly, but for production use, metal would be better. There are flanges at the ends and the headstock end is best driven by a faceplate (Fig. 17-12G).

The squares that are to be turned go between the flanges and are sufficient to fit all around the cylinder. Their ends are held by straps, which could be metal pieces with bolts, but are most simply made by joining a sufficient number of worm-action pipe clips. The larger the cylinder, the more squares that can be fitted and the nearer their finished cross-sections will be to flat, but the clearance of the lathe will be the limiting factor.

The desired shape is turned on the exposed surfaces. When this is satisfactory, the straps are released and the strips of wood moved through 90 degrees to expose another surface for turning. This is done four times to complete the job. Move each piece so cuts are from a surface already turned toward a plain surface. This minimizes the risk of breaking out on three surfaces. The fourth surface will need special care as cutting toward a finished surface cannot be avoided.

One attraction of this technique is that a series of pieces are made that must be identical, unlike turning individual round parts, which depend on skill and frequent checking to get uniformity between a number of parts. This means that a series of square-turned pillars can be used close together in something like a balustrade with the certainty that there will be no discrepancies in the final appearance.

Narrow and fine pieces in the form of decoration are best avoided because there is a risk of them breaking away when the fourth side is turned. There is no satisfactory way of reducing this risk, except by backing each place with a piece of wood fitted between the parts, and this would involve a considerable amount of extra work. It is better to avoid the sort of sections that would be expected to give trouble.

Chapter 18

Turning and Carving

Wood carving is a specialized branch of woodworking and in commercial production, the man who works at a lathe would not also be expected to carve. The amateur or craftsman working alone may find that some knowledge of carving is worthwhile to supplement his wood turning ability. If carving is to be taken far, it needs more knowledge and information than can be acquired from a book such as this, which can only deal with it as supplementary to turning. However, there is enough information in this chapter to show what is involved, so the enthusiast can follow this other line if he finds it interesting.

Some carving can be done with ordinary shop tools, as was shown in the instructions on twist turning in Chapter 16. Most of the work in twist turning is done with a fine saw, followed by chisel, gouge, and rasp or Surform tool. Besides twist turnings, there are other products of the lathe that can form the basis of carved work. Examination of many traditional types of furniture will show examples where carving and turning are associated or actually combined. For instance a turned leg may

also be carved, or a turned part may blend into another part that is carved. This type of carving, which includes stylized or natural forms of leaves and foliage or other intricate work, can only be done with tools designed for carving and nothing else.

An expert carver accumulates a very large kit of tools that may run into hundreds. Most of these tools are gouges of many sizes and different sweeps (Fig. 18-1). Fortunately, much can be done with a much smaller carving tool kit, but about 10 is the minimum, and this will be added to as the need for other tools is felt. There are uses for many ordinary woodworking tools, but such things as firmer chisels, used for general benchwork, do not have many applications in carving.

There are carving gouges, chisels, and a few special tools. They are made like bench chisels but are lighter in section. Traditionally, a tool has a tang to fit into a handle and a shoulder to press against the wood inside the ferrule (Fig. 18-2A). A turner can buy unhandled carving tools and turn his own handles. This has the advantage of allowing him to vary the handles so individual tools are easily

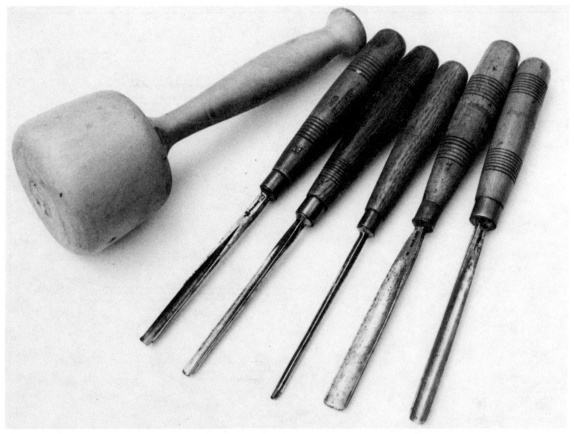

Fig. 18-1. Some carving gouges and a special carver's mallet are shown.

recognized. Bought handles are all the same, but even if your handles conform to basic shapes, you can turn different numbers of rings, beads, and other marks on them for identification. Different woods can be used, with one wood for gouges and another for chisels.

The most used carving tools are gouges. These are made in widths from 1/16 to 5/8 inch, but within each width there are many different curves or sweeps, going from near flat to quite a deep U-section (Fig. 18-2B). Makers define the curves by numbers, but the whole range of numbers in each size is no longer made. A middle curve, with an approximately semicircular section, is #9. Although different widths of gouges do not have the same curve for the same number, they are related, so #9, whatever its width, is near a semicircle in any size. Gouges with lower numbers have flatter curves and

those with higher numbers have deeper curves.

To further complicate things and add to the range of gouges that an enthusiast may have, there are differences lengthwise. The majority of gouges are straight and these serve for most carving (Fig. 18-2C). A gouge may be curved in its length (Fig. 18-2D). This will get into a recess and present the correct cutting angle to a lower surface in a way that a straight gouge could not. There are spoon gouges, which may be straight, front bent, or back bent (Fig. 18-2E), also for getting into awkward places. Very small gouges may also be known as fluters or veiners from their uses in cutting narrow grooves or the veins of leaves. A few straight gouges are all that are needed in a first carving kit.

A carver sharpens his gouges inside as well as outside. The thin section is ground and honed on the outside so the bevel blends into the line of the

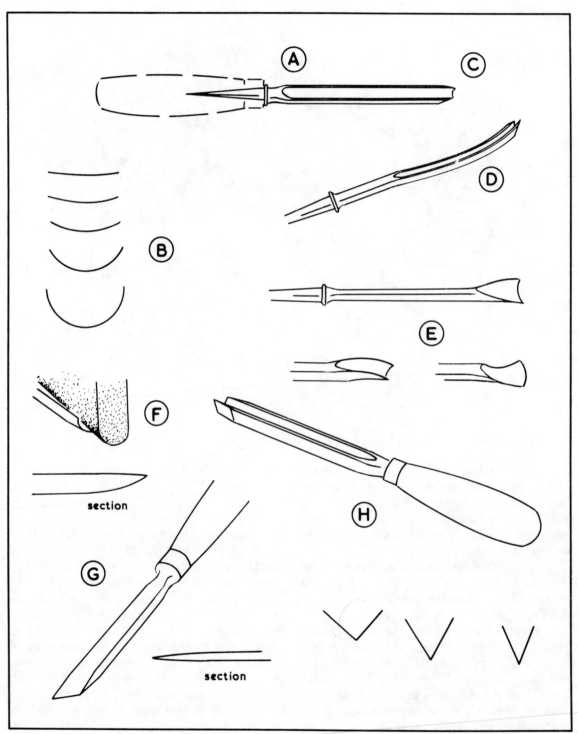

Fig. 18-2. A carver uses lighter gouges and chisels than a turner. They are sharpened on both sides. A V-tool makes grooves.

tool and does not have definite angles as used on turning tools. A slip is used inside to rub away metal to a slight angle (Fig. 18-2F) and not just to remove a wire edge as in turning or other bench tools.

Chisels for carving are less used than gouges. They have fairly thin sections and may be square or skew at the ends. Sharpening is from both sides, like a turning chisel (Fig. 18-2G). Besides straight chisels, there are curved and spooned versions similar to those described for gouges. A skew bent spoon chisel may be left or right handed, depending on which corner is forward. In an initial carving kit, one or two chisels are all that are needed, while for economy it may be possible to depend on any ordinary bench chisels at hand for the first carving work.

Of the special tools, only the V-tool need be considered in the initial kit. A V-tool is a sort of double-sided chisel and is normally straight (Fig. 18-2H). Several widths are made and the angle between the sides may be 90 degrees, although it could be more acute. V-tools are sharpened on the outside, but a knife-edge slip stone is needed to rub inside and remove the wire edges. It is also needed to remove the spiky point that sometimes occurs between the two sharpened surfaces. A V-tool is useful for outlining a pattern when it gives a straight edge instead of the curve from a gouge. One V-tool is worth having in the initial kit. Its width and angle is not important, but it could be 3/8 inch wide and any angle.

Much carving is done by hand pressure. The technique is familiar to a turner—one hand on the handle does the pushing and controlling, while the other hand over the blade assists in controlling and restrains if the tool starts cutting ahead too quickly or heavily.

For heavier work, the tool may be hit by a mallet. This is possible with straight tools, but those that are curved or lipped in any way are not intended to be hit, except very lightly. Any mallet can be used, but expert carvers favor a round-headed one (Fig. 18-1). Sometimes this is turned in one piece, but it is probably better made in two parts (Fig. 18-3A). The sizes given suit average work. Choose a close-grained hardwood. The han-

dle is turned between centers in the normal way (Fig. 18-3B). It is possible to stop the handle halfway through the head and wedge it there (Fig 18-3C), but it is better to go right through it and wedge on the outside (Fig. 18-3D), so shrinkage and wear can be taken up by driving the head on further and tightening the wedge.

The head should have its grain lengthwise. The block can be mounted on the faceplate or held in a self-centering chuck with the back center brought up to provide extra support. Drill through from the tailstock. It helps to bell out the end of the hole slightly with a scraper after drilling, so the wedge can spread the end of the handle to get a more secure grip (Fig. 18-3E).

Besides normal carving tools, there is always a use for a sharp knife. One of the type with replaceable blades is probably better than a conventional knife. For the modern type of carving with sweeping curves and little detail, much can be done with filing tools. Ordinary metalworking files soon clog on wood, but there are rasps intended for wood and Surform tools are particularly appropriate for this sort of work. They may have flat, half-round, or round blades. A traditional carver does all his work with gouges and other edge tools, but some carving today breaks with tradition and these other tools are useful.

Carving has to be done with tools given quite fine edges, much sharper than need be given to turning tools for many of their operations on the lathe. This means that carving tools should be protected so their edges are not damaged. A small number may be put in a tray or drawer with divisions. A fabric roll with pockets for the blades can be used, but as the tools are sharp, the material should be canvas or quite stout cloth that will resist cutting. They should also be protected from dampness as rust will spoil their edges. If kept indoors they should not suffer, but if there is any doubt, some silica gel crystals or paper should be included with the tools to absorb moisture.

There is not much use for power tools in carving, particularly in the type associated with turning. A power router can be used to remove waste wood, particularly in a sunk background. In nor-

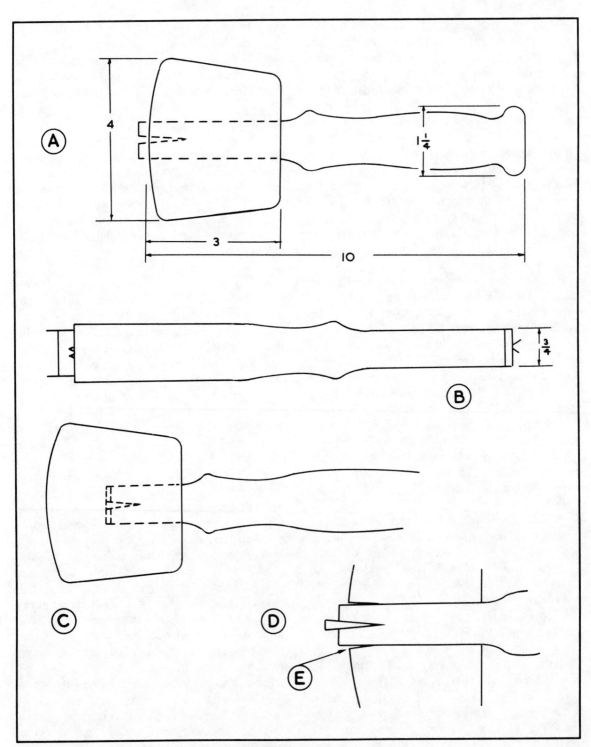

Fig. 18-3. A carver's mallet is round and can be made on the lathe.

mal carving, it is not considered correct to leave a surface as it comes from the router, although it may be geometrically more accurate than could be obtained with hand tools. A router normally removes the bulk of the waste and is followed by hand work with gouges.

There is a form of router work that is comparable to carving with tools. Lettering on name boards and similar items was carefully cut with carving tools and the best work is still done this way, but a router can be used to cut in letters that make an acceptable alternative. The router has a cutter with a semicircular end, and the tool follows around a guide to sink a hollow in the form of a letter. If the hollow is darkened, this emphasizes the contrast with the surface wood. Such work may not be done directly on turned wood, but a name board can be supported on posts that have been turned.

REEDS AND FLUTES

A reed is a raised curved piece (Fig. 18-4A) comparable with a bead. A flute is the reverse of this, being a curved hollow (Fig. 18-4B).

Turned legs may be given reeds or flutes lengthwise on part of their body. This is usually on a vase-shaped part and the treatment looks best if the part is turned smaller at its bottom than at its top. Only a part of the leg is treated. The rest may be fairly plain or decoration can be built up with the usual shapes around the leg and done on the lathe.

In a simple reeded leg (Fig. 18-4C), the part to be reeded is enclosed by beads and the ends of the reeded part is curved off to the depth that the reeds are intended to go (Fig. 18-4D). The outline of the reeded part is turned as smoothly and accurately as if it was to remain plain.

The next problem is dividing the circumference into spacings of equal width. As a general rule, a large number of narrow reeds will look better than a smaller number of wider ones. If the lathe has a dividing head, the reeds can be arranged to suit a number that is possible on this. A pencil drawn along the tool rest can be used to mark the division as the work is moved around in the appropriate steps (Fig. 18-4E). If the lathe is without this con-

venience, measure the greatest circumference by wrapping a strip of paper around and pricking through with a pin (Fig. 18-4F). Open the paper and divide the space between the pin holes into the number of divisions required. Put the paper back around the wood and use these markings as a guide when penciling along the tool rest.

Another way of dividing is to step off the intended width around the circumference with a pair of dividers or compasses. After the first experimental circuit, readjust the dividers and try again until the spacing is exact.

Grooves have to be cut along these lines. An expert would have the table leg on the bench or in a trough and cut along with a V-tool. A turner will find it better to have a pencil line just above the level of the tool rest, then lock the lathe at this position while the V-tool is guided along the tool rest (Fig. 18-4G).

With grooves cut at every position, the next step is removal of the edges with a chisel (Fig. 18-4H). Carve with the grain, which means that if the wood is straight-grained, pare from the thicker to the thinner parts of the wood in the same directions as turning. If the V-grooves had been cut to the full depth, as indicated by the turned rounding at the beads, this paring can be done carefully by hand, without benefit of the guidance of the tool rest, although it is still possible to slide a chisel along.

Get as good a shape as possible with the chisel. To ensure uniformity, do each step to each reed before moving on. Do one edge in one direction to each reed first, then the other way. Final smoothing can be done by sanding. A piece of wood hollowed to the curve of the largest part, but not as wide as the reed there, can be used as a pad for abrasive paper.

A variation on the reeded pattern on a bulbous part of a leg is to let the reeds follow a spiral course. It is inadvisable to make the twist too great, but an angle of 30 degrees at the center is about the limit (Fig. 18-4J). To get the shape, divide the two ends of the part, then stretch a string between pins to follow the intended direction (Fig. 18-4K). Make a paper or card pattern that will bend around the

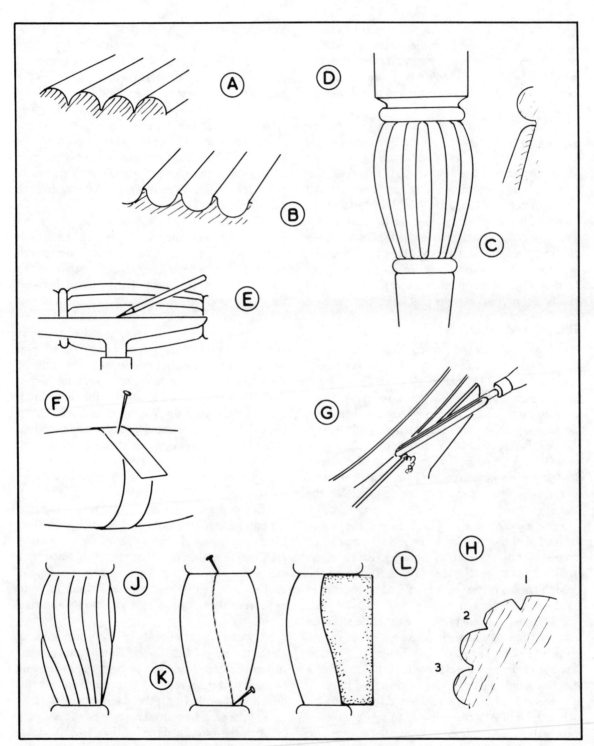

Fig. 18-4. Turned work can be embellished by carving lengthwise as shown.

wood. Put its straight edge along the string and press it around the wood so the location of the hollows at the end beads can be marked. Open the template and trim the edges on these lines. Now use the template to mark each reed line in turn (Fig. 18-4L).

It will not be possible to use any sort of guide for the tools, so the grooves between the reeds will have to be cut carefully by following the marked lines with the V-tool. The further steps will also have to be done freehand. Because of the twist, it is not always easy to see which is the correct way of the grain at every part, so make initial cuts very lightly to check the grain before slicing heavily.

For a pair or set of four legs, the spirals may all be the same way. Some observers may think they look better if they are paired, however, with the spirals of adjoining legs going opposite ways.

It is possible to work flutes in a very similar way. Marking out is the same, but the V-tool or a narrow gouge is used along the center of each flute (Fig. 18-5A) to settle the depth. This is followed by a wider gouge to remove some of the waste wood (Fig. 18-5B) and finally by a gouge of a section that matches the intended section of the flute (Fig. 18-5C). At the ends, the raised ridges will follow the profile of the turning and blend down into the edge of the bead. The deep part of the flute will merge into the bottom of the groove beside the bed.

This method of fluting has fairly acute-angled ridges running lengthwise. They should be rounded slightly, but they could be weak points that will suffer from wear and knocks. A variation that reduces the risk might be thought of as a combination of flutes and reeds (Fig. 18-5D) with the place of the sharp angle being taken by a curve that is usually not quite as much as that in the bottom of the hollow.

Flutes are also used in another way so they do not actually touch each other. This pattern can be worked on the square part of a leg or on a turned part.

On the flat surface at the top of a leg, the width to be patterned is divided so the spaces between flutes is about the same as the widths of flutes. The outlines of the flutes are penciled on (Fig. 18-6A). Deep flutes produce stronger shadows and are, therefore, more effective than shallow flutes. A

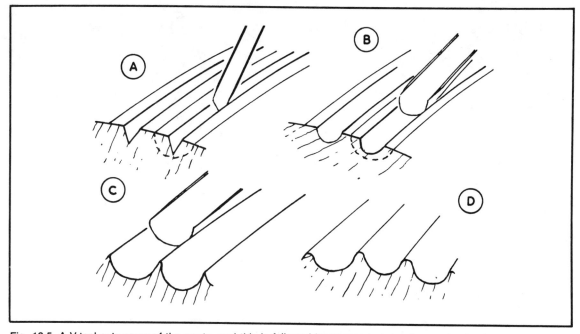

Fig. 18-5. A V-tool cuts some of the waste, and this is followed by gouges to bring the carving to shape.

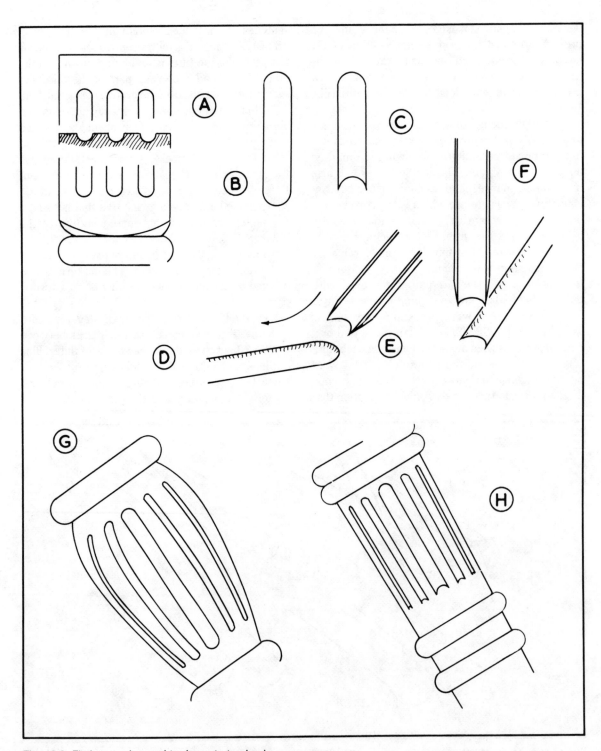

Fig. 18-6. Fluting can be used to decorate turning in many ways.

semicircular section is about right. A flute may curve in at both ends (Fig. 18-6B) or it can have a reverse curve at the bottom (Fig.18-6C).

Cut the grooves in the same way as for the close flutes, but be careful to keep within the boundaries at the ends. Deepen with a narrow gouge at first, then remove more waste with another gouge and finally make one sweep along with a gouge that fits between the penciled lines and makes a groove of the correct depth and shape (Fig. 18-6D). This can be done with only hand control, but it helps to clamp a strip of wood along one side of the groove and use this as a guide to feed the gouge along.

For a rounded end, this shape will come automatically as the gouge enters at a steep angle and starts to cut (Fig. 18-6E). For a reverse, cut straight in with the gouge (Fig. 18-6F) and work the groove towards this. There is less risk of damaging the wood if this cut is only taken part way at first, then some of the waste removed along the groove and the end cut deepened further. A mallet may have to be used on the gouge in both directions. Use the point of a knife to remove any fibers that lodge in the corner of a reverse curved end.

If this sort of fluting is used on a bulbous part of a turning, keep the flutes the same width throughout their length and let the differences in diameter be taken care of by variations in the spaces between the flutes. It is probably safest and neatest to divide the circumference at the smallest point, so the widths of flutes and spaces there are about the same. At all other points, the spaces between flutes will be wider than the flutes. This looks better than bringing the flutes very close together at the smallest part. In this form of decorating by fluting, the flutes are not taken to the ends of the part being worked on (Fig. 18-6G).

Flutes on a straight tapered part of a leg or post were often used on Victorian furniture and shop fittings. These were usually made in mahogany or wood of a similar appearance (Fig. 18-6H).

Parallel flutes of semicircular section can be worked with a router cutter of suitable shape. The problem is one of setting up and guiding the tool. Where flutes are to be made on a flat straight surface, the router can be guided from the edge and

the work is comparatively simple.

For similar work with the router on a shaped turned part, the wood can be mounted in the lathe and locked with the part to be cut on top. It may be possible to support a board to act as a guide behind the lathe, then the router is kept straight by running along this.

CABRIOLE LEG

The club-footed leg turned with a taper that is offset is a variation of the cabriole leg or Queen Anne leg. This is more shapely and is more of a smooth carving than a turning exercise.

As with the club foot, the inner corner of the leg is almost straight from the square top to the foot. The outer corner and its adjoining surfaces have the most shaping. The top may be square, but in the traditional form, the two inner surfaces are left square to join against rails, but the outer surfaces curve back from a greatest thickness at about the level of the bottom edges of the rails (Fig. 18-7A).

It is advisable to make a card or plywood template of the proposed shape of the outer surfaces (Fig. 18-7B). The actual foot is bulbous and adjoins the inner surfaces. This is marked on the end and turned (Fig. 18-7C) using a center at the top in the same relative position on the end. This is the only lathe work.

Use a template on one surface and cut the outline with a bandsaw. If a bandsaw is unavailable, reverse the template on the other side to provide a better guide if the waste wood has to be removed with hand tools. With the outline cut in one direction, use the template in the other direction, then cut that to shape (Fig. 18-7D).

The wood now has the correct profile when viewed two ways. Further steps are the removal of the angles to leave curved sections for all the length except the top. A bench firmer chisel can be used bevel-downward to pare some of the waste away. Work from the high parts into the hollows. This can be followed with a half-round rasp or Surform tool used with a sweeping action, so it goes along the surface as well as across it. Shaping could also be done with a spokeshave. Note that the turned foot becomes part of the leg and not a separate feature as in the club foot.

Follow by thorough sanding. First use strips of abrasive cloth pulled around the leg in all directions to remove tool marks. When high spots and all roughness have been removed, change to shading lengthwise until all of the cross-grain sanding marks have gone. Work through successively finer grades of abrasive to get the best finish.

Because these legs are normally wanted in sets of two or four, it is advisable to work all of them together so they will end with a uniform shape and finish. Turn all of the feet. Saw all of the shapes one way and then the other. Rough the sections to shape, then do all of the sanding. This is the only simple way to get legs that match.

A further variation on the club foot or the cabriole leg is to work a ball and claw on the bot-

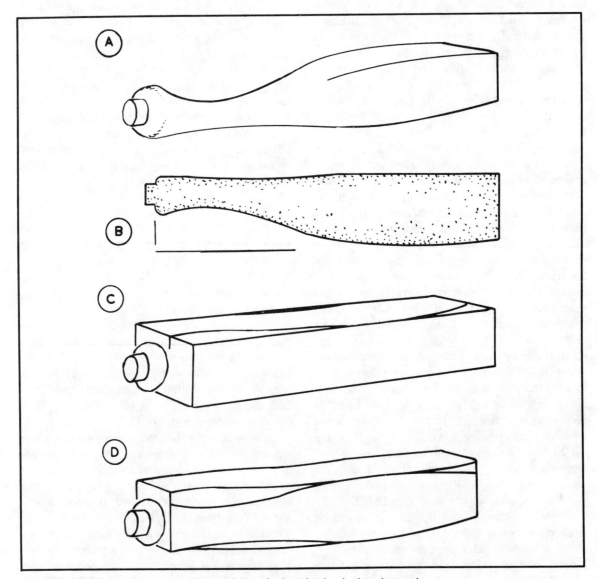

Fig. 18-7. A cabriole leg can be partly turned, then further shaping is done by carving.

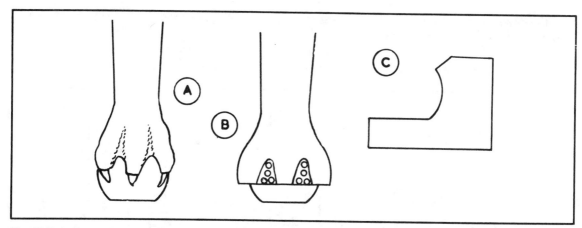

Fig. 18-8. A claw and ball foot is first turned to the outside dimensions, then it is completed by carving.

tom of the leg. Although the ball should be reasonably spherical, it cannot be turned and has to be carved inside the claw. It is usual to arrange three claws (Fig. 18-8A) with the center claw pointing toward the outer corner of the chair or table. The leg is either turned like a club foot or made as a cabriole leg. In both cases, the foot is turned large enough to allow carving the claws. If the outside that will enclose the claws is approximately spherical, the recesses showing the ball can be drilled from this surface. Use a drill without a spur and have a depth stop. Use gouges and chisels to remove the waste between the claws to the depth shown by the holes (Fig. 18-8B). This should leave the ball in a reasonable shape, but a template can be used for final shaping (Fig. 18-8C).

With the ball shaped, the wood forming the claws can be reduced to the shape of a bird's foot with extended claws by using mostly gouges. There is no need to aim at a smooth surface; the pattern left from careful tooling will look better.

CARVED POSTS

When carving gets beyond the formal and stylized patterns, it becomes as much an art as a craft. Some of us may not be artistic, but we can achieve attractive results with formal carving. Anyone who is artistic will soon want to carve figures of humans or animals. Their field is then away from turning. There is one form where lifelike

or stylized carving can be combined with turning and that is in a turned post with a top carved in the form of an animal or bird. Much depends on the artistic skill of the carver, but even a nonartistic worker can produce attractive results.

At the top end of the scale—in size—is the totem pole. A totem pole may not have been turned, although many patterns could have been. A more reasonable size is a post, maybe 2 inches in diameter, that stands in the yard or garden, possibly as part of a fence, then the carved top is there as a pleasant surprise for a visitor. An even smaller version might form one of a pair of uprights supporting a mirror with a carved top instead of a turned finial.

The simplest type of figure is an upright bird, such as a penguin or owl, preferably with few fine details or thin extending parts. An expert may add other pieces of wood for wings, but the beginner will do best with a compact upright figure. The post could be turned with the top also turned parallel ready for carving, but it is easier for a beginner to get a good shape if he works on wood of a rectangular section. The end of the wood could be left square (Fig. 18-9A) or the carving can be a separate piece of wood. In that case, it is convenient to turn a dowel on the post and have a matching hole in the carved part (Fig. 18-9B). This is better than having the hole in the top of the post as it avoids the need to mount the carved wood in the lathe to

223

turn the dowel, and that wood can be left long to grip in a vise until after carving is finished. If it is not convenient to turn a dowel on the post, there can be a hole there as well as in the carving, and a separate piece of dowel rod used to make the joint (Fig. 18-9C).

One way of arriving at a satisfactory design is to first model the shape in clay, then measure this

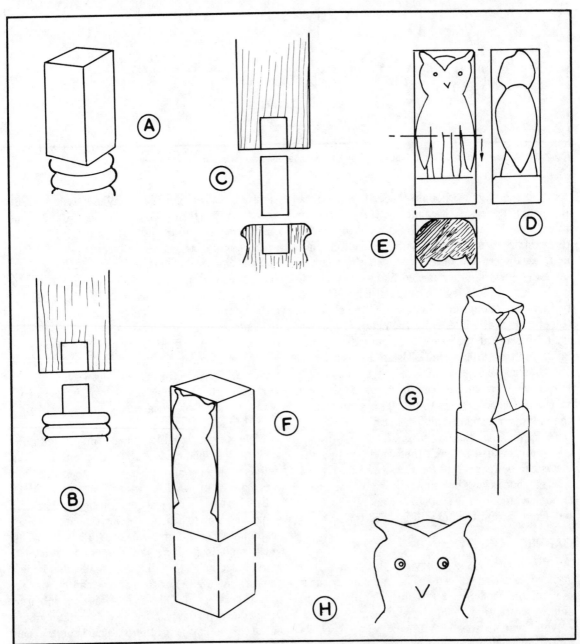

Fig. 18-9. There can be a carved end on a round spindle when carving an animal. This is easier to do if the wood is left square, than if it is turned for the full length.

and carve the wood to match it. It is possible to work from sketches, but it is difficult to properly visualize a three-dimensional shape from flat drawings. Drawings showing two or more views are helpful (Fig. 18-9D). One or more sections give a clue to the shape the wood has to take (Fig. 18-9E).

If the wood is made to the section shown to enclose the two views, but with some extra length to grip in a vise, the shape can be transferred to one surface (Fig. 18-9F). It may be helpful to make a reverse outline on the opposite side. Cut the outline to shape. How this is done depends on available tools and the size of the work. A bandsaw is best for moderate sizes, but a coping saw or fretsaw will be better around the outline. Make many saw cuts with a back saw toward the outline, then use a chisel, or even a knife if it is very small, to remove the waste.

When the first outline has been cut, mark the shape in the other direction on it (Fig. 18-9G). Because this is on a surface that is no longer flat, much of the marking will have to be done freehand using measurements from the drawing. Cut that shape.

Looking at the wood from right angles to either surface gives a correct appearance, but in all other directions, it is angular and too large. If you have a drawing of a view from the top, you may trim to that shape. For many models, you cannot draw a third view that will be any use in subsequent work, so from here on, the work has to be done by eye.

First remove parts that are obviously not needed. Everything will be rounded, so the flat and angular cross-sections have to go eventually, but you may be glad to retain some surfaces at first as a guide to shapes and sizes. Aim to get the overall shape close to what it will finally be, but do not bother about fine details at this stage. Use a fairly wide gouge and pare away, mostly diagonal to the grain. Use a mallet when needed. Decide on what has to come off and remove it with bold strokes rather than with a series of nibbles. However, keep the corners of the gouge above the surface; otherwise, the gouge will dig in and split the wood.

If there is much hollowing or space between the legs, drill through or into the hollow, then work carefully with a suitable small gouge or even the point of a knife. Be careful of grain direction when working inside recesses. With most of the waste wood removed, look at your carving from all directions. This will show you what final shaping needs to be done. Make sure main outlines are correct. It is no use making a good job of some fine detail if the wood you are working on, should have been cut back further before the detail work.

Most of the final shaping is done best by hand paring with suitable sharp gouges. Be careful of the correct placing of eyes. They may be drilled holes in a small carving, but getting them just a little out of position can spoil the effect of a bird or animal (Fig. 18-9H).

What finish is given to the carving depends on the carver. A good tool finish may be best, but if it is more of a symbolic outline then a true rendering, it may be better sanded smooth. If the result is a piece of furniture in which the turned and other parts will be polished, it may be advisable to finish the carving in a way that will accept the same polish.

Be careful to true the bottom of the carving when the surplus wood is cut off, so it will fit truly on the top of the post. In some figures, it may be advisable to leave some outer wood at the bottom of the carving that can be carved after fitting to the post, so the carving blends into the turning and the joint between the two parts is not obvious.

SPOONS AND FORKS

The Welsh have carried the carving of spoons to a fine art with their love spoons, which are given as a token by a suitor to his intended. These did not include turning, but there are turned wooden ladles and forks that may be decorative or useful in the kitchen and for serving salad.

Such a spoon or fork may have a turned handle and a shaped end, that has to be carved (Fig. 18-10A). The handle could also be carved as a twist turning and the top end could also be carved.

To make such a spoon or fork, a piece of wood with sufficient length on it to carve the end is needed, but it can be cut down for the handle part

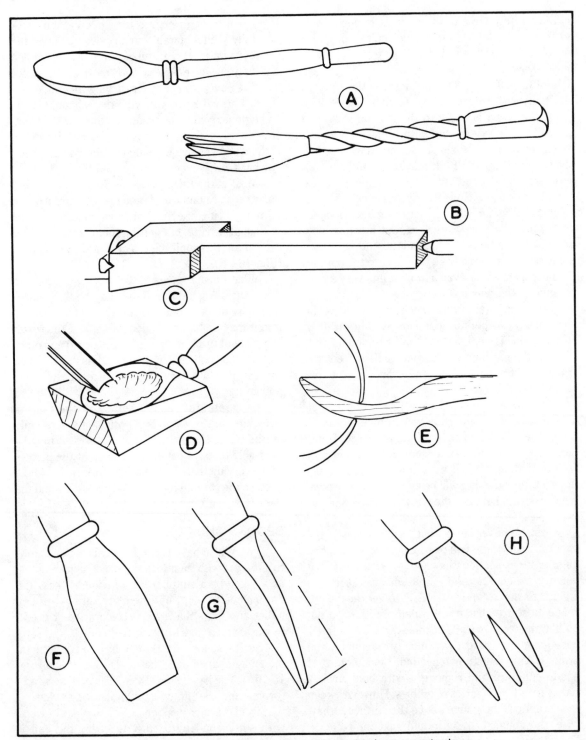

Fig. 18-10. Spoons and forks can have turned handles, then carve the bowl or prongs to shape.

to avoid having to turn a large amount away (Fig. 18-10B). This is mounted between centers. Have the large end near the headstock; this minimizes vibration and makes turning the other part easier (Fig. 18-10C). If the handle is to be slender, do turning near the ends after getting the whole handle round. Leave the finishing work at the center until you have completed turning elsewhere so as not to weaken that part and cause it to flex. If the handle is long and slender, it may be necessary to use a "steady" as the middle is turned.

When the handle has been turned, smooth the upper surface of the spoon and draw the outline of its bowl. Grip the block in a vise or use a holdfast to secure it to the bench top. Remove the waste with a gouge working all around toward the center (Fig. 18-10D). As the work progresses, use the gouge slightly diagonally to the grain and avoid cutting so far that the edge is beginning to cut upward into the opposite grain, because this might start a split.

Tool marks can be removed inside by using abrasive paper wrapped around the thumb, but a sharp scraper, as used for turning the inside of a bowl on the lathe, can be drawn around the inside of the spoon to scrape away gouge marks before sanding. Hold it upright so its cutting edge approaches the wood at the same angle it does when turning a bowl.

When the inside is satisfactory, cut the outline of the spoon bowl. Pare away the outside to a pleasing shape. If the bottom of the spoon is kept thicker than the edges, a pair of calipers can be used to test thickness (Fig. 18-10E). The outside is easily sanded smooth. Round the edges to complete shaping.

The end of a fork is simpler. Cut the outside shape (Fig. 18-10F). At right angles to this, cut the top and bottom of the blade (Fig. 18-10G). Smooth all of these surfaces. Mark the cutouts needed to produce two or three prongs and saw these (Fig. 18-10H). If a very fine saw is used, only the minimum of sanding with a strip of abrasive cloth will be needed between the prongs. Round all exposed edges and finish by sanding the blade in the direction of the grain.

There are many possible variations to the spoon and fork, using the long turned handle and an end

Fig. 18-11. A long-handled shoe horn and a blank prepared for a similar one.

shaped from a block after turning. The block has to be large enough for shaping, but by careful planning it need not be too big. A problem comes if it has to project to one side, as it would for a ladle, which is really a bent spoon; then there is the risk of this eccentric part causing vibration as the wood revolves. The Eastern back scratcher is another variation, with only a little wood needed in the block for carving. A shoe spoon or horn with a long handle (Fig. 18-11) will be appreciated by anyone having difficulty in bending. The carved end is made in the same way as a spoon but with the open end taken to a fairly thin curved edge. Several items used in the kitchen can be made with turned handles or shafts and carved or whittled ends. With some items, it may be better to make the handle to dowel into the carved end. It is then possible to use different woods, such as a heavy working end and a light handle or a light-colored wood for contact with food and a dark wood for the handle.

Chapter 19

Finishing Preparations

The term *finishing* in connection with woodwork refers to all of the processes of bringing the wood to a good finish and giving it a protective and decorative treatment. Paints, varnishes, polishes, and similar coverings are all *finishing materials*. Turned wood may have to be finished to match other parts to which it is attached, but where the turned item is an independent article, its finish may be applied without reference to other furniture.

The wood you are considering is shaped by rotating in a lathe and that action can be used in some processes of polishing. With ordinary furniture, there may have to be fairly strenuous hand work to achieve a good finish. A similar effect is obtained by holding the hand still and having the work rotate against the cloth or other polishing medium. This is a limited, but satisfying, use. A problem is the presence of dust. The action of turning produces a considerable amount of waste, ranging from shavings down to the finest dust and this settles everywhere in the vicinity. Any method of cleaning cannot completely eradicate the dust, so a finish that is affected by dust cannot be applied

successfully on the lathe. Most methods of finishing are best applied somewhere away from the shop where the atmosphere and surroundings are as free from dust as possible.

This chapter provides a guide to the various ways of finishing turnings. Finishing in all its ramifications is a big subject.

CHOICE OF FINISH

There are some general characteristics of all woods, but they come from an enormous variety of trees. Broad divisions are softwoods and hardwoods. These terms apply to the categories of the woods and are not descriptive of relative hardness in all cases, but nearly all softwoods are softer than nearly all hardwoods. The finish that can be applied to a really hard, close-grained hardwood may not be applicable to the open-grained texture of a softer wood. Most turning is done in hardwood, so most available finishes are appropriate.

The use of the finished work must be considered. If it is mainly decorative, any high-quality finish is appropriate. If it will have to stand up to rough use and knocks, protection may be more appropriate than appearance. If it is something for use with food, it may be better to leave the wood without any applied finish, so it can be scrubbed clean.

Appearance may be the first thought, but there are other considerations. Wood is porous material, and it will absorb moisture and dirt. An applied finish covers the wood pores and prevents absorption. Bare wood is also easily damaged by knocks or abrasion. Damage can only be removed by working away the surface, and this is not usually possible. A finish on the surface provides protection and a barrier to damage. Most finishes are harder or more resilient than the wood underneath.

Finishes may show the wood grain, or they may be opaque and hide it. The most favored finishes for turned work are transparent or translucent. Anyone with a feeling for wood usually wants to be able to admire the beauty of the grain in the final work. Sometimes the wood may be of uneven color. Sometimes the natural color is not what is wanted. Stains are used to alter wood color. They do this without hiding the grain. Usually they darken the wood. Most antique oak furniture is a darker brown than the natural color of the wood. Similarly, most mahogany furniture, so popular in Victorian days, is a deeper red than the natural wood. It is unusual to try to lighten the color of wood. This can be done by bleaching, but the process is less common than staining.

Paints and associated finishes are opaque and hide the wood so its grain and color do not affect the final appearance. Toys, outdoor woodwork, and some other items may be better painted. For most turnings, a transparent finish shows the quality of the craftman's work better and is more appropriate for furniture. Paint, particularly with a gloss finish, gives the greatest protection to wood, so it is appropriate when rough usage is anticipated. It is also more suitable for pieces made of softwood, which does not usually have the attractive grain of hardwoods, and its tougher surface gives the maximum protection.

In the past, many finishes were prepared by their users and many craftsmen kept the recipes as trade secrets. Today, it is better to buy these items ready-made. However, some finishes are quite simple to make, and there is a satisfaction in making your own, even if it is not much cheaper.

WOOD PREPARATION

The success of any finish is not dependent only on what goes on top. Whether this has the best possible effect or not depends a lot on what goes before, particularly how well the wood surface has been prepared. An expensive finish over poorly prepared wood may be a waste of money. Paint may hide the wood surface more than a clear finish, but its smoothness is still dependent on the evenness of what is below it.

Sanding has been mentioned in other chapters, but here you need to consider it in relation to the finish. Wood is a fibrous material and as the wood is turned, the fibers are cut through. No matter how sharp the tool is, some of the fibers will be left bent or projecting raggedly. This roughness may be quite slight and not visible on casual observation, but the aim of finishing is to reduce the raggedness of fibers to the absolute minimum, so for practical purposes, the wood is smooth. Sawing wood or the first gouge work of turning may produce ragged fibers that are large or obvious. Planing or later turning with a chisel reduces the roughness. The better the tool finish, the less dependence there is on sanding. Sanding—no matter how thorough—over a poorly tooled surface, will not produce as good a final surface as much lighter sanding over a good quality tool finish.

Sanding is a term carried over from the distant past when sand was used as an abrasive grit for wood. This has fallen from use, but the name persists. Abrasive paper is often called *sandpaper*, but this is incorrect and best avoided. There are now a number of natural and manufactured grits used as abrasives for wood.

There are several ways of grading grit sizes. Some of these are traditional. A more scientific way that is increasingly being used gives a grade number to the grit on abrasive paper or cloth. This indicates the number of grits per square inch. With the coming of metrication this may change, but the numbers are an indication of relative size of grit. Fifty grits per square inch is very coarse. Three hundred grits is fine, but the numbers may go on in fineness to 600, although the very fine grits are unsuitable for wood and are used on metals and glass.

Some relative grades in the various systems are shown in Table 19-1. Beside these grades, there are two traditional divisions. Papers used on bare wood are *cabinet* papers. Those used to rub down applied finishes are *finishing* papers. The term "paper" is sometimes applied even when the actual backing material is cloth.

The abrasive that followed sand was powdered glass. Glasspaper is still a good abrasive paper for wood. A cheaper grit is flint, made from quartz and silica. This is not advised for turning as it wears quickly and clots with dust. Garnet paper is fast cutting and will have a good life on turning. Aluminum oxide paper is mostly in finer grades and is used for rubbing down finishes rather than working on bare wood.

Silicon carbide grit is used on finishes. This, and most of the other abrasives, are attached to their backing with waterproof glues, making what are often called *wet-and-dry* papers. These papers can be soaked in water or other solvent. The use of water allows dust to be flowed away, which makes for clean cutting when rubbing down hard finishes.

Some abrasives, particularly glasspaper and some garnet paper, have the grit held to the backing with nonwaterproof glue. This means that a damp atmosphere can soften the glue and cause grit to break away from it. Warming the paper before use will drive away the moisture in the glue and give the abrasive a longer life.

Abrasive paper is made in several forms, but for hand sanding it is produced in sheets measuring about 9 by 11 inches. Most sanding on the lathe is done with this paper, because the rotating wood has a similar effect to using a power sander on stationary wood. However, strips intended for belt sanders and other forms can all be used for hand sanding wood in the lathe.

Abrasive grit can also be bought loose. This does not have much use in turning, but it is possible to use grit on a cloth for sanding irregular shapes.

Table 19-1. Abrasive Grades: Approximate Equivalents.

Use	Grits	Traditional	Glasspaper	Emery Cloth
Finest (for finishes)	400	10/0 (ten nought)		
	320	9/0		
	280	8/0		
Very fine (for bare wood)	240	7/0		
	220	6/0		
Finest (commonly used on wood)	180	5/0	00 (flour)	0
	150	4/0	0	FF
Medium sanding	120	3/0	1	F
	100	2/0	1 1/2	1
Usual first sanding	80	0	F2 (fine 2)	1 1/2
	60	1/2	M2 (middle 2)	2
Rough sanding	50	1	S2 (strong 2)	3
	40	1 1/2	2 1/2	4
	36	2	3	

For economy, it is common to tear a standard sheet of abrasive paper into four equal parts. One of these, folded in half, is convenient for most hand sanding. The friction of sanding can have a softening and even charring effect on the glue and backing, and the abrasive paper should be moved in relation to the wood, so different parts of the surface come into contact. It is usually best to have the tool rest out of the way and hold the abrasive paper underneath (Fig. 19-1A). For broad turned surfaces without detail work, it helps to use a long strip of abrasive pulled around the wood, so it is moved up and down as well as sideways (Fig. 19-1B). Besides reducing wear and making the greatest use of the abrasive, this serves to take out inequalities from tool work (Fig. 19-2).

In the same way that a cabinetmaker aims to get as good a surface on his work as possible from his tools and not depend on sanding to disguise poor workmanship, a competent woodturner should try to get the shapes and surfaces as accurate as possible, so sanding is only a brief final step. His tools should always be sharp and surfaces should be cut on work between centers with the slicing action of a chisel in all places where this is possible. In particular, long sweeping curves should be cut with bold strokes of the chisel and not short cuts that leave ridges. In faceplate turning, scraping tools should be honed to a good edge, but where the wood has its grain across the diameter, some slight roughness where end grain meets the tool will have to be sanded. If the direction of rotation can be reversed, much of this roughness can be reduced with tool work before sanding. If the outside of a bowl has to be turned with the base away from the faceplate and it is then reversed to have the base gripped with a chuck or hollowed block, the outside will then be rotating the opposite way and further sanding outside will deal with the rough grain that was left at the first sanding.

If there are beads, quirks, ridges, or other unevenness turned in the wood as decoration, care is needed in sanding to avoid spoiling these outlines. Too enthusiastic sanding with a broad piece of abrasive paper spanning over several high parts, will soon lower them and the intended effect may be spoiled. If these parts have to be sanded while the wood is revolving, it is better to use a folded edge of abrasive paper in angles, but the grit on the fold will not last long, so be prepared to frequently refold. You can roll a strip of abrasive paper to sand in a hollow. You might put a nail or piece of dowel rod through the roll to apply pressure. So far as possible, move the paper backwards and forwards to spread the sanding. Holding it in one place could quickly wear away the grit or even heat the wood so much with friction that angular parts become charred.

Steel wool also has possibilities for preparing a surface. This is not the type used for domestic scouring. It comes in grades from 000 (finest) to 3 (coarsest) and only those grades up to 1 are likely to be needed on turned wood. Steel wool will get into shapes too intricate for abrasive paper. Care

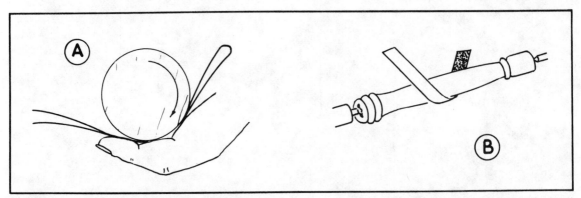

Fig. 19-1. Sanding should be done with the tool rest out of the way. A piece of abrasive paper can be held in the hand or a strip moved about on the turning.

Fig. 19-2. Abrasive paper should be held so that it cannot pull out of your hands and moved constantly on the rotating wood.

is needed with some woods. There will be discolored marks on oak if tiny particles of steel get trapped in the grain. Wiping with a damp cloth should remove these.

Sanding following good tool work can be started with 80 or 100 grit. This can be followed with 180, and it is rarely necessary to go finer than this. If the tool work is not so good, it may be necessary to start with a slightly coarser abrasive or continue longer with the other grades. Sanding should be done enough at each stage to remove all marks from the previous grade.

Of course, sanding revolving wood does the work across the grain and in only one direction. If the lathe can be reversed, a change of direction for sanding will be beneficial as tiny fibers that have been bent one way in the first sanding should be caught in the other direction and be cleaned off.

This is particularly valuable with faceplate turning with the grain across the diameter. This often results in rough patches where the tool opposes the grain. Reversing rotation makes it easier to get these parts as smooth as the rest of the wood.

Even when the wood is apparently smooth, there is still a risk that some tiny fibers are still bent into the grain and may stand up when the finish is applied. If the wood is moistened and allowed to dry, these fibers will be made to stand up and can be sanded away. The final sanding will leave scratches so fine as to be invisible to the naked eye, but these scratches are at right angles to the direction of the grain. There is a risk that they may show through a transparent finish. If the final abrasive is very fine and each stage has been thorough, there is little risk of this happening. The places likely to suffer are the broader sweeps, like the plain curve of a bulbous leg. On these areas, it is a help to give a final hand rub with the lathe stopped, working lengthwise with the grain.

Many turners give the wood a final rub with shavings held in the hand. It is difficult to see how this can improve the surface, but it is a common practice and expert turners claim it does something to the wood. It is worthwhile picking up some shavings from the work in hand and holding them under the revolving wood.

It is common to give a complete sanding to a piece of work as the final stage before taking the wood out of the lathe. However, if the wood has to wait some time before finishing is taken further, it may be advisable to leave final sanding until just before the next step to that part. This may apply to a turned part that is to be built into something else not yet ready, or when only one of a set is turned and others will be made later at intervals. Early turning left about may absorb dirt and not finish as good as is possible, or the piece may not come up with exactly the same finish as its partner finished immediately after making. If a turned part is to be finally sanded later, it should be left with the ends to fit the lathe centers still in position.

Abrasives, by their definition and nature, are grits harder than most other polishes you use. It is unlikely that you will be using abrasive grits so extensively that they would do damage to your lathe or hand tools, but bear the possibility in mind. Do all tool work on the wood before changing to abrasives; otherwise, particles of abrasive grit in the wood could take the edge off of the tools. Headstock bearings are usually well-protected, but if abrasive grit got into them, it could do damage. Grit embedded in the end grain of wood could wear away a plain tailstock center.

Cleaning a lathe after each turning session is good practice in any case, but brushing away the mixture of wood dust and abrasive grit will reduce any risk of grit damaging the bearing surfaces of the lathe bed and other parts. Wiping with an oily cloth has a mixed effect. It is a good way of preventing rust and easing the movement of sliding parts, but it does attract dust as soon as you start turning again. Keep the film of oil thin—certainly much less than the heavy oiling often used on a metal-turning lathe.

STOPPING AND FILLING

We would like our wood and workmanship to be perfect, but wood is a natural material and may contain flaws. It may also be given knocks or cuts that cause blemishes. It is not usually possible to disguise flaws completely, and it would be better to avoid them if possible. Sometimes it is necessary, however, to treat an otherwise finished part so it can be used instead of discarded.

A dent in wood does not mean wood has been removed. Instead, it has been compressed. Sometimes it is possible to bring the hollow back to its original shape. Hot water put in the dent may be all that is needed to make the wood fibers swell. Steam will penetrate the less-absorbent woods better than water. Put water in the dent and dip a hot piece of metal into it until steam appears. With the usual shape of a dent, a heated spoon is a good thing for applying the heat needed to produce steam. This may have to be repeated several times. Let the wood dry, then sand the surface. If this does not work, it may be possible to sand around the dent so it is less obvious. Otherwise, it will have to be filled in the same way as cracks and other flaws.

There are several compounds to fill cracks, joints, sunken nail holes, and other flaws. Some of the older mixtures have been superseded, and it is now usually better to buy prepared compounds, which are described as stoppings or fillers.

The choice of compound depends on the finish. It does not matter about color if the finish is paint, but for a transparent finish the filling should match the wood—meaning it should match the stained wood if that is the treatment. Not all fillings take stain the same as the surrounding wood and may show. There are colored fillings intended to be applied after stain. Other fillers go into bare wood and can be expected to match the surrounding wood after staining.

Stick shellac or plastic fillers (sometimes called *beaumontage*) are good for covering nail and screw heads and similar small holes. They do not take stain and must be used after staining, when they are melted by heat and dropped into the hole, like sealing wax. Oil putty (whiting and linseed oil) has been used, but is not recommended; the oil soaks into surrounding wood and discolors it. Drying takes a long time, and the putty eventually becomes powdery.

Plastic water putty is effective. A thick paste is made with water. It sets rapidly after being pressed in. Test it for matching color if it is to be stained. A similar filler is wood compound.

Plastic wood (wood plastic) sets with some of the qualities of wood. Within limits it can be shaped after setting, so it is possible to not only fill a flaw, but also do a modest amount of building up to sand to shape to match a broken part.

All of the fillers so far described are just that. They fill a space, but do not contribute any worthwhile strength. Modern synthetic glues are only satisfactory when the meeting surfaces are fairly close. If there is a gap to be filled, plain glue will craze when it sets, so there is a pattern of hairline cracks in it. These weaken the joint to the point where the glue is ineffective.

Glue can be used to fill and strengthen a crack if it is reinforced with sawdust, preferably from the same wood. This prevents crazing. Sufficient sawdust is worked in to make a thick paste, which can be pressed into the open joint like putty. Leave some excess to sand off later, and the finished joint should match the surrounding wood. However, the glue-sawdust mixture will not take stain.

If softwood is turned, it may contain pockets of resin or knots. These may not show up until the shape is formed. Such a turning can be given a painted finish, but it is unlikely to produce a very satisfactory result under a clear finish. The snag with a painted finish is that resin tends to continue to work to the surface and will come through the paint if nothing is done about it. After any filling or other treatment, the problem area should be given a coat of shellac to act as a barrier to the resin.

Bleaching is unlikely to be often practiced by a turner, except there is sometimes a problem of uneven color in a piece of wood. A dark streak may be reduced by treatment with household laundry bleach. Read and follow any directions, but usually the mixture is 12 parts water and 1 part bleach. Avoid metal containers. Use rubber gloves and be careful how the mixture is used. Apply with a cloth on the dark part as frequently as necessary until the right color is obtained. Wash the surface with clean water to remove any remaining bleach and allow the wood to dry completely before taking further steps in finishing.

Chapter 20

Finishes

Most turning is done because the beauty of the wood is appealing and any finish applied should emphasize that beauty. It is usually only the more utilitarian items that are painted. Consequently, a turner who finishes his own work is more concerned with the transparent finishes.

STAINS

Wood does not have to be stained, but this treatment often improves the appearance and may be necessary if the turned work has to match something else. It may also be necessary if different woods are used in a turned assembly and they have to be bought to a matching color and appearance.

Staining is not a way of making one wood look like another. Anyone with much knowledge of wood can see differences in grain pattern, even when the color has been altered. It is sometimes necessary to stain when a part made in one wood to match the color of another wood, but it is no use turning an item in an inferior wood and staining it to the color of a quality wood with the hope of passing it off as being better than it is.

Usually staining is better done to deepen the existing color. It is normally unwise to attempt a change of color. This means that it is safest to keep to the various hues found naturally in wood. It is possible to get stains in such colors as blue and green, and they may have applications for special effects, but the approach to their use should be very cautious.

Stains differ from paints and other opaque finishes in coloring the wood by allowing details of the grain to show through. A stain should penetrate the wood. Most are made with pigments dissolved in a solvent. Several solvents are used, and it is the choice of solvent that mainly affects the choice of stain.

Oil Stains

Many popular stains have light oil as a solvent, such as benzene, naphtha, or turpentine. Ready-made stains available are mostly described by the name of the wood they are intended to be used on or to represent. The actual colors include a variety of browns, reds, yellows, and oranges, as well as black.

Oil stains penetrate quickly, and initial drying may be swift, although full drying takes close to a day, and the work should be left that long before further treatment. Application should be fairly quick by brushing or spreading with a cloth pad. Spread is fairly even, but work with the grain and lift the brush over a previous part. Put on plenty of stain and aim to cover everywhere before dulling shows drying has started. So far as possible it helps to have the surface being covered horizontal. If the work is done while the wood is in the lathe, it can be brushed on top and turned progressively by hand. It helps to work in a cross light so progress can be seen and checked.

There may be a problem of uneven absorption, resulting in parts that have absorbed more, thus finishing darker than others. This can happen with sapwood, which will absorb quicker than heartwood. Stain can be wiped off the sapwood when it is judged to have taken enough, or more can be brushed on the heartwood. This is less likely with turned work than with the broader surfaces of cabinetwork.

A problem more likely with turning is the increased absorption in end grain. With the varying curves is turned work, parts of a shape, such as a pronounced curve and bulbous shape, may have part with the grain and part across the grain. This can happen with smaller curves, such as beads, but darkening at the bottom of a groove between beads may not be regarded as a disadvantage, as it may emphasize shape, as is also done by shadows. Quick wiping of end grain before much stain has soaked in is usually the only treatment needed to keep the color there similar to that on side grain.

Dried oil stain will look darker than it will finally appear under a clear finish. This should be allowed for. If it is required darker, more stain can be applied over a dried earlier coat. Lightening is best done by wiping with a cloth while the stain is still liquid. If it has been allowed to dry and the color needs to be reduced, it may be possible to use a cloth soaked in solvent, but there is a risk of leaving a patchy appearance.

One interesting finish is to deliberately make high parts a lighter color than elsewhere. This makes a piece of furniture look as though it has suffered from wear over a long time and may be done to improve the appearance of reproduction work. Before the stain has fully dried, wipe the high parts with a cloth. This can be done in the lathe with the work turning slowly.

The solvents used in oil stains are flammable. The small amounts used on turnings are unlikely to be hazardous, but the obvious precautions should be taken and rags soaked in stain should be destroyed. An accumulation of soaked cloths in a confined space, such as a trash can, could start a fire by spontaneous combustion.

Water Stains

Most turners will find oil stains fill most of their needs, but water stains have possibilities. They come as powders that are dissolved in water. Instructions are provided, but with most of these stains, mixing is simply a matter of pouring the powder into warm water. The water must be stirred continuously. The intensity of the color can be adjusted by the strength of the mixture. Mixed stain can be bottled and kept almost indefinitely. A strong basic solution can be kept and thinned as needed.

A very large range of colored powders are obtainable, and it is possible to buy certain basic colors and blend your own stains. It is also possible to buy water stains already compounded to match certain woods.

With water as a solvent, drying time has to be sufficient for it all to evaporate before further treatment. Water does not have the penetrating power of oil, so it does not go as deep, but the color and effect are adequate. It soaks into softer woods better, and it is not as suitable as oil stain for the very hardwoods.

Water will raise grain so little fibers that had bent under sanding stand up. To minimize the risk of this happening when water stain is applied, it is advisable to wipe the wood with clear water and allow this to dry before giving another light sanding before the application of water stain. This problem is greater with softer and more open-grained woods, then with the denser hardwoods.

Water stain does not even out the color by itself as so conveniently as oil stains, which will often put right any errors in brushing by flowing to form a reasonably even spread. Brush water stain on. For a very dark finish, it is easier to get an even result if two coats of lighter stain are used instead of one dark one. As with other staining, work as quickly as possible. Be careful of splashing stain onto wood yet to be treated. Spots of stain that have partly dried are not so easy to disguise as with oil stains. Surplus stain can be removed with a cloth. Any excess stain in a groove between turned parts can be lifted with the edge of a cloth or a dry brush.

Spirit Stains

Colored powders may be dissolved in spirit (alcohol) to make stains in a more limited range of colors, which include blue, green, and yellow—not associated with the other types of stain. Colors can be blended. Powders are available to make your own stains, which can be kept in concentrated form and thinned for use.

The quick-dry quality of alcohol is both an advantage and a disadvantage. Further work can follow almost immediately, but it is very difficult to get an even finish, particularly over a big area. It is almost impossible to stain a large area and avoid brush marks. This is more of a problem with the broader expanses of cabinetwork, but it could affect a large piece of turned wood. Spirit stain is better than the other stains for spraying, but this is unlikely to be of much value in dealing with turned work, unless a considerable production quantity is being dealt with.

In turned work, spirit stain is useful for smaller items where there is little risk of streaking from brush marks. Brushing should be done rapidly and the brush kept full, rather than dry to spread each lot to the maximum. Try to work onto a wet edge as much as possible.

Besides its use for staining small items of new work, spirit stain can be used for touching up. It can be used over other stains to touch up flaws or

damage due to use. It will also penetrate some finishes, so it may be tried on old work that has become marked.

Other Stains

There are other ways of coloring wood, and there are occasional fashions for unusual treatments. Diluted paint can be used to partly penetrate and partly hide the grain through a translucent coloring. There have been ways of chemically changing the color of wood, but most of these have been superseded by simpler oil and other stains.

Oak and chestnut can be given a deep brown color with ammonia that is different from anything obtainable with stains. The wood may be put in a closed cabinet with a little ammonia, or it might be possible to brush on ammonia in a very well ventilated place.

Permanganate of potash dissolved in water is cheap and safe to handle. It will turn most woods a medium brown if used as a stain.

FILLERS

All woods are porous and some have visible crack-like openings along the grain. If this wood is finished without anything being done to fill the grain, there may be at least some of these openings showing through the finish, or even if covered by the finish, the surface may be poor.

These woods have to be prepared by filling. Not all woods need this treatment, although if there is any doubt, filling can do no harm. Fillers are broadly divided into paste fillers for the more open-grained woods and liquid fillers for those woods that are more close-grained although not so much as to not require filling.

Some fillers will absorb stain at the same rate as the wood. They can be used before the wood is stained. Other fillers are better used after staining, then their color has to be chosen to match the stained wood. Of course, the problem does not arise if the wood is to be finished without staining and a filler is chosen to match the wood.

The actual filling material is a fine powder that

is deposited in spaces in the grain. Most modern fillers are made from a finely ground crystal called *silex*. This is formed into a paste with linseed oil or other binder, then fillers of other consistency can be formed by thinning. Some examples of the consistency of filler normally required are shown in Table 20-1.

Paste fillers can be bought in many colors. They can be mixed. It is wiser to choose something slightly darker, rather than lighter, than you want as there is a tendency to dry a shade lighter. Paste filler can be applied with a cloth or an old hair brush. Work in all directions to fill the grain. Leave the filler long enough to become dull, then wipe over with a piece of course cloth, mainly across the grain. This can be done with the lathe turning slowly. Finally, wipe lengthwise with a soft cloth.

If excess paste filler becomes hard, it can be wiped off with a cloth soaked in benzene. If you have doubts about having completely filled the grain, another application can follow. Leave a filled surface for a day before applying a finish.

Liquid filler to apply with a brush can be made by thinning paste filler with benzene or turpentine. Brush it on and wipe with a cloth after the surface has dulled. Shellac can be used as a filler on some woods. There are clear and orange varieties. Brush on and allow a short time to dry, then lightly sand the surface to leave shellac in the pores. Shellac will not fill larger spaces. Clear white (bleached) shellac can be used on many bare woods, but it should not be followed by stain, which it will not absorb. Orange shellac can follow many darker stains. If the wood is to be varnished, many woods will use the first coat of varnish as a filler and no other preliminary filling is needed.

WAX POLISHING

Very old furniture was polished with oils and waxes and the attractive patina only resulted from many applications of polish over a very long period. Consequently, this method of finishing is rarely used on furniture today, mainly because of the considerable labor involved in achieving a worthwhile finish. The turner has one great advantage—having the labor performed for him when the wood revolves in the lathe. Instead of having to rub the wood hard, he keeps his hand still and the wood does the rubbing. Because of this, wax polishing is a good way of finishing turned work. Oil polishing is less applicable because of long pauses between applications.

A great many waxes have been used for polishing. Paraffin wax alone is not very effective. Beeswax is the main base of wax polish. There is also a very hard carnauba wax that comes from a Brazilian palm tree. It is too brittle to be used alone, but it can be mixed with other waxes to make a very good polish. Although it is possible to mix polishes, as most waxes dissolve in turpentine; a turner is better advised to buy ready-made polish. Most polishes are in the natural wax color. It is possible to add coloring matter, but too much of this will affect the polishing effect. It is better to use wax as a clear finish over wood that is already the color desired.

Wax relies on building up a surface film, which is polished. Wax does not penetrate the grain to any

Table 20-1. Filler Requirements of Some Types of Wood.

Paste Filler	Medium Filler	Liquid Filler	No Filler
Ash	Butternut	Bass	Aspen
Chestnut	Korina	Beech	Cypress
Elm	Mahogany	Birch	Ebony
Hickory	Rosewood	Cedar	Gaboon
Lacewood	Sapele	Fir	Hemlock
Oak	Tigerwood	Gum	Holly
Padouk	Walnut	Maple	Magnolia
Teak		Poplar	Pine
		Sycamore	Redwood
			Spruce

appreciable extent. Consequently turned wood that is to have a wax finish should be prepared smoothly and with the grain sealed with a filler if necessary. There should be no gloss on the surface to be waxed.

The first steps are the application of wax without any attempt to produce a shine, but an uneven build-up should be avoided, particularly in the sharper hollows of a turning. This could be done with a cloth having plenty of wax on it and rubbed over the stationary wood, or it may be possible to do it with the cloth stationary and the wood revolving. However, at this stage, a coat of wax is what is being aimed at, and working with revolving wood can result in too much being wiped off.

Leave this first application on for ten minutes or so, then rub it with a cloth. It should begin to build up a dull sheen, which is characteristic of wax. Much of the rubbing can be with the cloth held against the revolving wood, but a final rub without the wood moving can be along the grain of larger parts. If the work being polished is in the form of a bowl, the extremes of size will affect the speed at which the revolving wood passes the polishing cloth. There will have to be more pressure and longer times near the center than at the rim.

When using a cloth on revolving wood, be careful of stray ends of cloth that may get caught and pulled around, possibly taking your hand with it. Turn under all edges of cloth and always work with a closed pad, rather than an open cloth (Fig. 20-1).

The first polishing will produce a modest shine. This can be left a short time and more wax applied, then polishing done over this. It is a build-up of coats of wax in the form of very thin films that gives the wood its characteristic polish.

Some prepared wax furniture polishes can be used, but these are not meant to be used on bare wood. Once a base of wax polish has been formed, it is possible to follow with one of these polishes. They are also useful for reviving existing polish. If something like a candlestick is wax polished and later suffers from finger marks, a wax furniture polish is the type to use on it.

VARNISHES

There are several brush-on clear finishes. They may have different make-ups, but they are applied in the same way. Traditionally, there were varnishes made from natural lacs and resins that could produce very good results, but there were snags concerning the sort of atmosphere at the time of application, working temperatures, and many other factors. Modern varnishes are compounded from synthetic ingredients and these difficulties have been overcome almost completely.

It is advisable to buy a varnish and read the instructions on the can. The best varnishes are usually described as boat varnish, although they are suitable for a great many other things besides boats. Modern varnishes should not be stirred or even shaken up. Use them directly as they come. Agitation causes minute air bubbles that may not disappear until they break on the wood surface and leave tiny blemishes.

Varnish is applied by brushing. For a turning with much of a pattern, it is advisable to brush around the circumference, although larger plainer parts are better brushed lengthwise. If the instructions for the chosen varnish say it should be *flowed* on, use the minimum brush strokes necessary to spread the varnish. Excess brushing may cause air bubbles or make the varnish suddenly become sticky and pull on the brush so an uneven finish results.

Usually the first coat of varnish will soak in unevenly and may feel rough when the hand is wiped over it. This is due to raising of the grain. Lightly sand and wipe off any dust before giving another coat. For the best finish a total of three coats is needed, sometimes more. Drying times vary and some varnish makers give a maximum as well as a minimum time for further coats to get the best finish.

Fortunately, most modern varnishes dry to a dust-free state in a short-time—possibly an hour. Up to that time, dust settling on the varnish will mar the surface. If an insect alights on wet varnish, leave it. When it is pulled off the hard surface there will be very little marking.

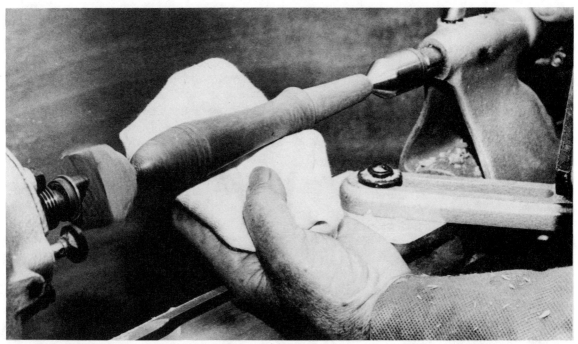

Fig. 20-1. When polishing, have the tool rest out of the way and fold the pad so that there are no exposed corners or edges to catch in the rotating wood. Hold the cloth underneath so you can see its polishing effect, and you can release easily if you have to.

Most varnishes are very light in color. Some are almost clear. The toughest and most durable varnishes have a slight orange color, which blends with most wood colors to give a pleasant result. It is also possible to buy varnishes that have been colored, usually in similar colors to wood stains. Such a varnish can be used over plain wood without staining first, so the stain color and the varnish are in one coat. This may be considered a saving of time, but expert wood finishers do not like using varnish stain.

When wood is stained, the coloring penetrates the wood and becomes part of a narrow layer near the surface. This may be covered by a clear varnish or similar finish. When a varnish stain is used, all of the color is in the varnish and the wood underneath is still its natural color. Doing the work in two stages is considered to give a better and more natural appearance. If the work subsequently suffers from knocks, chipping of varnish stain will leave the plain color of the wood showing through.

If varnish over stained wood becomes chipped, the damage is less obvious and the color is unchanged.

Although not strictly a varnish, shellac has some uses as a brush finish. Shellac is a lac that comes from India and is dissolved in alcohol to make a liquid something like varnish. It can be dissolved by the user, but it is better bought in various strengths. The strongest is called 5 pound cut and this can be diluted with alcohol if necessary. Shellac is brushed on. A first coat may act as a filler and have to be lightly sanded. Shellac dries quickly, so coats can be applied at intervals of about two hours. Application should be fairly quick, with the brush working toward a wet surface where possible. Do not brush excessively and use long strokes, so far as this is possible on the particular turning.

A shellac finish is not as tough as varnish. It is susceptible to moisture, so shellac should not be used if it is liable to get wet. The final surface will not have as high a shine or as good a surface as varnish. Shellac has the advantage of giving a quick cheap surface that is acceptable for some things. Shellac can be lightly rubbed down and followed with wax. It then takes the place of some earlier coats of wax and the final appearance is much the same as total wax polishing.

FRENCH POLISHING

This is a method of polishing that uses shellac and has been a traditional finish for good-quality furniture for some time. On furniture surfaces, the work is done by hand rubbing, so a turner using the technique has the advantage of his moving wood.

The finished appearance is considered superior to any other gloss finish, although other qualities may not be as good. French polish does not stand up well to knocks, heat, or moisture, but the majority of turned items are not likely to come up against these hazards sufficiently to suffer.

Polishing is done with a pad made of a piece of cotton batting inside an old lint-free cotton cloth. The special shellac mixture sold as French polish is without the resin found in ordinary shellac and is put on the batting. Screwing the cloth over it causes the polish to ooze through.

There are three stages in French polishing: bodying in, building up, and spiriting out. The wood needs to be brought to a good finish and filled if necessary. French polishing shows everything, so imperfections in the wood cannot be disguised.

To body in a turning mounted in the lathe, put polish on the batting and squeeze the cloth so it oozes through. Hold this against the revolving wood without too much pressure, but move it about so shellac is deposited all over the work fairly evenly without excesses in hollows or high parts rubbed thin. Recharge the *rubber* with polish as frequently as necessary. The action will cause the polish to harden on the wood almost instantaneously due to the friction generating heat. Fine steel wood can be used to even the hardened surface, but do not rub so much that the polish is rubbed away. Ideally, the work should be left for a day before proceeding, although this is not so essential with a turning as with a large piece of furniture.

Follow by building up. This is done in the same

way, but do not charge the rubber with as much polish. This may drag a little on the surface. It this happens, put a spot of linseed oil on the pad—just one spot applied with your finger. If pad marks show, you have used too much oil.

Work all over the surface several times. Recharge the rubber if necessary, but do not have it too wet. Do not rub too hard. If you stop the lathe, withdraw the rubber first. It must not stop on the surface. For a large plain part of the turning, it may be an advantage to do some rubbing with a circular action, but mainly lengthwise, with the wood stopped. To complete this stage, give one rub all over with the pad charged with polish that has been diluted with alcohol. Again leave the work before tackling the third stage. A few hours will be enough.

For spiriting out, use a small amount of alcohol on a new pad. Wipe, rather than polish, the surface all over with this. Change to a dry clean pad and do this again. The finished work should be left a few days before handling.

French polishing is mainly a treatment for large areas, although it will work effectively on the high parts of turned wood. If there is much intricate work, it may be necessary to use a narrow brush to put polish into the deeper parts.

PAINTING

Painting turned work has very little difference from any other painting. Any flaws in the wood should be stopped, but the color of the stopping will not matter. Open-grained wood should be filled and the surface brought to a smooth finish without needing to bother about even coloring. Shellac as a filler has possibilities under paint. It can be used with more than one coat to thoroughly seal the wood, but it must be sanded smooth before painting.

There have been changes in the compounding of paints. This is due to the replacement of natural ingredients with synthetic ones, which is to the advantage of the user and the improvement of the finish.

It is advisable to use a paint system from one marker and follow his instructions. For some paints there has to be a primer, but the place of this is turning can often be taken by the shellac filler. This is followed by an undercoat, which provides the base for the top coat. To get the best results, there may have to be more than one application of undercoat. Any build-up of paint necessary should be at the undercoat stage, so only one layer of top coat is applied.

It is inadvisable to apply paint with the work mounted in the lathe, although that may be a convenient way to mount a large piece that can be moved around by hand to present fresh faces to the brush. A snag with painting a turning is that it is too easy to get a build-up of paint in hollows and grooves. A total of three coats carelessly applied can almost fill some fine detail, so the beauty of the turned work is diminished. This should be watched. While sufficient paint has to be used, too much should not be on the brush at a time when dealing with detailed parts. Go back after dealing with other parts and look around grooves and hollows to see if there is a blob of paint accumulating anywhere.

Painting will usually be around the wood following the turned outlines. In general, deal with the finer details and leave broader parts to last. Some of these may be better painted with lengthwise strokes than around the circumference, but be careful that final stroked do not deposit paint in a groove bordering the plainer part.

Modern paint is like varnish in drying dust-free in a short time, but leave each coat for the time specified by the markers before applying the next. Gloss paint is tougher than other finishes, so it should be used when there is no reason for another finish. It is best for outdoor woodwork and more easily kept clean on toys and household equipment.

There are several special paint-like finishes that may have possibilities on turned parts, but check that they are suitable for the intended conditions and consider how they will look in the intended surroundings. Not all are suitable for hand application. Some need stoving to set them.

SPRAYING

Sprayed finishes are suitable for larger areas and fairly large production. Setting up the equipment for a single or just a few items is not worthwhile. With turning in particular, the shapes are unsuitable. More sprayed paint will be going to waste than onto the wood. Small aerosol-type sprayers may have possibilities for decorative effects with one color over another. Anyone already having spray equipment may find a use for it in putting a lacquer finish on turned work, but, otherwise, spraying is not a thing to associate with wood turning.

Chapter 21

Other Materials

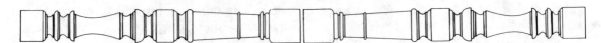

A woodturner sometimes finds the need to incorporate other materials in the pieces he turns. These may be complete items made of glass, metal, or plastic, or he may need to do some work in one of these materials as part of the design in hand or to make a manufactured part fit what he is turning. A woodworking lathe is unsuitable for heavy metal turning, and it is difficult to do more than just superficial work on iron and steel. The softer nonferrous metals can have more work done on them with hand tools. Many plastics can be hand turned and this also applies to such natural materials as horn and bone, which have similar turning characteristics to some plastics. Glass is not a material that can be turned. It has to be taken as it is and the wood adapted to suit it.

GLASS

The only working of glass that may have to be undertaken is the cutting of sheet glass to fit a picture frame. If it is a round turned rabbet, it will probably be wisest to get the glass cut by a profes-

sional. There is a sort of glass cutter compass that can be used to get a good true circle, but an amateur would be better advised to make a template of the shape undersized by the clearance needed by the cutter (Fig. 21-1A), and cut around this. It may also be advisable to make straight cuts to remove most of the waste (Fig. 21-1B) if you do not trust your ability to cut and make the circle otherwise. You can then nibble off of the circle with pliers. The edge left may not be very good, but it will be hidden in the rabbet.

If a cut glass is very ragged, it can be smoothed by rubbing on abrasive paper supported flat on the bench or another piece of glass. Be careful not to let the abrasive mark the surfaces. It may help the final appearance to stain or paint inside the rabbet dark brown or black. This stops reflections that could spoil the general appearance or show up (by reflection) any raggedness of the edge of the glass.

Another use of glass is in inset dishes and bowls. If these are accurately shaped, there are no difficulties, but if they are not as truly circular as could be hoped, be careful of using force. If such

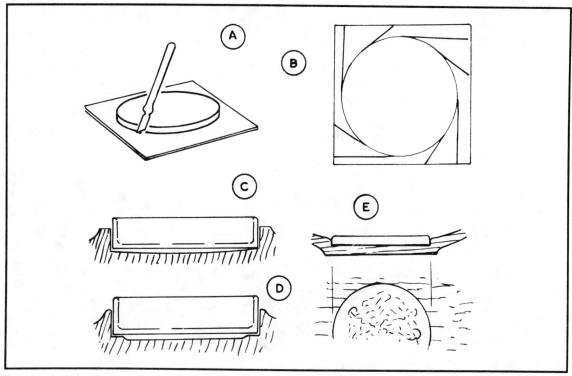

Fig. 21-1. Cutting a circle from glass is done in a series of straight cuts. A glass or tile insert can be fitted into a bowl or a tray.

a dish is forced into a turned recess, there may not be any immediate cracking, but later slight expansion and contraction of the wood might be enough to break the glass. A turned recess should be an easy fit on a glass insert. It is obviously important to have the glass part by you when you turn the recess to take it—you cannot be sure that a glass described, for instance, as 4 inches in diameter, will be precisely that size. This is very important if you have already turned the wood to take it (Fig. 21-2).

Another problem with some glass inserts is their lack of flatness. If the bottom is deeper at the center than around the rim, it will rock on a flat-bottomed recess. It is wiser to either turn the recess slightly dished (Fig. 21-1C) or with a ledge around (Fig. 21-1D) so the glass insert rests only around its circumference.

Sometimes tiles are let into the bottom of trays and bowls as decoration or to provide heat-resistant places to put hot dishes on a dining table. They can be treated in the same way as glass. They may

merely drop into place, so they can be removed for cleaning, or the recess can be turned deep enough to allow for a layer of the sort of mastic that is used to fix tiles to walls. There may even be some of this used around the tile to *grout* it so there are no gaps (Fig. 21-1E).

PLASTICS AND BONE

There are probably as many different plastics as there are kinds of wood, and their characteristics are even more widely different, so it is difficult to describe techniques that are applicable to all plastics. Those plastics that are available in a sheet and rods can usually be worked with hand tools—in fact, the use of power tools is discouraged for some as the heat generated by rapid work softens the plastic and causes it to grip the tool. This leads to breakages or a poor finish.

Transparent plastic sheeting has a use in place of glass for some things (Fig. 21-3). It is softer than glass and, therefore, more likely to suffer from

Fig. 21-2. Checking the fit of an insert in a tray mounted on a screw center is shown.

Fig. 21-3. The base of a trophy showing a paper insert and a transparent plastic cover to screw over it.

scratches. Some of it is supplied with paper loosely attached to the already brightly polished surfaces. This should be left on as protection for as long as possible while work is being done. It is also convenient for marking with a pencil.

This, and most other colored plastic sheeting, can be cut with a hand saw, which may be a woodworking back saw or a metalworking hacksaw. It is better cut flat than on edge, because more teeth are in contact and there is less risk of breaking out (Fig. 21-4A). If a power saw is used, feed slowly so the minimum heat is generated.

Some plastics can have straight edges planed by using a sharp, narrow-mouthed plane. It is more common to file edges, however. A fine file will quickly clog. It is better to get the plastic to size with a fairly coarse file and finish the edge by sanding. This can be done with garnet or other wood finishing paper. Work down to finer grades if a good edge is needed.

Drilling plastics should be approached cautiously. Mark the center with a square-pointed awl (Fig. 21-4B). In most plastics, it is possible to drill holes up to about 3/16 inch with drills intended for metal, but fed at quite a low speed and with only enough pressure to keep them cutting. Hand drilling is preferable. Because the material is soft, the work is easy. If a power drill is used, however, even on a low speed heat is generated, and the plastic around the holes softens to cling to the drill. This usually destroys the plastic.

There are special drills for plastics, which have a steeper angle to the flutes than those for metalworking. Unless much plastic work is anticipated, buying these is not justified. For holes 1/4 inch upward, it is better to adapt a metalworking drill by grinding the leading edge of the lip upright (Fig. 21-4C). If this is used at low speed with light pressure it will make a clean hole in most plastics. If you wish to turn plastic rod, the ends should be drilled and countersunk for the lathe centers, preferably with a combination drill (Fig. 3-3). This should be done either with the rod held in a headstock chuck and the drill in a tailstock chuck or in a drill press (Fig. 3-4).

Polish on plastic is a process more like metal than wood polish. With wood, the polish is obtained on something applied to the surface. With plastic and metal, it is the smoothness of the surface of the material itself that provides the polish. This means that polishing consists of breaking down the surface with successively finer abrasives until the marks left are so tiny that they appear to blend into each other and our eyes regard the surface as smooth.

When dealing with plastic, whether flat or turned, it is necessary to remove tool marks with abrasives, which may be in the form of abrasive paper, but sometimes it is more convenient to use loose grit on a cloth. Use successively finer abrasives. Make sure all particles of grit from one stage are removed before moving to a finer one, and

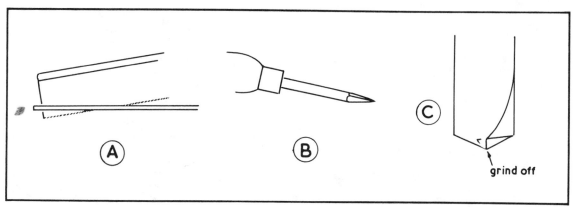

Fig. 21-4. Sheet plastic is cut at a flat angle and holes are marked with the point of an awl and drilled with a metalworking drill having the point ground vertically.

make sure each stage thoroughly removes the scratches left by the previous grades. The next step is the use of polishes, which are really even finer abrasives in a liquid. The makers of some plastics after two polishes. The first follows abrasives and the second should give the final gloss.

If the maker's polishes are unavailable, similar results can usually be obtained by starting with a polish intended for brass or similar metals and finishing with one intended for silver. It is also possible to use a domestic scouring powder for the first stage and finish with a metal polish. Turned plastic can be polished with hand polishes on a cloth. If power polishing is used, there are solid polishes that are intended for plastic. It is unwise to use a power polishing mop or other head for plastic after it has been used for metal. Keep equipment for use on plastic only.

Tools for turning plastics are like the scrapers used for bowl turning, but these scrapers are mostly too large and clumsy for the finer work usually entailed in turning plastic associated with spindle turning. Plastic parts are usually decorative rings or ends on wooden spindle turnings, or the turner may use plastic only to turn chessmen or similar items. Short small items of this sort are best held in a self-centering chuck, although slender pieces can be drilled to take the back center for extra support. Round hollow or tubular parts are better supported for turning on a wooden arbor (Fig. 21-5). This prevents distortion and reduces the risk of breakage. Ends can be trued, decorative rings can be cut, and the first steps in polishing can be done on the lathe.

A suitable tool is made for steel about 1/4 inch square. One tool can have a rounded end (Fig. 21-6A) and another may be angular (Fig. 21-6B). A pair with skew ends will be useful. The cutting angle is backed off at about the same angle as for wood scraping (Fig. 21-6C). The edge should be properly honed to get the best results. An edge that has only been ground may cut and remove material, but a honed edge brings ribbons of waste off in a continuous stream to leave a very smooth and almost polished surface on most plastics.

The metal part of the tool need not project

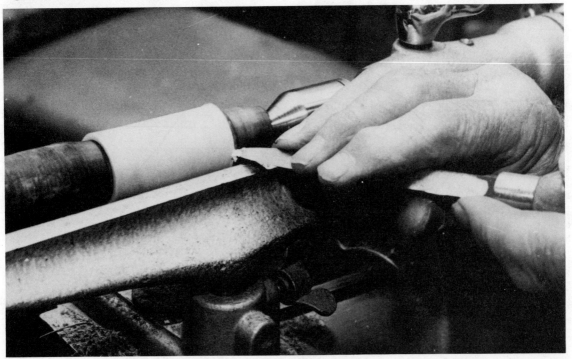

Fig. 21-5. A plastic tube mounted on an arbor is having its end trued with a graver.

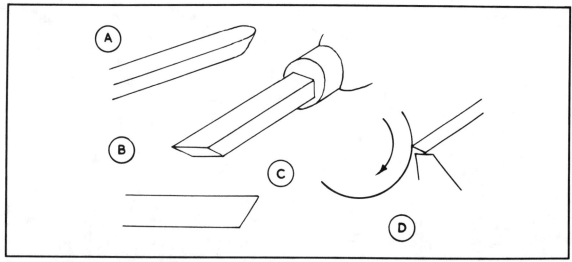

Fig. 21-6. Plastic parts are turned with small scraping tools.

more than a few inches from a handle, and the handle can be the normal type, although not very large, as leverage is never very great. The ordinary tool rest can be used, although a flat-top one for metal turning is better. The surface of the tool rest should be below center height, and the tool held on it so it presents a cutting angle at about center height (Fig. 21-6D). Experiment with the tool angle, but for most plastics, the top surface should slope a few degrees. The correct angle can be recognized by the smoothness with which shavings peel away. With a wrong angle either way, the tool may chatter and the waste may come away powdery.

Sheet laminated plastic, of which the best-known trade name is *Formica*, makes good kitchen and other working surfaces when glued to wood or particle board backing. A turner may need to deal with it when it is used on a round part. An example is a round hot pad or a larger circular board for a cook's use in the preparation of food. The material is hard but tends to be brittle, so there is a risk of cracking or chips breaking out from edges if tools are used incorrectly.

Plywood makes a convenient backing and the laminated plastic should be attached with the adhesive recommended by the makers, which is usually one of the impact type. Cutting and other hand work should be done as discussed earlier in this chapter regarding plastics. Work with the face surface upwards, so cuts break out at the other side. For a round pad, cut both wood and plastic fairly closely to size before mounting in the lathe.

The plywood and plastic edges can be turned with a wood-turning scraper tool, preferably sharpened with a slight burr and used lightly (Fig. 21-7A). Then give the edge of the plastic a bevel with a small scraper or graver (Fig. 21-6B). Aim to get a good bevel from the tool (Fig. 21-7B). Work back from the surface towards the wood to avoid breaking out. If you sand the turned edge, be careful that the abrasive does not touch the plastic surface and spoil its polish. Support the abrasive paper with a piece of wood (Fig. 21-7C).

Laminated plastic glued to wood may be fitted into a round wood rim to make a stand for a coffee pot, plant pot, or anything else that could damage wood with moisture or heat. In that case, it might be sufficient to saw the plastic and plywood to fit in the turned rabbet in the frame (Fig. 21-7D), although turning the edge of the insert would produce a closer fit. Cloth glued under any of these assemblies would provide a good finish and prevent slipping or marking surfaces. It would also hide screw holes if turning has been done on a faceplate.

There are some plastics that are not compatible with any glue, so they cannot be bonded to

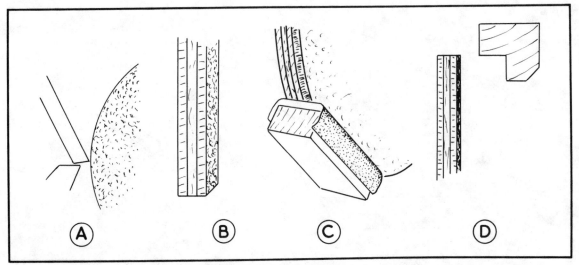

Fig. 21-7. Turning Formica on a plywood backing is shown.

themselves, wood, or any other material. Most plastics obtainable in sheet and rod form can be glued, usually with epoxy adhesive, unless the makers advise another adhesive. This allows the bright colors of plastics to be combined with the more somber wood colors.

An example of the use of colored plastic is a backing for a door knob (Fig. 21-8A). A black or red disc behind a wood knob provides contrast and prevents the wood around the knob being soiled from frequent handling. If only protection is needed, transparent plastic could be used. Cut the disc from sheet plastic and drill its center to clear the screw or dowel used with the knob. For turning, it can be mounted on a bolt, which is then held in a chuck. Usually, you will need two or more discs to make a set, and they can all be turned to size together (Fig. 21-8B). If you want to round or bevel the front of each disc, that should be done one at a time (Fig. 21-8C). Fine abrasive will make a reasonable edge surface, but if you want it brighter, you can use liquid polish on a cloth pad.

The knob discs will not need glue, but if you want to turn plastic with wood, there will have to be glued joints. A round tool handle could have a plastic end (Fig. 21-8D), either glued directly or drilled for a small dowel turned on the wood end. If the tool to be fitted has a round tang to go

through, or almost through, its handle, you can include one or more plastic rings (Fig. 21-8E). Turn the wood like a completely wood handle as far as roughing it to shape. Drill for the tang. Cut the wood where you want to put in the plastic (Fig. 21-8F). Use either the tool tang (if that can be mounted in the lathe) or a short metal rod to hold the glued parts together during turning. Grease or wax on the metal will prevent it sticking to the glued parts. If you were turning wood only, you would use a chisel; if you were turning the combination of wood and plastic, you would use a scraper.

Bone and horn are the traditional materials that were used before the coming of suitable plastics. It is interesting to experiment with turning them. Techniques are much the same as with plastic, but there is not the uniformity of texture of plastics, so results may not always be as successful. A piece of bone may turn well at one part, then crumble at another. Obviously, most work in these materials must be small. Even if you get large bones, the workable parts may be limited. Fine detail may be possible in small items, and the attractiveness of bone or horn is in making little handles for domestic and sewing items or miniature versions of what would be turned much larger in wood.

Some plastics will soften with heat. It is possible to soak a turned handle in hot water so it becomes limp. The tang of a knife or other tool can then be pressed into a hole that was drilled slightly undersize. When the plastic cools it will grip the tang securely. This cannot be done with other plastics and would be ineffective with bone. A hole for the tang should be drilled to make a push fit, then the tang secured with an adhesive. Traditionally, this was melted resin in bone handles, but it would be better today to use epoxy or other adhesives suited to the materials.

METAL

Most wood-turning lathes are not of heavy enough construction for serious metal turning. It is possible to trim the ends of a metal tube used as a ferrule on a handle (Chapter 7) or do other comparable light turning of metal without much difficulty. Turning heavier cuts, like a steel rod to a smaller size, requires a rigidity that most wood-turning lathes do not possess. A graver will trim brass, copper, or other soft metal tubing (Fig. 21-9). These metals can also be cleaned and polished

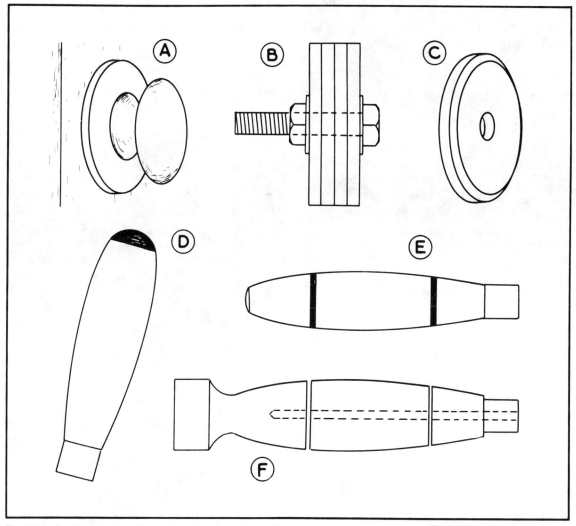

Fig. 21-8. Plastic sheet can form a backing for a knob. Several can be turned together on a bolt. Plastic may form an end or inserts for a wooden handle.

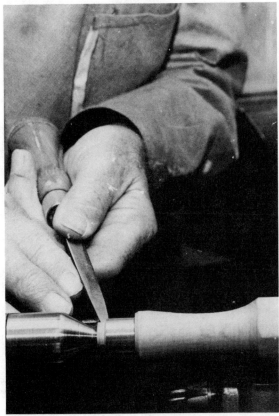

Fig. 21-9. A graver will true the end of a metal ferrule after it has been driven onto the handle.

get slide rests that allow limited metal turning. However, anyone seriously interested in metal turning needs another lathe.

Steel will turn well in a suitable lathe, but it is unwise to consider it on a wood lathe, except for squaring the end of a tube or cutting lines around a rod already of the right size. Attempting anything further would lead to disappointment. Copper and soft aluminum do not turn easily. Some of the alloys that contain copper, such as brass and the various bronzes, mostly turn well. Harder aluminum alloys may also turn well. Some suppliers of metal have grades they offer as *free-turning* or *free-cutting*.

If metal turning is to be very limited, this can be done with a graver. If more shaping is intended, as when turning ornamental ends of rods or even slightly reducing the diameter of a rod, the hand tools described for turning plastic are suitable for the softer metals. Use them in the same way. Make

while revolving by using abrasive paper or cloth (Fig. 21-10), followed by metal polish on a pad if necessary.

For heavy turning, the tool is held in a compound slide rest. This is a substantial assembly that mounts on the lathe bed and can be moved along it. The slide rest then has control handles to move the tool into and out of the work and in a direction parallel to the bed of the lathe. Such an arrangement allows quite heavy cuts to be made, and the tool is controlled to accurately cut into or across the metal or make a parallel cylinder with an accuracy measured to one-thousandth of an inch or less. There are further complications on even a simple metal-turning lathe, all are designed to control tools mechanically in relation to the work—that makes the usual woodturning lathe look naked.

For some woodworking lathes, it is possible to

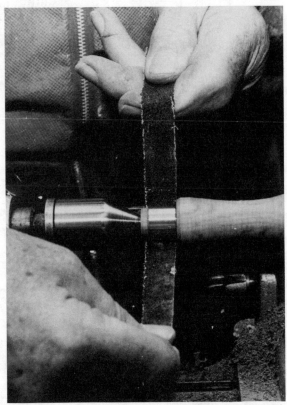

Fig. 21-10. Rotating metal can be polished with a strip of abrasive.

sure the metal is turning so it cannot vibrate and present the tool to the surface so it takes a light cut. Letting it merely rub without cutting will very quickly blunt it. Pressing too hard may cause it to dig in and damage both tool and surface. Let the tool pivot on the tool rest. Instead of trying to slide it along, as might be done with a wood-turning tool, pivot on the heel of the tool so the cutting edge makes a small arc, then move the tool and do it again if a long part has to be turned.

An expert metal turner may not consider filing in the lathe to be a good technique, but the woodworker using metal to supplement wood may find it worthwhile. If the end of a revolving rod has to be beveled or rounded, it may be better to do it with a few strokes of a file than with a hand tool. Do not merely rest the file on the metal. Sweep it across as if filing metal in a vise, so all teeth get a share of the work. The edge of a file can be used to make lines around metal, but do this with a sweep along the full length of the file. Merely putting the file in one position on revolving metal may be enough to blunt that spot on the file.

Metal can be polished in the lathe. Rust or corrosion may have to be filed off while the metal is revolving, and this can be followed by several grades of abrasive paper or grit on cloth, then by polish. Keep any cloth tightly folded so there is no risk of a corner catching in the work and being pulled around.

If metal has to be drilled in the lathe, it is best held at the headstock end by a chuck. Driving in any other way can be risky. Use a tailstock drill chuck. Whatever size hole is to be made, start with a short piece of drill that does not project much from the chuck. Feed this into the work just enough to make a dent. This is the equivalent of a center punch dot, and it is there to ensure that the drill makes the hole starting centrally.

A wood-turning lathe runs faster than a metal-turning lathe. To drill holes, run it as its lowest speed, but feed the drill fast enough to keep it cutting. As with other metalworking, letting the edge of the drill merely rub inside the hole will quickly blunt it. If you are drilling steel, it helps to lubricate the drill with soapy water dabbed on with a brush.

Another use of metal is in providing weight in the base of something that might not be steady enough if left as wood only. This is important with table lamp standards and candlesticks; their appearance is enhanced by being slender, but they might be unstable without a weighted base. This also applies to any wood turning that has a bulbous shape above a bottom of smaller diameter.

Lead is the metal that lends itself to this use. It can be melted without special heating facilities. Put small pieces of lead in an old can and heat it over a flame until the lead melts. Impurities can be skimmed off the top as *dross*. Then pour the melted lead into a mold of any shape, and it will set to this shape. Obviously, care is needed in handling, but it is a process that only needs common sense.

If a weighted base is required, the bottom of the article can have a recess turned (Fig. 21-11A). It does not matter much whether this is broad and shallow or narrow and deep. If it is a lamp standard and holes have to be made for wire, a broad shallow hollow is better. Another way is to turn a groove (Fig. 21-11B) instead of a central hollow. It may be considered better to have the weight spread near the rim in some assemblies, but steadiness is a combination of the breadth of the base and the pull of gravity on the weight. Providing the weight is there, it does not much matter how it is arranged, providing it is not off-center.

It is inadvisable to pour molten lead into the actual recess that is to take it. Charring of the wood cannot be avoided. Turn a matching recess in scrap wood and use this as a mold (Fig. 21-11C). Melting can be done in an old can, which can be discarded, although a proper iron ladle would be better. If a can is used, squeeze one side of the rim with pliers to help in pouring (Fig. 21-11D). Make sure sufficient lead has melted, but do not continue heating unnecessarily. Then, pour it into the mold. The wood will smoke and char. If it actually flames, have a damp cloth ready to dab on it, but do not pour water on it. Water may make the lead spurt dangerously or prevent the lead from setting in a good shape.

If you are not satisfied with the first shape, melt the lead and try again. Leave the lead to harden in

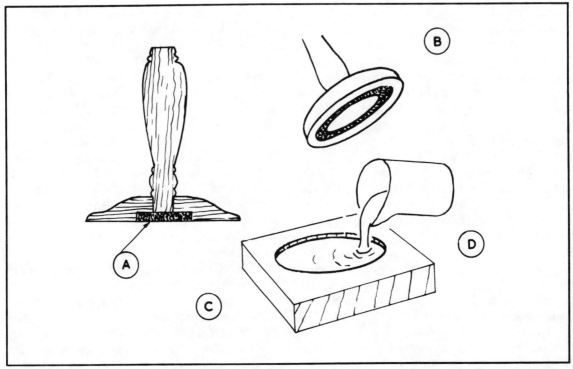

Fig. 21-11. If weight is needed in a base, lead can be melted into a similar sized hole in scrap wood then screwed in the base.

its mold. When it is obviously hard and cool enough to touch, final cooling can be accomplished by dipping it in water.

There are several ways of fixing the lead weight. It must be fixed securely or it will drop loose or right out. One way is to use epoxy or another suitable adhesive. It is probably better to use screws. Lead can be drilled and countersunk, then screws driven through into the wood.

So far as possible, the lead should be level with the bottom of the wood, but it is better for it to be slightly below the surface than above it. It is common to cover the bottom with cloth so that the lead does not show.

Chapter 22

Design

Everyone has their own ideas as to what looks attractive and beautiful. If everyone had the same opinions, there would be such uniformity that the effect would be lost by monotony. This means that what one person regards as good design may be considered most unattractive by another. It does give turners the opportunity of producing almost any form that they may claim is good design, even if the majority of other people condemn it. But most of us want to make things that the majority of people regard as good design, so we should attempt to follow the rules—such as they are.

FASHIONS IN DESIGN

Fashions in design change, and we have to follow current trends. Through it all, there are features that are necessary for good design, and they overcome extravagances of the moment and can still be picked out as the reason for the attractiveness of an object long after the fashionable feature has passed away. Some of the early civilizations knew about design. Greek and Roman pillars

that were made many thousands of years ago are still regarded as leading examples of good design.

It is not easy to pinpoint what gives something the mark of good design, while another thing is generally regarded as bad design. To a certain extent, it depends on the artistic appreciation of the viewer, and he would have difficulty in saying what it was that pleased him. Any rules are really guidelines capable of variations. If this were not so, anything made to rigid rules of design ought to be perfect, yet it would be more likely to fail than something made with knowledge of the rules, but using a free interpretation.

It is necessary to be aware of fashions in design. In less than a century, there have been considerable changes that concern woodturners. Furniture in Victorian days was very ornate. It seemed that designers were concerned to cover every piece of wood with the maximum of detail. Carving was very popular and used often in unlikely places. Any turned piece had beads and grooves everywhere and any generally large sweep of outline was broken by turned detail. Much of this work was very skillful, and a modern turner may find difficulty in following it if he wants to make reproduction furniture.

Modern furniture is much plainer. To a certain extent this is a reflection of the coming of the machine age. When most furniture making was done with hand tools, it was easier to include detail than to make long straight parts or have a broad expanse with no detail. Maybe plainness has been taken too far, and there is a return to more shaping in woodwork. Such turned work as is included in modern furniture follows the general trends and still has some detail, but long flowing curves that depend on their outline and the grain features are used more than formerly.

DESIGN TRENDS

A woodturner, like other artist-craftsmen, should keep an intelligent eye open to check on design trends. Furniture shops and catalogs can be examined to first observe overall appearances and then to look more at details and see how the better furniture has detail work that complements the broader and longer plainer parts. Without these details, the furniture would look more boxy and unattractive. Notice, too, how proportions are what play the biggest part in making a piece of furniture attractive. Although it may be a large cabinet that is being looked at, with little or no turning on it, features that make you feel it is a good or bad design can also be applied to what you turn on your lathe.

It is important to consider design as a whole. This may mean what is being turned has to be looked at in relation to what it will hold or what it will form part of. It is no use making a lamp standard that looks good on its own, but looks out of proportion when a shade is put on it (Fig. 22-1), or making nicely-proportioned slender pillars that are then built into something of fairly heavy construction. Fortunately, many turned items are complete in themselves, but if other things or wooden parts are involved, it is no use just thinking of the design problems of the turning only.

This points to fitness for purpose. If a turned piece will not do what is intended, it is bad design,

Fig. 22-1. Turned parts should be designed by keeping in mind the other items that will be attached to them.

no matter how ornate or decorative it seems to be. There were some extravagances in Victorian days where the function was obscured by unsuitable shape and decoration, so the whole purpose was lost. The first consideration in design should be suitability for the intended purpose. Even when the item has no utilitarian purpose and is not intended to perform a function, such as supporting or holding something, there is still the need to look at stability, size in relation to other furnishings, and other factors concerned with the mere presence of the item being designed. It is no use making an ornamental turning that will fall over at the slightest touch, or one that is so big that there is on suitable place to put it.

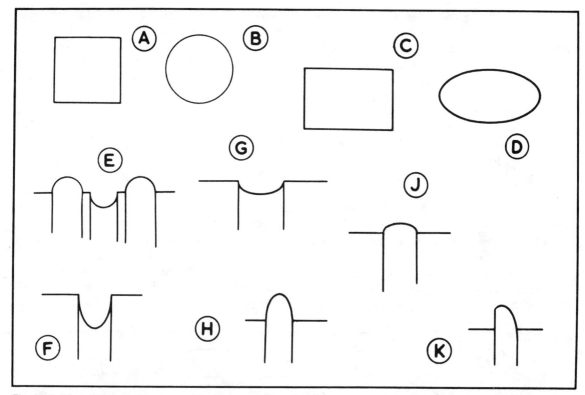

Fig. 22-2. It is better design to use a rectangle or an ellipse than a square or a circle. This applies to hollows and beads.

Fitness for purpose is most important and should be an overriding factor in design. Fortunately, the ability to do its job in the best way usually results in a pleasing shape. We have become used to certain general shapes for particular functions and these are recognized as good design.

There are some general rules that apply to all design, and they can be applied in many ways to turned work. The same measurements in both major directions, in a square or a circle (Figs. 22-2A and 22-2B), are not as pleasing to the eye as proportions like 1 1/2-1, as in an oblong (Fig. 22-2C) or an ellipse (Fig. 22-2D). In turned work, this is not always easy to apply, and there are cases where measurements have to be symmetrical. If the general outline is longer one way than the other, it will be better than if the general mass of the turning offers about the same dimensions. Most turnings are longer one way than the other, but if something like a bulbous lamp stand is being made,

a generally elliptical section should look better than a spherical one (Fig. 22-2D).

This can be applied in detail work. Beads and hollows are usually parts of circles in section (Fig. 22-2E). Because they are often quite small parts of an overall design and are unlikely to be examined closely as design features, this does not matter. However, if some traditional turned work is examined, even these details will have been treated as design features.

A hollow given a section like half of the end of an ellipse (Fig. 22-2F) is better than a semicircle and will cast better shadows to throw up the shape. If it is part of the article that does not need emphasis the hollow could be like the side of an ellipse (Fig. 22-2G).

Semicircular beads are usual, but they can have similar treatment to the hollows, with a section like the end of an ellipse for maximum prominence (Fig. 22-2H) or a flattened shape when too much attention is not wanted (Fig. 22-2J). Another way of dealing with a projection like a bead is to let it overhang with the underside flat (Fig. 22-2K) or even hollowed. On a pillar with the usual lighting coming from above, this casts a good shadow to emphasize the shape. It is something like the undercutting practiced by carvers to make something look deeper than it really is.

Much wood turning design can be regarded as "an eye for a curve." Much successful turned work is produced on the lathe following what the turner has in his head. He may work without any drawing, or just one that gives overall dimensions. A shaped part does not have an even curve both ways if it is to have the best appearance. Instead its greatest diameter is off-center (Fig. 22-3A). An example is a chair rail that would have to be given a symmetrical curve if turned without embellishment (Fig. 22-3B), but if a bead or other feature is

turned at the center, there can be two asymmetrical curves to the ends (Figs. 22-3C and 22-4).

Many turned pieces of pillar form, like the legs of a table or a candlestick, have the main feature largest and with a flowing curve. Sometimes the greater diameter is below the center of its length (Fig. 22-3D). This is acceptable, particularly if weight has to be kept low—then function is a main consideration. Usually this type of curve benefits from a turned out lip toward the top (Fig. 22-3E). It is considered more pleasing and, therefore, better design to have the greater diameter above the center of the curve (Fig. 22-3F). This can be seen in Grecian and other old pillars.

In a turned leg, there is no other closely-related turning to consider, but in something like a lamp, there is a base as well. If the base is fairly large, as it should be for stability, the whole thing should look better if the greater bulk of the stem is kept

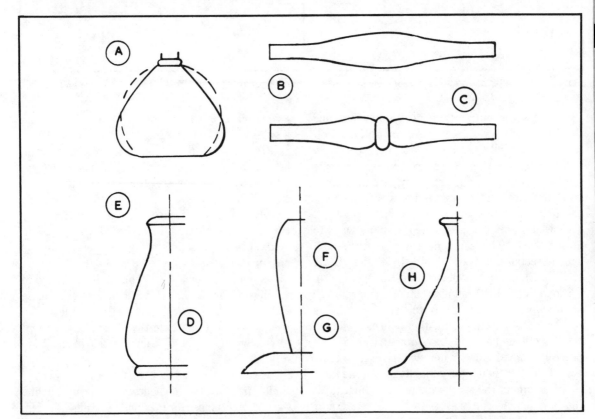

Fig. 22-3. Most things look better with the outline having its greatest diameter off-center, rather than being symmetrical.

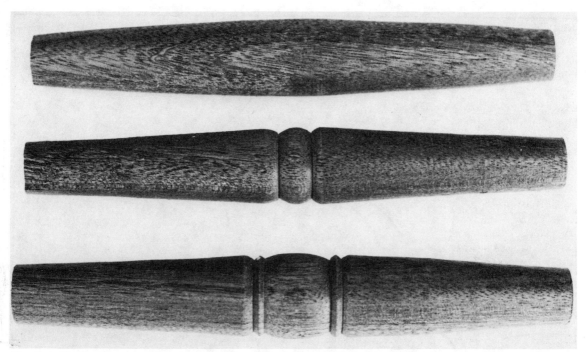

Fig. 22-4. Three chair rails showing the effect on appearance of beads at the center.

away from the base (Fig. 22-3G). If the base and more bulky stem are to blend more into each other, there may be a reason for keeping the greater curve low (Fig. 22-3H).

Even more does the eye for a curve come into its own with the design of bowls. It is usually better to work by eye than to templates, except when more than one of a design is to be produced. There is need to check thicknesses of wood and other practical considerations, but the curves inside and out are what the turner is visualizing rather than an attempt to follow a set pattern.

As with other sections, a symmetrical section is not wanted. The section at the outside of a bowl would not be very satisfactory if it was part of a circle (Fig. 22-5A). Sometimes it can be close to this, particularly if there are beads or other decorative features to break up the outline, but it is usually better to depart from any part of a sphere.

Usually a flatter curve from the base becomes tighter towards the rim (Fig. 22-5B). The rim may be nearly sharp and the upper part cylindrical (Fig. 22-5C). It looks better if the top curves in more

tightly towards the rim, and it is attractive if the actual edge is not part of a circle (Fig. 22-5D).

The size of the base is important. It must be broad enough for the bowl to stand firm. It is no use turning an ornate base that is tall and narrow (Fig. 22-5E) if that makes the bowl unstable. A broader and shallower base is better (Fig. 22-5F). In any case, it is the shape of the body of the bowl that is a design feature, and the base does not normally attract any attention.

In most bowls, it is the grain features of the wood that supplement the overall shape to give a pleasing design. Consequently, a modern bowl is best made with a flowing attractive curved section and no added turning embellishment. This may even be good enough with plain wood when shape is all that is needed for satisfaction.

If some added turning seems necessary on plain wood, this should be confined to a molded or beaded rim and possibly some shaping of the base (Fig. 22-5G). It is usually unwise to turn parts on the curve of the bowl (Fig. 22-5H) unless it is reproduction work where the older craftsman broke up the

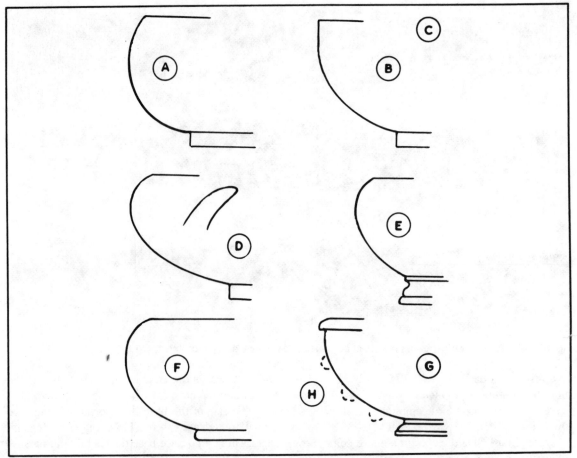

Fig. 22-5. Bowl outlines should follow elliptical or other uneven curves rather than parts of a circle. Usually, a bowl gains by a sweeping plain curve, which is better than one embellished with many turned smaller decorations.

curve with a mass of features. If the sweep of the curve is broken today, it is probably better to have a series of beads in descending sizes, or something similar, all over, rather than isolated turning on an otherwise plain surface.

As can be seen from the foregoing, you are largely on your own when it comes to designing your own turned work. Take every opportunity to look at other work, not necessarily turned. If something appeals to you, try to analyze what there is about it that is attractive. If what someone else thinks is good offends your good sense, again try to see what proportions, features, colors, and other aspects are not what you like. Compare design features with the few rules and see how the designer has used variations to get his effects.

Wood turning is one branch of craftsmanship where you have a great opportunity to express your own individuality. You do not have to shape wood the same as someone else. What you produce is an expression of your own design sense—or lack of it! However, do not be put off by sometimes producing unattractive items. The best training in designing for turning is turning. It is not something that can be put on paper completely. By all means make drawings and sketches, but a flat picture is not the same as the piece in the round. Practicing turning, even if some of the output has to be scrapped, is the best way to learn how to produce turned work of good design.

SECTION II
THINGS TO MAKE

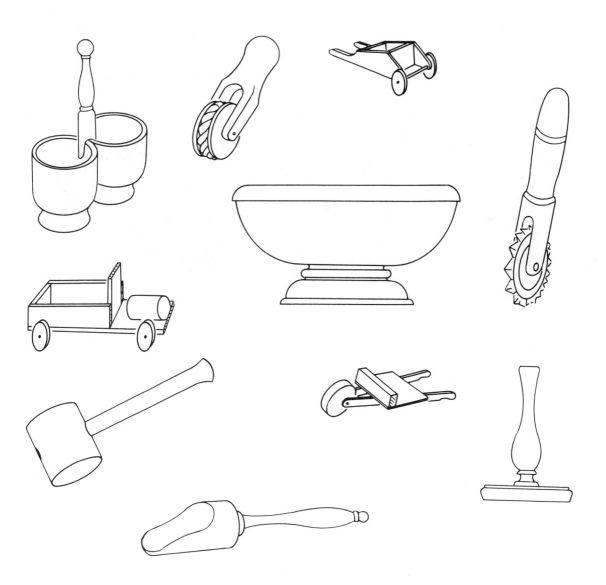

Chapter 23

Spindles and Legs

Much lathe work consists of making spindles with the wood supported between the driving center of the headstock and the back center at the tailstock. Almost any work done in this way can be called spindle turning, but items that qualify for this name in particular are turned lengths, often with square ends, used in banisters, ballustrades, room dividers, screens, book shelves, and anywhere that turned spindles or pillars would enhance furniture or room fittings. Usually the spindles are used in a series of identical patterns. Sizes may be anywhere between a few inches long for spindles in a gallery surrounding a border of a desk to room height for dividers. Sections may be anything, depending on whether the effect wanted is solid and strong or long and slender. There is a practical limit due to the need to consider stiffness when turning. The thickness should be enough to stand up to tool work without undue bending.

SPINDLES

Spindles may be turned with curves that blend into each other (Fig. 23-1A) or with steps between most curves (Fig. 23-1B). The latter has been the accepted way for a very long time and sometimes regarded as the mark of the expert turner. However, today shapes without these intermediate steps are sometimes seen in keeping with the plainer lines of much modern furniture.

Spindles are often symmetrical about a central design (Fig. 23-1C). Sometimes a section of design is complete in itself (Fig. 23-1D), but more than one section may be used on each side of the center of a long spindle. For an upright spindle, there may be more sections below what would have been the central design, although height in a tall spindle is more likely by having the lower square part longer than the upper square part (Fig. 23-1E).

Most spindles have long sweeping curves between shorter pieces of decoration. These allow variations in length to be taken care of. The smaller features may be unaltered, but it is possible to compress or lengthen a sweeping curve and still retain its attractive appearance (Fig. 23-1F).

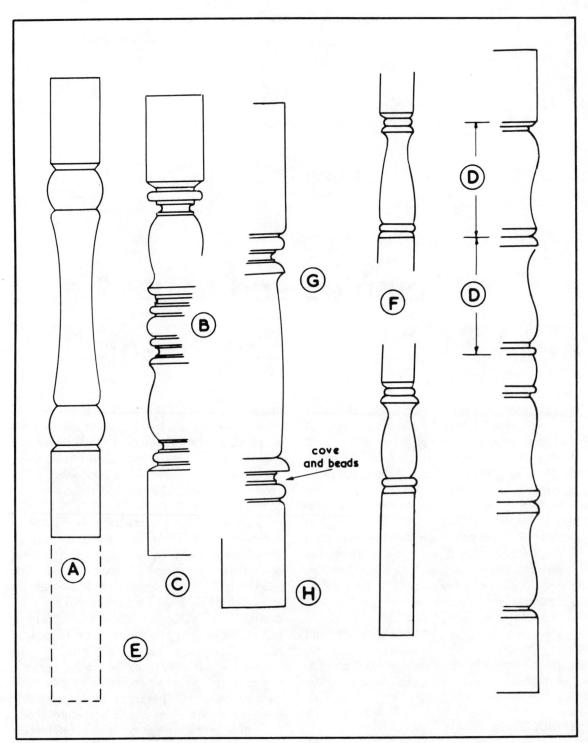

Fig. 23-1. Suggestions for spindle designs are given.

Classical spindles used in a series may have had their greatest diameter central, with decoration symmetrical about this point. A common ballustrade spindle had the greater size lower than the middle and a sweep to a turned out fairly slender neck (Fig. 23-1G). In stone these tended to be rather thick, but a similar theme is seen in Colonial spindles (Fig. 23-1H). The long sweep is a curve and should not be turned as a straight taper if it is to be most effective.

At one time, considerable detail was turned into a spindle or pillar, some of it supplemented by carving. Such work was a test of the turner's skill and would not be done in such detail in modern furniture, but the examples shown indicate what might be turned in reproduction furniture (Fig. 23-2). For a total height more than the capacity of the lathe, a dowel joint can be made at one of the turned details and should be invisible when the work is finished.

Spindles may be used in gates, in galleries, around sideboards and similar things, in chairs, and as a kitchen valance. These spindles may be only a few inches long or up to a few feet, but they tend to be slender. Some of the foregoing patterns are possible, but a few simple spindle shapes are shown (Fig. 23-3). There may be square ends or the spindles can be turned with dowels to fit into holes in rails.

These spindles, and most others, have to be considered for their mass effect. A spindle is not viewed as a single piece—except by another turner looking into details—but is part of a pattern made by a series. Normally the spindles are identical and arranged all the same way, but it is sometimes worthwhile using a different design at the ends of the row or anywhere that a break comes in the furniture. It is also sometimes effective to turn alternate spindles upside down. This has to be done with caution, and even then not every viewer will regard the arrangement as attractive.

It was in Victorian days that turned pillars became complicated. If furniture of earlier periods is examined, some of the great designers used much simpler outlines (Fig. 23-4). Some of these outlines will be seen to include quite long straight sections.

A straight part needs more care in tool handling than a curved shape. Although the aim should be to get a curve perfect, a slight variation from the originally intended outline may be modified so it does not show. There is none of this tolerance with a straight part, which should be perfect. If a mistake is made, the only cure is to reduce the whole section, but if it is a series of spindles, there cannot be one thin one amongst the others.

NEWEL POSTS

Spindles fit between other parts. There may be an intermediate rail, but the ends are closed by sections of the furniture and the spindle end is doweled or otherwise jointed there. In some constructions, a spindle stands up and its top is unsupported. There are usually attachments lower down, but the extremity of the turned part points upward without being fixed to anything else. In most constructions, this is called a *newel post*. A newel post may form the side support for a mirror. It may be a corner bed post. It can come anywhere in an assembly where it would be better for the post to continue upward overlapping what it is attached to, instead of the other part overlapping it in spindle form.

The main part of a newel post can be turned in the same patterns as spindles. In some constructions, the main part of the newel post may have to match a series of spindles, but its top goes above the rail at which the spindles stop. More often the newel post is one of a pair, so the turner is freer in his choice of patterns. Some traditional ones are shown (Fig. 23-5).

A square section near the top allows for joints to other parts or the pivot fitting for a mirror. Usually there is a need for lightness in appearance. This is obtained by a general taper toward the top, and the greatest thickness of the turning low down.

The decoration above the square part can carry on with a design that matches that lower down or it can be a knob or other projection. In general, the projecting piece above the square should have no part larger in diameter than those parts just below the square. In most cases, the top is at or just below eye level, so the finish of the end should be good. This means that you should be careful turning to-

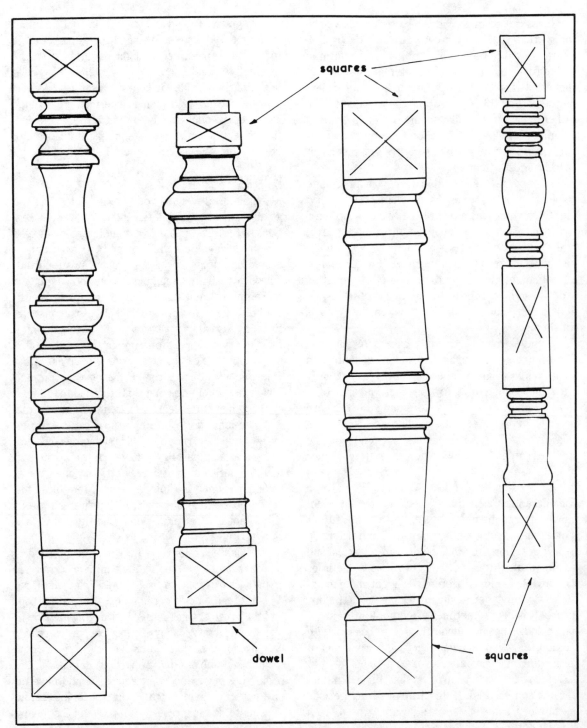

Fig. 23-2. Further suggestions for spindle designs, which incorporate square parts for attaching rails and other parts of furniture, are shown.

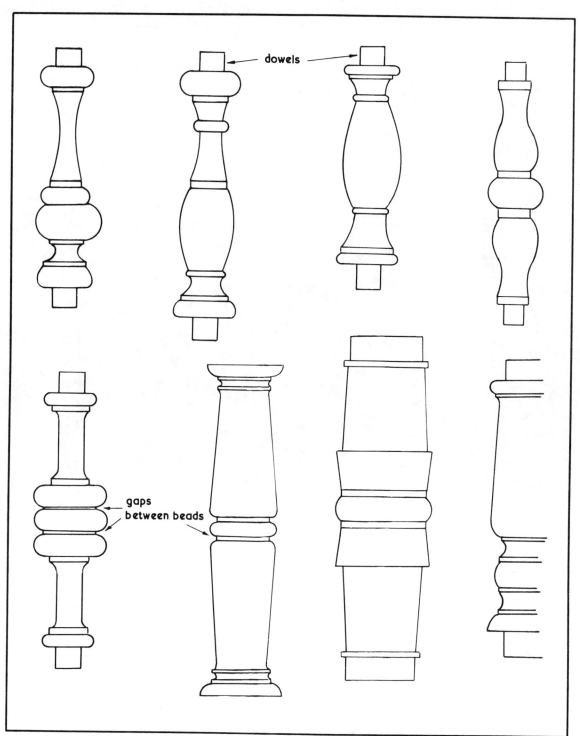

Fig. 23-3. Pictured are some spindle designs following traditional and modern outlines.

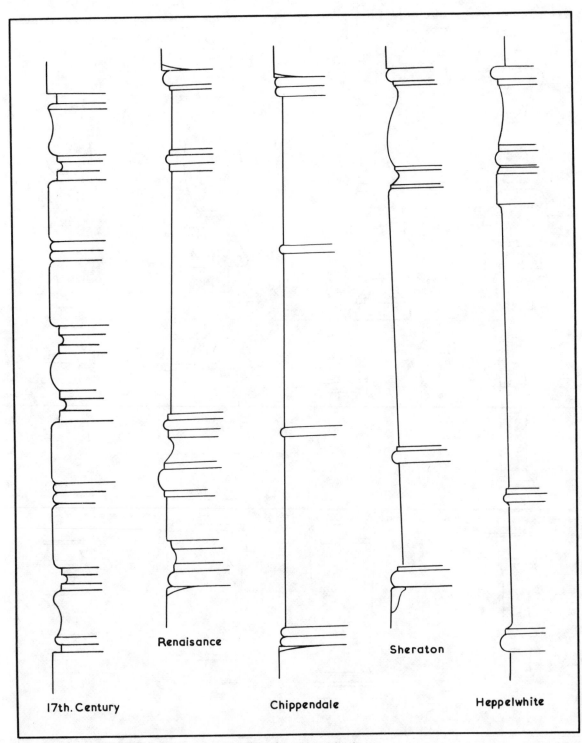

17th. Century   Renaisance   Chippendale   Sheraton   Heppelwhite

Fig. 23-4. Here are some examples of spindles used in traditional furniture.

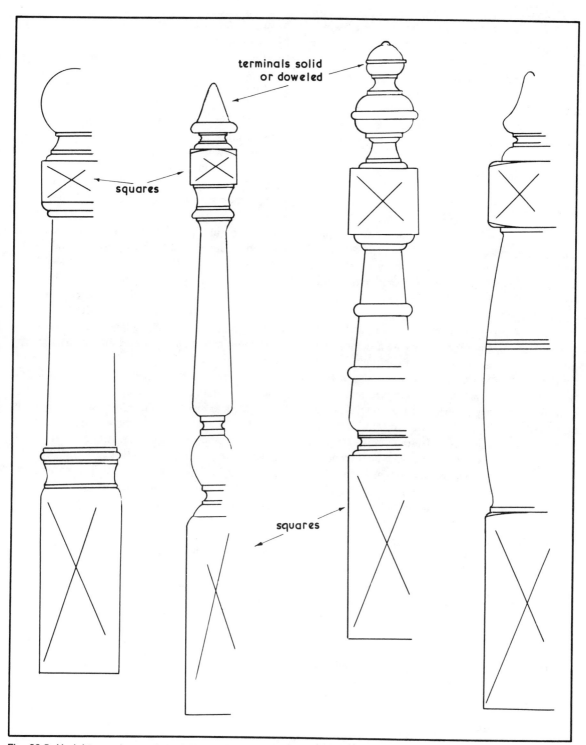

terminals solid
or doweled

squares

squares

Fig. 23-5. Upright newal posts intended to support mirrors and similar objects are featured.

ward the back center as a final step, with accurate parting off and probably a little hand sanding over the end to remove any uneven marks.

It is possible to turn the spindle part of a newel post as a unit and make the decorative end as a separate piece. This will be a finial or terminal, made with a dowel to fit into a hole in the top of the spindle. The end post of a banister can be made in this way with the banister rail joined into the square top of an extended spindle, and a knob fixed above that.

LEGS

Turned legs have much in common with spindles and newel posts, in fact some legs can be made to newel post designs, except for the end which forms the foot. Other legs may have spindle designs to match spindles elsewhere in the furniture.

The making of legs has been, and probably will continue to be, the main output of a commercial turner, and it is likely to be a main activity of many amateurs. Legs are nearly always in sets of four. Some chairs may only have two turned legs at the front and other shapes at the back. Some tables may be so large as to need six legs. In any case, the turner needs to make sets. He may make the first leg to a pattern that pleases him, but he then needs to use a rod and calipers to ensure that further legs will match. Fortunately, legs are usually further apart than spindles in a gallery, but variations of any consequence will still be obvious.

Legs are broadly divided into those with square tops deep enough to take a rail and wide enough to provide stiffness and those that are expected to take rails lower down. In most cases, there are square sections where the joints come, although a few legs are needed round throughout their length. This occurs with Windsor chairs and others of that type, where a round leg has a dowel top into the seat (Fig. 23-6A). Lower rails also have ends that dowel into the round legs.

Some legs are made of softwoods. These do not take such fine detail as hardwoods. They also tend to be thicker for the sake of strength. Softwood legs may be used in tables that are more utilitarian than

beautiful, but some decoration is still welcomed. Many lathes have a capacity about 30 inches between centers. This is to accommodate table legs. A softwood table leg with a top up to 4 inches square is as much as most of the lighter lathes will take. A hardwood leg of this size might be managed, but the work could be tedious due to the need to take light cuts.

For softwood legs there should be bold outlines and no prominent turning of thin section that might soon suffer from knocks (Fig. 23-6B). Rely on fairly broad beads and flowing curves that do not leave thinner edges outstanding. Although the foot looks more graceful if it tapers to a small size, it has to take all of the weight with its partners and this is better fairly broad (Fig. 23-6C).

A softwood leg with squares should have the round parts roughed to a circular section with a gouge (Fig. 23-7). You should tilt the tool at the ends of the cuts near the squares, so it cuts away from them and the risk of breaking away the corners is reduced. The curved ends of the squares are trued to shape with a chisel on edge, then beads adjoining the squares are shaped and the dowel top is reduced to size (Fig. 23-8). The center part is turned to shape with bold curves and no fragile detail. The foot is shaped, leaving a short length of waste at the fork center (Fig. 23-9). When the shape has been checked as satisfactory and the round parts sanded, the foot is cut off with a parting tool (Fig. 23-10).

Legs in hardwood mostly have the larger part of the design toward the top (Figs. 23-11 and 23-12). Prominent beads and other projections should still be avoided if the table can be expected to receive knocks; they should only be included with harder close-grained woods.

Some legs on antique furniture will have squares smaller than the largest diameter turning. These can be built up, as described for bulbous legs, but where the size is not very different, the squares may be bandsawn to the reduced size and planed. If a leg is to be fitted with casters or other fittings, this should be allowed for in the overall length. It is important that a table finishes at a comfortable height for use, so the thickness of top and depth

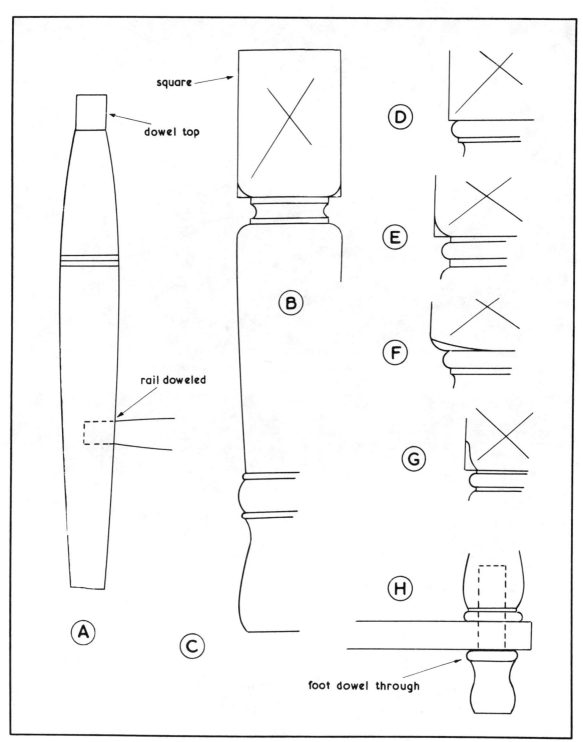

square

dowel top

rail doweled

D

E

B

F

G

H

A

C

foot dowel through

Fig. 23-6. The legs shown are intended mainly for softwood and therefore have a bold treatment.

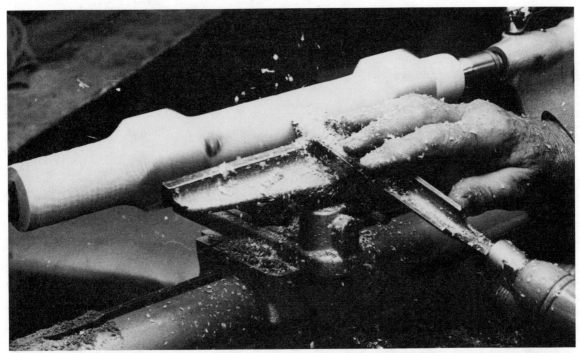

Fig. 23-7. The first step in making a softwood leg with squares is to rough the round parts to shape with a gouge.

Fig. 23-8. The ends of the squares are cut and adjoining beads shaped. This leg has a dowel turned to fit into a table top.

Fig. 23-9. The main part of the leg has been shaped, and the foot is being tapered.

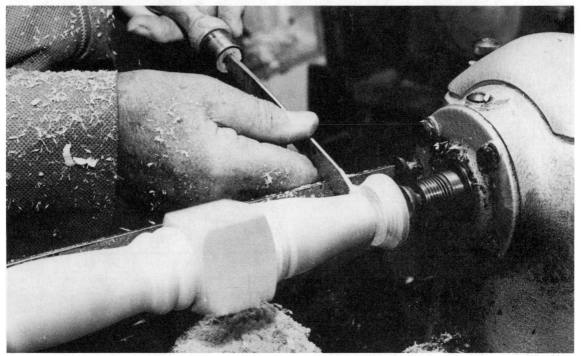

Fig. 23-10. When all of the parts have been completed, the foot is parted off.

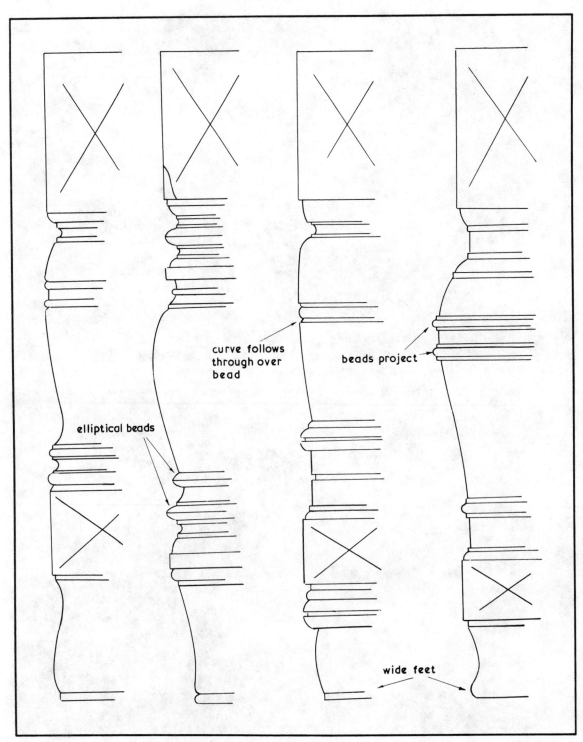

Fig. 23-11. Intricate turning suitable for hardwood legs is shown.

to go too deeply anywhere so as to weaken the leg (Fig. 23-12).

The proportion of the lower square, if there is one, needs care. It looks best if its length is at least as much as its width. Too shallow a depth is not usually as attractive. The ends of the square part can be cut square (Fig. 23-6D), but taking off the corners softens the effect (Fig. 23-6E). This blends into a curve (Fig. 23-6F) or there can be decorative cuts at the corners (Fig. 23-6G).

The usual rails tenon or dowel into the legs, but in some occasional tables, there may be a lower shelf or under frame. The lower shelf or under frame is more conveniently fixed by making the leg in two parts, with a dowel from one part going through the frame into the other part (Fig. 23-6H).

Legs up to about 4 inches in diameter can be expected to keep their form and not crack if properly seasoned wood is used. With thicker legs, there is a risk that they may check and crack, particularly if they are used in a very warm room where they dry excessively. One way to reduce this risk is to drill a central hole right through the leg similar to drilling for the wire in a floor lamp standard. A hole about 3/4 inch in diameter is advisable, although a smaller hole would be better than nothing if that is all that can be made with available equipment. A plug may be glued in the bottom of the hole.

In reproduction work, a part of the leg may have to be carved. If so, the turning should be almost completed and the leg removed from the lathe without damaging the center marks. Carving may then be done and the wood returned to the lathe for final cleaning up—in particular the removal of any marks from a vise or clamp used when carving.

Fig. 23-12. Shown is the application of turned legs with square parts in the construction of a small table.

of rail should be known before planning the turned part of a leg.

Legs for lighter occasional tables are more slender than dining tables. The outlines can be generally similar, however, although care is needed not

Chapter 24

Pedestals

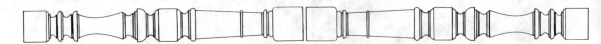

There are a large number of turned items that have a main part in a central column, which may be supported by a broad base, have legs, or in turn support a table or other top. The pedestal may be adapted to hang, when it can support arms that hold lamps. It may be cut down the middle so it forms part of a wall bracket. In a few instances, all of the pedestal is turned from one piece of wood. More often the main part is a spindle turning, which is joined to a base and other parts are joined to it.

CANDLESTICKS

Over the centuries, some of the most attractive products of the lathe have been candlesticks in a multitude of different forms. Wood does not often endure for long periods, but there are brass candlesticks in churches and cathedrals that show their origin a great many years ago as they were cast from wooden originals. In many cases, the wooden candlestick would have been just as serviceable, if not as durable, as the brass version made from it. These candlesticks provide examples

of design which would still be worth following.

Candles are no longer an essential of life, but candlesticks are still sought after for their decorative value and for use as table centers on special occasions. The fashion for ornamental candles has brought a revival of interest in things to hold them, and this is an opportunity for the turner.

When planning a candlestick design, it should be related to its use. If it is only expected to be decorative in itself with possibly an occasional use with a plain candle, the design is self-contained. If a very ornate candle is to be used with it, the woodwork may be supplementary to the candle and the total effect would benefit by having the woodwork fairly plain.

In its simplest form, the central column is turned with the socket in the same piece of wood (Fig. 24-1A). The hole in the end should suit the chosen size of the candle. It will be between 3/4 inch and 1 inch for standard candles, but it is advisable to check on locally available candles before starting work.

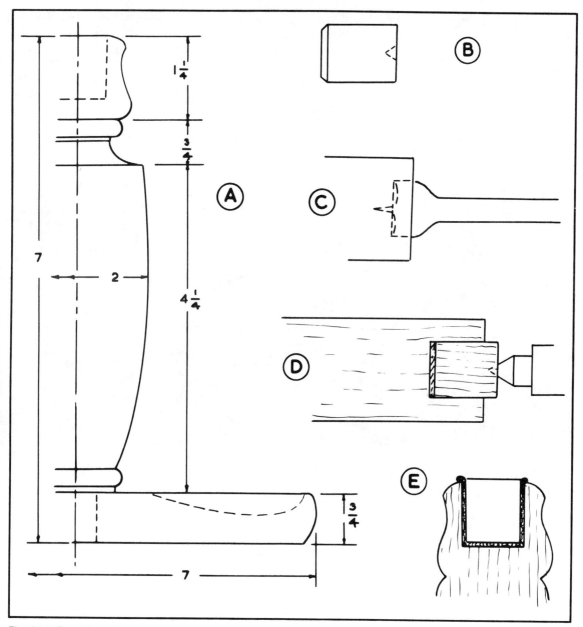

Fig. 24-1. Steps in making a wooden candlestick.

Make a plug to represent the end of the candle. Let this be a little longer than the socket to be drilled and retain its center hollow (Fig. 24-1B). Rough-turn the piece of wood that is to form the column, then drill the hole for the candle using a drill in a tailstock chuck (Fig. 24-1C). Push the plug into this hole and do the rest of the turning with the plug in place (Fig. 24-1D).

Further turning is straightforward. Drill a hole in a piece of scrap wood and use this to check the dowel end of the column, either directly or by using it as a guide to caliper setting.

Metal candle sockets can be bought to fit in the top of the column (Fig. 24-1E). If one of these is used, that will settle the size hole to drill. A metal socket makes a neat mount for the candle, but check first that it matches available candles.

There are many developments on this basic candlestick. If serious use is intended, there should be a drip ring to catch candle grease. This improves the appearance of the candlestick in any case, even if candles will rarely be lit. A good way to include this is to let the actual candleholder and the drip ring fit over a dowel end on the column (Fig. 24-2A). Both parts are drilled to a size to suit the candle and the top of the column turned to fit.

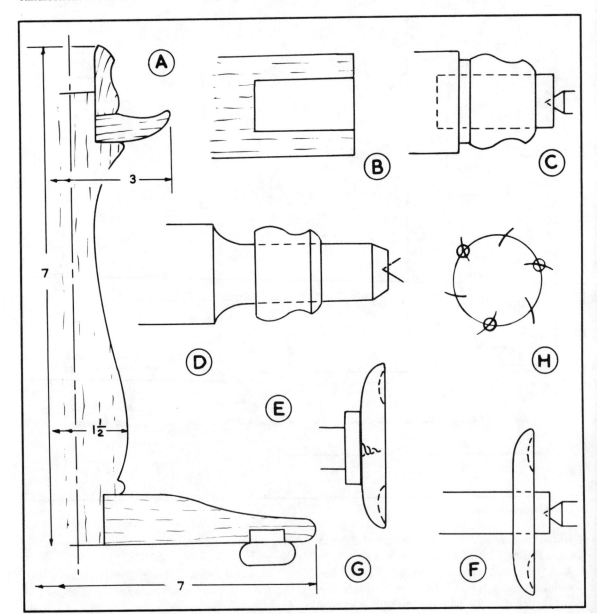

Fig. 24-2. Details of a candlestick with feet and a drip ring.

The candleholder has its grain lengthwise. If a self-centering chuck is available, the blank can be held in this to drill through. Otherwise an overlength piece can be made cylindrical between centers, then drilled from the tailstock (Fig. 24-2B). The outside can be finished with a plug in the hole (Fig. 24-2C). Alternatively the blank can be mounted on a mandrel (Fig. 24-2D).

If the drip ring is not very large, it may also have its grain parallel with the hole, but for most sizes, it will have to be turned from a disc with its grain across. It may be possible to turn it on a screw center so the flat part can come on the underside (Fig. 24-2E). The hole is drilled after turning has been completed. The screw hole will center the drill accurately. This may leave too large an area of flat for some purposes. It may be better then to do all of the turning with the ring mounted on a mandrel (Fig. 24-2F).

A flat surface on the bottom may be satisfactory as most candlesticks stand on level surfaces. Cover the bottom with cloth or one of the self-adhesive clothlike plastics. Alternatively, turn the bottom hollow so it rests on the rim. If it is a tall candlestick, it may be advisable to increase stability with a lead block in the base (Chapter 21). Another way of ensuring standing level, whatever the surface, is to arrange the weight to be taken on three feet, which will rest without wobbling no matter how uneven the surface. The feet can be turned with dowels to fit into holes in the base (Fig. 24-2G). To get an even pitch circle, draw a circle of the desired size and step off the radius around it. As the radius goes exactly six times, the dowel holes are at alternate points (Fig. 24-2H).

The steps involved in making a similar candlestick (Fig. 24-3) are shown in the photographs. The base is turned on a faceplate (Fig. 24-4), and the hole for the dowel on the stem is drilled from the tailstock. The stem is turned between centers. On it, the dowel that will pass through the drip ring and candleholder can be checked for size with a hole in a scrap piece of wood when the tailstock is withdrawn, but the dowel that has to fit in the base must be tested with calipers (Fig. 24-5). The candleholder is a simple exercise in outside turn-

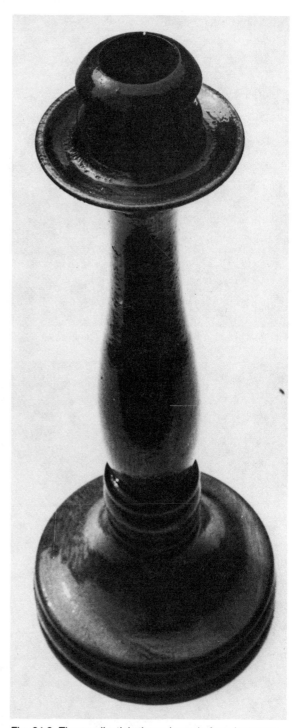

Fig. 24-3. The candlestick shown is made from four parts: base, spindle, drip ring, and candleholder.

Fig. 24-4. Turning the candlestick base mounted on a pad on a faceplate.

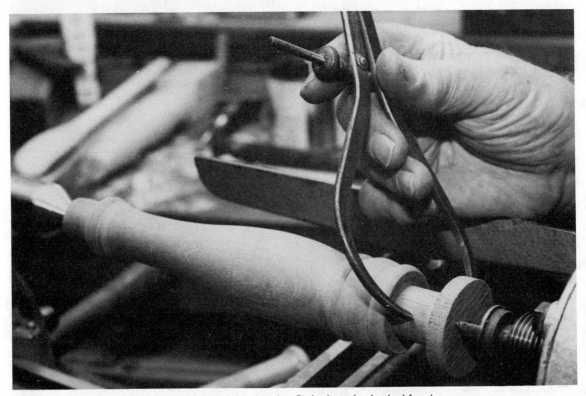

Fig. 24-5. The pedestal has been turned, and the dowel to fit the base is checked for size.

ing on an arbor (Fig. 24-6). The drip ring is made from a disc with its grain across and has to be turned carefully on both sides (Fig. 24-7).

A candlestick does not have to be tall. For the decorative candles that are individually-made, it is better for the holder to be little more than a block of wood with a hole in it (Fig. 24-8A). Anyone with a lathe will want to do something more than just have a plain block, but excessive turning detail should be avoided, and the finished work should have a broad base if the candle is very large (Fig. 24-8B). Blocks could be built up with different colored woods.

This is an opportunity to use up offcuts of wood too small to be built into anything large. In some cases, it may be advisable to join two pieces so the actual holder is mounted on another piece forming a base (Fig. 24-8C). This could be developed further and the base turned up like a bowl to hold small items and look like the candlestick that people used to light before the days of electricity. To complete the illusion, there could be a handle let into the rim (Fig. 24-8D). Another treatment would be a turned handle doweled into the base (Fig. 24-8E).

Single-block stands can be made to suit the small candles used as Christmas decorations, but the bottom should be broad and heavy (Fig. 24-8F). A lit candle, of any size, could be dangerous knocked over.

It is possible to make a stand for more than one candle. The result is a *candelabra*. Not all of the work is done on the lathe, but it is possible to design

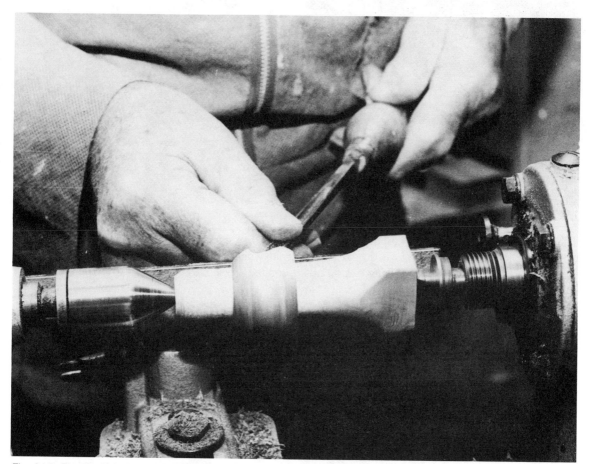

Fig. 24-6. The candleholder is made from a drilled block mounted on an arbor.

Fig. 24-7. The drip ring on an arbor has to be turned on both sides.

a stand for two or three candles with mostly turned parts (Fig. 24-9A). The base is turned to be fairly heavy to give stability. A part-turning can mount on this (Fig. 24-9B). This may be turned as a circle on the faceplate, then the piece needed cut off (Fig. 24-9C). One circle will cut two of these parts.

It would be possible to fit the candleholders with drip rings, but in the simple assembly shown, each holder is a drilled blank turned on the end of a mandrel (Fig. 24-9D). This could be done with the mandrel between centers or it could be a turned block on the screw center. The center of the holder is drilled through for a fixing screw, countersunk inside (Fig. 24-9E). Obviously, the candleholders should be turned to match each other.

The supporting piece can be bandsawn from flat wood (Fig. 24-9F) and the edges thoroughly sanded. Assembly is with glue and screws.

LAMP STANDS

Electric table or floor lamp stands obviously have an ancestry in candlesticks. It is possible to adapt candlestick designs to suit electric light fittings. It is even possible to get electric lights that look like candles. The basic method of construction has been described earlier in the book, but there are many possible designs, and one of the joys of wood turning is in producing your own designs.

For a table lamp stand turned from one piece

of wood, the shapes of classical and other vases can provide a starting point for design (Fig. 24-10A). Remember that the stand will have a lamp above it and there may be quite a large shade. This means that the base should be broad and may have to be weighted with lead to give adequate stability (Fig. 24-10B). Allow for drilling through in two directions. Make a large hole in the base so the wire can be manipulated between the two holes (Fig. 24-10C).

Breadth of base is easier to obtain if the column dowels into a separate piece of wood (Fig.

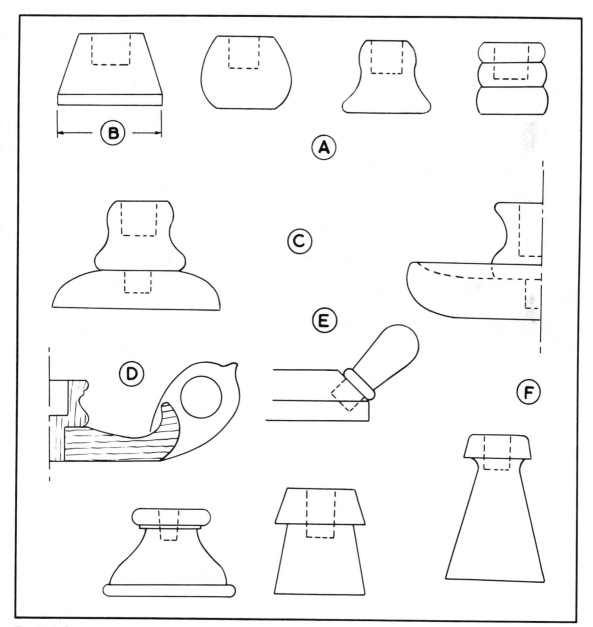

Fig. 24-8. Some examples of small candlesticks.

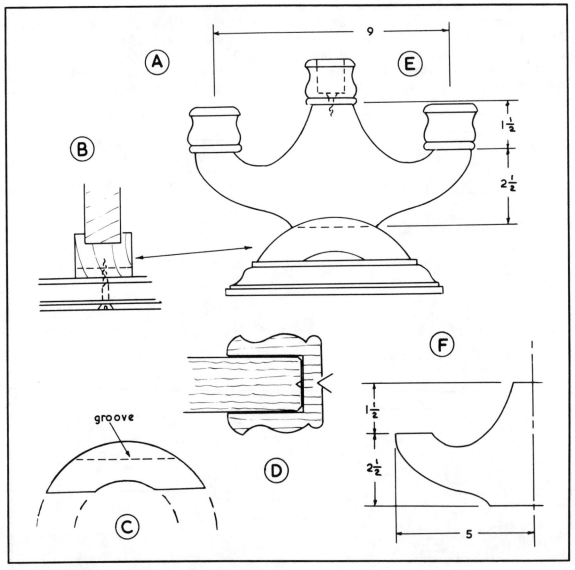

Fig. 24-9. A multiple candlestick on a round base is shown.

24-10D). Although having the greater diameter of the column high conforms to modern ideas of good design, it may be advisable to keep the bulk low if maximum stability is a main consideration. Keep the dowel shorter than the thickness of the base wood so the wire can be worked through (Fig. 24-10E).

A floor lamp can be a similar construction; its greater length would be the only complication.

Breadth of base is important. If the table lamp design is followed, the disc forming the base is reasonably large and thick, without much turned away, so it retains its weight. The use of three feet is advisable (Fig. 24-11A). Floors are not always as level as table tops and any unevenness is exaggerated in movement of the lamp.

With this sort of base, the column can follow traditional form with fairly elaborate turning. The total length will be in three or more parts doweled together. Besides making a long length possible on a short lathe and permitting drilling with limited equipment, this also allows different sizes of wood to be used. Appearance is improved by a large diameter near the base (Fig. 24-11B). This can be

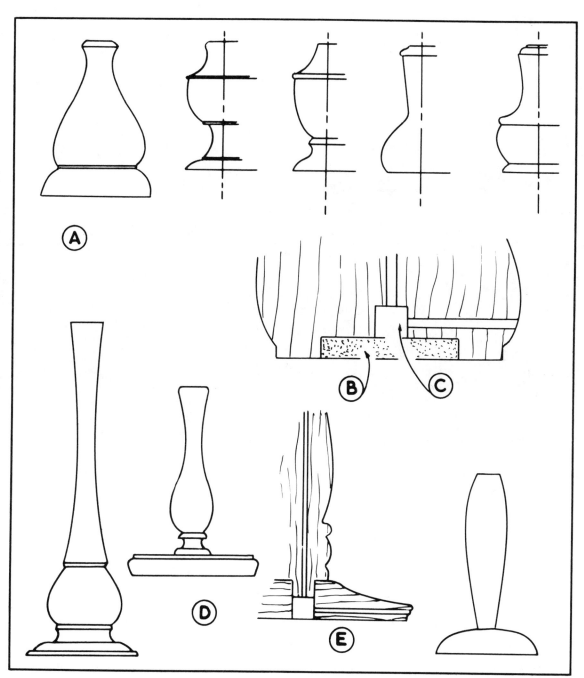

Fig. 24-10. Some outlines of lamp standards based on traditional candlestick lines.

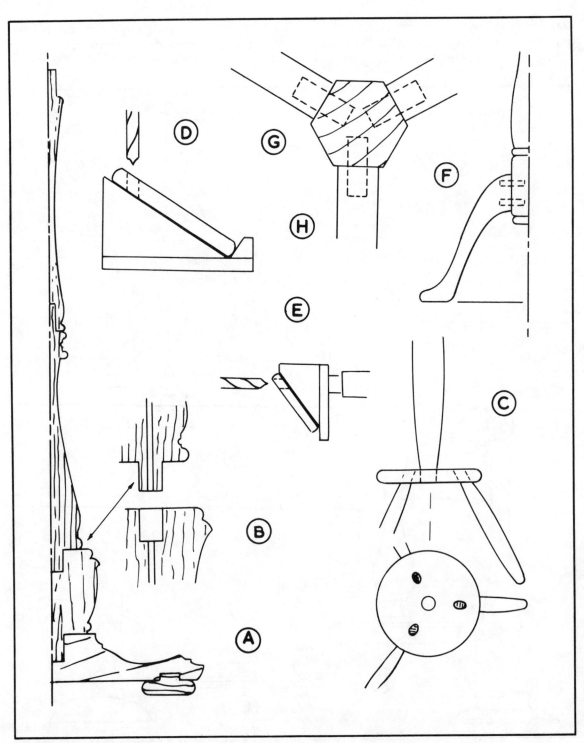

Fig. 24-11. Floor lamp standard details, with methods of getting height without having the main shaft too long, are given.

a separate thick piece of wood, so other parts do not have to be turned to waste as a higher section of it.

Getting a long slender spindle assembled straight is not very difficult, but the problem is reduced if the spindle part is kept short. If legs are used, it is possible to support the lamp at the same height but with a shorter spindle. One way of doing this is to turn a stout disc to fit on the bottom of the column and arrange this to take three legs. The effect is like a milking stool (Fig. 24-11C). The main problem is in getting the holes for the legs in the right places and at the same angles. Positioning is by stepping off the radius around the pitch circle. To get the angles right requires a jig. If a drill press is available, the disc can be mounted on a wedge-shaped piece of wood (Fig. 24-11D). If a drill press is unavailable, something of the sort can be made to plug into the tailstock and this can be fed toward a drill in a headstock chuck (Fig. 24-11E).

With that sort of base, the column looks best with wide flowing curves and an absence of fine turned detail. For a more traditional spindle, the support may be in the form of three shaped legs joined directly to it (Fig. 24-11F). The legs can be bandsawn and the edges cleaned, but the major problem is in mounting the legs evenly on the column.

It helps to plane the wood for the bottom of the column hexagonal before turning and leave a sufficient length unturned (Fig. 24-11G) where the legs are to come. This gives a positive location and dowels can be used into alternate faces (Fig. 24-11H). Dowel positions can be staggered to miss each other and allow deeper holes.

If the legs have to be attached to a round part, it should be of sufficient thickness to take the dowels and be a parallel cylinder for the length the legs will cover. If the lathe has a dividing head, mark lines along the column where the legs will come. Alternatively find the circumference and push a pin through a piece of paper wrapped around. Straighten the paper and divide the distance between the pin holes into three. Return this to the wood and mark the leg positions from it. Another way is to measure the diameter with calipers then set dividers to half of this. Step the dividers around the cylinder. If necessary, make minor adjustments until the points step around exactly six times then put the legs at alternate steps.

TABLES AND STANDS

A combination of a top and a pedestal, made up of a column with legs, can form a small table, sometimes called a candle table from its original use in providing somewhere to put down a candlestick. Such a table is useful today as a side table, a stand for a vase of flowers, or for smokers' requirements.

The top need not be turned, but with the usual three feet it would not look right if square. To match the leg layout, it should be hexagonal. If the lathe available will permit a large enough diameter, a turner will find more satisfaction in a round top (Fig. 24-12A).

The top of the spindle should have a fairly broad form so the table top bed is level (Fig. 24-12B). There can be a boss turned to fit under the top (Fig. 24-12C), so a dowel turned on the spindle has a good depth to fit in. With some tops, it may be better to cross two braces under the top and let the dowel go into them (Fig. 24-12D). Keep these braces shorter than the top diameter and taper their ends so they do not normally show.

How the top is treated depends on its purpose. It can be flat with a molded edge (Fig. 24-12E). It could be turned with a lip to prevent things from falling off (Fig. 24-12F). Traditionally, many of these tables were turned with a slight recess made just deep enough to take a large disc of leather (Fig. 24-12G). Leather may not be feasible for most use, but it could be a piece of plastic with a simulated leather appearance.

An interesting development of a pedestal with joints in the column is to make a stand with round shelves at intervals (Fig. 24-13A). The dowel joint is then arranged long enough to take in a turned shelf (Fig. 24-13B). This is sufficient for a light shelf, but for a stronger structure, one piece can go through a larger hole and the other dowel into the end of that (Fig. 24-13C).

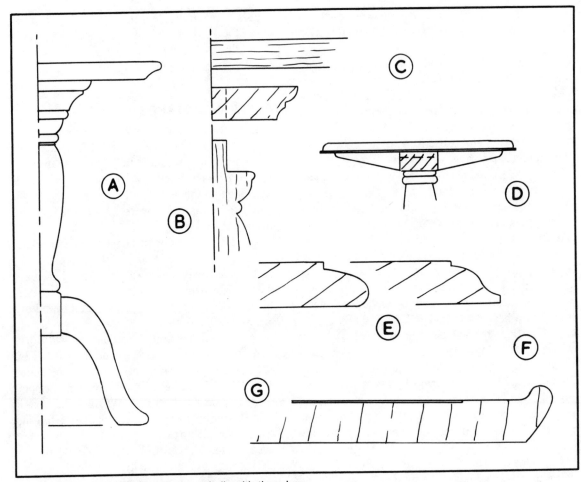

Fig. 24-12. A turned table based on a spindle with three legs.

Similar lower stands can be used for food or plants. A top, like a small table, is turned to mount on a low spindle with a base wide enough to stand firm. Although the outer part of the top may be turned to a light section, it helps to keep the center thick enough to fit firmly on a dowel on the spindle (Fig. 24-13D).

Such a stand can be tiered, with a small top and one or more intermediate shelves included in column joints as just described (Fig. 24-13E).

A further development is a lazy susan with the tray top able to rotate on the base. The first requirement is the fitting, which is screwed to the two parts so one will turn on the other. This settles the sizes of meeting parts, and the rest is up to your preference in design (Fig. 24-13F).

MULTIFITTINGS

Hanging lamp pendants may be made in several ways, but most turners will favor a construction that uses turned parts as much as possible. A three-armed pendant with equally-spaced arms projecting from a boss below a central spindle is the usual arrangement.

One of these fittings can be made almost completely on the lathe (Fig. 24-14A). The boss is the main part to which other parts are fixed. This can be turned on the faceplate and a hole made at the center. Locate other holes at three equal spacings for the arms and drill for wires (Fig. 24-14B).

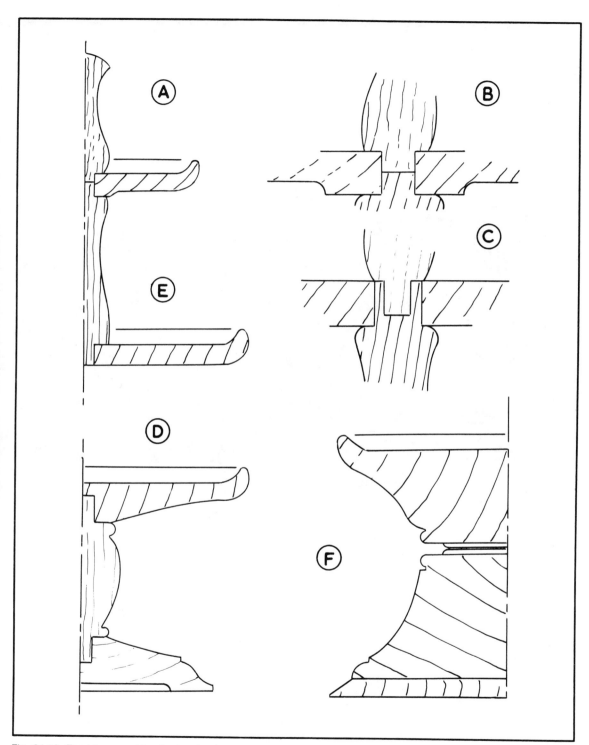

Fig. 24-13. Food trays and bowls showing how to build up.

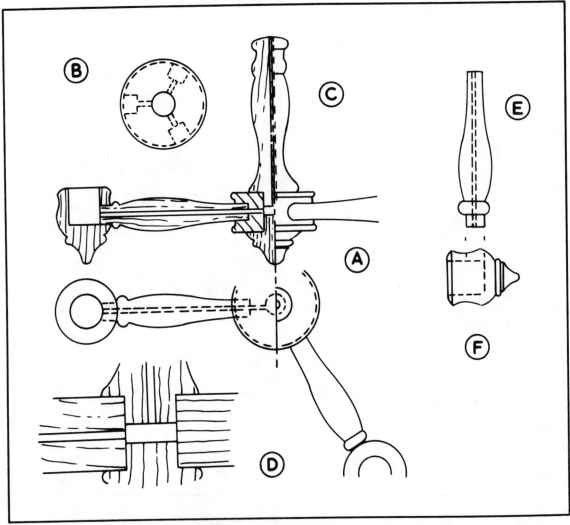

Fig. 24-14. A method of making a hanging, three-part lamp pendant.

The central spindle should be fairly deep in order to keep the assembly upright when hanging from the wire (Fig. 24-14C). It appears to go through the boss, but its dowel only goes part way and a button below also has a dowel (Fig. 24-14D). There should be a gap between the dowels in the central hole to permit wiring to be arranged before the bottom is fixed.

The arms carry on a similar turned theme to the central spindle. The inner end of each arm fits a hole in the boss and the outer end is doweled to fit the lamp carrier (Fig. 24-14E).

Each lamp carrier is drilled to suit the lamp fitting. This may determine the size of wood to be used. Turning can be done on the end of a mandrel. The underside can match the button below the center of the fitting (Fig. 24-14F).

Holes drilled in the sides of the boss and the lamp carriers may be done after turning if the circle can be supported in a V-block, either on a pad at the tailstock or under a drill press. The alternative is to prepare carrier blanks as squares, then drill at right angles to a surface for the side holes. For the carrier, the blank should be a hexagon, so

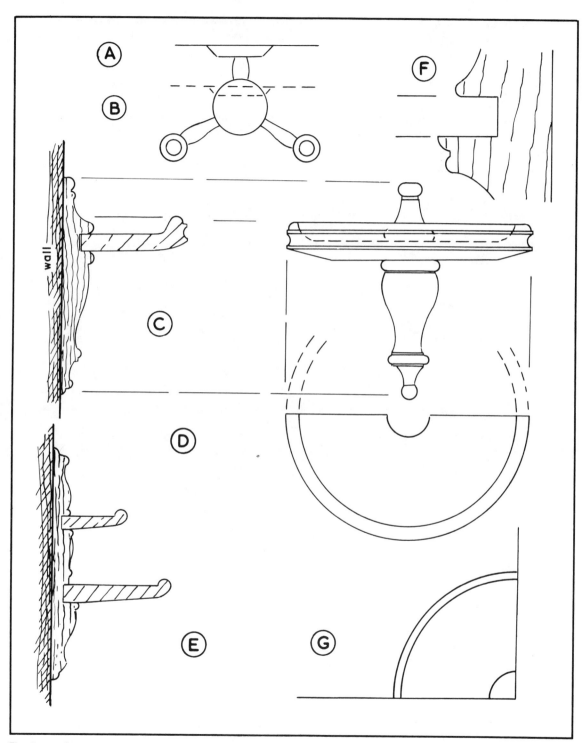

Fig. 24-15. Shelves and lamp fittings to go against a wall.

careful centering will bring the holes true.

A lamp fitting, as just described, can be converted to a wall bracket. This is possible by having two arms for lamps, while a third arm goes to a wooden plate on the wall (Fig. 24-15A). A further step is to do without the third arm and cut the boss to fit against the wall plate (Fig. 24-15B), which may be a turned disc or sawn to another shape.

Interesting wall brackets can be made by what amounts to cutting a pedestal in half. There is half a spindle with half a tray (Fig. 24-15C). The pedestal may go directly against the wall, or there may be a shaped piece of plywood or solid wood behind it to improve the appearance or protect the wall. The spindle can be turned from a solid piece of wood then sawn down to give two slightly less than semicircular pieces. It can also be made from two pieces with paper glued between them, so they can be levered apart after turning and the backs cleaned off. The tray cannot be made in this way, but if it is cut across the grain with a fine saw, it should match the spindle, whichever way it is produced (Fig. 24-15D). Of course, turning produces parts for two brackets, even if you only want one.

The idea can be taken further. There can be more than one tray on a deeper spindle (Fig. 24-15E). The tray can be larger if the spindle is made from thick enough wood to support it (Fig. 24-15F). The bracket can go into a corner with only a quarter of a circle employed (Fig. 24-15G).

Chapter 25

Bowls and Trays

Much spindle turning gives opportunities for artistic expression, but there is a limit to individual design. A lot of the detail work is bound to be common to many other designs. The arrangement of these parts and the way larger curves flow can be planned by the turner, but there is a limit to the way he can express himself. A bowl may seem an even simpler thing. There are certainly not as many details, but there is an infinite variety in the differences of curves inside and out. There is also the opportunity to make use of the grain detail of a particular piece of wood in a way that would not be possible in the longer and narrower spindle turning. This can be featured so it is the appearance of the wood, at least as much as the shape of the bowl, that provides appeal to a viewer.

The design of a bowl starts with the size of the available block of wood (Fig. 25-1). After the circle has been sawn, the general proportions can be seen, and there may be a case for a preliminary sketch of what is to be made (Fig. 25-2A). There are the practical problems connected with the method of mounting in the lathe. The pitch circle

of screws through a faceplate may limit the size of a base. If the lathe does not permit outboard turning, the possible maximum diameter is limited by clearance above the bed. With practical considerations taken care of, a few experiments with freehand curves will give an idea of a possible outline. The finished bowl may not be exactly that shape, but for a newcomer to bowl turning, the sketch is a starting point. Anyone with experience may start straight in with a gouge and work to a shape what is being visualized.

Some possible shapes are shown in Fig. 25-2B. Curves may be modified to suit larger diameters (Fig. 25-2C) or thicker blocks (Fig. 25-2D). What bowl thickness to work to depends on the wood. There must be clearance over the points of fixing screws, but a dense hardwood can be taken thinner than a lighter wood (Fig. 25-2E). If the blank is laminated or built up from blocks in any way, it is inadvisable to go as thin as with solid dense wood.

Actually, thinness is a relative thing. Some turners make bowls very thin, mainly as an expression of skill, but apart from risks of breakage in use,

Fig. 25-1. A tray, a deeper bowl, and a small bowl showing the effect of simple curved sections.

a thin shell may warp and twist due to taking up and giving off moisture from the air. It is better to have most of the bowl thick enough to give stability, but the edge may be thinned (Fig. 25-2F). This gives a delicate appearance as the thicker lower part is not obvious.

CURVES

It is possible to make a bowl to almost any curve and get an acceptable result. The tightness of the curve should vary. If it closes toward the top, the popular turned-in shape results (Fig. 25-3A). If the curve is less near the bottom, the bowl will have better capacity (Fig. 25-3B) for things like piled-up fruit. For a complete break from the more enclosing bowl, the section can go out almost conically, but it is unwise, from a design point of view, to have straight lines in the section. It looks better for everything to be curved—even if only very slightly (Fig. 25-3C).

Most wooden bowls in normal use are viewed from above, possibly at about 45 degrees, but unless the bowl is put on a high shelf, its profile is not usually the main feature. What is seen is the inside and a short distance down the outside from the lip. This should be kept in mind when turning these curves. Obviously, the shape should be pleasing all over, but if the rim area—inside and out—has poor shaping, the whole bowl fails.

The base of most broad bowls is rarely seen. Consequently, a simple small projection is all that is needed (Fig. 25-3D). This also suits mounting, because there is no need to turn the bowl over to work on the base. However, there may be designs where a recess below is needed; this can be turned first and the block mounted on a turned pad as described earlier. If a bowl is broad in relation to the size of its base, it may be advisable to turn a recess to take a lead block (Fig. 25-3E) to provide stability. This would also be advisable if the base is high or the bowl is more like a cup in its proportions.

294

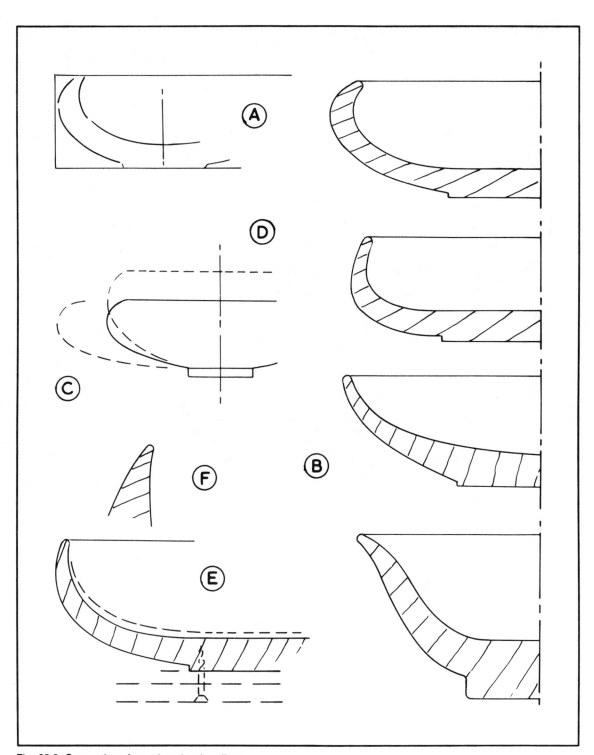

Fig. 25-2. Suggestions for various bowl outlines.

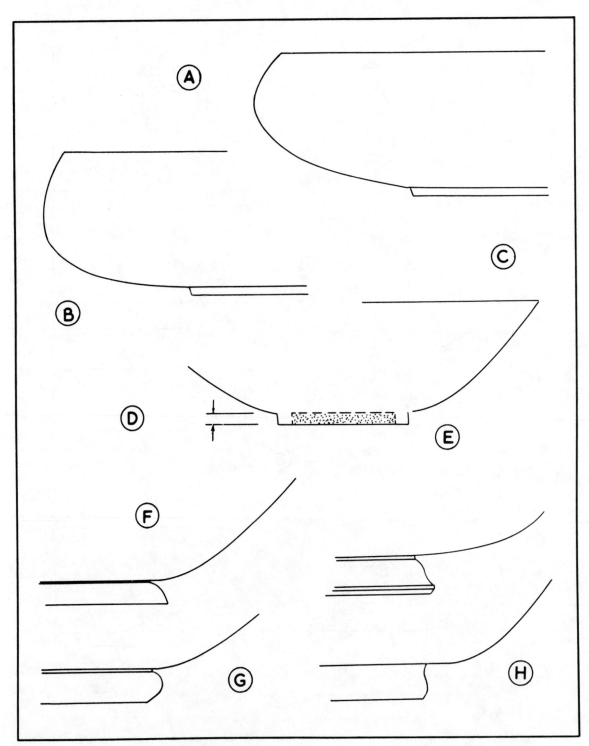

Fig. 25-3. Suggestions for relating the base to a bowl.

Almost any pattern can be turned on a base if it is to be a feature. In general, it looks better if its top is narrower than its bottom (Fig. 25-3F). That is also more stable than the less attractive narrower bottom (Fig. 25-3G). If there is not much depth in the base, a fairly plain outline (Fig. 25-3H) is better than one turned with many flourishes.

If a deeper base is used, its design becomes more like spindle turning (Fig. 25-4A). The bowl above can have a plain curve, but if there are beads and hollows in the base design, the bowl may complement this. There can be a double curvature to the bowl outline and a comparable molding outline to the base (Fig. 25-4B). If there are beads and other curves in the base, it may be considered better design to have a lip with a thickened edge (Fig. 25-4C).

SMALL BOWLS

Bowls do not have to be large. Pin bowls and trays for oddments need only be a few inches across. Whether the grain runs across the wood or parallel with the lathe bed depends on the available blocks. Both are possible, but if the diameter is much more than the depth, it is preferable to have the grain across.

These small bowls can be turned on a screw center. If the screw center has holes for other screws to be driven through for extra support, it is possible to turn discs up to about twice the diameter of the screw center.

Many outlines are possible (Fig. 25-5A). A difference between these small turnings and large bowls is in the relatively thicker section, at least for the bottom. Although there can be a base, usually of the size of the screw center disc, good patterns can be without bases (Fig. 25-5B). The outline need not conform to the hollow inside and might be turned in some other way than that used for large bowls (Fig. 25-5C). If the whole thing is kept bulky for its size and given a smooth hollow, it is easy to scoop small items out without the bowl moving (Fig. 25-5D). Some variations are possible. A central tapered spindle will take rings (Fig. 25-5E).

PEN TRAY

This tray (Figs. 25-6 and 25-7) is turned with a raised center to take a trumpet-type pen holder. It is the sort of project that could be made any size to suit oddments of wood, but it should have some weight and width to provide a steady base when the pen is removed or replaced. A second matching tray could be turned without the raised center as part of a pair to provide additional storage of pens and paper clips.

The way the pen holder has to be mounted affects details at the center of the bowl, so that should be obtained before starting work. Usually, a screw goes from below into the threaded base. In many cases, however, it is not very long, so the head needs to go into a counterbored hole in the base to allow just enough of its end to project above.

You can use your own ideas about the shape of the tray. It can have a flared bowl shape outside, but the flat bottom should be kept fairly wide for stability. There could be a rounded or turned-in edge, but the inside is best with a smooth deep curve, so items inside can be scooped out easily with a finger. Turn the central knob lower than the rim with enough flat area to take the metal part. Even if a screw center is used, and that locates the hole position on the other side, mark the hole center on the front with the tailstock center before removing the wood from the lathe.

Drill the hole so that it will be a fairly tight fit on the screw, so the metal fitting cannot be moved about later. Counterbore underneath to take the screw head; allow space for a small washer under it to prevent the head pulling in. After varnishing or polishing, make sure the pen holder has been mounted tightly before covering the base of the tray with a cloth disc.

BOWL STAND

Small bowls can be made in sets that fit into holes in a disc that is given a central handle (Fig. 25-8A). On a desk, a small version would hold pins and clips. On a dining table, it could hold nuts and small fruit. The disc would need thickness near the center for the dowel from the handle (Fig. 25-8B),

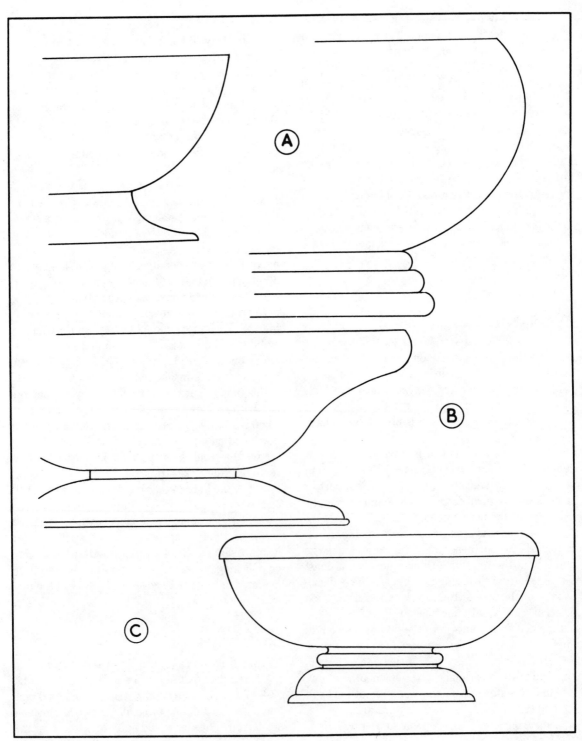

Fig. 25-4. Some bowl shapes with more elaborate bases.

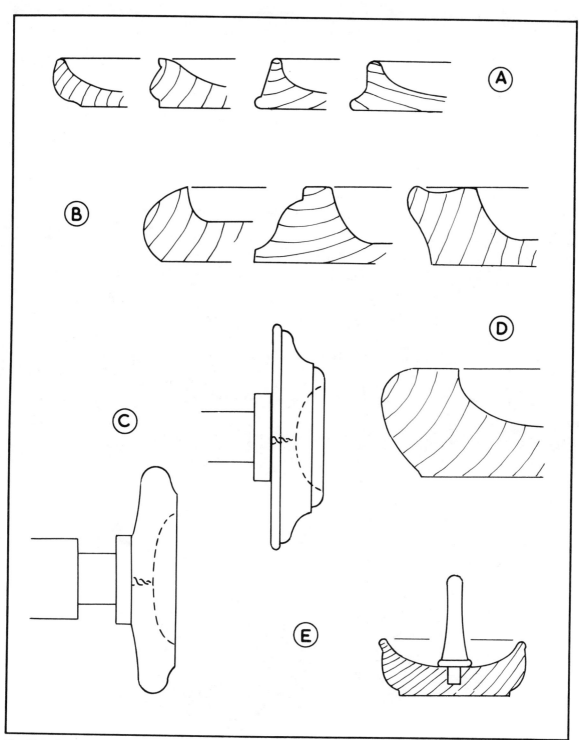

Fig. 25-5. Sections and shapes for small bowls.

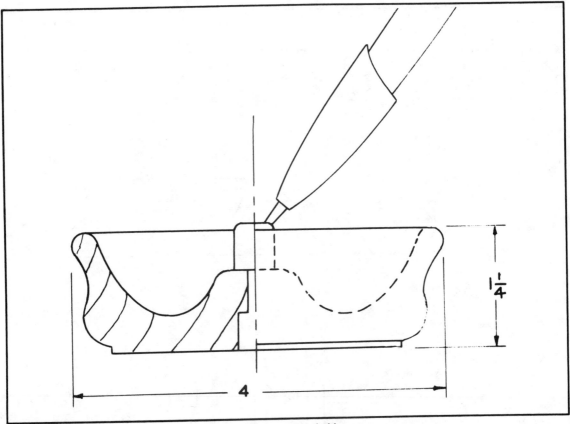

Fig. 25-6. Suggested shape for a small tray to mount a pen in a holder.

Fig. 25-7. Two bases and a completed pen tray.

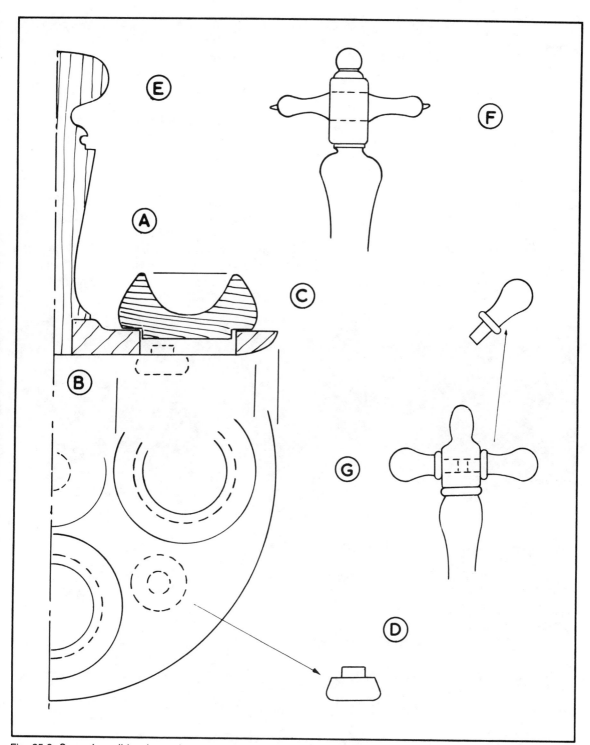

Fig. 25-8. Several small bowls can be mounted around a central handle.

but it should be thinned toward the rim so it looks lighter (Fig. 25-8C). Plywood could be used for the disc, but it might need thickening at the center and feet put between the bowls to give clearance on the table (Fig. 25-8D). The top of the handle can have a knob (Figs. 25-8E and 25-9) for lifting, although a more secure grip comes from a peg through a hole (Fig. 25-8F). If the peg is turned with the ends of smaller diameter than the center, it can pass through in one piece, but if there are to be larger parts outside, the peg can be made in two pieces with dowel ends (Fig. 25-8G).

AVAILABLE OPTIONS

Although it is possible to give a wooden bowl a finish that will withstand liquids and can be washed without affecting the wood or the contents,

it may be better to let the wood enclose a glass or plastic dish that can be removed. The wooden bowl is then more of an insulated container. Most suitable glass bowls have flat bottoms and vertical sides, so the wooden part has to be designed accordingly. Instead of the curves of the popular bowl, the inside must conform to the glass, which should usually stand above the wooden rim (Figs. 25-10A and 25-11). The bottom inside may be padded with cloth or plastic, and the glass should be an easy fit in the woodwork.

The outside may be curved (Fig. 25-10B) with or without a small base. If the wood has an attractive grain, a simple cylindrical shape outside (Fig. 25-10C) may be all that is needed to given an attractive appearance. Alternatively, there may be one or more beads or raised parts turned into the bowl (Fig. 25-10D).

Fig. 25-9. A small fruit bowl with a central handle for convenience in carrying.

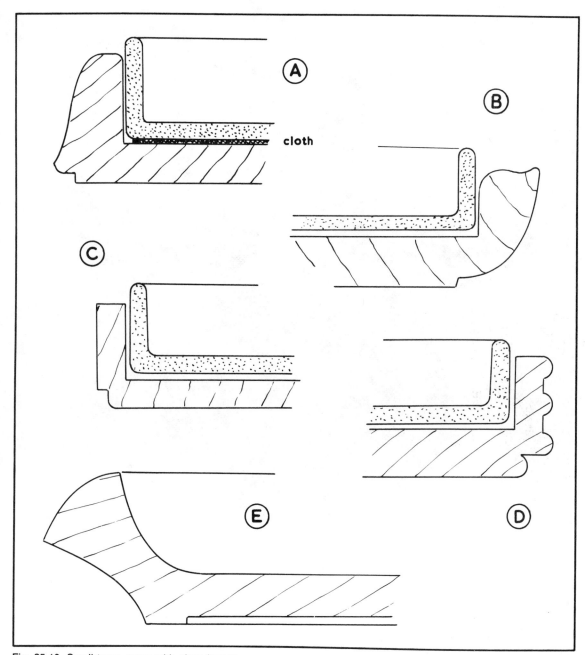

Fig. 25-10. Small trays, some with glass inserts.

Although the beauty of most bowls is in flowing curves, it is possible to get attractive shapes with angular outlines (Fig. 25-10E). Even then, the lines of the section should be curved rather than straight. This type of bowl benefits from a broad base. It is unwise to make the inside angular; a flowing curve is better even when the outside has several faces.

303

Fig. 25-11. Small turned trays with painted glass inserts.

PRESERVES STAND

This is a stand that holds three jars of preserves, jelly, or other foods, together with three spoons, all with a central spindle and a knob handle at the top (Figs. 25-12 and 25-13). The stand could be made to hold four jars, but three will probably take care of most needs. Sizes depend on the jars or pots that are to be held. The height of the spindle will depend on the sizes of spoons to be used. It is best to obtain the spoons and jars first and then design the stand to suit them. As shown,

the stand is about 12 inches high and 8 inches across and is made to suit jars about 2 3/4 inches in diameter and 4 1/2 inches high with spoons about 7 inches long.

Any close-grained hardwood can be used. There is no fine turning that might produce weak sections in open-grained wood, except for the disc to hold the spoons. If you want to use a weaker wood to match furniture or a table top, that disc might be made of a different close-grained wood in a contrasting color.

Fig. 25-12. A stand to hold three jars of preserves and three spoons, with a knob at the top for lifting.

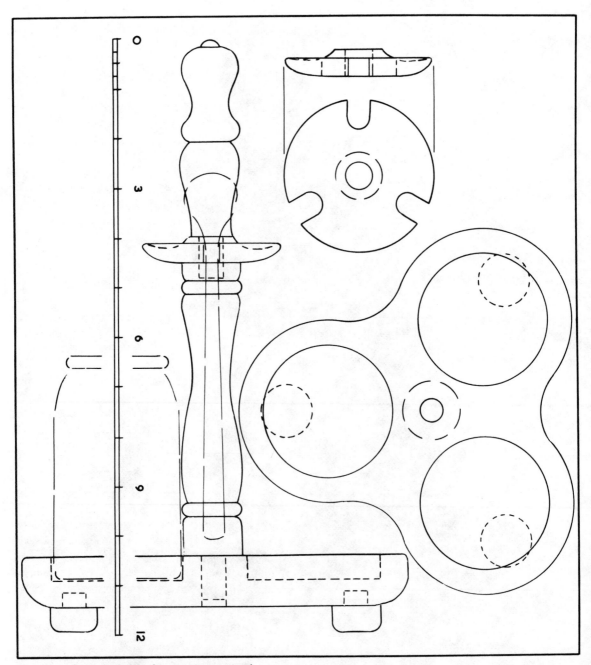

Fig. 25-13. Suggested sizes for a preserves stand.

The base is shown with a shaped outline. It could be round, but that makes a rather large disc if intended for three jars. If there are to be four, the round area has less blind spaces between the jars, so it does not look so bulky. The base could be made from one piece of wood and the hollows cut with an expanding bit or a hole saw, but it may be easier to make it out of two 1/2 inch thicknesses, then the holes can be cut without any disfiguring marks in their bottoms. However, the bottoms of the holes could be covered with cloth or plastic discs. It would be possible to turn the hollows, but that would mean mounting the wood three times on the faceplate; it would be rotating eccentrically with a risk of vibration and possible damage.

If the base is made in two parts, arrange the three sections at 120 degrees to each other and cut the holes in the top part before bandsawing or jigsawing the outline. When this shape is satisfactory, use it to mark on the lower piece. Glue the parts together and shape their combined outlines. Rounding the lower edge lightens appearance. Drill 1/2 inch holes for the feet and the central spindle. The feet can be turned to any shape you wish, but as they do not show much, a simple outline is sufficient.

The disc for holding the spoons could be turned on a screw center and drilled for the central dowel afterwards. Another way would be to saw the wood circular and drill the dowel hole, so it can be slid onto a slightly tapered mandrel to be mounted between centers. An advantage of this latter method is that the outline must finish concentrically with the hole, where a slight error in drilling in the first method could cause the disc to assemble askew on the other parts. The underside of the disc should be flat where it fits against the main spindle (1 1/4 inches in diameter). The upper surface should be turned hollow with a curve that will blend into the handle part that fits against it (1 inch in diameter). The hollow helps to keep the spoons from falling out of their slots.

Mark the centerlines of the spoon slots at 120 degrees to each other. What size you make the slots depends on the necks of the spoons. As shown, the slots are 5/16 inch wide and cut into the bottoms of the hollow. Drill the bottoms of the slots and saw into them. Carefully clean the slot edges and round the entry corners.

The main spindle is basically 1 1/4 inches in diameter. It is shown with a narrow neck and two beads, but this is a part where you can use your own ideas, although most of the spindle will be hidden by the spoons and jars. Turn a dowel at the bottom to almost go through the hole in the base and drill a hole at the top for the peg from the upper part.

The top is shown with a knob 1 1/4 inches in diameter, but you could turn a larger one if you wish. Make a dowel to go through the spoon disc and into the hole in the main spindle. Turn the lower edge with a curve to blend into the hollow of the disc.

When you glue the parts together, make sure the spoon slots come midway between the hollows to take the jars. A waterproof finish is advisable, because spilled preserves may have to be washed off.

The beauty of turned work is usually in its circular form. It is possible to give an undulating line to the rim of some bowls. Whether this is good design or not is a matter of personal opinion. The section should be fairly uniform for the depth below the turned rim that is to be shaped (Fig. 25-14A). The rim can be divided into any number of divisions, but four gives a satisfactory effect. Draw a circle of the size of the rim on paper and put two diameters across it (Fig. 25-14B). Invert the bowl on the circle and mark where each diameter meets. Draw curves on the rim at opposite marks to about halfway to the next marks. Cut these hollows (Fig. 25-14C). Blend the curves into the high spots that come between the hollows. The hollows can be cut with a coping or fretsaw, thus being less likely to damage the bowl than a power saw. Finish the edges with a spokeshave or a Surform tool, followed by a drum sander or hand work with abrasive paper. Avoid excessive shaping—hollows 1/2 inch deep on a 10-inch bowl are enough. Get a uniform rounded section to the shaped rim (Fig. 25-14D).

FROM BOWL TO TRAY

A broad shallow bowl may be regarded as a tray. The dividing line is vague. A tray can be turned from thinner material so that an offcut from some other piece of work may be used. Usually it is best to have a broad base (Fig. 25-15A). This can often be mounted direct on a faceplate without a pad if the surface has already been planed flat. However, for the sake of standing steady, there could be a recess turned with the wood reversed (Fig. 25-15B), then the wood put the right way and carefully centered on the faceplate for the rim and hollow to be turned.

If the piece is to be a tray, the central area should be flat (Fig. 25-15C). This can be done by careful finishing with a straight-edged scraper. Use a straight piece of wood that fits across the inside for checking. If the wood is tray-shaped, but intended for something like serving nuts or sorting pebbles, it will be better turned with a slight hollow

(Fig. 25-15D). This is more easily shaped with certainty than a flat bottom. The gouge can be given a swing from the center outward, and the finish can be with a scraper of moderate curve used in the same way.

What is done to the rim depends on preference and the purpose. It should stand high enough to hold the intended contents. Usually it will sweep up from the inside (Fig. 25-15E). The outside may be plain curve or with detail turning (Fig. 25-15F). If the tray is large in relation to the finished

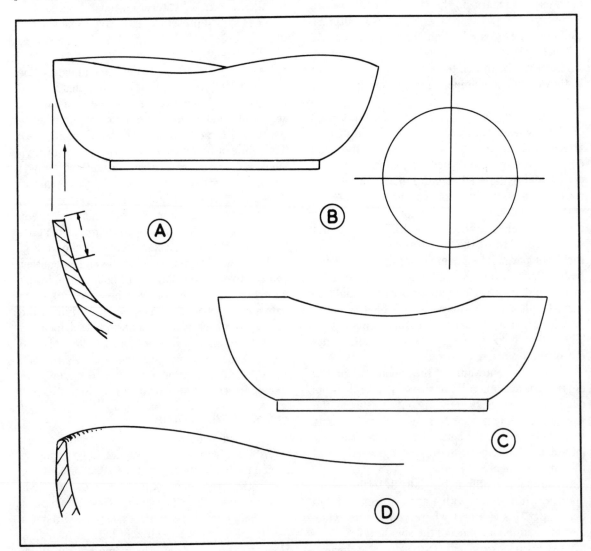

Fig. 25-14. A bowl with its edge given an undulating shape after turning.

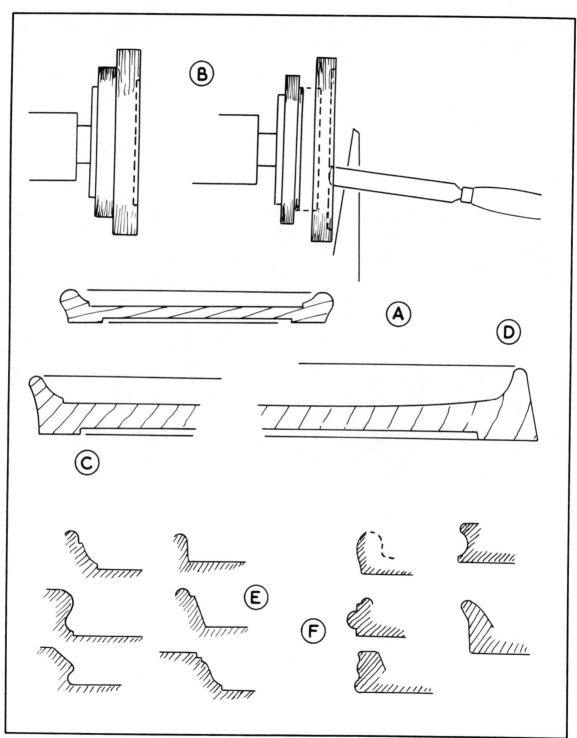

Fig. 25-15. Patterns for large plates or trays.

thickness, there is always a risk of it warping later. If the wood has been properly seasoned, the risk may be slight, but keeping the rim fairly thick does help to reduce the risk of warping.

We may not eat off wooden platters as they did in the Middle Ages, but there are uses for wooden plates, such as for taking the collection in church. A plate differs from a tray in having a broader rim. The general shape can be plain (Fig. 25-16A). This follows modern trends, but a traditional or a reproduction plate will give elaborate turning, both above and below the rim (Fig. 25-16B). How the inside is treated depends on the use, but for coins and similar objects, it helps to turn a shallow re-

cess for a piece of leather or plastic (Fig. 25-16C).

A similar form can be used to provide something better than the usual coaster as a stand for a glass or cup (Fig. 25-16D). The shape is like a plate, but with a hollow that is a very easy fit on the base of the glass. It is not intended that the stand should grip the glass. The inside can be covered with soft plastic. Thin cork or a piece of plastic floor covering can also be used. The outside may be turned with a molded outline toward the bottom, but leave a space to get fingers under for lifting (Fig. 25-16E). There is scope for a great many outside patterns to be made. Even in a set, there can be variations. So long as the overall

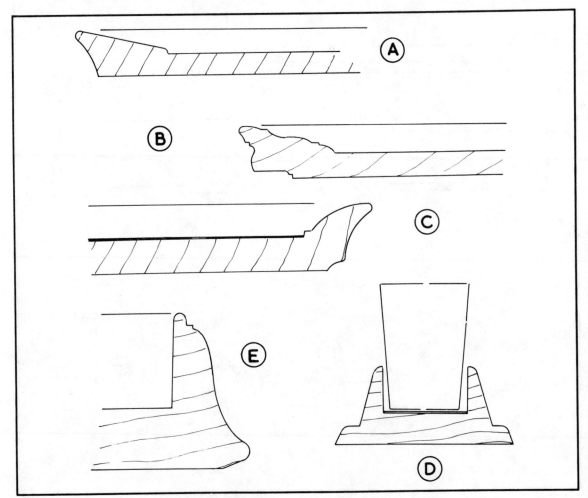

Fig. 25-16. Plates can be turned with broad rims used for making glass stands.

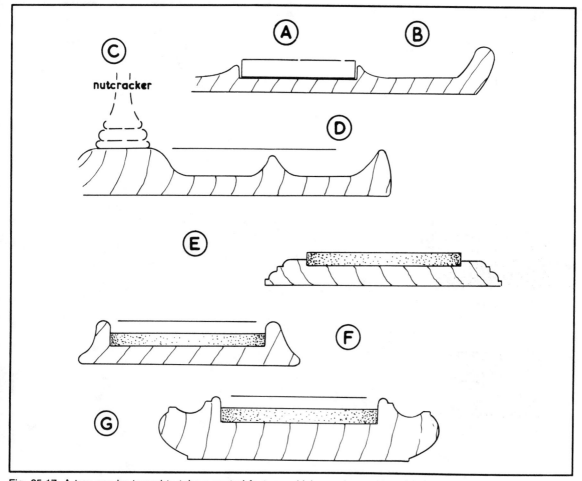

Fig. 25-17. A tray can be turned to take a central feature, which may be a nutcracker or a piece of tile.

dimensions are the same, individual treatments will not detract from the matching appearance of many stands.

Similar stands can be made for use in the shop. They do not need decoration to do their job, but a nicely-made article always inspires better workmanship and gratifies the maker. These stands can be made to support cans of glue, varnish, or anything else liable to be knocked over. They benefit from being tight fit so their broad bases provide steadiness. Small trays and bowls are also useful for nails and tacks. A curved inside makes it easier to scoop out the contents than trying to pick nails, screws, or other objects from rectangular boxes.

Not every bowl or tray is a simple container with a smooth interior. There may be a tile in the bottom. There are also other things that can be inset. A circular box of cheese sections may be accommodated in a recess with a lip around it, and the outer part available for crackers (Fig. 25-17A). A circular tile in a raised center of a tray will become a cheese platter. The same idea can be used with a taller container. The rim then serves to catch crumbs or as somewhere to put a spoon (Fig. 25-17B).

There are some nutcracker fittings to mount on a base. One of these could be located on a raised center in a bowl (Fig. 25-17C). A further refinement is to turn the inside of a broad bowl with a division,

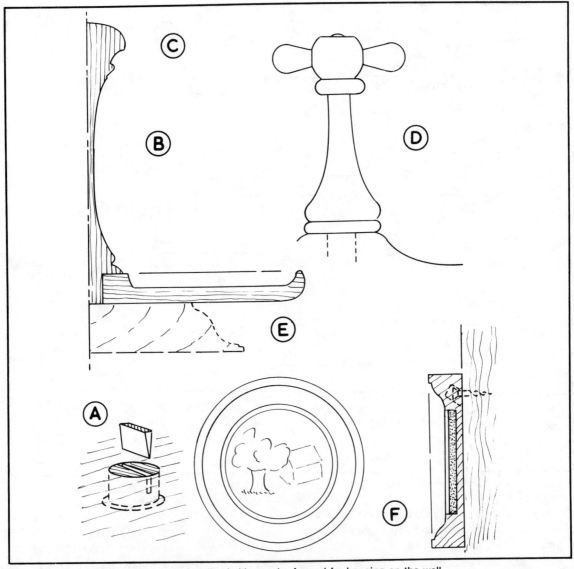

Fig. 25-18. A tray can have a central handle. A title can be framed for hanging on the wall.

so uncracked nuts are in the outer part and broken shells fall into the inner part (Fig. 25-17D).

A stand for a coffee or tea pot is a development of the bowl. The central part should be something heat resistant. It could be a plain piece of cork or plastic, but a round tile with a decorated center looks neat. The tile could stand above the wood (Fig. 25-17E), but with its shiny surface, it is better to provide a rim around it to prevent the pot from sliding (Fig. 25-17F). There can be a narrow molded outer edge or the wood may be turned with a hollow rim (Fig. 25-17G).

A bowl or tray that is to be used for serving food can be given a central handle. There are metal handles available that merely bolt through a central hole. Such a plated handle may serve to accentuate the beauty of the wood. Because it is slim, it does not take up room on the tray.

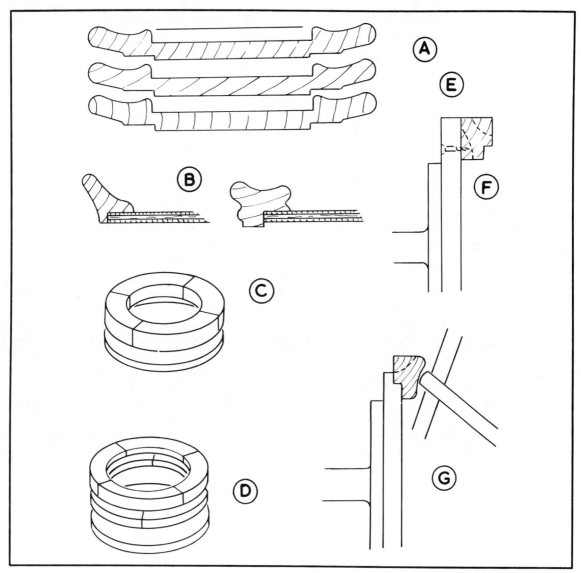

Fig. 25-19. Plates can be turned to stack. Larger plates and trays can be made with laminated rims and plywood bases.

A turner may prefer to make a wooden central handle (Fig. 25-9). This can be doweled through the base. For the strongest joint it should have a saw cut arranged across the grain of the bowl, so a thin glued wedge can be driven in and cut off flush (Fig. 25-18A). Let there be a fairly broad shoulder above the dowel, but in most designs, it is advisable to keep the main part of the handle stem quite slim (Fig. 25-18B). It can broaden into a knob (Fig.

25-18C) or there can be a turned peg (Fig. 25-18D). Make the handle high enough to keep the hand well above any food piled on the tray or bowl.

To give a balanced appearance to the assembly with its handle, there may be a rather deeper base than usual. This could be turned with the bowl or tray, or it could be turned separately and glued on (Fig. 25-18E). Obviously, making it too high and narrow should be avoided so that there is no risk of the contents being tipped over.

Plaques have a family connection with trays. A circular tile with an attractive design may be framed to hang on a a wall. Because the finished item will hang and not have to stand on a table, the outline can be more like the section of a picture frame (Fig. 25-18F). A metal piece can be used to hang the plaque or a plate with a keyhole slot although a suitable method of hanging is to drill a hole large enough to clear a screw head sufficiently on (Fig. 25-19A) will permit stacking. Besides keeping the diameters right, it is necessary to arrange that no part of the bottom curves below the base upper edge and no part of the top will interfere with the next plate nesting closely.It may even be possible to include design features that will mate, one with the other.

The examples given in this chapter have been shown as if being turned from solid wood. Most of the work can be done with laminated blocks or with bowl patterns built up from blocks of different color woods as described earlier. Some of the designs with inset tiles or those that serve as stands for other things look particularly good with patterns of contrasting woods.

Another way of building up is with a base of plywood rimmed with solid wood. What is possible depends on the lathe. Trays up to maybe 10 inches in diameter are just as well made from solid wood. Smaller trays could have plywood centers, but the advantage in larger trays is in the resistance to warping. It also becomes possible to use plywood with special surfaces. The lathe's limitations determine the maximum size that can be turned.

The rim must have a section something like a picture frame (Fig. 25-19B). The form is simple and capable of many variations, but the work has to be done in stages. The rim has to be built up in several pieces. These can merely meet (Fig. 25-19C), but it is stronger to overlap laminations (Fig. 25-19D). The outline is turned with the rim temporarily mounted on a piece of still plywood, which acts as a pad. This is not the final base. The rim may be glued onto paper, or screws might be driven into wood that will be turned away later (Fig. 25-19E). The inner surface is also turned and the rabbet made (Fig. 25-19F).

Remove the rim from the pad and turn the pad down to fit in the rabbet, where it can be held with glued paper or screws (Fig. 25-19G). This allows completion of the turning of the rim. The plywood base may be carefully sawn to fit or it might be mounted on the pad and its edge turned with more precision. Cover the bottom with cloth, even if three feet are to be spaced equally around the rim of a large tray to give firm standing.

Chapter 26

Boxes and Lids

Turned wooden boxes can have an attractive appearance, whether the wood is plain and the appearance is enhanced by turned details, or the beauty comes from the grain markings and the wood is turned to a simple pattern. Such a box may be complete in itself and made without a lid, but a lid will usually add to the utility of the box and improve its appearance. Lids may also be made for other things—a wooden lid can be fitted to a round metal or glass article. It is also possible to make a turned wooden box to enclose a glass tray or jar, which may then have a lid fitted.

The possible variations are endless. Besides producing attractive items, making boxes and lids provides the turner with an interesting exercise. The need for parts to match and fit gives something more to think about than just turning an artistic pattern.

Most boxes are turned with flat bottoms to their interiors (Fig. 26-1A). This is done by opening out a hole made with a bit in a tailstock chuck, with the wood on a screw center if it is small enough or mounted on a faceplate if it is larger. Such a box

usually has a basically parallel cylindrical outside (Fig. 26-1B), but the outside does not have to conform to the inside. If the contents are to be small items that have to be scooped out with the fingers, it is better to give the bottom a curve (Fig. 26-1C). If it is a shallow box, it may become more like a bowl, both inside and outside (Fig. 26-1D).

If there is to be a lid, regard both parts together as a total design. The box will normally be viewed with the lid in place, so the two should match. Because the lid needs to be positioned by the way it fits, there can be a recess in the edge of the lid (Fig. 26-1E) or in the edge of the box (Fig. 26-1F). Much depends on the final appearance required. If the lid is to overhang the box, it is easier to recess the lid than the box.

The bottom of a box can be finished in several ways. If it is a cylindrical type, the method of treating the bottom should be chosen so it can be done at the same time as the box is parted off. This avoids the need to part off and then reverse the box to finish the bottom. If the section of the lip of the box is comparatively thin in section, as it usually

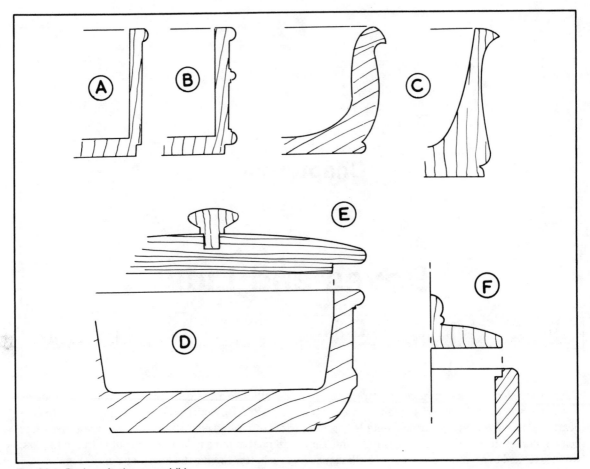

Fig. 26-1. Designs for boxes and lids.

is, there might be difficulty in chucking it without damage in the reversed direction.

Some possible bottom treatments are shown (Fig. 26-2A). So a box will stand level, the bottom should be turned slightly hollow (Fig. 26-2B). This can be done by tilting the parting tool or using a chisel point-downward after cutting in with the parting tool.

If the lid is to be shallow with a knob added (Fig. 26-2C), it will usually be turned with the grain across. If the design calls for a deeper lid with the knob integral with it, the grain may be better lengthwise. Usually the bottom of the lid is kept flat and this allows fixing to a pad with glued paper, so there is no need to reverse the wood and everything can be done in one operation (Fig.

26-2D). If the underside is to have any shaping, this should be done and the edge recessed first. It can then be pressed into a hollowed pad for the top to be turned (Fig. 26-2E).

Usually the knob will be the same wood as the rest of the lid and box, but appearance may be improved in some cases by using contrasting wood or staining the knob darker than the rest of the box. Another way of making a feature of the knob is to separate it from the lid with something of a contrasting color. This could be a metal washer (Fig. 26-2F). Plated metal gives an enhanced appearance to most woods. It could be a colored or clear plastic disc. Many plastics can be turned with wood scraping tools, so it may be possible to put a sawn disc in place, then glue the parts together and turn the

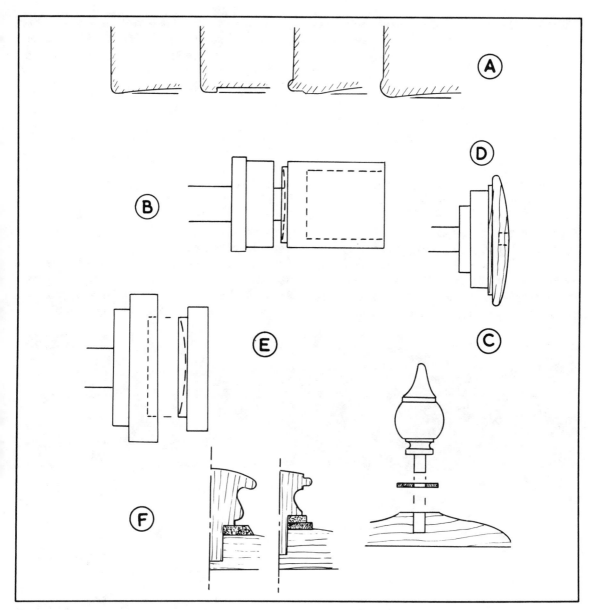

Fig. 26-2. Details of box and lid constructions.

plastic to a true circle with the wood. It is also possible to turn the knob completely in plastic. Polishing can be done in the lathe, with successively finer abrasives, followed by metal polish on a cloth. Another alternative is to use bought metal knobs. If the wooden boxes are to form part of a set to stand on another piece of furniture, it may be possible to buy matching drawer and box knobs.

MORE LID POSSIBILITIES

Lids can be made for other items besides turned wooden boxes. A wooden lid to fit a glass jar or even a plastic container may produce an interesting total design and put into use something that would

317

otherwise be disposed of. This is possible with glass jars that were bought with food in them and would normally be thrown away. The wooden lid may fit into a suitable jar or it may enclose a screwed metal or plastic lid (Fig. 26-3).

The first lid is made in the same way as for a wooden box, but the second lid has to be made to enclose the existing lid without looking too bulky when finished (Fig. 26-4A). The recess should be turned so the old lid is a tight push fit in the wood (Fig. 26-4B). If there is a rim to the metal lid, let that come outside of the wood. When the turning is finished, the metal or plastic lid can be pressed in with a little glue in the joint.

This sort of lid can be decorated on top. It may be possible to turn and let in a disc of wood of contrasting color. This should be slightly too thick when it is glued in, then a light skim made over the surface with a turning tool (Fig. 26-4C).

A variation on this is to turn a recess deep enough to take a piece of paper with a transparent piece of plastic pressed in above it. Details of the contents can then be written on the paper. If the plastic is only a press fit and there is a small notch at one side (Fig. 26-4D), it can be lifted out if the contents are to be changed.

This type of lid can also have a decorated center. If a patterned round tile of suitable size is available, that can be let into the wood (Fig. 26-4E). To reduce the risk of damage to the tile if the lid is dropped, the wood should either be level with the surface of the tile, or the design arranged so it stands above (Fig. 26-4F). Such a lid with a tile could be also used as a coaster.

A glass jar can be completely enclosed in a wooden box. This provides an attractive and hygienic food container. How this is arranged depends on the jar. If it is with a plain outline, ei-

Fig. 26-3. A turned lid for a glass jelly container and a metal screw top covered with a wooden rim and a tile insert.

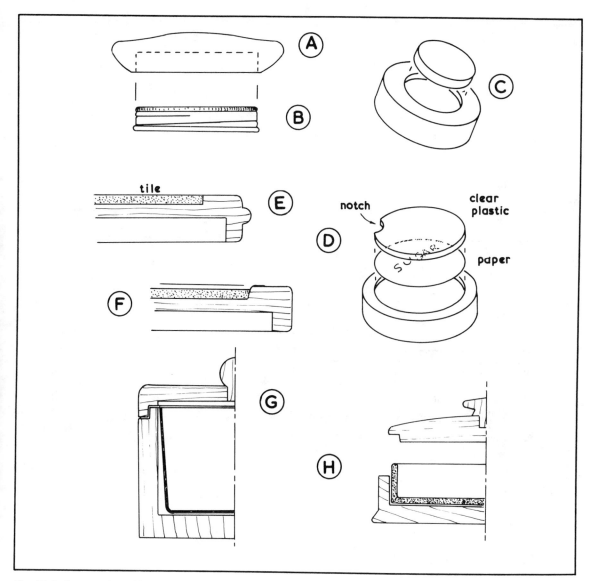

Fig. 26-4. Construction of a lid for a glass jar and boxes for glass containers.

ther parallel or tapered, it can merely stand in a full-depth box (Fig. 26-4G). If it has a shaped top, it may be better to have the wooden box only part of the height of the jar, so it encloses enough of it to be stable, then let the lid fit the jar (Fig. 26-4H).

Something like this can be done with broad shallow glass dishes or trays. The glass may be fully contained and covered by a lid that fits the wooden box (Fig. 26-5A). Alternatively, the glass may pro-

ject above the box (Fig. 26-5B) and have the lid fit into it (Fig. 26-5C) or over it (Fig. 26-5D). Whatever the construction, the lid should be an easy fit, and the glass should be tight enough not to move about, although it should be possible to remove it for cleaning. If possible, the wood should be finished with a treatment that is resistant to moisture, fruit juices, and other liquids that might otherwise mar the polish or stain. If this cannot be arranged,

319

there should be little risk of the contents coming sufficiently in contact with the wood to do damage anyway.

MULTIPLE BOX USES

Not every turned box is a single item. Several similar boxes or glass jars with lids can be further grouped in a tray (Fig. 26-6A). If the circular containers are to fit without moving about, there should either be three or six (Fig. 26-6B). With four, or another number, there could be movement to disturb a balanced appearance.

A box could also be raised on a pedestal. It might be made in the form of a goblet with a lid (Fig. 26-6C). Designs of presentation silver and similar cups will provide ideas for goblets in wood, but the amount of decoration will have to be reduced to suit the change in material, although general proportions could be the same.

A further step is to support a broad box on a pedestal made with a base and column (Fig. 26-6D). A broad shallow tray supported in this way can become a container for small items alongside a chair. A suitable inner part may be used as an ashtray or a place for small sewing items. A glass container on a pedestal could serve as a vase. Such a

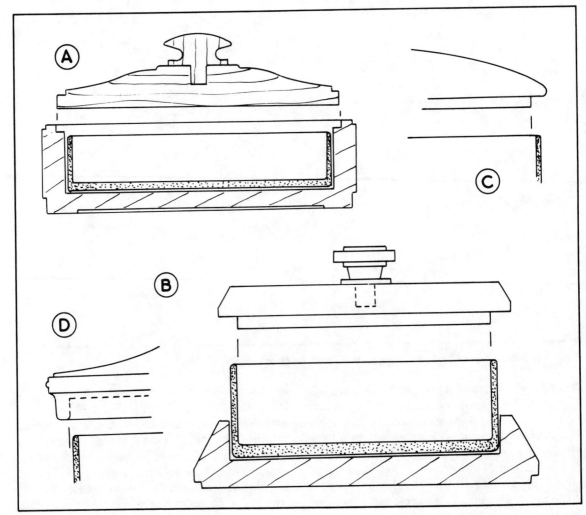

Fig. 26-5. Fitting lids to glass parts.

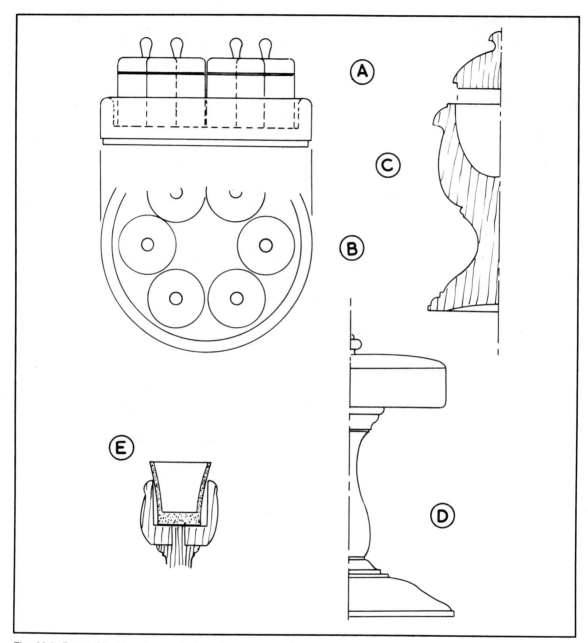

Fig. 26-6. Boxes fitted to a tray and others built up on pedestals.

pedestal stand helps in making a flower arrangement attractive (Fig. 26-6E).

VASES

A wooden vase is an unusual item, but several costs of a fully waterproof varnish make wood as suitable for holding water as glass or plastic. Shapes can be modeled on those used for glassware (Fig. 26-7A). Keep bases broad for stability, and shape the interior to suit the stems of flowers, usually with a conical shape (Fig. 26-7B). However, if any of the flower arrangement holders are to be used, the vase can be broader and allow for a more scattered arrangement (Fig. 26-7C).

Although it is possible to make a wood vase and treat it with a waterproof sealant or varnish inside, there is always the risk that this may fail and allow water to soak into the wood. It is better to use a glass insert. In this example, the vase is proportioned to take an insert of about 1 3/8 inches in diameter and 4 inches long (Figs. 26-8 and 26-9). The vase is in two parts. The two parts may be of the same type of wood, or the base could contrast with the other part. The proportions shown should suit most purposes, but if there may be a large floral display, a wider base could be turned. If you want to make the vase taller, the base diameter should be increased.

Turn the base on a screw center or faceplate. It might also be made by drilling a wood disc and

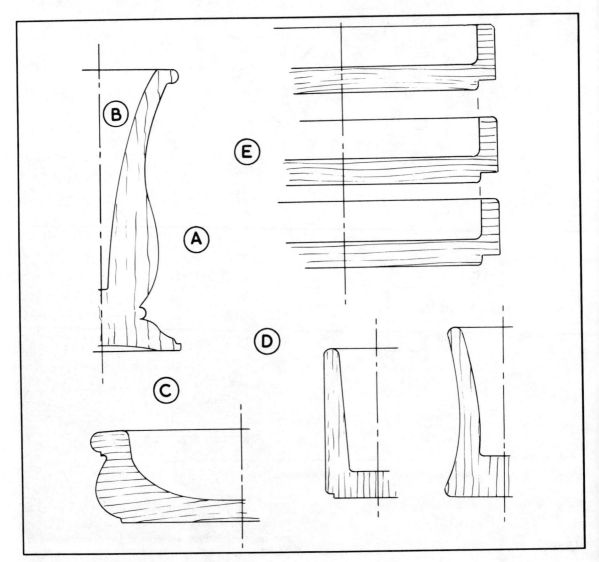

Fig. 26-7. Deep turning shapes and nesting trays.

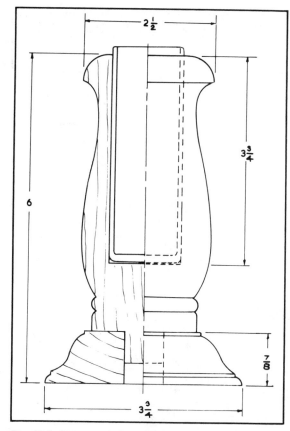

Fig. 26-8. Suggested size and shape for a vase to take a glass insert.

wards the tailstock. You may turn the dowel end by checking the size with calipers, or you can reverse the wood so that the spur center drives the plug while you turn and check the dowel at the other end, with the actual hole in the base as a gauge.

Glue the parts together and put a disc of cloth under the base.

There are other boxlike containers that can be made in the same way. A dice shaker is an example (Fig. 26-7D). This is turned with a flared interior and a broad enough base to let it stand steady, although still a reasonable size to hold in the hand. For games and other purposes where several identical round boxes are needed, it is convenient for storage if they are arranged to nest. This is done by making the bases a suitable size to fit into the tops (Fig. 26-7E).

At one time, the cuspidor or spittoon was en-

mounting it on a mandrel between lathe centers. This method allows a large base to be turned hollow underneath so that it should stand more firmly. Keep the surface that has to be in contact with the upper part flat. There are, however, other possible edge designs that could be turned instead of the one that is shown.

The hole for the glass insert is the important process in the upper part. Carefully center the wood and drill it for the insert. Use either a drill press or a drill chuck in the lathe tailstock. Make it an easy fit and allow for about a 1/4 inch of the glass to project above the finished vase so that it can be gripped and pulled out. Turn a plug with a slight taper to push into the end of the hole and project a short distance with its own center dot. Mount the wood between centers with the plugged end to-

Fig. 26-9. Vase with a glass insert. This is made from two pieces of wood with the grain of the base across.

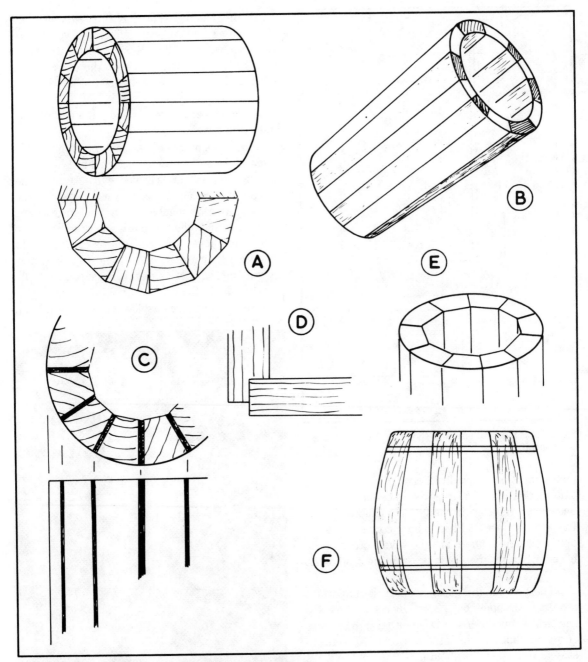

Fig. 26-10. Using lengthwise laminations to build up a cylinder.

cased in what was really an elaborately turned wooden box. This Victorian piece of barroom furniture may not be regarded as essential today, but one of these containers could be turned and used as a stand for a plant pot.

As with the making of bowls, most of the boxes described could be made from blanks built up with laminations or joined blocks of different wood. In fact, a deep box will be stronger if made with several laminations set across each other (Chapter 12) than if made from one piece of wood, even if all laminations are the same wood and the joints are not obvious. This also allows a large box to be made from many small pieces of wood. Lids can also be built up from contrasting woods if that is done with the box, or a lid made in layers of wood of different colors may look good on a glass jar.

It may not be as easy to get a smooth interior with woods that are contrasting in grain characteristics as well as in color. If it is important that the inside be smooth, woods chosen should be a similar hardness and quality as far as possible.

One way of building up a box shape is by lengthwise laminating. This is rather like a cooper making a barrel (Fig. 26-10A). Obviously, the angle of lengthwise joints should be cut as accurately as possible, but this method of construction has the advantage that the glue is able to grip on side grain,

which is much stronger than on end grain. Shapes need not be parallel (Fig. 26-10B). The parts (*barrel staves*) can taper, but the angles between the faces will remain the same. A further variation is the inclusion of parallel strips in the joints (Fig. 26-10C). These can be anything from veneer thickness upward, and preferably in colors to contrast with the other wood.

If a three-jaw, self-centering chuck is available, it is helpful to have the number of pieces a multiple of three, so the jaws can grip the end of the assembly before it is turned round. A recess can be turned in one end to take a bottom (Fig. 26-10D). The inside can be turned round or it can be left with a polygonal shape (Fig. 26-10E). The outside can be turned to any of the shapes suitable for boxes made of solid wood. Because the attraction of the finished box may focus on the different woods, it is better to keep the outside fairly plain (Fig. 26-10F). A bulbous barrel shape is appropriate.

Chapter 27

Kitchenware

In the not very distant past, many of the domestic items used in the preparation of food were wood, and most of these were the products of the local woodturner. In some cases, the articles were entirely turned, while others had parts made by hand tools on the bench. A Welsh collective name for such items was *treen*. There may be less need for some of these things today, but they still have uses or can be regarded as reproductions or articles of general interest. Although there may be alternatives for some of the jobs, it is a fact that professional cooks often still favor the older wooden tools. In any case, making some of this *treen*, or wooden kitchenware, provides interesting projects for a woodturner.

Wood to be used in contact with food should be close-grained, so there are no crevices that could harbor small particles. It should be free from resin and without smell. It should not be too absorbent as it will have to be washed and could take a long time drying if it soaks up water readily. It should be as light a color as possible because of ap-

pearances. A maple color looks more hygienic. Exceptions might be the head of a mallet or the end of a pestle, where a darker color gives an impression of greater weight.

The choice of wood depends on what is available locally. Welsh treen was mostly turned in beech, which has all of the required qualities, although some of it can be darker than may be desired. Sycamore is lighter in color, but otherwise similar in characteristics. Holly and box were two other British woods used for treen where fine detail and weight were needed in light-colored woods.

Softwoods are not generally suitable for kitchenware, except parana pine, which is from Brazil, and may have some uses. Other softwoods are mostly too easily damaged, and they suffer from water. Besides the hardwoods mentioned already, maple has possibilities and so does basswood. Because wood is a natural product, there are variations between specimens. One piece of wood may be suitable for use with food, where another piece of the same species includes flaws, resin pockets, or other unsuitable characteristics.

BOARDS

A cook needs a board to cut and chop on. Before sliced bread, the usual board to support a leaf being cut was turned. A similar board can still be used for cutting other things in the preparation of food.

A simple board (Fig. 27-1A) has a flat center and a molded rim. The rim serves no purpose except decoration, so it can be shaped as you like. A small board may be given a handle. This could be fitted into a hole drilled into a fully-round board, but it is better to plane off a short flat side (Fig. 27-1B) and plug a handle into that. This type of board would also be suitable for serving cheese.

Any boards for use with food should be finished without any added stain or varnish. The wood should be finished to as good a surface as possible and left at that. The boards will have to be washed

in use, and it is advisable to remove any stray fibers by wetting the wood before giving the final sanding.

Chopping Block

The expert in a kitchen prefers a chopping block with an end grain surface made in the butcher block manner. It could be square, but a turned outline is attractive and this allows a small amount of rounding of the edges, which makes handling easier. Obviously the wood must be a type that is safe with food, and it should be hard and close-grained to resist heavy chopping blows. Sizes can range from about 6 inches up to quite large boards for professional use. The specimen suggested (Fig. 27-2A) could be made of 1 1/2-inch square pieces to give a board about 10 inches in diameter with seven squares across.

A pattern of squares with a circle drawn on them (Fig. 27-2B) shows that the corner blocks are not needed. Although, you may prefer to include

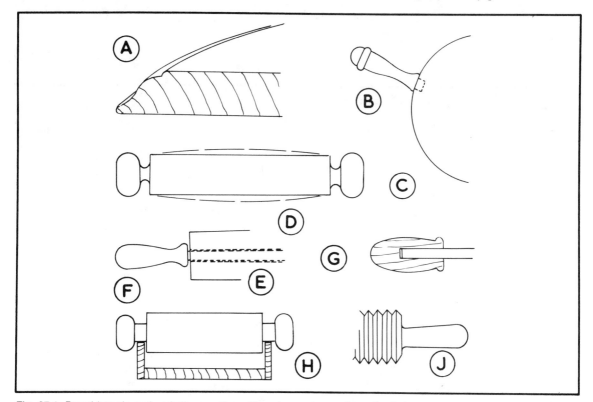

Fig. 27-1. Bread boards and variations on the rolling pin can be made on the lathe.

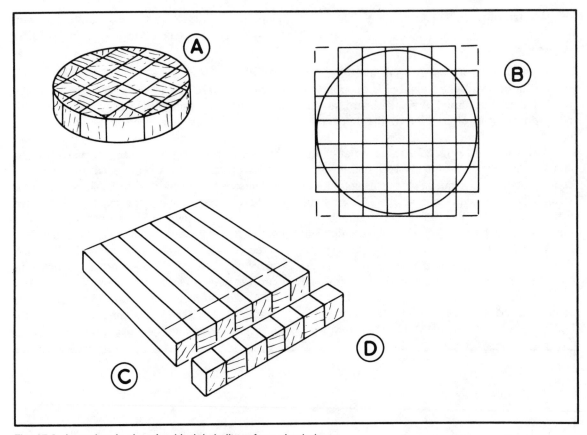

Fig. 27-2. An end-grain chopping block is built up from glued pieces.

them in the first assembly, particularly if you are using wood of other sections. This is an opportunity to use odd pieces of wood, not necessarily square, although they should all be the same width. For instance, you could adopt 1 1/2 inches as a standard width but might then include strips thinner or thicker to make up the size the other way.

If the block is to have seven squares across the diameter each way, prepare enough strips to cut the seven pieces. Whatever size squares you use, allow for the finished board to be at least 1 1/2 inches thick (Fig. 27-2C). You will notice (Fig. 27-2B) that with the size of the board and the squares suggested, you could use only five strips and allow for cutting off seven parts. Join the strips together. Use a waterproof glue. When the glue has set, level the surfaces, and then cut off enough sets of blocks (Fig. 27-2D). Glue these edge-to-edge to

make up a big enough area to let you draw the circle. Saw a disc ready for mounting on the lathe.

The cook will want to use both sides of the block. You could mount it with screws through a packing on the faceplate, and then plug the screw holes later. Or, another way would be to plane one end-grain surface flat, and then mount it by gluing it to a wood block on the faceplate with paper in the joint, so that it can be eased off after turning. That allows you to turn the rim and the other surface. Besides sanding on the lathe, the two working surfaces should be rubbed smooth on a piece of abrasive paper resting on a flat surface.

Before it is used, it is advisable to sufficiently soak the wood in vegetable cooking oil to impregnate the grain. This will reduce any tendency to split or warp and will be hygienic for working with food.

Cheese Cutting Board

The expert way to cut cheese is with a wire on a grooved cutting board. The board may be any size, but the suggested size is about 9 inches in diameter and 1 inch thick (Fig. 27-3A). The wood should be close-grained and safe for use with food. The cheese board could be built up from square pieces, as described for the chopping block, if you want to make matching kitchen equipment; otherwise, this is unnecessary and a board with its grain across is suitable. If you can find a quarter-sawn piece of wood (with the end grain lines about square to the broad surface), there will be less risk of warping, but any properly-seasoned piece of wood should keep its shape without giving trouble in use.

Saw the disc and turn it on a pad on the faceplate. The underside will not normally be seen, so you can screw on and plug the holes later. Round the circumference edges slightly. How the groove is cut depends on your equipment. Size is not critical, but 1/4 inch wide and 1/4 inch deep would be suitable. With a router you may be able to cut a groove with a rounded bottom.

The cutting wire should be spring steel and not thicker than 20 gauge. Ideally, this should be stainless steel, but more likely it will be plain steel, often sold as "piano" wire. Model shops may have it. A length of twice the diameter of the board will be more than enough (Fig. 27-3B).

You can make the handle however you wish, but a simple form is shown (Fig. 27-3C). It is 3/4 inch in diameter and 4 inches long to give a comfortable grip. Take the wire through a central hole and bend the wire over its end to drive it into the wood.

At the end of the groove across the board, drill a hole no bigger than necessary to clear the wire. Do this at a moderate angle in the direction of the pull (Fig. 27-3D), then groove along a short way underneath to where the wire can be trapped under a screw head (Fig. 27-3E).

The board may be left untreated, so it can be washed occasionally, or it could be wiped over with vegetable oil to provide a finish. Let the oil dry com-

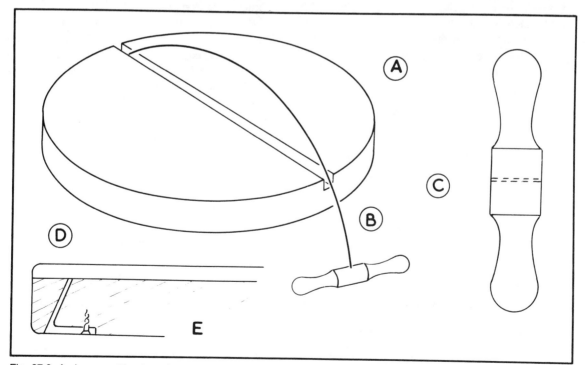

Fig. 27-3. A cheese cutting board uses a wire through a groove.

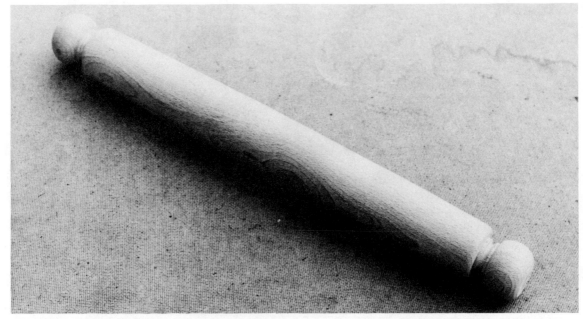

Fig. 27-4. A rolling pin is a simple spindle turning project.

pletely before cutting cheese, so the taste is not affected. To use the board, put a piece of cheese centrally on it with the wire out of the way, then lower the wire into the end of the groove and pull down. You can get a cleaner cut on most cheeses than you can get with a knife.

ROLLING PIN

Expert cooks prefer a wooden roller for working on pastry, and many prefer the roller be made in one piece with knobs at the ends (Figs. 27-1C and 27-4). The roller may be parallel for most of its length with a slight curving at the ends, or it may be made slightly bulbous (Fig. 27-1D). Both types have their uses in food preparation.

With the one-piece roller, the end knobs have to be allowed to turn in the hand. An alternative is to let the roller revolve on an axle with handles at the ends (Fig. 27-1E). The roller is turned and drilled through with a hole that will make a loose fit on the axle. If it is necessary to drill from both ends, leave some waste wood on each end to accommodate the driving center until after the hole has been made. The axle may be turned with one of the handles, with an extension to fit in the other handle (Fig. 27-1F). An alternative is to use prepared dowel rod for the axle, and drill both handles to take it (Fig. 27-1G).

Basically similar rollers were used for other domestic purposes. One with parts to run along guides at the edge of a wooden tray was used in butter making (Fig. 27-1H). An oatmeal roller is made in either of the ways just described, but its surface is ribbed (Fig. 27-1J).

BUTTER WORKERS

A handled disc was used to work butter, but it can also be used to press moisture out of vegetables. The main part is a stout disc with a rounded surface (Fig. 27-5A), with a handle doweled into it (Fig. 27-5B). A suggested size is given but a well-equipped kitchen might have two sizes available.

Similar in general shape are butter prints. These press a pattern onto a circle of butter or margarine. The turned part has the handle and print made from one piece of wood (Fig. 27-5C). The end is carved with the reverse of the pattern to be pressed on the butter (Fig. 27-5D). Many patterns are possible, from simple geometric shapes to animals and rural scenes (Fig. 27-5E).

The ordinary print is used on a block of butter that has already been brought to a cylindrical shape with butter *pats*, which is like a pair of flat bats. Another type of print can also round the butter. The print slides inside a hollow cylinder of the size the butter is to be (Fig. 27-5F). The handle has a parallel part sliding loosely through a hole of sufficient length to allow the completed pat of butter to be pushed out (Fig. 27-5G).

The end of a butter print could have a turned pattern instead of a carved one, or there may be a turned rim to frame the carving. It is possible to press patterns on other things besides butter, but it may be necessary to coat the surface with grease to prevent sticking. An impression might be made

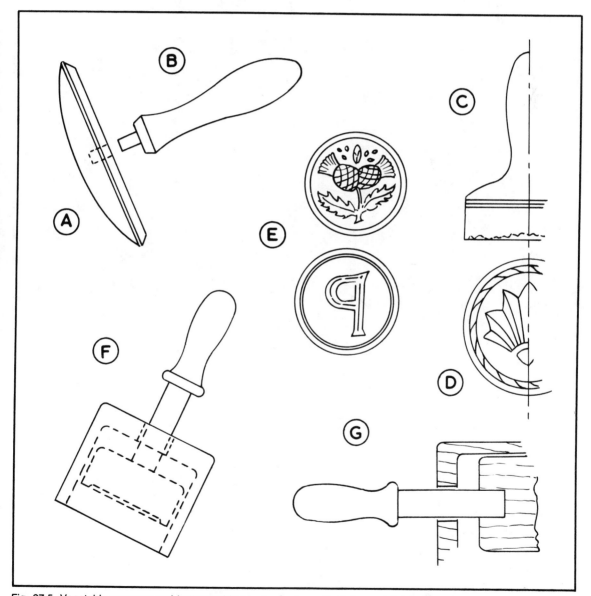

Fig. 27-5. Vegetable pressers and butter molds can be made on the lathe and finished by carving.

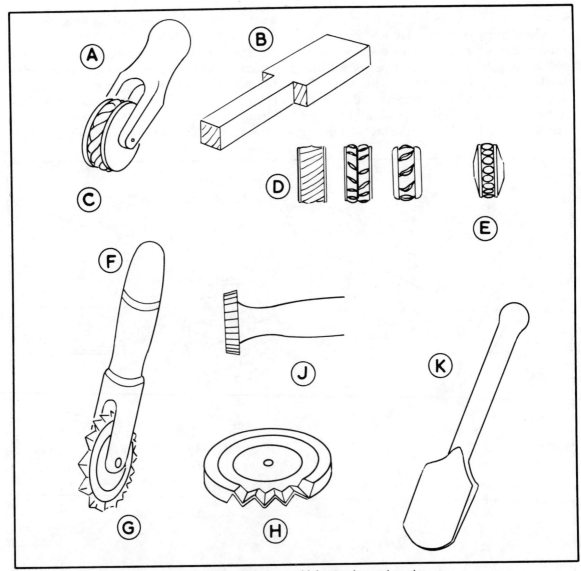

Fig. 27-6. Rollers for butter and pastry can be made by combining turning and carving.

on pastry or on cheese before it has hardened. Prints cut with royal coats of arms and other devices to show ownership were used on cheeses as recently as Victorian days.

Another type of print works as a roller. It can mark a strip of butter, which is then cut into pieces, or it can be used to mark around the edge of pastry. The roller is held by a forked handle (Fig. 27-6A). This is turned from a strip of rectangular section (Fig. 27-6B), with the work on the forked end done after the handle has been turned. The roller is a simple cylinder, around which a pattern is cut (Fig. 27-6C). Turned patterns are possible, but the most effective patterns are carved and vary between simple lines to carved foliage (Fig. 27-6D). Cutting of these and plain butter prints should be bold. Pastry does not take such a sharp and detailed pattern as butter.

The axle should be stainless steel wire or other noncorrosive metal that is stout enough not to bend under the pressure needed. Drill the roller for it in the lathe.

It is probably best to fit a roller permanently to a handle, but it is possible to use one handle for a selection of rollers in order to allow pattern changes if the axle can be pushed out. It will probably be sufficient to use a plain wire axle with enough projection to grip with pliers and pull out, or there could be a bolt and nut. If different width patterns are to be used with one handle, the gap in the handle should suit the widest and the other rollers should be made this width and tapered to the patterned rim (Fig. 27-6E).

A variation on the roller is a pastry marker or jigger (Fig. 27-6F). This has a narrow roller, and it can be accommodated in a cut in a turned handle (Fig. 27-6G). The disc is turned like a wheel with a thinner part between the hub and the rim. This allows cuts to be made in the edge so a wavy line is made as the roller goes around the edge of a pastry pie cover (Fig. 27-6H). A few different patterns can be arranged.

Another type of jigger has the pattern turned on the enlarged end of the handle (Fig. 27-6J), and there is no revolving part. The whole tool is rolled around the pastry edge. This could be combined with a roller jigger, so the fixed pattern is at one end and the roller at the other end.

Other simple kitchen tools are spatulas. These are like flat spoons and are used for stirring and mixing. Turn from rectangular section wood and pare the blade to shape after turning the handle (Fig. 27-6K). A long spatula (about 15 inches) is needed for large mixtures, while one half that length is better than a spoon for smaller quanities.

MALLETS AND MORTARS

Mallets are used in the preparation of meat. A fairly heavy head and a handle not as long as might be needed for woodwork are common. The head can be round with flat or slightly domed ends and the handle may be straight, although a swelling at the end will stop it from slipping through the hand. It is better taken through the head and wedged,

than only part way through (Fig. 27-7A). Some chefs prefer a mallet face with a pattern of small cones (Fig. 27-7B). This is made by drawing lines across the face to make squares. These are sawn down, and then V-cuts made into them both ways (Fig. 27-7C). Clean the sawn wood with a chisel and abrasive paper wrapped around a piece of wood with its edge planed to slightly less than the angle between the cones.

Another type of chef's mallet has a round head of greater length than the handle, which is turned in the same piece of wood (Fig. 27-7D), although it could be separate piece doweled in. The head has a slight conical taper that appears straight in outline, but it is better turned with a moderate convex curve.

A pestle and mortar was once an essential part of kitchen equipment. It still is needed by anyone preparing food from natural materials straight from the field. It serves two functions: pounding grain and similar things to powder and mixing assorted powders. Even if rarely used today, the pair make an interesting kitchen decoration as well as a challenging project for a woodturner.

The mortar is a stout wooden bowl (Fig. 27-8A). The inside is the important part. This should have a curve slightly less than that of a bottom of the mortar (Fig. 27-8C). The middle of the end of the pestle should always make contact with the inside of the mortar at any angle it is held. It would not do its job properly if the curve of its bottom was flattened.

The pestle needs to be fairly heavy (Fig. 27-8B). It is given a taper and a knob handle. The bottom should have a curve slightly less than of a bottom of the mortar (Fig. 27-8C). The middle of the end of the pestle should always make contact with the inside of the mortar at any angle it is held. It would not do its job properly if the curve of its bottom was flattened.

An interesting alternative way of making the pestle is to use two woods. The lower part is heavier, while the top part can be a lighter wood of attractive appearance. The two pieces are first turned cylindrical with a substantial dowel on one piece mating with a hole in the other (Fig. 27-8D),

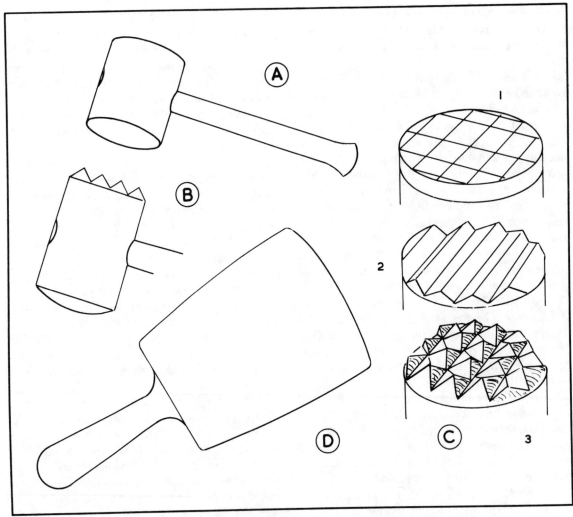

Fig. 27-7. Kitchen mallets may be plain or with serrated ends.

then the shape is turned after they have been glued together. The joint should come above the rim of the mortar when the pestle is placed in it.

A pestle is not very different from the second mallet (Fig. 27-7D). It is possible to make this a dual tool by rounding the end of a mallet so it can act as a pestle (Fig. 27-8E). The mortar should be wide enough to provide some clearance around the mallet, which needs to be moved to angles a little each side of vertical.

MEASURES

At one time a cook used wooden measures.

Reproductions make decorative items, even if the modern cook uses metal or plastic measures. Outlines are utilitarian rather than decorative, although the turner can test his skill by making a set of nesting measures that fit inside a decorative container (Fig. 27-9A).

Another type of measure is dished (Fig. 27-9B) in the form of spoons of various capacities. They can be just this, or handles may be added, either from the same piece of wood (Fig. 27-9C) or doweled in at an angle (Fig. 27-9D). A long shallow wooden spoon is still the chosen item for stirring a large container of cooking food.

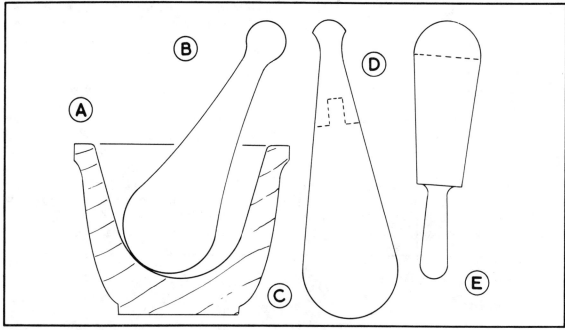

Fig. 27-8. A pestle and mortar.

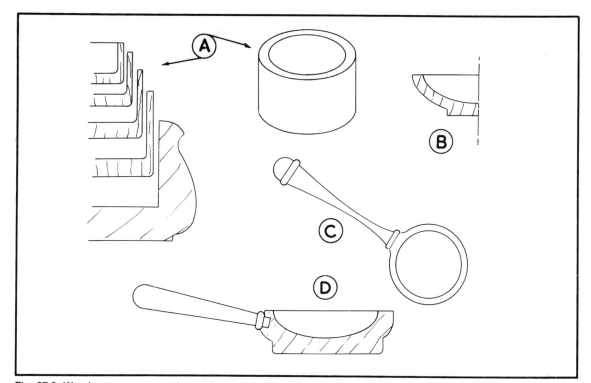

Fig. 27-9. Wooden measures can be made to nest or fashioned as spoons.

SALT AND CONDIMENTS

Salt, in the quantities needed in the kitchen, was kept in turned boxes with lids, similar to those already described. However, it would be better today if a reproduction salt box is to be made, to fashion it around a metal or plastic round box with a lid so the contents will be kept dry. The inner container could stand in the wooden box, so its lid could be lifted easily after the wooden lid had been removed (Fig. 27-10A).

For table use, there are condiment containers that can follow traditional outlines with detail turning (Fig. 27-10B), or they can be more severe in a modern manner (Fig. 27-10C). At one time, salt for the table was in a small bowl with a matching small spoon to transfer some to the side of the plate. Both could be made in wood and treated with a waterproof finish. It is more common today for salt to be in a shaker.

A simple shaker has a parallel hole through it, which is closed by a cork or rubber stopper (Fig. 27-10D). It is common to provide a single central hole for sprinkling salt, while a pattern of smaller holes is used for pepper (Fig. 27-10E). A pair of shakers can be mounted on a stand with a central spindle as a handle (Fig. 27-10F). The two shakers can be located by turned rings (Fig. 27-10G), or they can have recesses deep enough to fit over shallow discs (Fig. 27-10H).

If a shaker of greater capacity is needed, the

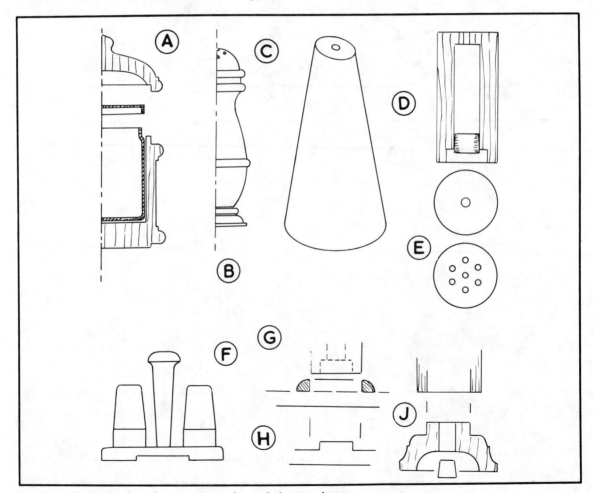

Fig. 27-10. Containers for salt or pepper can be made in many forms.

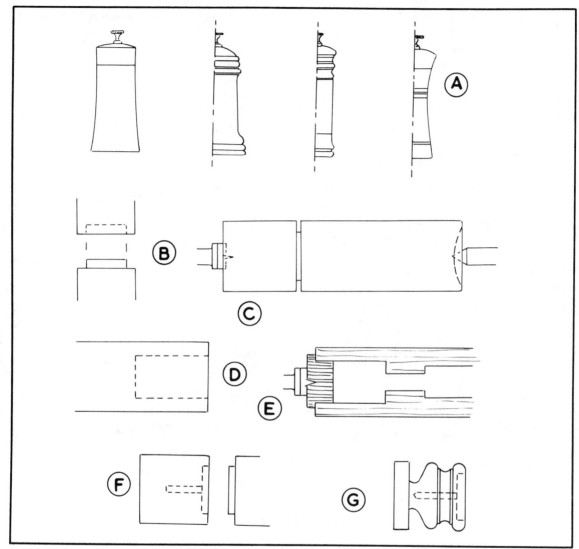

Fig. 27-11. Pepper mills make interesting lathe projects.

inside can be turned larger. This also allows a smoother interior than might be obtained in the smaller sizes with some drills, because there is room to use a scraper and abrasive paper inside. A plug is turned for the base, and this may continue along the same lines or broaden to form a stand. Then the filling hole is made in that (Fig. 27-10J).

Another way of dealing with pepper is to actually mill the peppercorns on the table. The design of the interior of the pepper mill depends on the mechanism, so this should be bought first, but many outside patterns are possible (Fig. 27-11A).

The body of a pepper mill for the usual mechanism is in two pieces with the operating part of the mechanism mounted through a hole in a cap. The cap fits over a projection on the body (Fig. 27-11B). The interior details will be made to provide a space for the peppercorns and give fit and clearance to the mechanism, but most of it can be done by drilling from the tailstock.

It is convenient to first turn both parts in one length of wood with a little spare length for final turning of the cap. The cylinder is squared at the tailstock end and slightly hollowed, then a length sufficient for the body is parted off (Fig. 27-11C). The body can be chucked or driven by a center, while a hole large enough to accommodate the mechanism is made in what will be the top (Fig.

27-11D). A plug is turned to fit if a chuck is not being used, and the piece reversed to drill the other end and right through (Fig. 27-11E).

The top of the body is shouldered in readiness to take the cap. The piece of wood for the cap can be mounted in a chuck or on a screw center, then a recess is made to fit over the projection on the body, and a hole is drilled through for the stem of

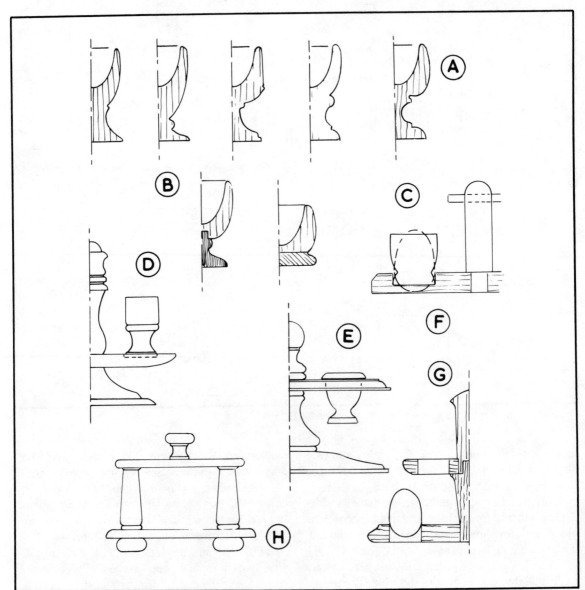

Fig. 27-12. The variety of eggcups and egg stands are infinite.

338

the mechanism (Fig. 27-11F). The outside can then be turned to the required shape and parted off (Fig. 27-11G.)

Shaping of the body can be done at an earlier stage, or the mill can be assembled to the cap before it is parted off, so that the tailstock center keeps the parts pressed together while the body is turned. This is the best way if the cap is to continue the same size as the body in a plain outline, but if there are beads and other shaping, turning together is not as important.

EGGCUPS AND RACKS

The making of eggcups has been described (Chapter 9), but a selection of designs are shown here (Fig. 27-12A). The choice is broadly between those with stems and those that are lower. Interesting effects can be obtained by mixing woods, with the stem part different from the cup and a small dowel between them (Fig. 27-12B). Something like this could be done with a lower cup on a base of a different wood.

If many eggs in cups have to be moved, it is useful to have a stand to accommodate the normal number. This may range from a simple disc with a central handle (Fig. 27-12C) to a more elaborately turned stand following traditional lines (Fig. 27-12D). Usually, the eggcups stand in hollows in the disc. In one traditional stand, the cups have rims so they can fit through holes in a raised disc (Fig. 27-12E). Any stand with a base should be broad enough or heavy enough to make the risk of tipping minimal.

Eggs can be stored and carried in a circular rack very similar to one used for eggcups. A single disc with holes is simplest. This needs feet to give clearance underneath. One ring of holes may be enough (Fig. 27-12F), although a larger disc can have a double ring of holes, staggered so as many positions as possible can be arranged. Holes of the sizes needed are most cleanly made with a saw tooth bit.

An egg rack can be two-tiered (Fig. 27-12G). Placing and removing eggs from the lower part is facilitated if the upper tier is a smaller diameter. This means that there can be more holes in the bot-

tom. The bottom may be thick enough so there is no need for feet, but the top may be tapered toward the rim so the overall effect is not heavy. An alternative to a central pedestal is an arrangement of three pillars with the handle only attached to the top disc (Fig. 27-12H).

CONDIMENT SET

This is a combination of two eggcuplike containers with a central handle that could be used for salt and pepper to be spooned out, or the cups could hold herbs if you want to put them on the dining table. It would not be difficult to arrange three cups with the handle between them, all held together with glue, but a pair of cups are easier to make (Fig. 27-13A).

Make the two cups identical. They could be turned on a screw center, because the hole left in the middle of each bottom will not matter. The holes could be plugged or hidden by discs of cloth. The insides can be any hollow shape you wish, but the outsides should have about 1/2 inch parallel below the rims so they fit together with their bottoms flat (Fig. 27-13B). Where they touch could be planed flat to give a better glue area. Arrange the inside shaping so the wood becomes fairly thin (not more than 1/8 inch) towards the rim; otherwise, you will have to make a thick handle to fit over it and that would look clumsy.

The handle (Fig. 27-13C) is simple spindle turning, and you may prefer to work a shape of your own design. Arrange a knob or other formed top for a finger grip. As shown, the cups are nearly 2 inches outside in diameter and the total height is 5 inches.

Cut a notch in the lower parallel part of the handle to fit over the cups tightly, then glue the parts together. Check that the cups stand level and the handle is upright from whatever direction you view it. Give the wood a waterproof finish that will not affect food, or treat the set with vegetable oil.

SCOOP

This scoop might be used for powders, such as flour, in the kitchen, or it could be used on the din-

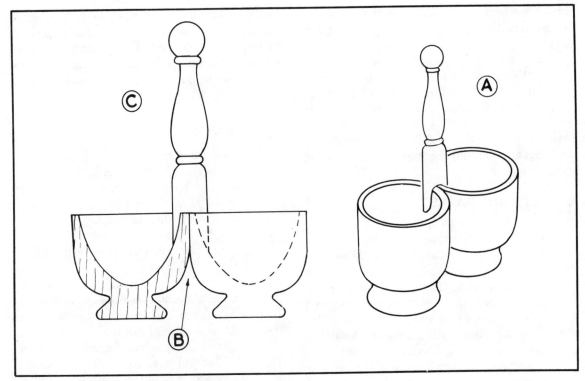

Fig. 27-13. This condiment set is made like two eggcups joined together.

ing table for various powders or granules, or even such foods as rice or peas. Even if you do not use it, it is decorative. Two versions are shown: one with a handle in line with the scoop and turned in one piece with it, and another with the handle at an angle and joined to the scoop part with a turned dowel. The second version allows the scoop to be used more easily inside a bowl or similar container with a better chance of getting a full load.

The end of the scoop is turned like an eggcup. Then, a shaped saw cut across it fashions the bowl for scooping. For the straight scoop (Fig. 27-14A), start with a piece of wood of the full diameter. True one end and mount that on the screw center. At the other end, which has to be turned hollow, use the tailstock center for support, then turn partly into the hollow. Leave some wood at the middle for support as long as possible by the tailstock center. Turn the end and the outside for a short distance. Withdraw the tailstock center and carefully turn away the remainder of the inside wood.

Mount a piece of scrap wood on the screw center or a faceplate and turn a hollow into which the end you have just formed can be pushed for a friction drive. At the tailstock, put the center in where the screw center had been, and turn the remainder of the outside shape completely.

Use a fine fretsaw or coping saw to make the outline of the scoop end. Then, trim that further with a file and abrasive paper (Fig. 27-14B).

For the scoop with an angled handle, turn the part that is to be hollowed first. Treat this like an eggcup with a short length of spare wood mounted on the screw center. When the hollow is satisfactory, turn the outside, including the curve that has to be shaped down to the point where you part off.

Drill for the handle dowel and make the handle to fit (Fig. 27-14C). Cut the shape to the scoop end in the same way as the previous example, but be careful that the dowel hole is central in relation to the shaped end. Glue in the handle to complete the scoop.

EGG TIMERS

There is a fascination about a sand glass egg timer, although logically it is outdated. Construction depends on the size of the glass part, so this should be obtained first. The reversible turned case of the first example has small parts, so this could be a project to use offcuts of attractive wood, and it could be made on the smallest lathe. Many variations are possible, but the usual egg timer (or hour glass in a larger size) has disc ends and three turned pillars (Fig. 27-15). The two end pieces grip the glass, and the pillars are spaced to give a small clearance to the glass part (Fig. 27-16A).

Draw a circle on a piece of paper or card of the greatest size of the glass. Outside this draw a pitch circle for the pillar positions. Step the radius around this and mark alternate places as holes for the ends

of the pillars. Draw another circle outside this as the actual size of an end disc (Fig. 27-16B). Use this drawing as a guide to size when turning the wooden parts.

There can be a shaped hollow in each disc for the glass (Fig. 27-16C) or a shallow hole will do (Fig. 12-16D). Because the timer has to stand on either end, these should be basically flat, although there can be a turned design (Fig. 27-16E).

The pillars look best if their thicker parts are near the center, opposite the narrow part of the glass. The ends can taper to dowels or be shouldered (Fig. 27-16F). If there is a taper without a shoulder, it is possible to have the holes a little too deep and adjust the distance between the discs so as to firmly hold the glass part. However, be careful that all pillars finish with the same length

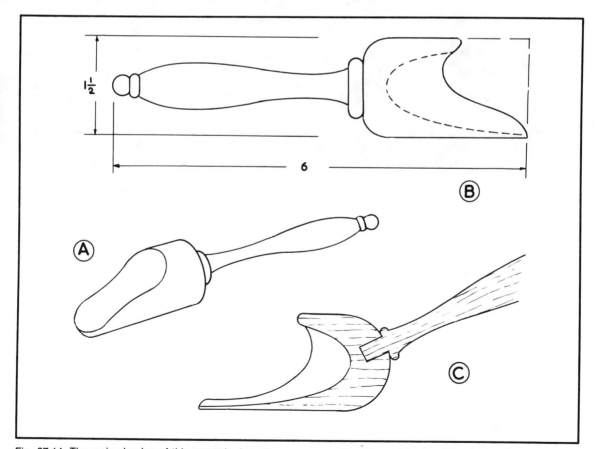

Fig. 27-14. The main shaping of this scoop is done like an eggcup, then the end is shaped and a handle added.

Fig. 27-15. An egg timer made with three pillars doweled into end pieces is shown.

exposed when glued and the timer stands upright. Shouldering the pillars automatically gets the discs parallel, but does not allow adjustment. A disc of card can be put at an end of the glass if slack has to be taken up.

It is advisable to polish or varnish the wooden parts before assembling with the glass; otherwise, it is difficult to get a satisfactory finish without marking the glass.

Tubular Egg Timer

This type of egg timer has the glass enclosed,

and the whole thing must be turned over to make the sand run the other way. Sizes will depend on the available glass, but the one shown suits a parallel glass about 3 inches long and 5/8 inch in diameter (Fig. 27-17A). Get your glass first and settle the wood sizes around it (Fig. 27-17B). Any wood can be used, but more care will be needed turning softwoods than the preferable hardwoods.

There are two possible ways of making the egg timer. A tube to fit around the glass could form one part, then separate ends glued on after the glass has been inserted. It is probably better to make the tube and one end as a single piece of wood, then turn the other end separately. This method is described below.

With this type of assembly, it is always wiser to drill the hole first. Make it an easy fit on the glass, but not so loose that it moves about. There should not be any need to glue or pack the glass. Drilling could be done in the lathe or on a drill press. Freehand drilling with an electric drill is not advised, because the hole produced may not finish truly in line with the wood. Have the piece of wood long enough to allow some waste at the headstock end (Fig. 27-17C).

Turn a plug to support the wood at the tailstock end (Fig. 27-17D). With this arrangement, you can turn the main part to size. Before you part off, check the fit of the glass inside and turn the other end so when the loose part is fitted, it will just touch the end of the glass and hold it.

To avoid having a hole showing in the separate piece, drill a shallow hole for the recess first. Do this so it can be pushed onto a plug of scrap wood mounted on a screw center or in a chuck.

The pair of cutaways in the tubular part should be made with a fine-toothed fretsaw or coping saw. Doing this will keep cleaning up with a file or an abrasive to a minimum. The amount removed should be enough for the state of the sand to be seen, but there is no need to cut far towards the ends of the glass tube. If you want to stain or polish the wood, that is best done before you finally fit the glass and glue on the end. To prevent the timer from slipping on a smooth surface, glue a disc of cloth on each end.

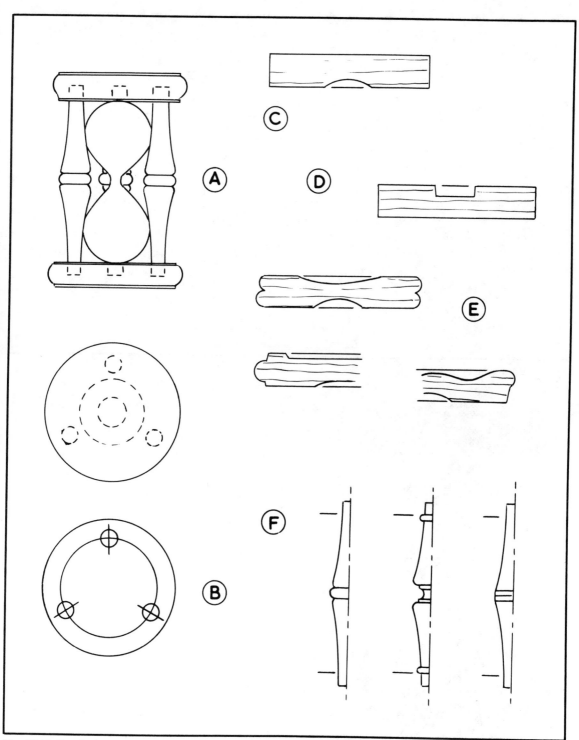

Fig. 27-16. Details for the invertible egg timer shown in Fig. 27-15 are given.

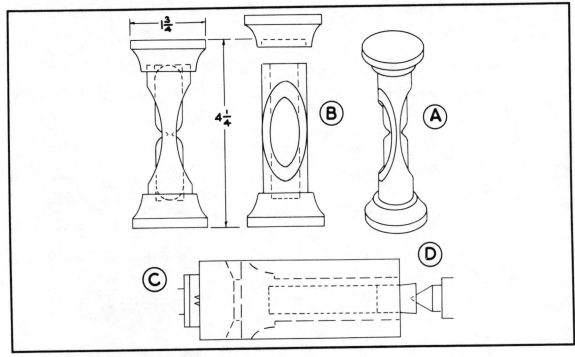

Fig. 27-17. A tubular invertible egg timer.

Fig. 27-18. A pillar egg timer with the tube on a rotatable disc.

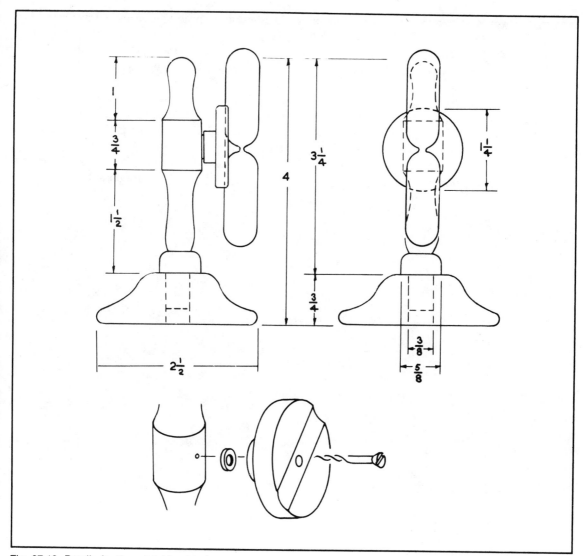

Fig. 27-19. Details for the rotatable egg timer.

Rotating Egg Timer

This egg timer uses a sand glass of the cylindrical type, which is sometimes mounted by its gripped center on a backboard or fitted between two end pieces joined by pillars. In this timer, the glass is mounted on a disc that can be rotated on a pillar projecting from a steady base (Fig. 27-18). The design suits a waisted sand glass about 3 inches by 1/2 inch in diameter, with a timing of 3 to 4 minutes (Fig. 27-19). The disc should be made of

close-grained hardwood in order to reduce the risk of the thin section breaking. The other parts can be anything you wish.

Turn the base on a screw center and drill it for the pillar. Turn the pillar between centers. A basic design is shown, but you can elaborate the pattern if you wish. Leave sufficient parallel section where the disc attaches, however. The dowel at the bottom need not go right through the base.

The disc could be made with its grain across

or through. If you want to make several egg timers, it would be easier to turn them along a cylinder with the one end faced and cut off ready for the same to be done to the next. Drill centrally for a slim screw 5/8 or 3/4 inch long.

Groove across the front of the disc. It need not be an exact match to the sand glass, but get it fairly close. Use a file or gouge. The glass will be fixed with epoxy glue, which has some gap-filling properties. Countersink lightly for the screw head in the groove. Drill an undersize hole for the screw to thread in the post. Flatten around that hole if you wish.

Glue the post to the base, then varnish or polish all of the wood, but leave the groove in the disc bare so that it will absorb glue. Put a washer on the screw between the wood parts and adjust the screw so the disc will turn easily, but not so freely that it might rotate when you do not wish it to rotate. Put a few spots of epoxy glue between the glass and the grooved disc. Leave the assembly on its side with a light weight over it until the glue has set.

Chapter 28

Domestic Turning

Much of the wood turning that can be done for use in the home is associated with the preparation of food, as described in Chapter 27. Some turned items have uses elsewhere in the home, however, and there are many utilitarian items that can be made on a lathe.

DARNERS

The mushroom (Fig. 28-1A) used to push into a sock being darned is similar to the vegetable presser, although smaller. It can be made in two parts (Fig. 28-2) or from one piece of wood. Obviously, the vital part is the large end, which should be smooth and well-rounded. Some bobbins used in lacemaking are very similar. Some workers prefer an egg pattern (Fig. 28-1B), and getting this shape with smooth ends is an interesting project for a turner. For use in darning the fingers of gloves, there are little double-ended tools (Fig. 28-1C). Any of these darners are best made in close-grained hardwood and finished by wax polishing, rather than applying any sort of varnish.

NAPKIN RINGS

The methods of turning hollow parts, such as napkin or serviette rings, on a mandrel has already been described. These rings offer scope for a variety of designs, and the size of the wood needed is small. Added interest comes from gluing wood or different colors together. These blocks can be built up with layers or with colored pieces outside a plainer square center (Fig. 28-3A). When the woods are turned through, interesting patterns result (Fig. 28-3B). So that individuals users know their own ring, blocks can be arranged to make different wood patterns, but the turned outline can be the same, so a set has a matched appearance.

Plain wooden rings can be made in matching designs, but different woods can be used for identification or similar woods colored with different stains before polishing or varnishing. Possible outlines are almost infinite, so the turner can exercise his imagination (Fig. 27-3C). Be careful not to go too thin at any point. Although a thin end to the hole looks neat, let the wood be fairly thick just

Fig. 28-1. Sock and glove darners.

behind the edge. If it tapers too gradually, the edge may be weakened.

Although it is easy enough to get an attractive outside on a mandrel after drilling through a block of wood (Fig. 28-3D), something ought to be done to the hole. Ideally, it should have as smooth an inside as the outside, and the ends should be belled to facilitate sliding in the rolled cloth (Fig. 28-3E).

It is possible to work the inside away from the lathe. The far end can be scraped with a curved knife blade (Fig. 28-3F), then rolled abrasive paper used to get the inside smooth. This is tedious and the result may not be perfect. It is better to turn the inside of the lathe.

This is done best after the outside has been turned, by using a wood chuck on a faceplate or screw center (Fig. 28-3G). Each end is turned separately with a scraper worked mostly from the center outward to conform to the direction of the grain. There can be central projection in the wood chuck coming halfway through the ring (Fig. 28-2H).

Fig. 28-2. Two parts of a mushroom darner.

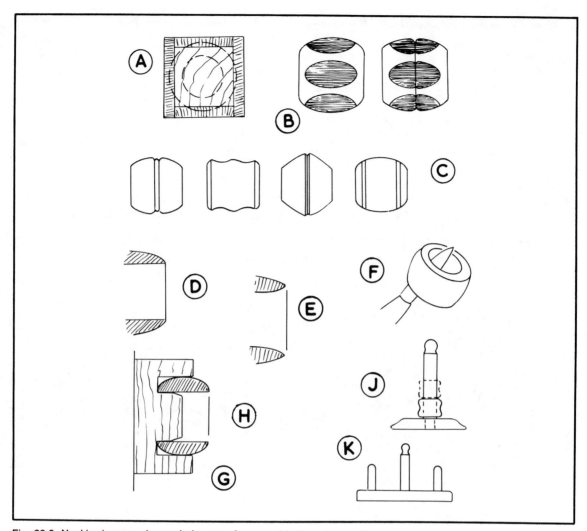

Fig. 28-3. Napkin rings can be made in many forms and built up from different colored woods.

A stand for rings can be made on the lathe. Simplest is a base with a length of dowel rod standing up, but it looks better with a turned column (Fig. 28-3J). If the height would be too great with a single column, there can be two or three on a square or turned base (Fig. 28-3K).

BOXES

Turned boxes have many uses. Even when a turner is just exercising his fancy without a particular aim in mind, it will be put to good use somewhere in the home.

A simple box with a parallel inside can be used as a stand for pencils (Fig. 28-4A). With trays and other things on an extended base, it will become a desk compendium.

At one time sewing needles were not as readily available, and they were kept in a case. This is still a good idea, it protects the user from the sharp points and the needles from damage. The basic design is a long box with a lid (Fig. 28-4B), but some traditional cases were given very elaborate external designs (Fig. 28-4C). The insides of the box and the lid can be drilled from the tailstock. If the top of the box is then turned to push into the lid, the two parts can be put together and the outside turned between centers as one unit. If any work has to be done on one of the parts separately, a plug can be turned to press in the end and provide a center.

String boxes are useful items that provide scope for considerable decoration. The basic box is something that will take the available ball of string with a lid that allows the string to be fed out as required (Fig. 28-4D). The box may have a flat or curved bottom, and the lid may be hollowed to clear the ball of string (Fig. 28-4E).

A pleasing shape can look like an apple (Fig. 28-4F). It might be a round house painted accordingly (Fig. 28-4G). The outline might be like a chessman (Fig. 28-4H). The hole does not have to be central in the lid or even at the top. A beehive pattern with a base to press in can have the string outlet where the bees would enter (Fig. 28-3J).

CLOCKS AND THERMOMETERS

A clock face is round so it lends itself to combining with turned wood. How it is mounted depends on its type. The older spring-powered

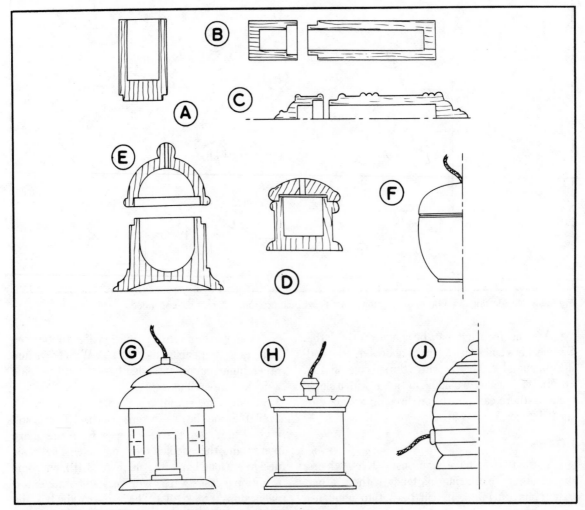

Fig. 28-4. Needle and string boxes offer scope for using many ideas.

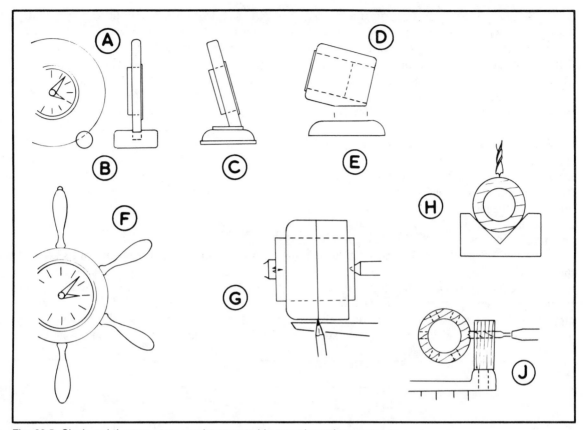

Fig. 28-5. Clock and thermometers can be mounted in turned wooden cases.

clock was often as deep back to front as its diameter and held in place with screws through a backplate. An electric clock has less depth, but the case may still benefit from being deeper than the minimum needed.

A shallow clock movement can be accommodated through a hole in a disc (Fig. 28-5A). This may notch into two cylindrical feet (Fig. 28-5B) or be mounted on a base, which could be turned (Fig. 28-5C) or be mounted on a rectangular or other piece of flat wood. Turned feet could be put below any type of base.

A deeper case could be turned from solid wood, like a box, or it might be better laminated from several pieces, either put together solid or already partly drilled to size before assembly (Fig. 28-5D). This could be mounted on a turned base after planing a flat on it. The flat can be made at an angle

so the clock is tilted up slightly (Fig. 28-5E).

A wall clock can be made in the form of a ship's steering wheel (Fig. 28-5F). If the clock is a full-depth movement, the inside can be turned through parallel. If it is a shallow movement, the whole depth need not be as great or only part need be turned out to accommodate the clock. In this case, it may be necessary to have the clock removable from the front if it needs attention, or a small diameter hole taken through to the back to give access.

The main problem with a ship's wheel design is in getting the handles positioned truly, because slight errors will be very obvious. The number of handles depends on the size of the whole thing. Six or eight are a reasonable choice, and five is the minimum. Handles of a genuine ship's wheel are all identical, except one is given an extra bead or other marking. When this is at the top, the rudder is straight. In a clock, this could also be at the top.

If the lathe has a dividing head, the positions of the spokes can be marked along the tool rest with its aid. Otherwise, a strip of paper wrapped around it to get the circumference, which can be divided when the paper is flattened, is the safest way of dividing.

Run a line around the cylinder by holding a pencil against the revolving wood (Fig. 28-5G). Holes for the handles can be drilled accurately if the cylinder is held truly on V-blocks, which may be improvised for the purpose (Fig. 28-5H). Another way is to mount a wood block in place of the tool rest and have a hole accurately drilled through this at center height. A hand electric drill can be used with this as a guide (Fig. 28-5J).

There are other round instruments that can be mounted in a similar way. These include thermometers, hygrometers, and barometers, all of which are shallow in relation to their diameters.

A simple mounting is little more than a hollowed disc to screw on the wall (Fig. 28-6A). The outside may be turned with a molding to give a more decorative appearance (Fig. 28-6B).

A tubular mounting can be made similar to a clock. In fact, it may be possible to make a clock and a thermometer or other instrument as a pair.

Another way to mount a round instrument is in a disc with another matching disc as a base. The case is planed with a flat for gluing and screwing that puts it at a convenient angle (Fig. 28-7) for viewing when standing on a table.

TROPHIES

Medals and other ornamental discs are often used as trophies and gifts within clubs and organizations. After presentation, the recipient may wonder what to do with his award. This also applies to unusual coins. The turned design shown is intended to provide a way of mounting any round

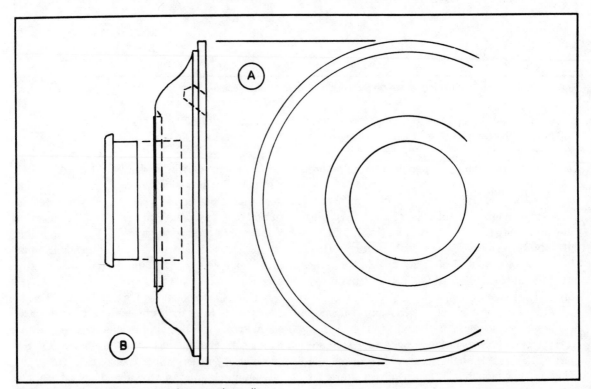

Fig. 28-6. A thermometer case to hang on the wall.

Fig. 28-7. Two thermometer stands and cases.

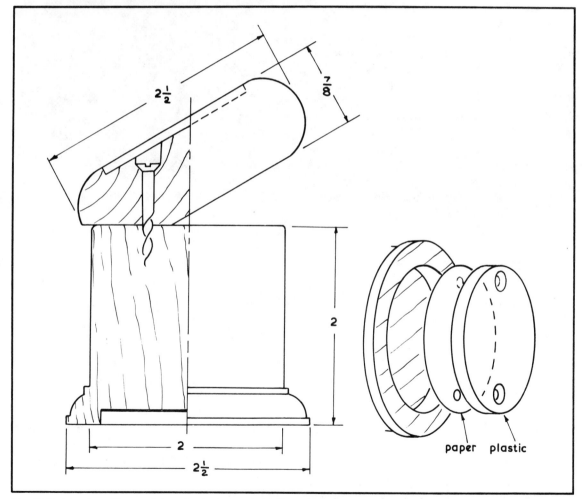

Fig. 28-8. A trophy with a medal set in the top and details under a transparent cover in the base.

metal disc of this sort and make it into a trophy, which could be used for regular competition or just a means of displaying what has already been won (Figs. 28-8 and 28-9).

The medal or coin fits into a recess in a wood disc, where it is glued, unless you want to be able to lift it out and examine the other side. Turn the disc with a rounded or molded edge on a screw center. The hole from the screw will not be very obvious underneath in the finished trophy, particularly if you fill it with stopping or drill it out for a wood plug.

The stand could be any height and is shown with parallel sides and a molded base. If the item is to be used for regular competition or you wish to keep a record of how the medal was won, there can be a paper in the base on which details may be written. Cut a circle of transparent plastic to go over the circle of paper. Turn a recess in the base deep enough for these to come just below the surface. Drill for two screws to hold the plastic and paper in, so they can be opened if a new entry has to be made.

If the trophy is to stand on a table, the top part should be at a flatter angle than if it is to go higher on a shelf. It is shown at 30 degrees to horizontal, which should suit a table position. Bevel the underside and drill for a screw. Use glue as well and also glue in the medal or coin.

FURNITURE

There are not many items of furniture which are purely lathe work. A great many rails and legs are needed for things completed by other woodworking processes, which cannot be included in a book devoted to lathe work only. The important part of the turner's work in relation to other woodworking is the accuracy of overall measurements and the diameters of doweled ends. If the turning is being done for work that someone else will complete, it is best to have some specimen holes from the other craftsman's tools in scrap wood for testing, rather than depend on measurements for dowel diameters. This is particularly true for a chair, where enduring strength depends on tight-

Fig. 28-9. The trophy showing the inset medal.

fitting dowel joints.

A round stool can be made with a turned top and either three or four turned legs. Four may be better for a smooth room floor, but if the stool may be used on an uneven surface, three would be your best bet. Angle the legs outward so their bottoms come outside a projection downward from the top, then there is no risk of anyone standing on one side tilting the stool.

A spinning wheel of traditional form is almost entirely turned. There are a great many parts, including the larger wheel, which is made by wheelwright methods. Such spinning wheels are now used mainly as decoration, but even then, they should be functional. Any turner attempting a spinning wheel should get a detailed plan and work from that.

Chapter 29

Small Items

Not all turning is big or even of moderate size. There is a lot of satisfaction to be gained from making smaller items. Some turners enjoy making miniature reproductions of larger items. It takes considerable skill to turn something like a cup with wood brought down almost to paper thinness. Such a piece may be more of a demonstration of the turner's ability. There are many other fairly small items that are useful and decorative that will be included in the turner's range of activities without resorting to modelmaking.

Although the average lathe can be used for small turning as well as large turning, small items are particularly appropriate to small lathes, which do not have the capacity to make table legs and other larger items. A lathe powered by an electric drill or just a small motor cannot deal with the load imposed by swinging a piece of wood of large diameter, but it may be as successful as a larger machine when used for making small items.

There is also the question of what to do with the accumulation of small offcuts left from larger work when turning, cabinetmaking, or doing some

other type of woodworking. It is possible to turn pieces of wood that most other woodworkers would regard as scrap. However, the number of odd pieces collected will be more than the turner can hope to deal with unless he has a few ideas to work on. It is these smaller items that are dealt with in this chapter.

BUTTONS

Round wooden buttons can be quite attractive, but they have to be made in sets that match, because there are not many uses for isolated buttons no matter how well made. If the button is to look different from a plastic button, it should have a prominent grain marking, so it is obvious that the finished button is wood. It is no use going to the trouble of making buttons on the lathe if most people look at the finished products and do not recognize them as anything more than common mass-produced buttons.

One way of making a number of buttons is to turn a cylinder to the diameter wanted. The

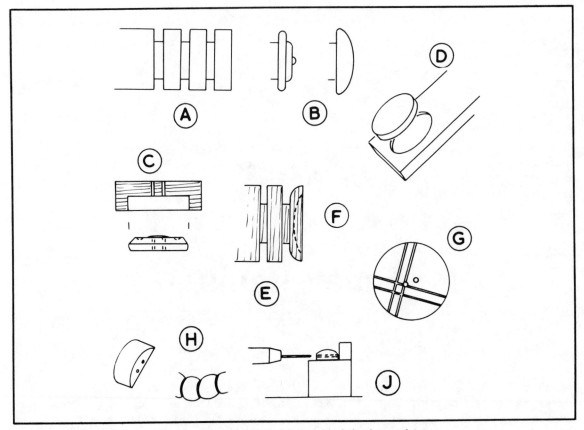

Fig. 29-1. Buttons can be made in a series and drilled with the aid of simple templates.

thickness of each button can be cut in a short distance with a parting tool (Fig. 29-1A). The piece of wood is then held at the headstock end with a self-centering chuck or by a wooden chuck made by drilling a suitable hole in a block of wood on the faceplate. The end of a button is turned. It may be simply rounded or there can be rings cut around it (Fig. 29-1B), then it is parted off. The surface of the next button is turned in the same way and so on until all of the buttons have been cut off.

A button has two or four holes for thread. The best way to drill these accurately is to make a small template. Drill or turn a hollow in a piece of wood to fit easily over a button, but do not have the hollow quite as thick as the button. Drill a pattern of thread holes in this. Use it over each button in turn to drill through (Fig. 29-1C). The holes in the buttons should be very lightly countersunk to

remove rough edges. This is best done by twirling a larger drill between the fingers. Using a power or hand drill might easily go too deep.

If the back of a button comes from the parting tool with a surface that is not smooth enough, it can be rubbed on a piece of abrasive paper on a flat piece of wood. It could be held against a disc sander. The problem then is holding a small button without also sanding your fingers. A hole can be made in a flat piece of wood that allows the button to stand above the surface, and this will serve as a holder (Fig. 29-1D).

Larger buttons are better made with the grain across. Usually, only a pair of these are required, and it is possible to turn them in the same way as the small end-grain buttons, with a block of sufficient thickness projecting from the chuck (Fig. 29-1E). With the larger diameter, it is possible to make the fronts hollow or with turned decoration (Fig. 29-1F).

Any of the buttons can be carved on the surface. In the simplest form, this can be lines cut across—not necessarily symmetrically—with a chisel or V-tool (Fig. 29-1G).

Buttons can be made into beads for a bracelet if fairly thick ones are trimmed with parallel flat sides and drilled through (Fig. 29-1H). A number of these can be threaded on elastic. Care is needed to get the holes uniformly spaced and straight through. One way is to have the drill chuck in the headstock and arrange a table and stop over the bed at the correct height (Fig. 29-1J). If lines are drawn

on the table opposite the button edges when it is in line for each of the holes, they should all finish to match.

BEADS

Plain wooden beads can be made in batches by turning a strip of wood between centers. Cuts with a parting tool mark the divisions (Fig. 29-2A). If a chuck is used, the wood is held by its end as the outside of the end bead is shaped. The tailstock center can support it, then a drill is used in the tailstock drill chuck (Fig. 29-2B). This can be taken deep enough to go through several small beads. Do all

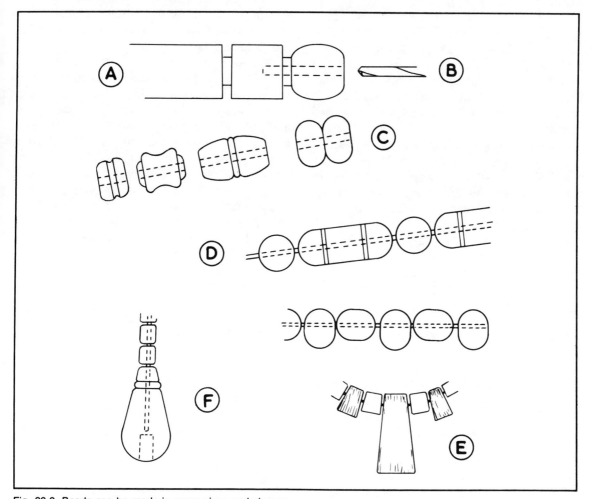

Fig. 29-2. Beads can be made in many sizes and shapes.

of the shaping and cleaning up of the end bead while there is still enough wood to support it, then part it off. Do the same with the next one.

These beads need not be plain, although attractive wood shows its grain best in a simple egg shape. There can be lines cut around or the outline cut to a different form (Fig. 29-2C). Not all beads on a string need be the same. Long beads can be separated by short beads (Fig. 29-2D). Two different colored woods can alternate. The beads can taper in size. A batch can start with a strip turned conical instead of parallel. For a long string, there has to be careful checking with calipers because the difference between adjoining beads will not be great.

The center bead of a string if used as a necklace, may be different or on edge (Fig. 29-2E). A hanging string of beads may finish in a longer and heavier terminal bead. This is best turned with a hole in the bottom large enough to let the knot at the end of the string go inside (Fig. 29-2F).

Fairly large beads can be used on a cord around drapes or curtains. With beads that may be up to 2 inches long, it is possible to use more elaborate turning methods. The wood can be built up in contrasting colors, rather like the napkin rings, or the outsides can have small versions of the beads and hollows used on the many examples of larger spindle turning in other parts of this book.

Where large beads are used, it usually looks best if they are separated by smaller plain ones to make a break in the design and ensure greater flexibility of the string.

KNOBS

Many knobs have been described in connection with other turned work in earlier parts of this book. Even when you have no immediate call for them, knobs are a worthwhile project for any turner looking for something to do, especially if there is a collection of small pieces of wood to use up. Although individual knobs have their uses, there are far more uses for sets of two, four, or more.

Most turned knobs are used with a dowel to glue into a hole (Fig. 29-3A). If there is no immediate use for a knob, its dowel should be made

long enough to allow for cutting off when needed. The alternative is a screw through from the back (Fig. 29-3B), although this may be combined with a short dowel (Fig. 29-3C). Knobs that have to be pulled tend to be wider than they are deep, with a good overhang of the top (Fig. 29-3D). In some applications, a taller knob is better (Fig. 29-3E). How much detail work is put into turning a knob depends on what wood is used and its size. Complicated turning in a knob of small size may give satisfaction to the turner, but it is lost on most viewers who only note the general outline. Well-marked wood may be more attractive if finished with a fairly plain outline.

Although the basic knob is a ball shape over a stem, there are many varieties possible (Fig. 29-3F) with hollow tops and other departures from the traditional form.

A knob with a good overhang of top provides plenty to pull on, but sometimes it is better to have a bar to grip. This can be arranged with a turned rod between two knobs. The ends of the rod dowel into shallow holes (Fig. 29-3G). The knobs may be traditional form or simple posts. The bar may be a parallel dowel rod, but it looks better if turned thicker near its center to provide a good grip. Another bar type handle is turned, then it is attached to the surface with bolts through spacer pieces (Fig. 29-3H). The bolt heads should be of a decorative type, or they can be sunk if the bar is thick enough, then the holes plugged over them (Fig. 29-3J).

If the normal type of knob is extended, it becomes a peg, which can be used as a coat hook or for hanging various things on it. A row of pegs driven into holes in a backboard will provide useful hanging facilities on a wall. The basic peg need not be very elaborate (Fig. 29-3K). The enlarged end prevents things coming off of it. A shoulder at the dowel contributes to the strength of the joint.

Alternatively, the pegs can be made without shoulders and the holes drilled so the pegs slope upward slightly (Fig. 29-3L). There is a risk that pegs inserted parallel with the floor may eventually develop a sag after they have been heavily loaded for a long time. A sloping peg need not have an enlarged end, but it can still be decorated (Fig.

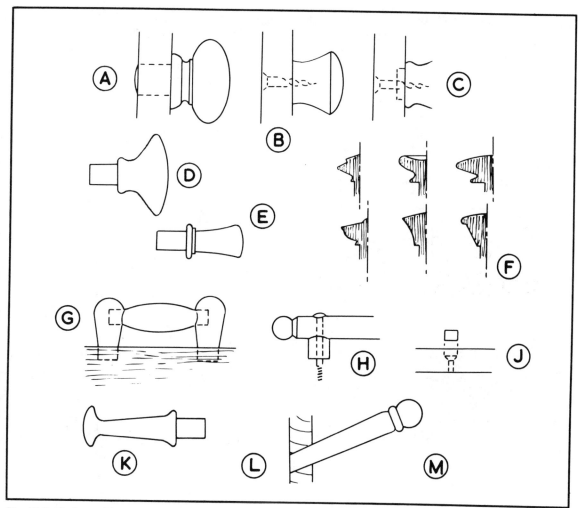

Fig. 29-3. Knobs and handles can use up small pieces of wood.

29-3M). Without the knob it is easier to hang clothing with small loops.

HANDLES

The making of tool handles has already been described. Similar techniques can be used for making handles for other purposes. Like knobs, a stock of handles can be built up when there is no more urgent work to be done. It is certain that they will find a use later on. Handles like those used on tools can be applied to many things, especially where a metal tang or other end has to go into the handle. Another type of handle has a doweled end to fit into

something else. This is like a knob, except that the handle is much longer than a knob. Such handles are needed in many sizes. Those up to about 1 foot long may fit some small garden tools, while the smallest suit more dainty items around the home.

There is scope for an infinite number of individual designs, but a utility handle should be shaped to suit the hand (Fig. 29-4A). For a more decorative handle, there should still be a greater diameter at the end furthest from where it attaches to something else (Fig. 29-4B). There are some things where the handle can be turned as part of the article, and there is no need to plug it in (Fig.

29-4C). Examples of both types are shown (Fig. 29-5) where the door wedge handles are plugged in and the sailmaker's seam rubber is made in one piece.

For some purposes, the handle may be given a shoulder to limit its penetration into the other part (Fig. 29-4D). In many cases, however, it is convenient to leave off a shoulder and give the end a very slight taper, particularly if the handle is being made for stock and its eventual use is unknown. If the wood shrinks or the eventual hole happens to be slightly oversize, it is possible to cut off the end so the thicker part of the handle makes a better fit (Fig. 29-4E).

Tradition has shown the best shape for a handle, and for most purposes, it is advisable to follow these lines. Although, it is possible to make departures and for some furniture very different outlines may be acceptable (Fig. 29-4F). In any case, handles and knobs are usually small features compared with the whole item of furniture. They contribute to the effect, but are not usually intended

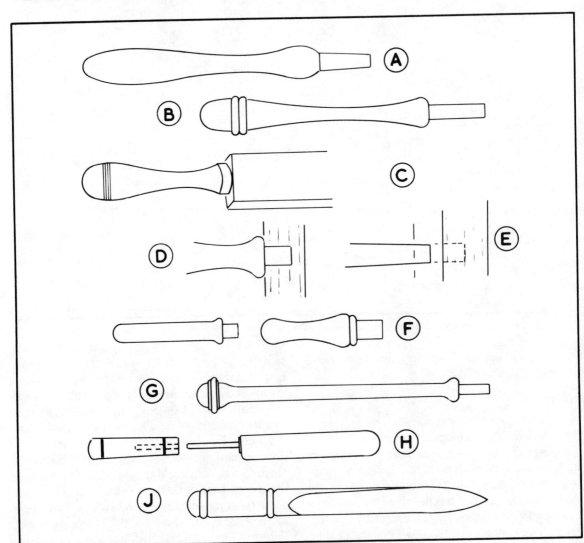

Fig. 29-4. There is a very extensive variety of handles that can be made on a lathe.

Fig. 29-5. A sailmaker's rubber and two door wedges showing how handles can be made from one piece with the other part doweled to it.

to be centers of interest.

In items where the handle is a feature, as in a long handle to a ladle, it is usually unwise to spread the decoration over the length. It is better to concentrate the main decoration on a thick part, which will usually be the grip, and let there be a sweep through most of the length from this (Fig. 29-4G). The handle might be turned or carved, then the fairly plain sweep lead to some minor decoration toward where the handle joins the other part.

Knife handles have possibilities. If a table knife loses its bone or plastic handle, it can be given a turned handle. Usually the tang of the knife is parallel and the original handle was shrunk on. The new handle can have a parallel hole drilled to make a push fit (Fig. 29-4H), then final fitting done with a little epoxy glue.

There are many slender handles on manicure and similar items. Mostly they are black and intended to look like ebony, but usually they are made of other wood and stained black. Except for their slim sections, they are made the same as other handles, and they are usually fitted over parallel tangs like knife handles.

Paper knives and letter openers can be made by adapting handles. The handle is turned with enough left on to make the blade, then this is planed and sanded down after turning is completed (Fig. 29-4J).

NAUTICAL ITEMS

The top of a mast or flagstaff may carry a sort of button, called a *truck,* in which there is a pulley wheel (*sheave*) for hoisting a flag (Fig. 29-6A). The size depends on the diameter of the top of the mast, but it is about three times this size. The top of the mast is reduced to go through a hole, and it is then wedged with the wedge across the direction of the grain in the truck. The sheave could also be turned from hardwood, although it is more commonly metal. The truck should be protected with paint or varnish, and there should be a metal plate over the end grain of the mast to stop rainwater from penetrating and causing rot.

Rope splicing is done with a *marlinespike* or a *fid*. The marlinespike is steel and is used for smaller fiber ropes and for wire ropes. For other fiber ropes, it is better to use a fid, which is a wooden spike made from the hardest wood available. One about 1 inch in greatest diameter and 9 inches long should suit yacht work (Fig. 29-6B). This is best turned with some surplus wood at the large end. Starting between centers, the point is turned down as far as possible before parting off at the tailstock end, then the thicker end is held in a chuck while the pointed end is completed. Finally, the large end is turned to shape and cut off.

A serving mallet is a sort of lever used for straining cord or stout thread, which is wound around a rope to protect it. It looks like a mallet with its head cut across, hence its name, but it is not used for hitting (Fig. 29-6C). The head is turned and drilled through—1 1/2 inches in diameter with 3/4-inch hole will do. It is then sawn in half. This provides heads for two serving mallets. The handle is made in the usual way and plugged into a hole (Fig. 29-6D). Considerable leverage may be put on the handle in use, so its joint should be good, and it should be stout enough not to break—hickory or ash would be best along with any close-grained

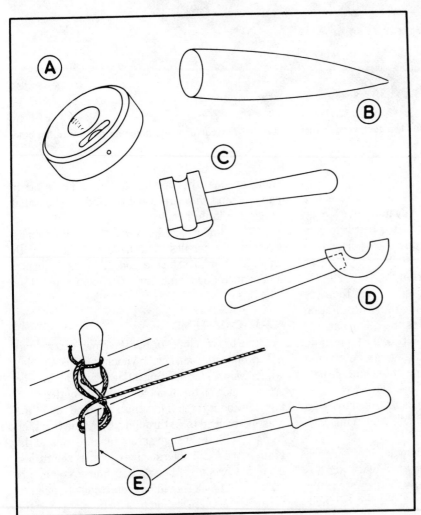

Fig. 29-6. A mast truck, a fid, a serving mallet, and a belaying pin.

hardwood for the head.

At one time, the ropes on a sailing ship came down to a row of belaying pins passed through holes in a rail, where they were secured by winding them around in a figure-eight manner. In many modern yachts, cleats serve the same purpose, but belaying pins are still used where the owner has a feeling for tradition.

A belaying pin may be anything from a few inches long to quite large. It should be hardwood. The two parts should extend above and below the rail about the same amount, so the handle part should be less than the parallel part (Fig. 29-6E), which passes through the rail. Actually, the parallel part should really taper very slightly, so it is easy to push through the hole in the rail, but comes tight when it is fully home. The difference in diameter between tip and shoulder is not enough to be noticeable.

MISCELLANEOUS ITEMS

Wooden clothespins may be considered obsolete, but they can be made on a lathe if only for old time's sake. The shape is turned solid and the waste cut out, preferably with a band saw (Fig. 29-7A). A length of 5 inches and a maximum diameter of 5/8 inch is about right.

A thick short piece of hardwood may be made into a door stop, or *porter*. It should be broader at the bottom, but its bulk should be kept as great as possible for the sake of its weight (Fig. 29-7B). If the weight of the wood only is not enough, a hollow can be turned in the bottom and a block of lead (cast in a similar hole in scrap wood) fixed in (Fig. 29-7C). This was described in connection with the making of lamp standards.

The handle may contribute to the weight by being made of heavy wood. If the weight there is not important, it can be any suitable wood, possibly contrasting in appearance with the block. Make the handle long enough to be used without the need to stoop (Fig. 29-7D).

Many craftsmen use a chalk line, which is a cord that is loaded with chalk and used to "strike" a line on the floor. This is wound on a reel or holder that has hollowed ends so it can revolve when held

between finger and thumb. Two types are used: one has a narrow and deep part for the line (Fig. 29-7E), the other is wider, but not so wide as to be difficult to hold between finger and thumb (Fig. 29-7F). It is important that the hollows are smooth, so they should be carefully cleaned after parting off. Although, it would be better to mount the holder finally in a chuck with each side exposed in turn, so it can be sanded while revolving.

A plumb bob can be hung on a line to check verticality. This is often made of metal, but it can be wood, particularly for use where a swinging metal bob might damage surrounding delicate work. Because wood does not concentrate weight like metal, it is common to make a wooden plumb bob longer. Size depends on purpose, but for indoor carpentry a length of 6 inches and a diameter of 1 inch in a dense hardwood should be satisfactory.

The body has a taper to a point, but to reduce the risk of damage this should be slightly rounded (Fig. 29-7G). The line goes through a plug with an enlarged top to provide a hand grip (Fig. 29-7H). This is a push fit in the body, and the hole is made deep enough to allow space for the knot in the end of the line. A refinement is to drill the hole much deeper and either load it with lead shot, or cast a lead plug to push in—both to increase weight (Fig. 29-7J).

Laminating and building up with different colored woods should be kept in mind when deciding what to do with oddments of wood. Quite small pieces can be glued together and made into interesting and attractive objects.

Desk pens are available with a screw fitting and a suitable base can be turned (Fig. 29-8). Usually the screw is intended for something thinner than a wood block, so its head can be let in by counterboring. If turning is done on a screw center, this will locate the drilling position, which can be done by hand after turning. The block can be screwed or glued to a desk set or used with a pad of paper, as shown.

A chairperson needs a gavel to call a meeting to order and to have in front of him as a symbol of his authority at the meeting. Gavels can be various designs and sizes. The one shown (Fig.

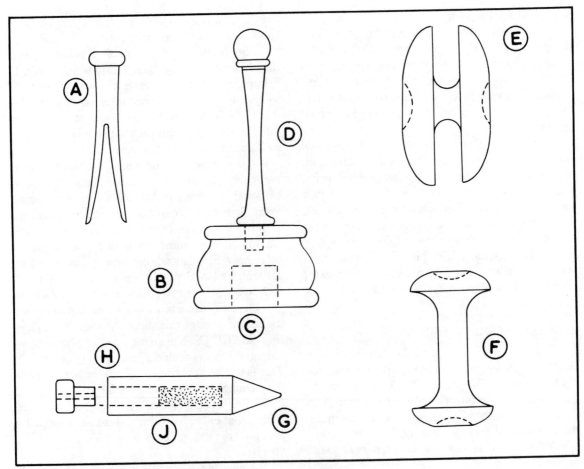

Fig. 29-7. A clothespin, a door stop, a chalk line reel, and a plumb bob.

Fig. 29-8. Two desk pads with pens in mounts on turned bases.

Fig. 29-9. A chairperson's gavel and striker plate.

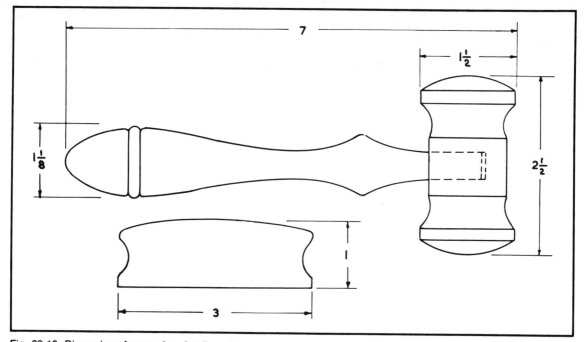

Fig. 29-10. Dimensions for gavel and striker plate.

29-9) is small enough to be carried with its striker plate or anvil in a pocket (Fig. 29-10).

Of course, a gavel is just a mallet, but it is usually made decorative. It may not have to stand the heavy use of a shop mallet, but it should be strong enough for the occasions when the chairperson of a lively meeting brings it down with some force.

The gavel head is best made of a dense heavy wood. The handle could be the same or of another wood. The striker plate is better for being dense and heavy.

As shown, the head is turned with slightly domed ends and the center diameter is less than the ends. Do not reduce it very much or the joint to the handle will be weakened. The end of the handle could be taken right through and a wedge used, but it is shown in a blind hole, where glue should give sufficient grip. Shape the handle to be comfortable in the palm of the hand. It should be parallel where it goes into the head but tapered immediately outside. Drill carefully across the head, preferably on a drill press, with the wood supported on V blocks. A few saw cuts along the end of the handle that goes in the hole, but not so far as to show when the joint is closed, will allow air and surplus glue to escape as the parts are assembled and give a better spread of glue in the joint.

The striker plate can be turned on a screw center. Dome its top and groove the rim to provide a grip. It will sound louder if the bottom is turned hollow, but a flat bottom, with cloth glued underneath to prevent slipping, should create ample noise.

Chapter 30

Toys and Games

At one time, children relied on the local turner for many of their games. They would stop by his door, and he would produce a spinning top or other toy while they watched. Ideas about toys may be more sophisticated today, but a child often gets pleasure from simple things. His imagination provides the details that his parents think ought to be built-in!

SPINNING TOPS

Spinning tops to be whipped are certainly simple things to turn (Fig. 30-1A). If the point is to stand up to wear for long, it should be finished with a round-headed nail.

A further step is to make a top that can be spun by pulling a cord (Fig. 30-1B). The body for the top should be heavy wood for the longest spin and have its weight concentrated in the greatest diameter fairly low. The groove for the cord should be smooth, particularly around the edges, so the cord does not snag as it is pulled.

The handle could be made in one piece with the dowel, or a piece of hardwood dowel rod might be

let into a hole. It would also be possible to use a metal rod instead of the dowel rod. In any case, the bore of the top hole should be quite a loose fit. If the top is drilled right through, the point can be another piece of dowel or turned rod glued in the bottom with a round-headed nail driven in the end. Sizes may suit available wood, but a diameter of about 5 inches and a height just a little less should give a long spin, which is what the younger user expects.

Another way to make a top spin by pulling a cord is to give the top a stem instead of a hole (Fig. 30-1C). A handle is turned to fit over this, with a slot, to clear the cord wound around the stem (Fig. 30-1D). The stem may be a metal rod going right through the top to a rounded point, or it can be a hardwood dowel. Any pattern can be used for the top, providing it is a large enough diameter to give a flywheel effect.

An example of this type is based on a traditional design (Fig. 30-2). The young owner puts the stem of his top through the hole in the handle, then puts

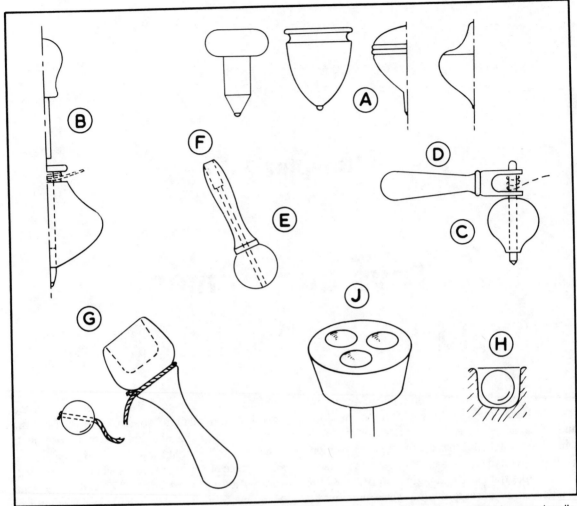

Fig. 30-1. Many children's toys can be turned on a lathe. Those shown include spinning tops, a skipping rope handle, and a ball game.

the string through the hole and winds it on several turns. With a good pull, he sets the top spinning and releases it to continue for some time. The drawing shows a top small enough to put in a pocket (Fig. 30-3). It could be bigger, and the design altered, but remember that a top spins like a flywheel, and it needs weight towards its circumference to keep it going, so there must be a bulbous part. Use close-grained hardwood to stand up to rough use.

Turn the top with the bulbous part stopping at a shoulder where the parallel stem starts. The bottom tapers to a point. For use indoors, a wood curved point will probably be sufficiently durable. If the top is to be used outdoors on stone, there should be a metal end. You can make the metal end by driving a nail into a slightly undersize hold, which may be good enough without further treatment, but it is better to turn the head after driving it into the wood. A nail with a thick head gives you more to work on. Shaping could be with a file or a graver, followed by abrasive paper.

Drill the hole in the handle to be quite a loose fit on the stem of the top. The string grip may be

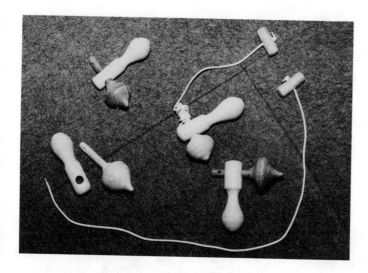

Fig. 30-2. A group of spinning tops based on a traditional design.

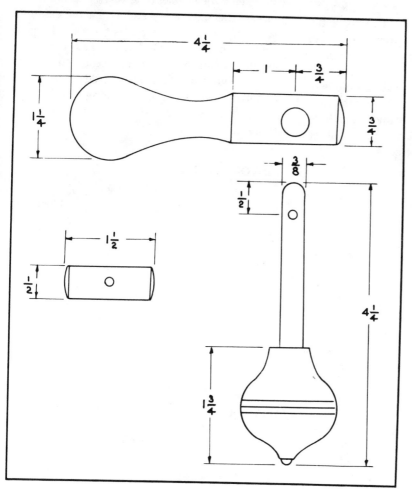

Fig. 30-3. Suggested sizes for a spinning top and handle.

a piece of dowel rod, or you could turn it more shapely. It might be made as a ball or bead. It is best to use flexible braided synthetic cord, 18 inches or longer. Drill a hole at the top of the stem so it slides through easily. Lightly countersink each side for a quick release. Do the same through the grip. Put the end of the string through the hole in the stem, and turn it some more and pull hard in order to prove that your top works.

SKIPPING ROPE HANDLE

A skipping rope handle (Fig. 30-1E) is a comparable turning project. A pair is needed, so there will have to be some careful checking to see that the second handle matches the first. In the traditional shape, a total length of about 5 inches and a diameter of about 1 3/4 inches should suit the young user's hands. The thickest part of the grip should not be too much to circle with the fingers—probably 1 inch in diameter.

The actual rope should be used as a guide to hole sizes, with a bore to slide easily over the rope and an enlarged end to clear a knot in it (Fig. 30-1F). Attractive wood could be varnished, but the usual finish is paint in a bright color.

BALL AND CUP

Rather similar in appearance to the skipping rope handle is a ball and cup (Fig. 30-1G). A few centuries ago this was a popular toy with adults as well as children. The objects is to swing the ball on its string and catch it in the cup. The ball determines the size of the other part, but a 1 inch ball is usually standard and the other part made from wood 6 × 2 inches would be satisfactory.

The ball is drilled to be fairly tight on a piece of cord about 2 feet long. Instructions for making balls were given earlier (Chapter 15). The handle is usually shaped like a skipping rope handle. The size of the cup depends on the degree of skill intended in catching, but there should be a reasonable clearance on the ball. The hollow should certainly be deeper than the diameter of the ball and a clearance of upwards of 1/4 inch is reasonable,

possibly more if the user will be a young child (Fig. 30-1H).

A variation is an end with more than one cup (Fig. 30-1J), so more skill is needed to catch the ball in the intended cup.

DIABOLO

Another game that was favored by adults as well as children was "Diavolo" or "Diabolo," which seems to have had a French origin. A cord is fixed between two handles. This is used to control a sort of spool (Fig. 30-4A), which could be tossed and spun by manipulating the handles.

The handles might be straight dowel rods, or have shaped handles and tapered stems, with the cord fixed through holes (Fig. 30-4B). Several variations on the spool are possible, but the essential feature in the design is large heavy ends and a quite small center (Fig. 30-4C). The spool has to revolve along a taut cord or settle with its center on the cord if tossed. Obviously, the center should not be turned too small so the spool breaks if dropped, but aim at the smallest diameter that will still retain strength.

YO-YO

A modern toy with family connections is the yo-yo. Various diameters are possible, but 3 inches is reasonable. The whole thing can be turned in one piece like a chalk line reel (Fig. 30-4D), or two discs may be mounted on a piece of dowel rod (Fig. 30-4E). The width between the disc sides should do no more than give a reasonable clearance to the cord, but the faces should be smooth and the outer edge rounded (Fig. 30-4F). It may be easier to get good inner surfaces if the dowel assembly is used.

BOARD GAMES

The making of chessmen has already been described (Chapter 14). Simpler are the pieces for playing checkers on the same board. Although they are simple discs that can be turned in quantity (Fig. 30-5A), they can be decorated on the surface (Fig. 30-5B) or given an individual treatment around the

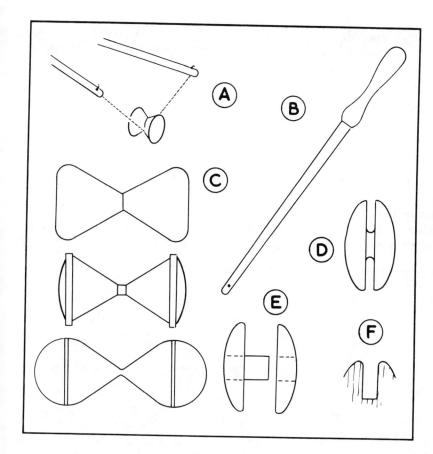

Fig. 30-4. Diabolo is a game that can be made on the lathe as is the yo-yo.

edges (Fig. 30-5C) to make them different from quantity-produced specimens. The set has to be in two different colors. They can be contrasting woods, but it is probably better to make all of the discs from a light-colored hardwood and stain one lot black or near-black, so the color difference is very marked. It is advisable to turn enough cylinders of the right size to make all of the discs so uniformity is maintained, but groups of four are probably as many as can conveniently be worked on together.

In medieval days, there were many games in which balls or marbles had to be moved between holes in various ways, either as a game between competitors or as a recreation for an individual. The one that has survived is usually known as *solitaire*. There are thirty three holes. Marbles or balls are put in all but one of them. The object is to remove all of the marbles from the board by "taking" a

marble by jumping over it with another into a vacant space. It is similar to taking a piece in checkers.

The board is a turned disc, which can have molded edges (Fig. 30-5D). The pattern of holes is marked out around two diameter lines crossing at right angles (Fig. 30-5E), with more lines drawn parallel with them and at each side of them. Holes come where they cross and at similar distances outside.

The holes can be made with an ordinary drill. The holes should be of a size that allows the balls to rest on top or go in to less than halfway (Fig. 30-5F). Traditional boards had rounded hollows made with a spoon bit in a brace. If one of these old bits is not available, a similar result can be obtained with a round-end router cutter (Fig. 30-5G). Another way of arranging the game is to turn thirty-two shouldered pegs to fit into smaller holes

(Fig. 30-5H). These are more likely to stay put and resist accidental tipping out, as might happen if the game is played while traveling.

For crib and other card games, pegs are used in holes in a board to record scores. These are quite tiny, but they provide scope for miniature detail turning (Fig. 30-5J). Normally, sets of four are needed (Fig. 30-6). Some boards have compartments for storing the pegs, so their capacity may limit sizes. Oddments of close-grained hardwood can be used. A peg can be turned between centers, to get support from the back center as far as possible (Fig. 30-5K), then an extension held in a chuck, which can be just a hole in a block of wood on the faceplate or screw center, while the point is turned (Fig. 30-5L). The holes in the board are usually drilled parallel, so the peg should be almost parallel for a short distance behind a rounded end.

RING AND BALL GAMES

Quoits and ring games can be made of wood. Traditional outdoor quoit games were played with turned wooden rings of quite large and heavy form. A ring might have a diameter of 12 inches with a section of about 3 inches (Fig. 30-7A). This was thrown over a post driven in the ground, similar to a game played with horseshoes.

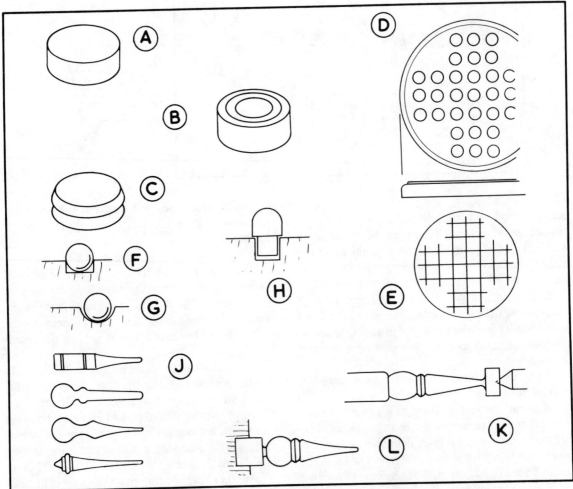

Fig. 30-5. Checkers, solitaire, and crib board pegs are amongst game accessories that can be made on the lathe.

Fig. 30-6. Crib pegs are small items that can be made from scraps of hardwood.

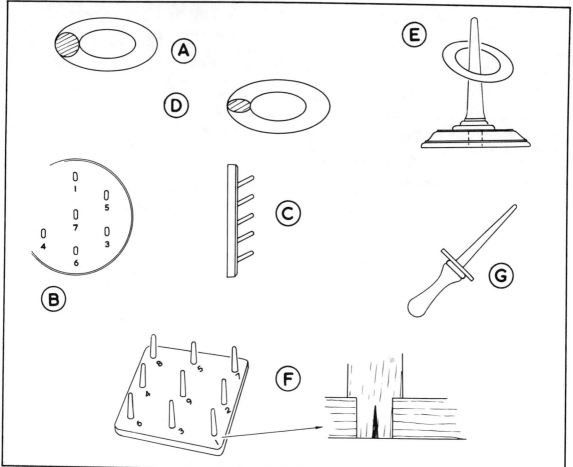

Fig. 30-7. Rings and quoits can be made for many games.

Smaller quoits can be used for a game in which the pegs project from a hanging board (Fig. 30-7B). Wooden rings against the board would bound off plain pegs, so they may slope upward and be given thicker ends (Fig. 30-7C). Quoits need not have round sections. If they are elliptical, this provides greater strength in the short grain (Fig. 30-7D).

A similar game to the outdoor one can be arranged indoors with smaller quoits and a post that is mounted in a turned base (Fig. 30-7E). If the underside of the base is covered with cloth, it could stand on a carpet without doing harm. The post should stand fairly high, otherwise quoits may bounce off, particularly if several are already on the post.

A further step is to have several pegs—usually a pattern of nine. They can be mounted on a square or round base (Fig. 30-7F). Alternatively, there could be strips of wood notched into each other with the pegs at their crossings. If the pegs are numbered, the highest score should be the center one and the lowest the front one. As with the single post, cloth on the underside of the stand will prevent damage to carpets and prevent the stand from slipping on a smooth floor. A variation of this could be quite a small assembly to be used on a table top with a throw of only a few feet.

Another ring game for two has a catcher. This game consists of a handle and a disc behind a stem, onto which the partner has to throw the quoits (Fig. 30-7G).

Skittles or pins have been in demand from the turner for centuries. Basic shapes are reversible with larger centers (Fig. 30-8A) or a pattern with a knob top (Fig. 30-8B). Turn deep hollows so the skittle stands on a rim (Fig. 30-8C) that will still be there after considerable wear and rough treatment.

Sizes can vary from those almost too large to carry to those small enough for table top use. A set of nine or ten are required, but a few spares are worth making. In some games, there is a king pin with something extra to identify it. The reversible pin may have rings or beads around it, or one with a knob can have an extra small knob on top (Fig. 30-8D).

Wooden balls should be made in a size proportional to the pins. Both pins and balls will suffer from impact, so they should be made from hard, close-grained wood. Open-grained wood would soon splinter and crack.

A form of table skittles uses a board with a post and a swinging ball (Fig. 30-8E). The skittles can be similar to those used for bowling games. The ball is made pear-shaped and the cord either goes through it (Fig. 30-6F) or is tied to a ring in its end. It is important that the ball and cord swing cleanly around the post, and it is best to use a small ball race. This could be enclosed in a wooden casing, either with a groove around or an eye for the cord (Fig. 30-8G).

A throwing game, based on throwing a line at sea, uses a pear-shaped ball, similar to that used for table skittles (Fig. 30-8F) on a long cord or rope. The target is a row of pegs (Fig. 30-8H). They could be posts pushed in the ground for a large game, but for indoor use, turned pegs in a board are better. Scoring is by numbers in the spaces, with the highest score at the center. The weighted cord is coiled and thrown in one hand, while the end is held by the other hand, so the weight goes past the posts and the cord drops between them.

WHEELED TOYS

The making of wooden wheels has already been described (Chapter 17). For a wheel to stand up to wear, it should be fairly thick; otherwise, it will soon develop a wobble on its axle. Normally, wooden wheels are only suitable for toys that are pushed or handled. They are not suitable for riding on—at least not for long.

A pull-along box on wheels can have a load of turned barrels or drums (Fig. 30-9A) for its owner to load or unload. There will be sufficient simulation of a truck for the imagination of the younger owner if a turned block comes in front of an upright piece (Fig. 30-9B). There can be a load of logs on a flat truck top with dowel supports (Fig. 30-9C). An old steam locomotive can have several turned parts (Fig. 30-9D).

In a large barrow, the owner can wheel other toys about in what is really a box with extended

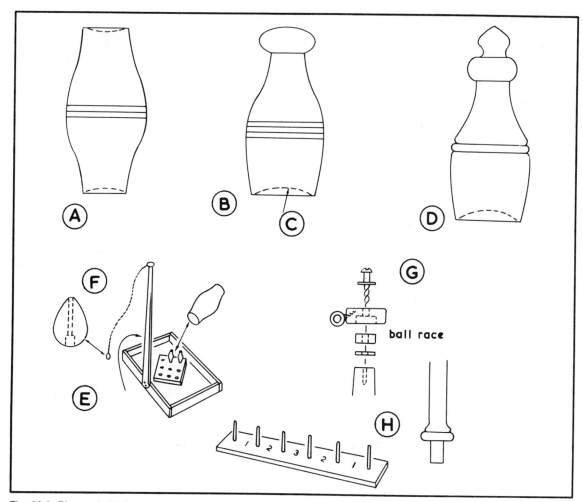

Fig. 30-8. Pins and skittles can be made in many sizes.

EQUIPMENT FOR GAMES

There are many turned items that can be used in various outdoor games and sports. The turner who is also a golfer may turn his own divots (Fig.

sides for handles and a pair of wheels (Fig. 30-9E). This is more easily managed than one with a single wheel (Fig. 30-9F). Such a single wheel can be built up with turned wooden extensions to take a steel rod that goes through as an axle (Fig. 30-9G). This makes a stronger assembly. In larger sizes,such strengthened wheels are still used by primitive people.

30-10A). For athletic high jumping, a cane rests on pegs in holes in uprights. These are turned with knobs (Fig. 30-10B). Tent pegs can also be turned in a similar manner (Fig. 30-10C).

Croquet mallets are turned like other mallets, but the head should be heavy and the handle long and slightly flexible (Fig. 30-10D). Ash or hickory can be used for the handles. This long slender design calls for the use of a steady in the lathe.

Baseball bats may not be up to the professional standard, but a turner can make them scaled to suit young players (Fig. 30-10E). Very similar are clubs used for exercising. Weight is concentrated in the end, and there is a rather slender neck to a ball end

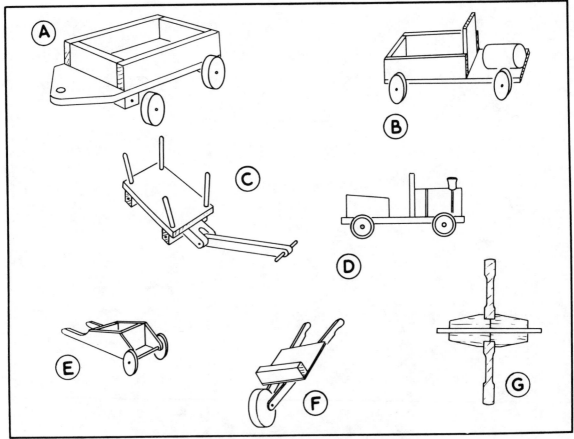

Fig. 30-9. There are round parts in many children's toys that can be made on a lathe.

(Fig. 30-10F). Dumbbells for exercising can be turned in wood and the ends hollowed so lead weights can be added (Fig. 30-10G).

Turned pegs can be made to mark stages around an outdoor course. A disc on top can be horizontal or sloping to show the number of the position (Fig. 30-10H). The turner might substitute a number of pegs in the disc to give a more weather-resistant alternative to a painted number (Fig. 30-10J).

PUZZLES

There are several educational toys that are really puzzles, in which the young user learns intelligent action by sorting parts. An example in a series of posts with many turned wooden discs of different sizes to fit over them (Fig. 30-11A). Usually the discs are painted different colors as well as being different sizes.

For the youngest user, arranging the discs in conical piles on a post according to color and size may be a sufficient test. For an older child, there can be the problem of sorting the discs with only one to be moved at a time. For added interest for the youngest, the whole thing could be part of a flat truck on wheels to be pulled around with a string.

A more advanced puzzle has several discs in a tray with one gap, and the discs numbered. A simple arrangement has eight discs (Fig. 30-11B). The problem is to sort the discs by sliding them into the space in turn until they have been put together in sequence (Fig. 30-11C). There can be a larger number to make things more difficult, providing

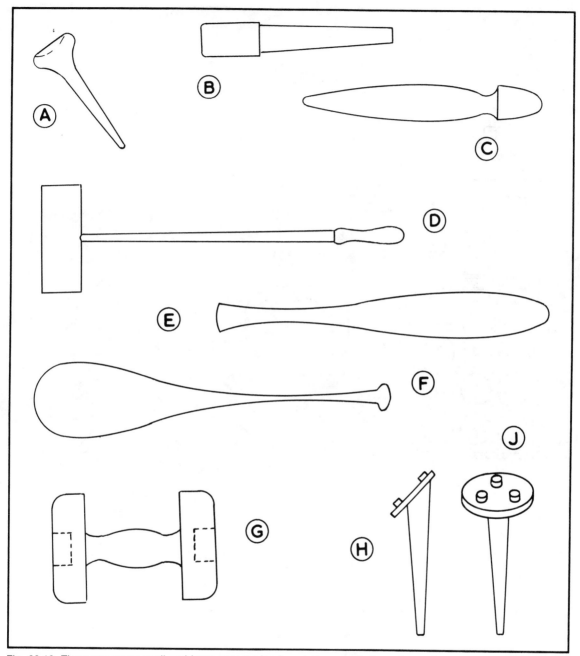

Fig. 30-10. There are many small and large accessories for adult games that can be made.

they fit into a rectangle with one spare space. To facilitate moving the discs, it is helpful to hollow the top of each, so the disc can be moved with a finger (Fig. 30-11D).

A puzzle that is more of a trick and will mystify your audience is one that has a cylinder with a hole through it and one end plugged with the ends of a piece of rubber band extending from it (Fig.

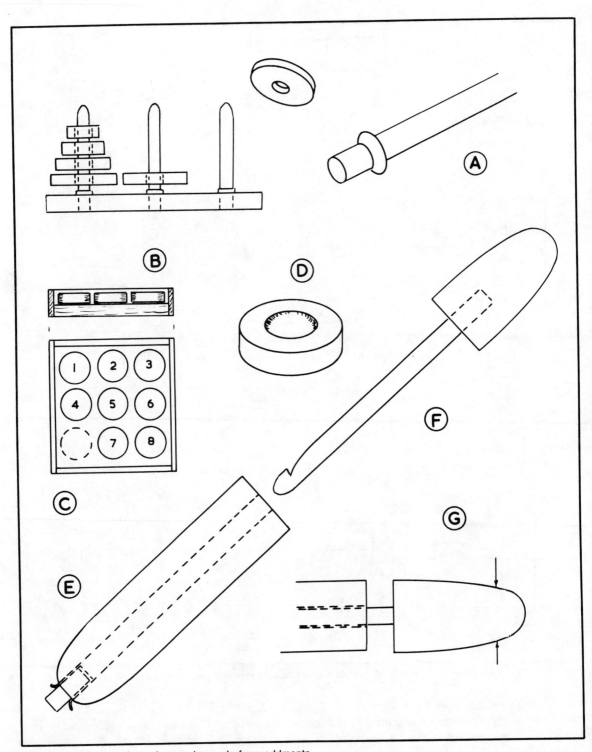

Fig. 30-11. Games and puzzles can be made from oddments.

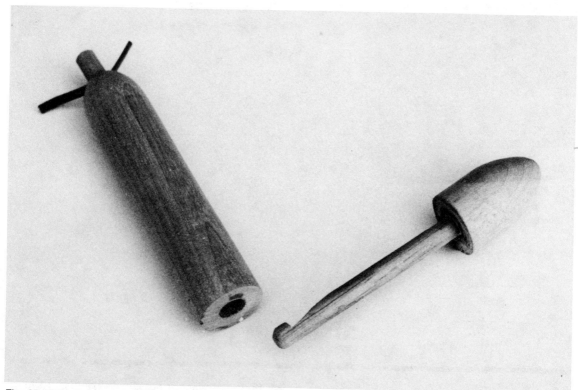

Fig. 30-12. Here are parts of the puzzle shown in Fig. 30-11E, F, and G.

30-11E). The other part has a rod with a hooked end to slide in the cylinder (Fig. 30-11F). Ask a member of your audience to try and hook the rubber band so the rod will spring back when it is pulled and released (Fig. 30-12). He will be unsuccessful, but you appear to do it with no effort, and the plunger springs back with a resounding bang.

Do not hook the rubber band. Instead, the end of the handle part of the plunger is turned with smooth taper; if you squeeze your finger and thumb

on this (Fig. 30-11G), the plunger will shoot back.

Construction is simple. The plug and rubber ends should project obviously because they form part of the deception. The rod should be a loose fit in the hole and have what looks like an effective hook in the end. It is the end of the handle that is important. Give this a curved smooth taper, but so this is not so obvious, give the rest of the puzzle an equally smooth finish. The end of the main part can be turned down to match.

Glossary

(Some of the words included here are obsolete or uncommon but are included in case the reader meets them elsewhere in conversation or in old books.)

arbor—In lathe work, a turned rod for holding hollow work. Alternative name for mandrel.
arris—The shape edge that occurs at an angle.
auger—Long drilling tool.

back gear—Gearing in the headstock to give very slow speeds. More common in metal-turning lathes.
back stay—Alternative name for steady.
bead—Curved section ring around turned work.
beading tool—Special chisel for turning beads.
bed—The body of the lathe on which other parts are mounted.
between centers—Spindle turning with work supported between the headstock and the tailstock.
bine—The raised part of a twist turning.
blind hole—A hole that does not go right through.

bodger—A woodturner specializing in turning chair parts on a primitive lathe.
boring—Making a hole, usually meaning using a hand tool and not a drill.
bulbous turning—Leg or other turning that is larger at the center than at the ends.
burnisher—A hard steel rod mounted in a handle and used for turning over the edge of a scraper.
burnishing—Rubbing rotating work with shavings. Turning the edge of a scraper with a hard steel rod.

cabinet scraper—Sheet steel tool with edge turned over for scraping a wood surface. Useful on raised fibers of cross-grained turned work.
cabriole leg—Form of club-footed leg.
calipers—Tool for measuring or comparing diameters.
calipers, combination—Inside and outside calipers in one instrument.
calipers, inside or internal—For measuring the diameter of holes.

calipers, outside or external—For measuring outside curves.

calipers, sliding—Calipers made with one fixed head and a sliding head on an arm.

capacity—The maximum diameter or swing (U.S.A.), or maximum radius (Britain) possible over a lathe bed.

carrier—Device to clamp on a rod to be turned to take drive from a catch plate or faceplate. Used more in metal turning.

catch plate—A type of faceplate with a projecting rod or slot to engage with a carrier to drive work. Used more for metal than wood turning.

center—Support for the end of the wood at its center.

center, back—The one which fits in the tailstock and does not rotate.

center cross—Driving center.

center, cup—Support for softwood at the tailstock.

center, dead—Alternative name for back center.

center, driving—The one that fits in the headstock end and rotates the work.

center, fork—Type of driving center.

center, live—Alternative name for driving center.

center, plain—One with a simple point.

center, prong—Alternative name for spur center.

center punch—Pointed tool for making dents.

center, running—A back center that revolves on bearings.

center, screw—Device for holding small work.

center, spur—A type of driving center.

center square—Tool for finding the center of a round object by drawing along its blade in two or more positions.

charring—Burning wood by friction to darken lines or edges.

chisel—Hand turning tool, flat in cross-section.

chuck—Device for holding work, drills, etc.

chuck, cup—One into which work is pressed and held by friction, or a pad for making balls.

chuck, flange—A small faceplate.

chuck, screw—A bell shape with side screws. Alternative name for a screw center.

chuck, self-centering—One with three or four jaws, all operating together by turning a key.

chuck, split—Wooden chuck with tightening ring.

chucking—Mounting work.

club foot—Leg with enlarged end.

cone pulley—Pulley with steps for varying speeds.

cove—Hollow cut around a turned piece.

combination drill—Drill to make a short hole and countersink it in one operation in order to match a lathe center (Slocumb drill).

compass—Adjustable tool for drawing circles. It has a point for the center and a pencil or pen for drawing a circumference. It differs from dividers, which have a second point instead of a pencil or pen.

dado—A straight groove, usually across the grain (a housing).

damping down—Moistening wood to raise the grain before final glass-papering.

distance between centers—The lengthwise capacity of a lathe.

dividers—A variation on a compass with two points. Should only be called a "compass" if one end is a pencil or pen.

dividing head—Arrangement for dividing the circumference into a number of parts, usually with a locating peg and holes drilled around a headstock pulley.

dowel—Parallel turned part, usually to fit a hole.

drift—Tapered punch to drive through a slot to release a tapered part.

drilling—Making a hole with a drill bit. If a hand tool is used, the method is more correctly described as *boring*.

drill pad—A pad that fits in place of a center to take the pressure off when drilling.

faceplate—Circular plate to screw on mandrel nose to hold work of a large diameter.

ferrule—Metal tube on handle end to prevent splitting.

finial—Decorative turned knoblike end to a long part. It normally points upwards.

flute—A curved hollow like a cove, except straight.

fox (tail) wedging—A wedge in a cut end of a dowel arranged to tighten inside a blind hole.

French polish—A layer of shellac on the wood.

gap bed—A lathe bed with a hollow below the mandrel nose to accommodate large work.

gauge—A testing instrument used for the same purpose as calipers, but of a fixed size.

gavel—Mallet used by a chairperson.

gouge—Hand turning tool with a curved cross-section.

graver—Handheld tool for turning metal, such as ferrules.

grinding—Sharpening a tool on a revolving coarse-grit stone. Grinding is usually followed by honing.

handrest—Tool rest.

headstock—The driving end of a lathe.

headstock, fixed—Old name for the headstock.

headstock, loose—Old name for the tailstock.

honing—Sharpening process on an oilstone or waterstone.

jig—Device into which the work fits. It is usually attached to an awkward shape to make turning possible.

laminated steel—High-carbon steel welded to low-carbon steel. This is done to make a tough tool that will keep its edge for a long time.

laminating—Building up wood in layers.

lead (pronounced "leed")—The amount of advance in one revolution of the thread of a screw or twist turning.

long and strong—Catalog description of heavier tools used especially for turning bowls.

mandrel—The headstock or tailstock spindle, or a turned rod (arbor) for holding hollow work.

mandrel nose—The end of the headstock spindle onto which chucks, centers, etc., are fixed.

Morse taper—Standard taper for plug-in tools such as centers and some drills.

newel post—Standing spindle with its top unsupported, as at the side of a swinging mirror.

oilstone—Natural or manufactured abrasive stone used for sharpening.

outboard turning—Turning at the left-hand end of the headstock.

parting off—Cutting off work in the lathe.

parting tool—Narrow, but deep, chisel for cutting off work or making narrow grooves as a guide for other tool work.

pedestal—Upright spindle, as in a lamp stand.

pitch—Distance from the top of one thread to the top of the next in a screw or twist turning.

pitman—Bar connecting the treadle to a crank on the flywheel of a foot-operated lathe.

pole lathe—One using a springy pole as a means of providing a reciprocating motion.

poppet head—Old name for tailstock.

pummel—Square left for joining rails on a leg.

profile gauge—Rigid or adjustable tool used for checking an outline.

Queen Anne leg—Form of cabriole leg.

quoit—Turned ring for use in games.

rabbet (rebate)—Recess cut in an edge, like at the back of a picture frame.

rake—Angle, in particular, the angle of a tool to the surface of the work.

rear turning—Alternative name for outboard turning.

reed—A raised curved section like a bead but straight.

rod—Strip of wood with distances marked. It is used for checking lengths of sets of spindle turnings.

roughing—Removing the bulk of the waste, usually with a gouge that leaves a rough surface.

roughing gouge—Gouge with its end sharpened straight across.

router—Hand or power tool for cutting and leveling grooves or recesses. The power tool can have a cutter to make reeds or flutes along turned work.

rpm—Abbreviation for revolutions per minute, which is the way of quoting the speed of a lathe or other machine.

rule—A measuring rod. A craftsman does not call it a "rule."

sanding disc (disk)—Circle of abrasive paper mounted on a wood or metal disc.

sandpaper—Common name for abrasive paper, but sand is no longer used as the cutting grit.

scraper—Tool with obtuse cutting edge, presented to the work with a negative angle.

screw center—Small pad to mount on headstock spindle with a projecting central screw to drive into the wood being turned.

skew chisel—A turning chisel with its cutting edge other than a right angle to its side.

slip—A shaped oilstone for sharpening inside gouges.

Slocumb drill—Alternative name for a combination drill.

spindle—The headstock shaft or mandrel.

spindle gouge—A gouge with a rounded cutting edge.

spindle nose—Alternative name for mandrel nose.

spindle turning—Turning wood with its grain parallel with the lathe bed and supported between the headstock and tailstock.

split turning—Turning two pieces temporarily joined that will be mounted on their flat sides as decorations.

spring bow—A spring top to force two arms out against an adjusting screw and nut as in some calipers and dividers.

square turning—Work that has a turned appearance in profile but is square in section.

squaring up—Truing the end of a spindle turning.

stay—Alternative name for steady.

steady—Support for slender work.

strop—Leather surface for fine sharpening.

swing—The largest diameter that can be turned in a particular lathe.

T-rest—A wood-turning tool rest.

tailstock—Movable support for the end of the work opposite the headstock.

template (templet)—A gauge for testing shape.

terminal—End decoration, such as a finial.

therming—Old name for square turning.

ticketer—Alternative name for a burnisher.

tommy bar—Lever for adjusting a chuck or other device.

tool rest—T-shaped rest mounted on the bed for supporting the turning tools.

treen—Domestic woodware of Welsh origin. Much of it is made on the lathe.

trough—Support for square wood while corners are planed off.

twist turning—Screw-like carved effect.

twist turning, open—A double or treble twist with the two parts separated.

waisting—Narrowness behind the cutting edge to give clearance, particularly in a parting tool.

waney edge—Natural edge of a board as cut from a tree with or without the bark.

waterstone—Abrasive stone for sharpening used with water instead of oil.

way—One side of a lathe bed.

whetstone—Any oilstone or waterstone used for sharpening.

whip—Bending of slender work.

wire edge—The sliver of metal rubbed off of a sharpened tool, but it may cling to the edge until cleaned off.

Index

V-tool, 215
varnish
  boat, 240
varnishes, 240
varnishing
  wood, 229
vases, 321
vegetable pressers, 331
veiner, 199
Victorian chess sets, 182
Victorian furniture, 180, 221, 255

W

wall bracket, 292

water stains, 236
wax
  beeswax, 239
  carnauba, 239
  Paraffin, 239
wax polishing, 239
Welsh treen, 326
wet-and-dry paper, 231
wheel
  spinning, 354
wheeled toys, 374
wheels, 203
whiting, 235
Windsor chairs, 174, 270

wood
  bleaching, 235
  filling, 234
  finishing, 229
  seasoned, 137
  stopping, 234
  unseasoned, 137
wood plastic, 235
wood preparation
  spindle turning, 91

Y

yo-yo, 370

Other Bestsellers From TAB

☐ **111 YARD AND GARDEN PROJECTS—FROM BOXES AND BINS TO TABLES AND TOOLS—Blandford**

Save $100's . . . even $1,000's . . . on more than 100 practical and exciting projects for your lawn and garden! Projects include: plant stands, storage shelves, climbing plant supports, benches, tables, window boxes, hanging planters and cold frames, gardening tools, fences and gates, garden carts, trolleys, and wheelbarrows, and more! 416 pp., 301 illus. 7″ × 10″.

Paper $16.95   **Hard $25.95**
Book No. 2664

☐ **BUILDING OUTDOOR PLAYTHINGS FOR KIDS, with Project Plans—Barnes**

Imagine the delight of your youngsters—children or grandchildren—when you build them their own special backyard play area complete with swings, climbing bars, sandboxes, even an A-frame playhouse their own size or a treehouse where they can indulge in their own imaginary adventures. Best of all, discover how you can make exciting, custom-designed play equipment at a fraction of the cost of ordinary, ready-made swing sets or sandbox units! It's all here in this practical, step-by-step guide to planning and building safe, sturdy outdoor play equipment. 240 pp., 213 illus. 7″ × 10″.

Paper $12.95   **Hard $21.95**
Book No. 1971

☐ **58 HOME SHELVING AND STORAGE PROJECTS—Blandford**

From a two-shelf book rack or tabletop organizer to a paneled chest, basic room divider, or hall locker . . . from shelves or a spoon rack to a period reproduction of a Shaker cabinet or a Welsh dresser, you'll be amazed at the variety of projects included. And, each one includes easy-to-follow, step-by-step directions, plenty of show-how drawings, and complete materials lists. 288 pp., 227 illus. 7″ × 10″.

Paper $14.95   **Book No. 1844**

☐ **THE WOODTURNER'S HANDBOOK**

Here's your source for step-by-step techniques for making a whole range of turned wood objects, gifts, accessories, toys, tools, utensils, and more! More than 220 exceptionally helpful photographs and drawings provide show how guidance! Expert tips on choosing, using, and maintaining a wood turning lathe! Practical advice on the types of woods for turning, and how to make your own cutting tools. It's all here! 224 pp., 233 illus. 7″ × 10″.

Paper $12.95   **Hard $21.95**
Book No. 1769

☐ **66 FAMILY HANDYMAN® WOOD PROJECTS**

Here are 66 practical, imaginative, and decorative projects . . . literally something for every home and every woodworking skill level from novice to advanced cabinetmaker: room dividers, a free-standing corner bench, china/book cabinet, coffee table, desk and storage units, a built-in sewing center, even your own Shaker furniture reproductions! 210 pp., 306 illus. 7″ × 10″.

Paper $14.95   **Hard $21.95**
Book No. 2632

☐ **THE COMPUTER FURNITURE PLAN AND PROJECT BOOK—Wiley**

Now, with the help of this first-of-its-kind handbook, even a novice can build good looking, functional, and low-cost computer furniture that's custom-designed for your own special needs—tables, stands, desks, modular or built-in units, even a posture supporting kneeling chair! Computer hobbyist and craftsman Jack Wiley provides all the step-by-step guidance, detailed project plans, show-how illustrations, and practical customizing advice . . . even basic information on tools, materials, and construction techniques. 288 pp., 385 illus. 7″ × 10″.

Paper $15.95   **Hard $23.95**
Book No. 1949

☐ **GLUE IT—Giles**

Here, in one easy-to-use reference is everything anyone needs to know about glues, adhesives, epoxies, caulkings, sealants, plus practical how-to's on when and how to use them! If you need to glue or seal anything—from plumbing to glassware or from toys and airplane models to a cabin cruiser, this is where you'll find the needed information! 112 pp., 32 illus. 7″ × 10″.

Paper $8.95   **Hard $14.95**
Book No. 1801

☐ **FASTEN IT!—Self**

Here in easy-to-use format is all the information you need to find exactly the right fastening method for almost every job imaginable. Plus, you'll get complete guidance on the tools you need for each type of fastener—from claw hammers to specialty chisels, from welding rods to drill presses, and more. You'll learn how to join any two objects together permanently, temporarily, flexibly, or rigidly. It's an indispensable sourcebook that no hobbyist, craftsman, or home handyman should be without! 304 pp., 364 illus. 7″ × 10″.

Paper $14.95   **Hard $23.95**
Book No. 1744

Other Bestsellers From TAB